While the principal purpose of human factors analysis is to adapt a given task to the capacities of the worker, the primary objective of personnel selection and training is to ensure that appropriate people are chosen and adequately trained to fulfill their part in carefully designed man-machine production systems. In actuality, the two are complementary and both are needed to derive an ideal system. In *Prediction and Development of Industrial Work Performance* emphasis is placed on the ways in which aptitude can be determined and skills developed, based on an analysis of the human requirements of a job function.

To develop a systematic and efficient basis for "fitting the man to the job", the authors analyze numerous facets of industrial employment, ranging from a description of the capacities and limitations of the individual worker to a critical evaluation of personnel selection procedures. Highlights of the book include—

- a detailed treatment of sensorimotor features in human performance and the acquisition of occupational skills
- the classification of industrial skills
- an explanation of the analysis of skilled performance in occupational tasks
- numerous case studies on industrial training
- and an evaluation of the ongoing developments in personnel selection techniques

Prediction and Development of Industrial Work Performance will be invaluable to those industrial engineers, human factors specialists, personnel managers, training officers and industrial psychologists who are responsible for predicting work performance and developing it by analytical training methods. It will also be of value to students and teachers of indust... agement and m

About the Authors

GAVRIEL SALVENDY is an Associate Professor in the School of Industrial Engineering at Purdue University. His previous positions include Assistant Professor of Industrial Engineering at the State University of New York (Buffalo), Research Associate of Engineering Production at the University of Birmingham (England), and Head of the Department of Management Services of Gunson's Sortex Ltd., London. A frequent contributor to the periodical literature on occupational psychology and ergonomics, Dr. Salvendy received his Ph.D. degree in Industrial Psychology at the University of Birmingham.

W. DOUGLAS SEYMOUR is an Honorary Research Fellow in the Engineering Production Department of the University of Birmingham. In addition, he is a Fellow of the British Psychological Society, a Fellow of the Institute of Personnel Management, and a consultant and contributor to the B. B. C. series on Training for Skill. He is also a frequent contributor to the periodical literature on industrial training and is the author of five previous books.

PREDICTION AND DEVELOPMENT
OF INDUSTRIAL WORK PERFORMANCE

Prediction and Development of Industrial Work Performance

GAVRIEL SALVENDY

Purdue University
U.S.A.

W. DOUGLAS SEYMOUR

University of Birmingham
England

A WILEY-INTERSCIENCE PUBLICATION

JOHN WILEY & SONS

New York · London · Sydney · Toronto

Library of Congress Cataloging in Publication Data

Salvendy, Gavriel, 1938-
    Prediction and development of industrial work performance.

    (Wiley series in human factors)
    "A Wiley-Interscience publication."
    Bibliography: p.
    1. Prediction of occupational success.   2. Job analysis.   3. Employees, Training of.   I. Seymour, W. Douglas, joint author.   II. Title.

HF5381.7.S24   658.3′06   73-5914
ISBN 0-471-75080-8

Printed in the United States of America

10 9 8 7 6 5 4 3 2 1

SERIES PREFACE

Technology is effective to the extent that men can operate and maintain the machines they design. Equipment design which consciously takes advantage of human capabilities and constrains itself within human limitations amplifies and increases system output. If it does not, system performance is reduced and the purpose for which the equipment was designed is endangered. This consideration is even more significant today than in the past because the highly complex systems that we develop are pushing human functions more and more to their limits of efficient performance.

How can one ensure that machine and machine operations are actually designed for human use? Behavioral data, principles, and recommendations—in short, the Human Factors discipline—must be translated into meaningful design practices. Concepts like ease of operation or error-free performance must be interpretable in hardware and system terms.

Human Factors is one of the newer engineering disciplines. Perhaps because of this, engineering and human-factors specialists lack a common orientation with which their respective disciplines can communicate. The goal of the Wiley Human Factors Series is to help in the communication process by describing what behavioral principles mean for system design and by suggesting the behavioral research that must be performed to solve design problems. The premise on which the series is based and on which each book is written is that Human Factors has utility only to the degree that it supports engineering development; hence the Series emphasizes the *practical application* to design of human-factors concepts.

Because of the many talents on which Human Factors depends for its implementation (design and systems engineering, industrial and experimental psychology, anthropology, physiology, and operations research, to name only a few), the Series is directed to as wide an audience as possible. Each book is intended to illustrate the usefulness of Human Factors to some significant aspect of system development, such as human factors in design or testing or simulation. Although cookbook answers are not provided, it is hoped that this pragmatic approach will enable the many specialists concerned with problems of equipment design to solve these problems more efficiently.

DAVID MEISTER
Series Editor

PREFACE

Meister, in introducing the series in 1971, stated that "the series emphasizes the *practical application* to design of human factors concepts" (p. viii). Although the emphasis on practical applications is continued, this volume concentrates more particularly on the procedures necessary to ensure that appropriate people are chosen, and adequately trained, to fulfill their part in carefully designed man-machine and other production systems. The principal purpose of human factors is to adapt the task to the capacities of the worker, and the principal purpose of personnel selection and training is to adapt the capacities of the worker to the task. The two are complementary to each other, and both are needed to derive an ideal system. The emphasis in this book is on the determination of an individual's aptitudes and the development of his capacities in relation to specified tasks.

Changes in the individual's abilities are considered here under the same terminology as elsewhere in the series, for example, Meister (1971): "Aptitude is capacity before it is trained; skill is capacity after training. Alternatively, we can think of aptitude as potential for performance, whereas skill is actualised performance" (p. 109). The aim of the present work is to explain how such aptitude can be determined and how skill can be developed, based on an analysis of the human requirements of a task.

The continually increasing rate of technological change and the simultaneous explosion of human knowledge precipitate many social, economic, and educational problems. Traditional career structures in service, teaching, banking, management, and other professions are being jeopardized by the fact that only the youngest entrants have had the opportunity to master the latest procedures; in other occupations, jobs and their skill profiles are changing so rapidly that the rate of human obsolescence will engulf our societies unless human learning and adaptation can outstrip it. In industrialized countries the philosophy that living is learning and learning is living must become established, and established effectively in action, if we are to survive economically without social disintegration.

The pattern of history since the industrial revolution has militated against the recognition of these truths. Two hundred years ago the factory system divided living from working, whereas in more primitive societies, the two were, and are, more socially integrated. Again, the development within the past century of state educational systems has tended to separate learning from living, whereas these two had been integrated under the medieval systems for training clerics, esquires, and apprentices.

This double divorce of learning from living and living from working underlies much of the social unease in an industrialized civilization. The reintegration of learning, living, and working in a dynamic era of social and technological change can only be achieved if—*inter alia*—people are enabled to learn and relearn their jobs many times in the course of a lifetime and thereby to develop an acceptable attitude of continuous learning.

In several countries, the continual need for reeducation throughout life is already being recognized and catered for by their educational systems with the use of the modern technology of education. The knowledge content required to cope with job changes in adult life can be provided by textbooks, programmed learning, and lecture courses now being produced in an increasing flood. However, methods for communicating *skills* still lag behind those for communicating *knowledge*, especially where skills depend on the use of nonsymbolic information, that is, upon the reception and discrimination of direct sensory information and not by symbolic translation and representation. Personnel selection and training for skilled performance in nonintellectual work still lags behind that available for intellectual activities which are more readily taught by traditional symbolic procedures through literacy.

This work thus contributes to the area, at present not adequately covered, where there is need to predict and develop the capacity of individuals for *doing* things, as distinct from their ability for *knowing* things. Such capacities cannot be adequately tested by written examinations, because they concern people's ability to behave in particularly skillful ways—whether it be in controlling a machine, restoring a tooth, or cutting a pattern in glass—rather than their ability to write answers about them.

A study such as this can, of course, contribute only the smallest mite toward the solution of our human problems in work situations. Attitudes to work are as important as the possession of the requisite skills and

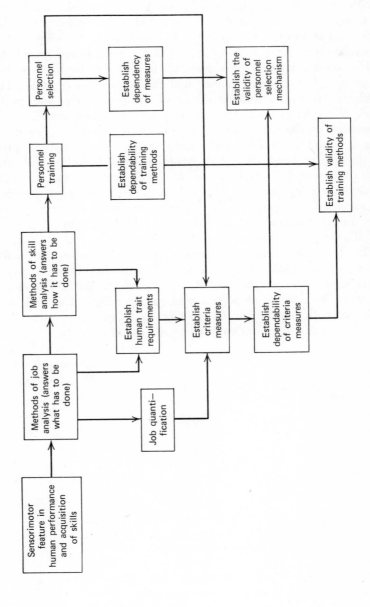

Figure 1. A schematic outline (as followed in this book) for adapting the capacities of the worker to the task.

ix

knowledge to perform it. But right attitudes to work are as useless without skill and knowledge as the latter are without the former. Attitudes depend on a complex of social, economic, and physical factors, many of which are determined outside the work situation and are the study of sociologists, social psychologists, and behavioral scientists. While they pursue their studies, it is possible to improve the development of work expertise by facilitating people's acquisition of skill and knowledge.

This book reviews (see Figure 1), first of all, the basic sensorimotor features in human performance and the acquisition of skills. These are fundamental to an understanding of all productive and professional work. Next, the methods for analyzing jobs are discussed. This leads to a discussion on the classification of work skills based on types of information flow and an outline of the techniques of skills analysis—procedures for developing productive skills based on these techniques are described with case studies illustrating each of the classes of work and each of the resultant benefits. Job and skill analysis are equally essential prerequisites of personnel selection. The procedures available for predicting performance on occupational tasks and the type of criteria utilized are discussed, and illustrations of ongoing developments are outlined.

This book attempts to contribute to the expanding technologies of selection and training and is presented in the hope that it may lead to an increasing success rate in "fitting the man to the job" and to an increase in the number of people who can speedily attain high work performance with satisfaction. Competence and confidence at work are still vital factors in individual well-being and social stability.

West Lafayette, Indiana   GAVRIEL SALVENDY
Clent Stourbridge,   W. DOUGLAS SEYMOUR
Worcester, England
January, 1973

ACKNOWLEDGMENTS

We wish to express our thanks to numerous colleagues, past and present, who have read the scripts and contributed greatly by their kind comments and criticism. We would particularly like to mention Dr. David Meister, Dr. Ben Davies, Dr. E. Megaw, John Fox, and John Pilitsis.

We are also indebted to Professors J. Barany, E. R. F. W. Crossman, N. A. Dudley, K. F. M. Murrell, and O. K. Buros, K. W. Tilley; and the late Dr. L. Brouha for permission to reproduce material from their texts.

Also, acknowledgment is due to the following publishers and organizations who gave permission to reproduce material from their publications: Engineering; MTM Association for Standards and Research; American Institute of Industrial Engineers, Inc.; John Wiley and Sons, Inc.; American Psychological Association; Pergamon Press; Taylor and Francis Ltd.; Gryphon Press, Inc.; Zoomar, Inc.; General Radio Company; British Steel Corporation, Consett Works; Digital Equipment Corporation; Western Electric Company; Eastman Kodak; and International Journal of Production Research.

Numerous firms and organizations have been kind enough to permit us to use case study material and results, and to conduct basic experiments with the cooperation of their employees. We particularly wish to thank the following for their permission to publish such material: Bairns-Wear Ltd., a member of the Courtauld Group; Cadbury Brothers Ltd.; Joseph Lucas (Electrical) Ltd.; The Knitting Lace and Net Industry Training Board; Mullard Blackburn; George Satter and Company Ltd.; Smith Corona Marchant; G.E.C.-A.E.I. Telecommunications Ltd.; T. Wall and Sons (ice cream) Ltd.; and Western Electric Company.

Our thanks go to Mrs. Pat Doeing, Miss Joyce Hinds, and Mrs. Sheila Lunt, each of who patiently and expertly typed parts of this manuscript.

xii

A major acknowledgment must go to our wives for their devoted assistance in improving and correcting the text.

G. S.
W. D. S.

CONTENTS

PREDICTION AND DEVELOPMENT
OF INDUSTRIAL WORK PERFORMANCE

I

THE NATURE AND ACQUISITION OF OCCUPATIONAL SKILLS

OVERVIEW

The importance of the sensori-perceptual and decision-making components in human performance of occupational tasks is emphasized and the basic features of such performance are restated. Some definitions of skill are quoted and skill is differentiated from human performance.

The nature of skilled performance in industrial tasks is discussed and exemplified, and the subjective changes that occur as skills develop are outlined in terms of movement and in sensory and perceptual terms.

Experiments on the acquisition of occupational skills started at the end of the nineteenth century and have been accelerated since World War II. Results of more recent researches are summarized, and results from factory observations are quoted.

The role of information theory in the understanding of skilled performance is outlined, and theories of the acquisition of speed skills discussed with particular reference to the sensori-perceptual components.

Methods derived from European and American studies for predicting output standards and learning times on occupational tasks are summarized, and the procedures for calculation are outlined.

HUMAN PERFORMANCE AND OCCUPATIONAL SKILLS

The fundamental features of human performance, which have been described in numerous publications (e.g., Murrell, 1969), are now becoming generally known. However, industrial managers and others concerned with human performance in work situations have been curiously slow to recognize the importance of the sensory and decision-making components in skilled performance. The early pioneers of time study, being engineers, naturally concentrated on the more mechanical aspects of work economy. Frank Gilbreth concerned himself with motion economy, and Lillian Gilbreth, in spite of her psychological training, did not in the early days emphasize the sensory component in skilled performance—probably the earliest to do this were Munsterberg (1913) and Pear (1924).

The need for new military and industrial skills in World War II led to a series of studies on human performance that gave rise to the development of human factors engineering, ergonomics,* skills analysis training, and other specializations, and all of these involve an appreciation of the sensorimotor features of skills. The general recognition of sensoriperceptual features is very recent; indeed, not until 1952 did *Motor Skills Research Exchange* change its name to *Perceptual Motor Skills Research Exchange.*

The sensory and other features affecting human performance at work have been well illustrated by Murrell (1969), as shown in Figure 1.1.

Certain essential features in the work situation—starter button, lever, dial reading equipment or material are perceived by the operator, and the equipment known as *displays.* The selection of data from the overall equipment and the display is important, since these items may contain information that is redundant or unnecessary. The selection of the most appropriate channel through which the sense data are to be admitted also contributes to an improved performance. The visual channel, which is principally used to perceive displays in occupational tasks, is limited, and data can be more readily assembled in the brain if some of them come by way of the sense of touch, or kinesthesis, or hearing. The incoming sensory data are dealt with centrally in the cortex of the brain, which initiates the effector processes by which action is achieved (Seymour, 1966). The forces exerted by the body arise from the contraction of muscle, which occurs when *neural impulses* (with electrical potential) from the brain reach the muscle groups to which they have been directed. The various body members amplify the small muscular contractions by means of tendons, joints, and bones, thereby enabling very small contractions to achieve quite large movements, as when the arm is raised above the head by relatively small contractions of muscles around the shoulder.

---

* Ergonomics (derived from the Greek for the "laws of work") is defined by the Ergonomics Research Society as:

"The study of the relationship between man and his occupation, equipment, and environment, and particularly the application of anatomical, physiological, and psychological knowledge to the problems arising therefrom."

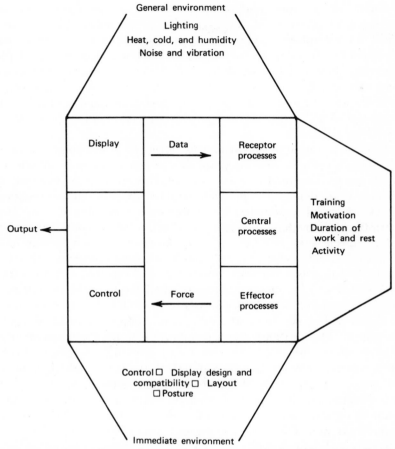

Figure 1.1. Factors affecting human performance at work. (After Murrell, 1969.)

The forces exerted need to be controlled if they are to be precise and effective. Such control is achieved by the counterpoise effect of contracting antagonistic groups of muscle; at the same time, *feedback* of information on how the activity is progressing is obtained through the visual, kinesthetic or other sense channels (see, e.g., Annett, 1969). The output of physical force from body movement achieves some quantum of the task objective, and *knowledge of results* that this has occurred provides the stimulus for initiating the next quantum.

Murrell's diagram also indicates other environmental factors, immediate or general, that influence human performance. These, although admittedly important, do not form part of the subject matter of the present work. The forms of physical energy and wave propagation that furnish the stimuli for exteroceptive perception, as well as the forces that produce proprioceptive perception, are dealt with in standard textbooks of physiology (e.g., Best and Taylor, 1963). Both the electrochemical processes by which the muscle is contracted and the mechanical means whereby the physical force of this contraction is amplified, controlled, and distributed, are described in textbooks on anatomy and ergonomics (e.g., Murrell, 1969).

The word *skill* has been defined variously (and is commonly used in many ways), yet none of the definitions is wholly satisfactory. We can more readily recognize skilled performance, whether in the arts, in sport, or in industry, than define it. The Oxford New English Dictionary defines skill as "practical knowledge in combination with ability"; but this is descriptive rather than definitive. Drever's (1965) *Dictionary of Psychology* calls it "ease, rapidity and precision (usually) of muscular action." Other writers defining skill have tended to concentrate more on its purpose when it involves complex, integrated, and directed activities. In exemplification of this viewpoint, two particularly relevant definitions are those of Guthrie (1952); "skill consists in the ability to bring about some end result with maximum certainty and minimum outlay of energy and time" and of Mace (1950): "skill is an ability to produce consistently an intended effect with accuracy, speed and economy of action." Welford (1968) wrote that skill is "concerned with all the factors which go to make up a competent, expert, rapid and accurate performance," and Kay (1955) again emphasized the aspect of economy—skill is "the ability to obtain maximum information from the minimum cues." The U.K. Department of Employment, in its *Glossary of Training Terms* (1971) adapted Welford's statements and defined skill as:

"An organized and co-ordinated pattern of mental and/or physical activity in relation to an object or other display of information, usually involving both receptor and effector processes. It is built up gradually in the course of repeated training or other experience. It is serial, each part from second to second is dependent on the last and influences the next. Skills may be described as perceptual, motor, manual, intellectual, social, etc., according to the context or the most important aspect of the skill pattern."

In the present work, the term *skills* is used in this sense and with special reference to the performance of occupational tasks (i.e., where the skills serve to provide services or make products for other people, and not solely for immediate personal satisfaction—as in sport).

Such occupational skills do not differ psychophysiologically from those employed in sport or in the military services; in all three cases we have to consider performance in terms of:

1. The reception of information by way of the senses.

2. The perceptual organization of this sensory information in meaningful form for the task.

3. The decision-making process by which the subsequent movements are determined.

4. The achievement of movement by means of muscular contractions evoked as a result of neural impulses from the cortex.

The two groups of occurrences—receptor processes by which information is channeled to the brain, and effector processes by which action is carried out—are linked by the equally important decision-making stage. The continuance of skilled performance, moreover, requires the feedback from the action undertaken in a manner that provides adequate knowledge of results to facilitate further decision-making.

How then are we to distinguish between the terms *human performance* and *skills*? This distinction can be pointed out most clearly by examples.

Anyone not physically handicapped can swing a golf club, but only those with the skills of match players can consistently drive the ball straight down the fairway. Similarly, anyone can use an electric hand drill, but only one with the skills of a dentist can drill a tooth for a filling. Many of us can take an automobile engine to pieces and reassemble it, but few have the skill to diagnose from the sound of the engine precisely what is wrong with it. Most of the jobs in industry are within the competence of most of the industrial population; but few people—even those of high intellectual ability—are immediately capable of performing even simple tasks with the speed and accuracy of the skilled worker.

We use the term *skill* for such differences in expertise, meaning thereby the ability to "produce consistently an intended effect with accuracy, speed and economy of action" (Mace, 1950). On the other hand, we use the term *human performance* to indicate the apparatus and its functioning whereby we do things. Swinging a golf club involves human performance; driving straight down the fairway requires skill as well. Skills are to be differentiated from human performance by noting that the former indicate the higher levels of the latter and involve complex learning processes by which the performance itself is changed in standard, nature, and degree.*

---

* Fitts and Posner (1967) have expressed this somewhat differently. "The study of human performance . . . analyses the processes involved in skilled performance, studies the development of skills and . . . seeks to analyse complex tasks . . . (p. 1).

Human performance requires the use of receptor, effector, and decision-making processes. *Skilled* performance—or, as we more briefly say, skill—consists in taking in information from the most appropriate cues at the most appropriate time and by way of the most appropriate sensory channels, determining which muscle groups are to be innervated, and contracting the right muscles at the right time to exert the forces that will most efficiently achieve the immediate objective. In any given situation the human operator possesses a wide repertory of possible motor responses for achieving his immediate purpose; but the identification, selection, and achievement of the most effective response (together with all that precedes this in organizing the receptor process and decision making) is a learned ability whose attainment constitutes skilled performance.

In all forms of human activity—constructive or destructive, in work or in play—man tends both to improve and to be dissatisfied with low levels of performance. In industrial and other occupations the standards of performance attained are economically important to the individual, the group, and the state. Thus the study of skilled performance, its nature, and its acquisition, is important in relation to almost all activities of mankind.

SKILLED PERFORMANCE ON INDUSTRIAL TASKS

In the performance of industrial work, with its infinite variety, almost all aspects of sensory, central, and effector processes are exhibited. There are still some occupations that require the exertion of considerable physical force—such as sawing, quarrying, and forging—but heavy work is becoming increasingly rare in industrial countries, where the limbs are used more and more to control forces and less and less to exert force. Almost all parts of the body are involved—the feet and legs to operate brakes and accelerator in truck driving, and the knees in operating some needle machines and type-soldering machines.

The increased mechanization of industrial work has led to a concentration of activity in the hands and fingers for the deft and delicate manipulation of material or of controls. The human operator has become increasingly a control element in man–machine systems, but the precision of such controls makes greater demands on the micro skills of finger movements, as in the testing and adjustment of electronic modules. Also, certain tasks in modern sophisticated industries demand the most delicate manipulation of material, as in the wiring of matrices for computer memories (see the Case Studies in Chapter 4 for a description of such tasks).

The higher levels of performance in repetitive industrial tasks arise not merely from swift and dexterous movements, but from the fine coordination of movements made by different body members. On completing a garment, for example, an experienced lockstitch machine operator raises the angle of her feet to stop the machine, lifts the needle foot by moving her knee sideways, removes the fabric with one hand, and brings her palmed scissors into the operating position with the other hand; all these movements are coordinated in space and time with the smoothness and precision of a ballet. Again as in dancing, industrial tasks may involve the coordination of movements of two operators, as in pipe tobacco spinning. The principal operator rolls the leaves of tobacco with the right hand before releasing them into the spinning roller, while at the same time selecting and rhythmically placing additional leaves with the left hand under the right thumb; meanwhile, a second operator, sitting opposite, picks up the other leaves of dark tobacco and places them "nose first" between the first and second fingers of the principal operator's right hand.

The relative importance of small, delicate movements and fine finger work for controlling machines and material in industrial work has increased as heavy manual work has decreased. Since fingers and thumbs have larger areas of representation in the brain than have those limbs whose movements are less precise, the human operator can produce with speed and precision the wide repertory of delicate movements required in fine work. The speed with which such movements are made results from more and more frequent contractions of precisely those muscle groups which facilitate the optimum performance of the element. Human performance in high-speed repetitive movements depends upon the consistency of repeated muscular contractions; this precision and consistency of activity also produces the consistency of quality standards required in batch or flow production in modern industry. Individuals differ in their ability to attain and to maintain the desired consistency of response, and some require many more repetitions before achieving it. This factor is important in the selection of workers for fine manual tasks. (See Chapter 7.)

In the *receptor* sphere, examples of the use of each of the senses can be found in many industrial tasks. Vision is the most commonly used of the senses; but the kinesthetic and tactile senses are involved in most tasks, and hearing is necessary in many. Just as coordination of *movement* is required for high levels of performance, so is coordination of the sensory input. Indeed, highly skilled workers differ from learners more in the way by which they organize their receptor channeling than in the way they move their limbs. In highly skilled performance, receptor organization involves:

1. The recognition of the locus of the cue from which sensory information must be derived.

2. The determination of the sensory channel most appropriate for its derivation.

3. The development of the appropriate state of adaptation within the sensory channel.

4. The timing of the derivation, so that the information is received and dealt with by the time it is needed (Borger and Seaborne, 1966, Chapter 7; Seymour, 1967).

These features can be identified in numerous industrial tasks. In capacitor winding, the correct winding of the first layer is critical in ensuring that the product comes out within the desired limits, and this necessitates the exact location of the cue and its kinesthetic appreciation. In many tasks, workers substitute other, more convenient, sense channels for vision as proficiency develops, as when a lathe turner learns to control the machine kinesthetically in order to concentrate the vision channel at the cutting point. In much fine work, the level of discrimination required is beyond normal levels and involves unusual adaptation; for example, in drawing very fine wire for electronic components, the wire, as it emerges from the die, is invisible to the uninitiated. Moreover, the wire is so fine that its pressure between the fingers cannot be detected by the inexperienced worker. Only when the level of discrimination in these senses has been adequately developed can work proceed.

Again, in the looping of sleeves and shoulders on fully fashioned knitted outerwear, sensory discrimination has to be highly developed (Figure 1.2). Fine vision is required to identify the course of stitches that must be run on to the points, and highly developed kinesthetic sensitivity is needed to determine when the fabric is correctly tensioned to allow the adjustment of each successive stitch to each successive point. The timing and coordination of the sensory input are equally important. The experienced looper glances ahead to see that the next few stitches are ready for running on; when this advance information has registered, kinesthesis takes over for the control of the fine coordinated movements of right and left thumb and fingers, which place the fabric in position. Meanwhile, the eyes glance back to the last section that was run on to check that the stitches have been correctly positioned. Such temporal patterning in the organization of sensory input is just as important in the attainment of skilled performance as the acquisition of the appropriate movement pattern by which the operation is achieved.

Even when the exact location of the cue from which the critical sensory information is to be derived has been recognized, the worker may need

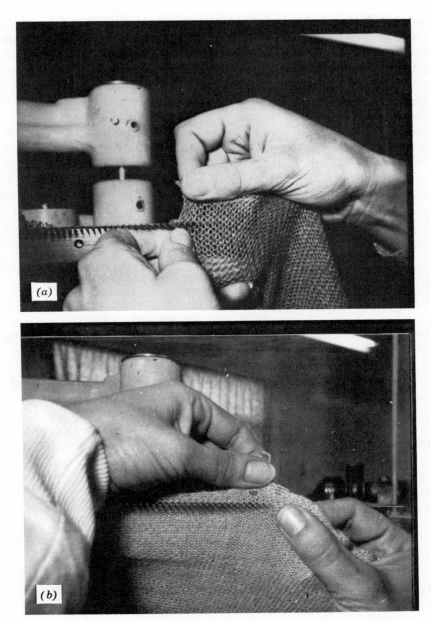

Figure 1.2. Looping fully fashioned outerwear. (*a*) Starting; (*b*) running on. (Courtesy of the U.K. Knitting, Lace, and Net Industry Training Board.)

to obtain the information indirectly. In work involving hand tools, this is particularly important, since the hands are not in direct contact with the material. The tool thus becomes not only a means by which material can be fashioned in ways unattainable with the bare hand but—equally important—the tool thus becomes a channel through which the experienced worker derives information. A commonplace example of this occurs in the fitting of the end of a screwdriver into the slot of a screw that is in a recess; the eyes cannot see the slot, but through the screwdriver the tactile and kinesthetic senses can derive the information by which the individual knows whether the screwdriver is correctly located. In machine tasks this "extended" sense channel is often more complex, as when the lathe turner feels the pressure of the tool on the workpiece through the arm of the star wheel, which he is holding. In process work, the operator is even more remote from his material and must sense changes in it indirectly—as when the sugar refiner puts his hand on the casing of a vat to judge the rate of boiling within. This may provide useful information in addition to what he learns from the pyrometer.

Skilled performance in industrial tasks provides as many examples of the variety of the central processes as of the receptor and effector processes. These central processes, coming between the sensory input and the muscular output, are concerned with various forms of decision making and prediction. The following are the principal features of the central processes:

1. *Selection of stimuli* to which attention is given. In every activity, the experienced worker has learned to ignore a mass of unnecessary or irrelevant information that emanates from the work. The greater the skill of the worker, the more he ignores certain information and concentrates on important stimuli (Kay, 1957). Experiments involving assembly task with two components have shown (Seymour, 1967) that the operator explores the various possible sequences of fixations by which the necessary information can be gained before settling on the most suitable one. Again, a proficient lathe worker concentrates vision at the cutting point of the tool in order to give maximum attention to the appearance of the swarf and what that is telling him. In selecting the stimulus to attend to, the skillful worker is unconsciously seeking the one that will give him earliest and easiest information, if one cue is dispensed with in favor of another, a change in channel may then become appropriate. This is exemplified in experiments on operating a capstan lathe described by Seymour (1967). Subjects initially determined the point at which the star wheel was to be reversed by bumping it on the stop, second by the sound of the "click"

of the release catch, and finally by proprioceptive kinesthetic information derived from the position of the arm. Such transition from the use of exteroceptive sense channels to proprioceptive (especially from vision to kinesthesis) is an important feature in the acquisition of skill.

2. *Determination of the muscle groups* to be innervated. A beginner makes movements randomly and, unconsciously, judges their suitability to his purpose. In subsequent repetitions of a task, he selects more and more frequently those particular movements and muscle contractions which seem successful, judged by feedback and knowledge of results. The speed of skilled performance and reduction of errors (i.e., fumbles) depends on this more and more frequent selection of optimum movements (see p. 17). Where the dimensions of materials on components used in a task are very consistent, as in electronic assemblies, the movement patterns are repeated with great consistency. Where the material itself is variable, as in the tobacco and food industries, a repertory of slightly differing motions is required, although these differences can usually be detected only by detailed film analysis of the task.

3. *Decision making.* Numerous decisions are made in the execution of even the simplest task—the choice of which hand to use, which fingers, which form of grasp, and so on. The human body, and especially the hands, are capable of such a wide repertory of movements that in every activity we must predict which is likely to be successful, and select the pattern of movement, or method, which proves successful.

In more complex tasks, such as machine setting and maintenance, decisions of increased complexity are called for from the central processes. The location and correction of faults in man–machine systems cannot be performed without diagnostic procedures whereby the worker decides the true cause of any stoppage or malfunctioning of plant or machinery. The basis on which such diagnosis is made is often quite complex; it entails an understanding of the machine system, a detailed recognition of the symptoms revealed by the fault and, where a fault could result from one of several causes, a sense of the probabilities involved.

The ability to derive the fullest information from a faulty product or machine manifests itself in the performance of most experienced craftsmen, who are able to recognize features that others fail to observe, to derive a meaningfulness from them, and to make judgments about cause and effect. Thus the mechanic on a packing machine carefully observes the details of a faulty carton and from these determines whether the folding mechanism, the corner-breaking mechanism, or the tucker blade is the cause of a fault.

4. *Translation of information.* In most activities (industrial work,

sports, military service, surgery, etc.), the human operator derives direct *nonsymbolic* information from the task by way of the senses (Seymour, 1967, 1968b). In some tasks, such as capstan and cold-forging machine setting and coil winding, external information in the form of charts, drawings and diagrams has to be used by the worker. This information has to be abstracted from its symbolic form and "translated" by the worker into a form meaningful for the task. The central processes are involved, and this feature of such tasks presents particular difficulty where there is frequent reference to external information. In the wiring of telephone and telecommunications gear, for example, the external information has to be "translated" into appropriate action for cutting, wrapping, soldering, and dressing wires (Seymour, 1967).

EXPERIMENTS ON ACQUISITION OF OCCUPATIONAL SKILLS

The study of the acquisition of skills may be said to have begun with the work of Bryan and Harter (1897, 1899). In their studies of the "telegraphic language" (Morse code reception and transmission), these investigators set "an entirely new standard in the scientific analysis of human learning" (Zangwill, 1965). Their discoveries that speed improved as subjects dealt with larger units (by progressing from letters to syllables, and then to words and whole phrases) and of the plateaux (or periods of no improvement) on the learning curve, constituted an important contribution to human knowledge about learning.

Subsequently Book (1925), in his comparable studies on the skill of typewriting, found similar features in the acquisition of skills. (More recent views on plateaux were given by Keller, 1958). Among the first to describe the basic physiological and psychological factors in the acquisition of skill was Pear, in his little book *Skill in Work and Play* (1924). Although he drew on existing knowledge, Pear for the first time clearly indicated the features of sensory input and motor output in athletic and industrial skills. His subjective analysis of ice skating was more detailed than that of any sport previously studied, and he emphasized the importance of the kinesthetic, as against the visual sense, in skilled performance.

During the 1930s the Industrial Health Research Board, which had been established in the United Kingdom after World War I, published several studies on industrial skills. Of these, the study of learning curves by Blackburn (1936) was valuable for the author's suggestion that the usefulness of different methods of training could be compared by plotting relative learning curves—a method that has been almost universally followed since then.

In 1934 Cox published his work entitled *Manual Skill*, which includes the most exhaustive introspective analysis of simple manual activities. He also graphed the times taken by subjects in assembling screws, insulators, containers, and wedges in making lamp holders and analyzed the improvement in relation to individuals and to tasks. He learned that there were features characteristic of tasks as well as of individuals, that the curves derived from groups of subjects were much smoother than those of individuals, and that the final ranking of subjects differed from the initial ranking. He also found an inverse relationship between variability and ability in these assembly tasks, and a positive correlation between variability and improvability. Cox's work was the first comprehensive psychological study of manual skills and of the factors involved in predicting human performance in manual tasks.

In Belgium, a contemporary, de Montpellier (1935) studied speed skills in hand movements by the use of Gilbreth's chronocyclegraph.* He found that in repeating a geometric pattern of movements, subjects started with straight lines but gradually progressed to smoother, curved, and ballistic movements.

In the United States, Barnes and others in 1938 initiated an important series of studies on more specifically industrial tasks at the University of Iowa. The experiments were interrupted by the outbreak of war, but they contributed an important step in introducing industrial tasks to the laboratory for the detailed study of the acquisition of skills. The research had started originally as *motion* study, but two experiments were especially important in relation to skills. Barnes and Mundel (1938) recorded the therblig (or basic motion) times for *reaching* to a contact plate, *grasping* a pin, *moving* it to a bush, and *positioning* and inserting it. Owing to the nature of the apparatus, it was not possible to separate all the individual therblig times, but the investigators did find that some elements improved more than others. A more extensive experiment in the laboratory by Barnes, Perkins, and Juran (1940) on positioning a relay spring with tweezers into a die provided valuable insight on the effect of practice on the performance of this factory task. Individual learning curves for the elements were plotted, and variations between subjects and the distribution of element times in relation to means were studied. A particularly valuable addition was the study of the visual patterns made

---

* A chronocyclegraph is a device developed by Gilbreth for recording and timing movement patterns by photographing a flashing lamp bulb attached to the finger, hand, or other part of the body (Barnes, 1968).

possible by film analysis. Barnes and Mundel found that the learning curves for various therbligs showed marked differences in characteristics, some being learned quickly, some slowly; thus the learning curve for the whole cycle depended on the proportion of quickly learned and slowly learned therbligs.

After the war, K. U. Smith and others at the University of Wisconsin initiated a series of investigations on motor skills (Wehrkamp and Smith, 1952). The results showed that manipulative elements in tasks improved more than movement elements and, moreover, (Smith, Rubrin, and Von Trebra, 1952) that these manipulative elements displayed uniform improvement, whereas movement elements underwent limited and inconsistent changes. Later, studies were made of perceptual factors in the acquisition of skills with specific relation to the role of sensory feedback (Smith and Wargo, 1963). This work continues, and during the past 20 years it has been extended to cover many spheres of human performance. Of particular relevance to human performance at work are those on motor learning (e.g., Smith and Sussman, 1969) and on delayed feedback (Smith and Sussman, 1970).

Another area of importance in training is that explored over many years by Fleishman and others—namely, the factorial analysis of changes in performance with increasing skill. Fleishman and Hempel (1954a) determined the percentage of variance represented by each of 10 factors (rate of movement, psychomotor coordination, specific coordination, etc.) at eight different stages of practice on the Complex Coordination Test, and found that the factors changed significantly as performance improved. These results were important, not only for selection (see Chapter 6), but also for training, and the authors concluded: "It is quite conceivable that the abilities contributing to individual differences in earlier stages of skill attainment in such jobs may be somewhat different than those contributing variance at more advanced and terminal levels of proficiency" (p. 251). These studies were extended by the same authors (1956) to the organization of abilities in perceptual motor skill using results from Air Force studies and again by Fleishman (1960) using results from rotary pursuit performance. Among other conclusions, Fleishman stated that "skill in later performance is more a function of specific habits acquired during practice on the task itself, relative to transfer from previous abilities, skills and habits" (p. 168).

Fleishman's point was followed by Hinrichs (1970) with the consideration that "it may be possible to increase the efficiency of skill training by concentrating throughout the training period on those abilities required for final proficiency rather than on those abilities required only in the early stages of skill acquisition." After analyzing the results of experiments on different methods and approaches in rotary pursuit tracking, he concluded:

"These results also point to the need for careful job analysis of the types of skills required for final proficiency in a task, and, if initial tests are utilized, designing the tests to measure these final proficiency skills to the extent possible. Also, there may be some very marked savings in training time by focusing primarily on skills required for final proficiency early in training, rather than employing a more gradual progression in training emphasis from early to final skill requirements" (p. 64). The even more important implications of the studies just described in *selection* are discussed in Chapter 6.

It will be seen that the analytical approach to training for skills discussed in the succeeding chapters is based on precisely the type of analysis considered by Hinrichs of the experienced workers' skills. At Ann Arbor, Michigan, Hancock and others have made detailed studies in analyzing the learning curves of the methods–time measurement (MTM)[*] basic motions with a view to using these curves in predicting the learning time required on tasks composed of these basic motions (Hancock and Foulke, 1963; Clifford and Hancock, 1964, see also pp. 35-37).

Further studies on skills began in the United Kingdom during World War II with the establishment at Cambridge of the Medical Research Council's Applied Psychology Unit (APU) under Sir Frederic Bartlett and Kenneth Craik. This group was originally concerned with problems of military skills. Since the war, however, it has broadened its scope, and the work has made a unique contribution to the understanding of the *nature* of skilled performance. Broadbent (1958) and others have also dealt with problems of the *acquisition* of skills, and studies on specifically *industrial* tasks have been reported by Siddall (1954), Conrad (1951), and numerous and subsequent workers in the APU. The work of the "Cambridge School" is perhaps best summarized in Welford's *Ageing and Human Skill* (1958) and *Fundamentals of Skill* (1968) and in Broadbent (1958, Chapter 11).

In Europe, where the theories of psychotechnique of Carrard (1949), Biasch (1953), and Silberer (1956) had influenced industrial training

---

[*] Methods–time measurement (MTM) is a procedure that enables any manual operation or method to be analyzed into the basic motions required to perform it, assigning to each basic motion a predetermined time standard dependent on the nature of the motion and the conditions under which it is made (Maynard, Stegemerten, and Schwab, 1948). Methods–time measurement is one of several pre-determined motion–time systems.

very markedly during and after the war, de Jong (1957, 1960) studied the change in cycle time required for repetitive tasks and derived a formula from which successive cycle times can be calculated.

In Great Britain during the 1950s the Medical Research Council and the Department of Scientific and Industrial Research (DSIR) sponsored numerous researches on industrial skills which were financed from Conditional Aid Funds. A summary of these researches is provided in the DSIR booklets *Training Made Easier* (1960) and that by Clay (1964).

Among the studies financed in part by Conditional Aid Funds was one on "The Nature and Acquisition of Industrial Skills," and this was carried out in the Department of Engineering Production, at the University of Birmingham, England (Crossman and Seymour, 1957; Corlett, 1960; Seymour, 1967). These studies, initiated in 1951 in the time of the late Professor T. U. Mathew and continued under Professor N. A. Dudley, have been pursued for 20 years, and reference is made elsewhere (Chapters 6 and 7) to more recent work. Of the earlier experiments, two types are particularly relevant to the acquisition of industrial skills (Seymour 1954a, 1954b, 1955, 1956, 1959, 1962, 1967). These are assembly experiments and machine control experiments.

Assembly Experiments

The assembly experiments aimed at determining the relative rates of improvement of the four main "assembly" therbligs (Reach, Grasp, Move, and Position)* in industrial assembly tasks and the way in which improvement was attained within each therblig. Preliminary film analysis of industrial tasks had shown that not all therbligs improved equally: Grasp and Position (the more perceptually stringent† therbligs in the cases studied) improved more than the transport therbligs Reach and Move. Subsequent experiments with a three-hole connector component (part of an automobile fuse box assembly), using current through the body technique and electronic timing apparatus (the SETAR; Welford, 1952) confirmed these points and led to the following conclusions (Seymour, 1967, p. 131):

1. The basic elements of a task—reaching for an object, grasping it, moving it, and positioning it—do not improve equally nor at the same rate as overall performance improves.

---

* An excellent study of the development of these skills in children is given by Kay in *Principles of Skill Acquisition*, Bilodeau and Bilodeau, (Eds., 1969).
† The term *stringent* is used to indicate perceptual situations where either the load (in bits of information to be processed) is high, or the level of discrimination (in a particular sensory channel) is unusually fine, or both.

2. The stationary elements (grasp and position) contribute more to overall improvement than movement elements (reach and move) *not* because they are stationary but because, in the typical situations examined, they involve greater perceptual stringency.

3. Generalizing from the two previous items, those elements which involve most perception improve most, and those which involve least perception improve least, during overall improvement on a task.

4. Those elements which improve most also manifest the greatest variability: the greater the variability in the time taken to perform an element, the greater is its improvability.

5. The range of times and the minimum time of elements show little change. The reduction in mean performance time of the elements does not arise from an overall lowering of these times; rather, it is due to a shift in their distribution, whereby the shorter times are achieved more and more frequently and slower times less frequently. Apparently, higher rates of performance come not from going quicker but from going slowly less often.

6. Salvendy (1968, 1969b; see Chapter 7) subsequently performed experiments using similar experimental techniques and high-speed filming, in order to analyze the improvement of subjects' therblig times in performing O'Connor, Purdue, and other tests. He found that "stationary" elements did not improve more than "transport" elements, but that those elements which "exhibit the highest perceptual load improve the most." His results also showed that improvement in the higher levels of performance were accompanied by:

(a) A decrease in knowledge of results.
(b) Greater smoothness within and between movements.
(c) Simpler motion patterns of fingers and thumb.
(d) Better timing and channeling of sensory information input.
(e) A decrease in frequency and duration of fumbles.

Machine Control Experiments

The machine control experiments were designed to determine the effects of different conditions of learning on the attainment of subjects' speed skills in a typical machine tool task, namely, operating a capstan lathe.* The first experiments on this task were done with student subjects.

---

* With the introduction of automatic attachments and computer control, the operation of capstan lathes is seldom done by workers, now, but the findings from the experiments can be considered generally valid for similar manually controlled machines.

Since these individuals might be unrepresentative of factory populations, however, the experiments were repeated using young factory workers.

Fourteen student subjects were divided randomly into two groups: the members of one were shown the task and asked to repeat it as rapidly as possible without errors (which would result in scrap components) the other group were shown the total task but asked to practice each element separately until it could be achieved correctly to a target time before combining the elements into the total job. Each subject worked for half an hour a day for a week and was given knowledge of results in terms of times and errors. At the end of a week a test run of 15 min. (target performance: 20 complete cycles per subject with no errors) was attempted by all the subjects. The results appear in Table 1.1.

Table 1.1   Results Obtained[a] by Student Subjects

Method	Subjects	Correct Cycles	Turret Errors	Cross-Slide Errors
Whole	7	77	47	17
Part	7	121	28	9

[a] Total χ^2 with 2 degrees of freedom $= 16.13$ $p < .1$ percent.

The performance of those following the part method was superior to that of those using the whole method, both in terms of greater number of correct cycles completed and in smaller number of errors. In this experiment, as in many industrial tasks, subjects were in effect penalized for errors; that is, if they spent 30 to 40 sec. on a cycle and then made an error, the time was irrevocably lost and their score of correct cycles in 15 min. was thus reduced.

Each individual element for each subject was recorded on a kymograph* and the results graphed. Those on the whole method exhibited improvement on all elements, whereas those on the part method showed little improvement for simple elements; but for those elements which involved greater perceptual stringency, much greater improvement was observed. Comparisons of subjects' individual cycle times indicated that those using the part method were less variable and slightly quicker; moreover, they required less repetition to attain target time. Transfer from

* A kymograph is an apparatus consisting essentially of a rotating drum; it is used for obtaining graphic records of physiological and psychological processes (Drever, 1965).

the component parts to the whole operation was accomplished with very little diminution in performance.

Subsequently the experiment was repeated, with some variation, using young workers from a box factory who were unacquainted with the capstan lathe. For this experiment 15 subjects were divided at random into three groups; the first and third group were given the whole and the part treatment as before. The second group was given an intermediate treatment (i.e., after initial demonstration they practiced the two perceptually stringent elements—operate cross slide and turret—then went directly to the whole operation). This was called the isolation method, since the difficult elements were isolated but the job was not fully divided into parts. Subjects again practiced for 30 min. each day for a week and then had a 15-min. test run. Scores are given in Table 1.2.

Table 1.2   Results Obtained by Factory Workers

Method	Subjects	Correct Cycles	Turret Errors	Cross-Slide Errors
Whole	5	56	18	13
Isolation	5	96	13	5
Part	5	103	4	4

Again, the subjects using the part method scored much higher than those using the whole method, and those using the isolation method were not significantly below those using the part method, as Table 1.3 indicates.

It is noteworthy that learning the *sequence* of the operation did not appear to present any difficulty to these subjects—this knowledge was acquired long before speed and accuracy were attained.

Table 1.3   Comparison of Results of Three Methods

Comparison of Method	Value of χ^2	Degrees of Freedom	Probability
Whole vs. isolation	11.468	2	$p > .01$ (very significant)
Isolation vs. part	5.090	2	$p > .05$ (not significant)
Whole vs. part	25.011	2	$p < .001$ (highly significant)

Results

The results of the machine control experiments may be summarized thus:

1. Part methods may have an advantage over whole methods for a more difficult or complex task (i.e., one in which the perceptual requirements of certain elements are stringent, or highly coordinated).

2. The terms "part" and "whole" are not, perhaps, very suitable for distinguishing methods of learning industrial tasks, since the more important distinction seems to be that between the more perceptually stringent elements and those less perceptually stringent.

3. The difficulties in learning a task of this kind appear to be not in mastering the sequence but in learning precise control. The problem in this appears to be one of perceptual learning, in identifying cues and appreciating feedback, rather than one of motor learning.

4. The way in which information is "channeled" to the operator from the task is an important part of the development of skills.

5. The maintenance of the speed of performance, which was more readily attained on isolated elements, did not appear to be unduly difficult when these elements were combined; that is, there did not seem to be an appreciable loss in performance in transferring from the components of such a task to the task as a whole.

6. The superiority of a part method in the more complex type of task arose not only from a reduction in the time per correct cycle but also from a reduction in the time occupied by cycles which contained error.

7. The greater consistency of results from the part method is attributable to the larger number of repetitions of elements that needed them; on the other hand, less time was spent practicing elements that could already be accomplished satisfactorily at target speed.

Further evidence from these results indicates that the primary difficulty in acquiring speed skills on such industrial tasks lies in the field of the receptor rather than in the area of the effector processes. This is an interesting corollary to the findings in the complementary studies on the acquisition of skills; namely, that differences in element times accompanying changes in overall performance occur more in perceptually stringent elements than in elements involving less perception.

On the basis of the results of these and other experiments, Crossman (1959) proposed a mathematical model for a theory of the acquisition of speed skill. These results have also formed the basis for the hypothesis (see Chapter 7) that changes in the distributions of performance times provide a measure for the prediction of the rate of acquisition of speed skills (Seymour 1959, 1967; Salvendy, Seymour, and Corlett, 1970).

FACTORY OBSERVATIONS ON THE ACQUISITION OF SKILLS

Changes in the distribution of element times during subjects' improvement on assembly tasks have been reported from laboratory studies (e.g., Barnes, Perkins, and Juran, 1940; Crossman and Seymour, 1957; Clifford and Hancock, 1964; Seymour, 1967). Few, if any, have been published from observations in a factory, however. During the practical learning situation in industry, it is seldom possible to record changes in the distribution of element times owing to the difficulties of achieving separate timings for individual elements. However, in "off-the-job" training where skills analysis training procedures (see section "Implementing a Training Course," Chapter 4) are used, trainees practice perceptually stringent elements of a job in isolation before combining them into the total job. This provides an opportunity to observe and record distribution changes in the times for small, critical elements. Such a situation arose in training capacitor winders in a telecommunications factory, where time records of successive attempts on two elements were analyzed.

Two elements were selected from the training buildup of the Mark II capacitor winding machine—the welding operation (WL) and winding to zero (Z). These two were chosen because most data were available on them and because the trainee (the same in both cases) had special difficulty in mastering these two parts of the whole job. The operator, a girl aged 16 years, had joined the firm from school and had spent 13 months on a different type of operation. The procedures were as follows:

1. *Welding* (WL) consists of selecting, with one hand, two leadout pins from a tray on the left-hand side of the machine at about shoulder level (operator sitting) and welding one pin to one foil and the second to another foil. The foils are fed off separate spools and wound between two layers of insulation plastic to the winding mandrel. The welding heads are operated by two foot pedals operated by right and left feet, respectively. Picking up the pins involves the selection of just two pins by feel (decision making depends on the orientation of the flattened welding ends) and pin changing in the hands according to the decision made. This aspect was specially trained in a preliminary exercise and the whole operation was practiced about 20 times before timing began.

2. *Winding to zero* (Z), the element that follows the welding operation, consists of winding the mandrel with the right hand and observing a meter reading. The right-hand wind has a 2:1 gear ratio, and a coarse control of the needle is obtained. Fine control is achieved by finally reach-

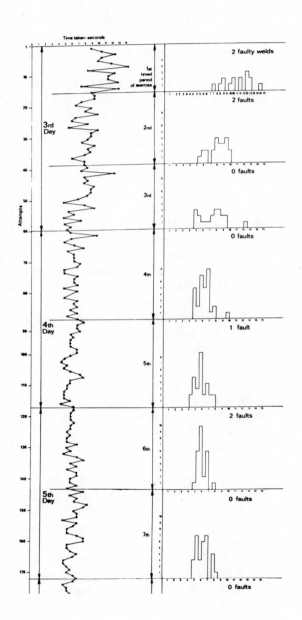

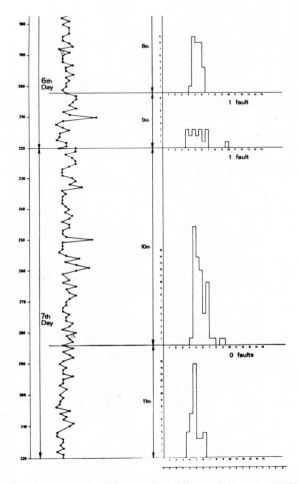

Figure 1.3. Capacitor winding: element WL. (From Seymour, 1968a.)

ing a turning point, using the left hand to turn the winding mandrel directly by means of a knob on the shaft.

The most difficult part of the operation consists of winding and anticipating the actual turning point of the meter needle, since winding past it is undesirable. There is no special exercise for this element, but the element itself was practiced for about 20 attempts before timing commenced.

23

Results

The results are shown in two ways (Figures 1.3 and 1.4). The individual times are presented graphically, and each day's attempts are also arranged in histogram form, with means and standard deviations.

The trainee's progress—from a mean of 3.6 sec to 0.6 sec for the Z element, and from 1.9 sec to 0.5 sec for the WL—is clearly indicated; but in each case this is followed by an increase in mean time. The curves in each case become less variable. The initial distributions are very roughly normal, although there are gaps in both cases; the distributions become more skewed, ending as almost vertical columns.

UNITARY CONCEPTS: PERCEPTION AND INFORMATION THEORY

Although the outline of human performance so far depicted—that of sensory stimulus, decision making, and motor response—is essential to the understanding of skill, it is far from complete. To conceive of skilled performance as comprised solely of separate responses to individual stimuli is inadequate (Lashley, 1951). Skill is more complex than such brief terms can indicate; and the need to find a unitary basis for understanding it has given rise to many researches.

Human skill is the more difficult to comprehend because so many dissimilar and apparently incompatible forms of energy are involved in it. The sources of physical stimuli that impinge on the sense organs (e.g., sound and light waves) are entirely different from the ear and eye which they stimulate and different again from the sensations they arouse. The afferent and efferent neural impulses are different both from the stimuli that initiate them and from the sensations to which they give rise. Again, the activities in the cortex, about which we know least, are different from the electrochemical changes in the muscle, whose contractions produce the effector response.

The complexity of skilled performance is particularly exemplified in the receptor processes. At any given moment, an operator's receptors are being bombarded by innumerable stimuli from many sources. Most of the stimuli reaching any given sense organ are disregarded because they are filtered out before they reach the final channel, thus failing to elicit a response. Those which elicit a response, or are recognized, are said to be *perceived*. Drever (1965) defined perception as "the process of becoming immediately aware of something; usually employed of sense perception, when the thing of which we become immediately aware is the object affecting a sense organ." Perception is something more than sensation—it is indeed the meaningfulness which the individual attaches to the sensation. As Holding wrote "Perception is the processing of information" (1965, p. 11).

The literature on the psychology of perception, and particularly that of the special senses, is very extensive, and the subject is treated in text books of psychology. (e.g., Sidowski, 1966). Five features are common to all the senses, and these are important in the understanding of human performance:

1. In accordance with the "law of specific irritability," each sense responds only to its own type of stimulus, and conveys only one type of information. Thus the eye cannot respond to sound or the ear to light. When an organ of special sense is stimulated in an abnormal way, it conveys only its normal form of sense information. For example, a blow on the eye produces the sensation of light and we "see stars" (but it still hurts!).

2. The synapses in the neural path between end organ and brain permit impulses to travel in one direction only. There is a variety of connections between the neural paths, and this gives rise to a summation of the sensory information in the final common path.

3. There is no resemblance between the form of the stimulus and the resulting sensation. The physical stimuli of light waves of various wavelengths bears no similarity to the corresponding color sensations they arouse, and there is no similarity between sound waves of different lengths and the sensations of pitch resulting from them.

4. For each sense there is a limiting threshold of stimulation below which no sensation is detected; there is also a minimal difference between stimuli below which no difference of sensation is recognized. Increases in stimulus do not give rise to similar increases in sensation—the stimulus increment required to give rise to a just-detectable difference of sensation bears a constant relation to the original stimulus intensity (Weber-Fechner law). The proportionate increases in stimulus required to produce a just-detectable increase in sensation are different for each sense; the relative amounts of such proportionate increases are quoted in the appropriate texts (e.g., Mowbray and Gebhard, 1958).

5. The sensory mechanisms are all subject to adaptation; that is, to changes in the excitability of the sense organ resulting from the continued application of a constant stimulus. Visual adaptation to conditions of lower illumination is a matter of everyday experience: when we move indoors from the sunlight, many objects are at first invisible, even though the room may be quite well lit; gradually, as the eye adapts itself, the objects are clearly seen. Similar adaptative changes occur in the other senses, although they may be less readily recognized. Sensory adaptation

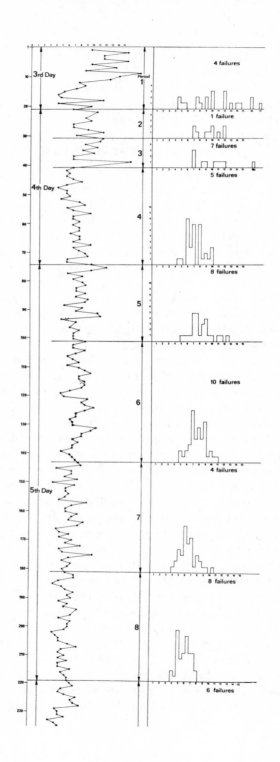

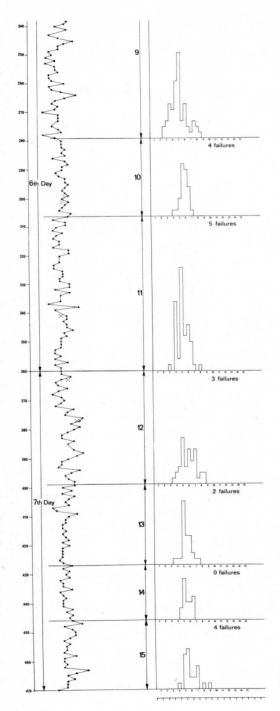

Figure 1.4. Capacitor winding: element Z; time taken–seconds. (From Seymour, 1968a.)

is fast for touch, relatively slower for pressure, and slowest of all for vision.

Crossman (Crossman and Seymour 1957) has listed five phases in the perceptual processing required for any activity:

1. Plan.
2. Initiate.
3. Control.
4. End.
5. Check.

Every activity involves some degree of *planning*. When picking up a pencil, the brain needs to perceive where it is and to determine with which hand it is to be grasped and by what positioning of thumb and fingers. Then the movements are *initiated* by the brain's (unconscious) determination of the muscle groups that are to be innervated to accomplish this. During the movement of the hand it has to be *controlled* so that it does not overshoot or undershoot the objective, and corrective adjustments are made if necessary during final deceleration. The movement is *ended* when the brain perceives tactually that the pencil has been reached. Then the achievement of the objective is *checked*—and it is a feature of skilled performance that this checking of achievement becomes briefer and more facile as skill develops.

Crossman (1964, p. 33) has analysed diagrammatically the component functions of the human receptor system in the form shown in (Fig. 1.5)

It will be seen that Crossman postulates first a filter process, then a temporary store for data from previous fixations, then a local pattern recognizer linked with a permanent store of pattern elements, then a temporary store for local pattern symbols followed by a recognition center, linked with a permanent store, for complete objects, into which center data from other channels can be fed. The ultimate perceptual response, in Crossman's diagram, emanates from a temporary store for recognized objects, and this perceptual response he describes as "giving a summary description of the environment in a pre-arranged code."

Perceptual processes in skilled performance give rise to decisions regarding the particular effector reaction to be initiated. At any given point the operator has available to him a range of possible effector actions and he must choose between them—by chance, by using stored information, or by current information arriving by way of the senses. The operator has to select from a large number of available alternatives and from a small class of successful motions. The need to select between various motion patterns and the degree of that selection constitutes the perceptual stringency

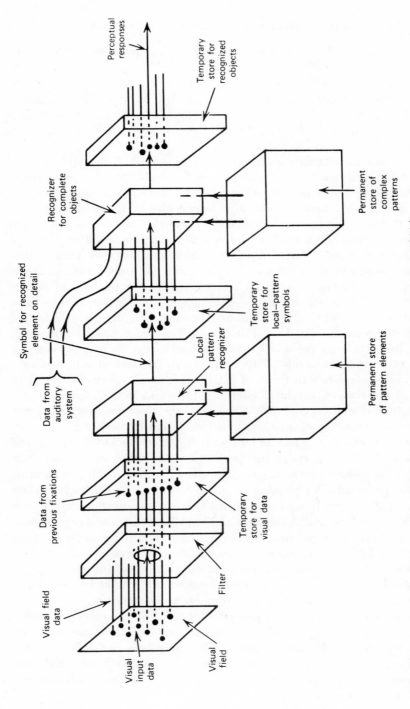

Figure 1.5. Component functions of the human receptor system. (From Crossman, 1964.)

29

(or perceptual load) of a given element of work (Crossman and Seymour, 1957).

Crossman (1964) has also set out a schematic organization of the human effector system showing the theoretical steps by which information is dealt with from the receipt of receptor signals to the initiation of limb action. The import of this in relation to performance on industrial tasks has been discussed by Seymour (1967).

The desire to establish a *unitary* basis on which skill could be considered, given its multivariate complexity, has led to the use of information theory (or communication theory) in the explanation of human performance. By this theory we are able to conceive of the whole receptor, decision-making, and effector processes as a single communication system by which information is received by way of the senses, dealt with by the brain, and used to initiate responses. Since this involves control, the information processing also includes cybernetics (Wiener, 1949), the term derived from the Greek word for steersman. For the purpose of understanding skilled performance, the concepts of information theory have proved more helpful than the stimulus–response (SR) theories of learning principally derived from Hull (1952). As Broadbent (1958) remarked, the "cybernetic language is as great an advance over S–R terminology as arabic over roman numerals." Fitts commented: "Behaviour can be understood more completely in terms of the processing of information than in terms of the transformation of energy" (Fitts and Posner, 1967).

By information theory we thus conceive of the receptor–effector process complex as consisting of a communication system transmitting a unitary medium: information. This communication system includes the stimuli and their physical properties, the processes of the sense organs and their neural connections with the brain, the cortical decision-making apparatus, and the organization of physical response by muscular contraction. The precise technical meaning of *information* in this context is that which reduces uncertainty and determines choice. Where there are two equally probable alternatives, one unit of information is required in order to make a choice; and this unit is known as one *bit* (derived from *binary digit*) of information. The most felicitous exemplification of this term was supplied by Kay, who noted (1957) that when a mother is told that her new-born child is a boy or a girl, this supplies one *bit* of information.

Information implies anything that enables a choice to be made between alternatives and reduces uncertainty or *entropy*. In the human operator, it is transmitted by the nerve paths, which constitute *channels* having a limited capacity in terms of bits per second that can be transmitted, and this transmission may be disturbed by noise (i.e., random events conveying no information).

Thus information theory provides an appropriate conceptual framework for studying skilled performance, since it is a function of the sensory, central nervous, and motor systems, which are largely concerned with processing and storing information. Crossman (1964) has outlined a systematic approach to the problem under these three headings. The work of the receptor processes consists in providing the brain with sufficient information about the environment to enable it to determine the course of immediate action and to establish a store of information for use in prediction. All but a small proportion of incoming data are rejected by peripheral filtering; the remainder are used to decide between a limited series of alternatives, and the process is smoothed by the use of temporary storage to facilitate discrimination.

In order for objects to be discriminated, they must differ in at least one sensory dimension; to be recognized, they must be compared with "templates" or stored patterns, whose collection commences at an early age but increases with perceptual learning. The recognition process develops both spatially and temporarily, as when the young reader progresses from characters to syllables, from syllables to words, and from words to sentences. In industrial tasks the perceptual meaningfulness derived from sensory stimuli similarly develops with increased skill. For example, a tube of toothpaste may appear perfectly satisfactory to a customer, although the crimping at the base might be recognized by the machine operator as uneven, and the same feature might indicate to the machine fitter that (a) the machine needed to be adjusted and (b) if not attended to, the fault would get progressively worse. In addition to this perceptual development, there is, for complex patterns, an integration of the detail percepts, which involves temporary storage while the total picture or perceptual pattern is built up. The evidence on this process of perceptual selection and integration has been surveyed by Welford (1968) and summarized by him (1970) thus:

1. Perception is not to be understood as a matter of sensory data alone but in terms of constructs or frameworks.

2. The process of selection and integration seems to be designed to secure economy of decision.

3. Incoming data are treated in both spatial and temporal terms.

Gregory (1964, 1970) has suggested that perception is a process of selection of internal models and that sensory data are used to modify behavior in terms of these models. Emphasizing that objects, as perceived, are more than statistical groupings of sensed events, he stated: "Sensory inputs are grouped according to the repertoire of behavioural skills of the owner of the perceptual system. One man's object may be another's pattern—or be nothing but randomness." (Gregory, 1970, p. 31.) Thus, in the previous example of the toothpaste tube, the fault is random and meaningless to the customer; it is recognized as a fault by the operator, but for the fitter it is associated with the complex mechanism whose malfunctioning has caused it.

It is further suggested by Gregory (1970) that the acquisition of skills is aided by the construction of these "internal models" resulting from the storage of information ("latent learning"). This affects the ability to discriminate and, later, makes it possible to deal with information in larger units, as when the pianist recognizes whole chords as units and is able to play them at a speed that could not be attained if the notes had to be read separately, owing to the limited rate of information transmission in the human system. Our abilities to select essentials and ignore irrelevant detail, to identify patterns and to ignore redundant information, enable us to attain a higher performance that could otherwise be reached, given our limited capacity to transmit information and make individual decisions. This capacity to ignore redundant information enables performance to be predictive, to continue functioning when there is a temporary lapse in information input, to cope with changes of input, and to generalize behavior to deal with situations similar to those for which a "model" was developed (i.e., to attain a positive transfer of training).

The concepts and terms used in information theory are helpful in the understanding of human performance and the acquisition of skills. They are similarly useful in the understanding of the analytical selection and training techniques discussed in later chapters of this book. In particular, their use is exemplified in the following ways:

1. For job analysis and skills analysis—in identifying task components that are perceptually difficult (i.e., those involving high perceptual load as expressed in "bits" of information; e.g., Fitts, 1954).

2. For training—in providing a basis for the design of training "exercises" on task components with high rate of information transmission and, correspondingly, for determining which components will need less attention because of their lower rate of information transmission or perceptual load. Information theory is also useful in training as a basis for comparing the complexity of tasks (Konz, Dickey, McCutchan, and Koe, 1967).

3. For selection—in the development of improved tests for predicting ability on manual tasks. For example, the One-Hole test (Chapter 7) was developed to reduce the "noise" resulting from the inconsistency in movements used in performing the Purdue Pegboard (and other) tests.

4. For criteria—in determining the relative difficulties of tasks that can be measured, for example, in kilocalories or in terms of "bits" of information.

THE PREDICTION OF OUTPUT STANDARDS
AND LEARNING TIME

Since the days of Taylor (Barnes, 1968), more precise means for measuring work and for predicting performance have been sought. Timing with stop watches and portable time recorders has made it possible to study work in elemental detail (e.g., Barnes, 1968). It is also possible to predict the times required for basic motions, derived from those proposed by Gilbreth, from the results of such studies and by filming (e.g., Maynard, Stegemerten, and Schwab, 1948).

Difficulties in predicting the time required for a task—even if it is assumed that element times are additive[*]—can arise if the perceptual load and stringency of the task differ from those within the tasks from which the data of the pre-determined motion–time system were derived.

The measurement of the perceptual component in skilled performance on existing tasks, and its prediction in new tasks, remains a considerable problem in the study of work. As Welford (1958) stated, the sense organs themselves take very little time to function, but effector action usually takes a great deal—so much so that industrial time and motion study "has often attempted to obtain analyses of performance essentially in terms of the times taken by overt movements," whereas "the limits to speed of performance . . . are usually set by the time required for the central mechanisms to act in discriminating one signal from another in carrying out the translation process, and in selecting responding action" (p. 31).[*] Thus in predicting the time required for a task, or a movement, we need to know the perceptual as well as the spatial requirements, since "the speed of motor performance is seldom determined by the time required to execute the movements themselves, but by the duration of the sensory and central processes controlling them (Welford, 1964, p. 65). This is well illustrated by the differences in time taken to move the hand 16 in. under differing perceptual loads (Seymour, 1967).

Early work on the study of perceptual load and performance (Seymour, 1954a) led to the consideration of methods of measuring perception in industrial tasks, and for this the concepts of information theory seemed to be appropriate. At the time it was considered that the human operator's rate of processing information was constant (e.g., Hick, 1952). If, then,

---

[*] Additive—for discussion of this topic see pp. 272.

[*] Doubts and criticisms about the inadequacies of early time study techniques were expressed as much as 50 years ago by psychologists (e.g., Myers, 1922), who as Broadbent (C. S. Myers lecture, 1970) pointed out, showed that early practitioners of time and motion study had misunderstood the nature of human beings.

the perceptual content of a task could be determined in bits of information, and if the proficient human operator were to deal with these at a constant speed, it would be possible to predict the ultimate, irreducible time for a task and to measure an individual's performance in relation to this.

However, subsequent work by Crossman (Crossman and Seymour, 1957) and others indicated that information rates varying from 4 to 6 bits/sec were to be found in symbolic tasks and from 10 to 25 bits/sec or higher in nonsymbolic tasks. At least for the present, these findings have prevented the development of predictive techniques for performance and learning time based on the information analysis of industrial tasks.

The measurement and illustration of improvements in performance by means of learning curves was commenced by Bryan and Harter (1897) and continued by Book (1925), Cox (1934), Blackburn (1936), Barnes and Mundel (1938), and others. More recently, in Europe, the work of de Jong (1957, 1960, 1964) has been concerned with the reduction in time required for consecutive work cycles where no technical or organizational change in work has occurred. From a review of a considerable range of industrial tasks, de Jong has demonstrated that work measurement times can be calculated for a particular work cycle in accordance with the formula

$$T_s = T_1 \left(M + \frac{1-M}{S^m} \right)$$

where T_1 is the time for the first cycle of a task, T_s is the time for the sth cycle, m is the exponent of the reduction, and M a "factor of incompressibility" that is dependent on the nature of the work and on the operator's initial skill and familiarity with the work.

Crossman (1956b, 1959) obtained curves similar to those plotted by de Jong in a studies of cigar making and capstan operation. Crossman also found that the decrease in time for individual elements of a task follows the same curve, a finding confirmed by Fitts (1962). From a study of the reduction in cycle times and of the times for their constituent elements from the machine control experiments described earlier, Crossman developed a theory of the acquisition of speed skill (Crossman, 1959).

In the United States, learning curves have been used for more than 30 years in the prediction of time required for the manufacture of aircraft and other systems. The basic theory derived from the curves is that when any operation is repeated, the time for the operation will decrease by a certain fraction each time the number of repetitions is doubled. This fraction is of the order of 0.8 in aircraft manufacture; but is not the same for all industries or for all operations and may vary between 0.7 and 0.95.

Corlett and Morcombe (1970), quoting Blakenship and Taylor (1938), reported early studies in the Jantzen Knitting Mills, Portland, Oregon, dating from 1938, showing differing improvement factors within this range for three different needle machine operations. Since then, hundreds of examples have been reported in Europe (e.g., Rohmert and Schlaich, 1966), in the United Kingdom (e.g., Glover, 1966a; Cooke, 1967), and in the United States.

It is in the United States that, during the past decade, the most extensive studies of the predictive value of learning curves have been carried out by Hancock (1967) and others at Ann Arbor, Michigan.

This research is a natural concomitant of predetermined motion time systems for determining and predicting the time necessary for performing operations at prescribed standards. The research has been carried out for the M.T.M. Association for Standards and Research, Fairlawn, New Jersey, and is based on the standard system of MTM (Maynard, Stegermerten, and Schwab, 1948). Using the MTM basic motions, the experiments aim to provide data on the learning rate for each basic motion so that the time and number of repetitions required to attain MTM standards can be predicted.

It is assumed that learning rates for basic motions are additive and that the learning time for a complex operation can be derived from the learning times of its constituent basic motions. The research has been restricted to the study of *reinforcement* learning, which is distinguished from *threshold* learning. Threshold learning is "that phase during which the operator commits to memory an organized sequence of elements or motions and the length of this period, unfortunately, cannot be predicted at present." Reinforcement learning during which the operators' responses progressively become automatic can be predicted as the result of the research, and "depends primarily upon two variables: (1) the number of practice cycles and (2) the kind of motions performed" (Foulke, 1966).

The initial experiments (Hancock and Foulke, 1963) were conducted in the laboratory, with student subjects as part of the project, "to develop better methods of predicting the rate and manner in which people learn and attain standard performance times." Subjects carried out 1000 cycles of assembly operations involving different types of Reach, Grasp, Move, and Position. Learning curves for each motion were constructed and equations were derived from them. It was recognized that these experiments had numerous limitations: they were performed only by right-handed men, for a maximum of 1000 cycles, and only linear regression curves were fitted (except for the Reach data, where negative exponential curves were also fitted). Subsequent industrial studies reflect more accurately the practical problems in industry. As the authors stated, "the learning curve equations developed in the laboratory were found inadequate for predicting what actually happened under industrial conditions" (Hancock and Sathe, 1969, p. 6).

The earliest experiment reported from an industrial situation (Clifford and Hancock, 1964) was concerned with a machine operation involving Reach, Grasp, Move, and Position with both hands. Again, learning curves for the basic motions and for the cycle were constructed for each of the eight subjects, and these were compared with the predictions arrived at from the laboratory studies. Since the latter were derived from single-handed motions, which had been found to differ from two-handed learning more in the first 500 cycles, curves were drawn separately for the periods before and after this halfway point. The operators, four male and four female, ranged in age from 18 to 50 years, and the age factor was found to be significantly related to learning rates. Other factors of importance in learning also were identified (e.g., previous experience and length of practice period between breaks).

In the same year, Paine (1964) published a report of an experiment on operator learning at the Thompson Ramo Woodridge plant. The investigation was designed to extend the previous laboratory experiments (which had attempted to provide means for predicting the expected learning time of a task from its motion content) to an industrial situation. At the same time, it was desired to measure other factors, including:

1. The effects of environment.
2. Simultaneous motions in a more complex operation.
3. The characteristics of skilled and unskilled male and female operators as compared with student subjects.

The operation involved checking the dimensional characteristics of a triangular block by inserting it in a fixture, checking the dimensions on gauges, removing the block, and placing either in an *accept* or a *reject* chute.

Subjects were instructed until they passed the threshold of learning (defined as an ability to perform five cycles without reference) and timing then began. Graphs were constructed for subsequent performance until the MTM standard was attained, and the figures were compared with predictions calculated from the previous laboratory experiments. The experimenters' conclusions can be summarized thus:

1. The learning equations derived from laboratory studies were generally inadequate predictions of learning rate or cycle time.

2. Linear regression equations were poor predictions of early learning; exponential curves would be better.

3. Linear equations proved to be accurate predictions of slope in the range of 500 to 1000 repetitions.

4. Patterns of learning of experienced and inexperienced workers were different.

5. There was no difference between the performances of industrial and student subjects.

6. Age of subjects appeared to be a significant factor, but sex did not.

The two studies just mentioned and an additional one on a clerical operation are discussed at length in a report by Hancock and Sathe (1969); simultaneous movements and eye functions are considered, and methods for computing learning curves when eye movements are involved are included. This report also contains an appendix giving accounts of research on selection tests for manual operators, and it describes experiments comparing the learning rates for manual operators, and it describes experiments comparing the learning rates for simultaneous motions with those for single-handed motions.

Appendix A of Hancock and Sathe's report (1969) also contains the basic equations needed to predict manual learning rates. These are summarized in tabular form for each main MTM element and are given separately for 0 to 500 and 500 to 1000 cycles and for one-handed and simultaneous conditions.

In making predictive calculations from the tables, a basic assumption is involved; namely, that the learning curve for a given element is proportional to the magnitude of the MTM standard. Although the computation of times from these equations may appear involved, simpler explanations have been provided by Foulke (1966), Hancock (1967), and Hancock and Foulke (1966). In the last of these, a detailed example of calculations from linear data is provided to show how the number of cycles required to attain 100 percent and 120 percent performance is determined. In addition, the calculations are given from the exponential learning equation:

$$T_N = K \times T_S \times N^{-a}$$

where T_N = time for the Nth cycle
T_S = standard time (0.0001 min)
N = cycle number
a = learning exponent, which depends on the number of cycles to standard

Further study of the data arising from Hancock and Foulke's factory and laboratory experiments (1969) has indicated that:

1. Linear curves give as good a fit as exponential curves if a split is made at 500 cycles. Computations with linear curves are less complex.

2. The rate of learning of elements in combination is a function of the number of eye fixations used. As performance improves, the operator recodes the information and relies less on the visual channel (a view supported by numerous observations and experiments, e.g., Seymour, 1967). When new curves were fitted, allowing for the reduced number of eye fixations with practice, and when allowance was made for the more frequent repetition of elements occurring more than once in each cycle, a much better agreement was obtained between observed and calculated times.

3. Age is a significant factor in the rate of learning. This has important implications for the assignment of workers, since younger persons are more flexible in their adjustment to job change and quicker at learning new tasks; older workers are more suited to stable jobs.

Hancock[*] and his associates have temporarily suspended their experiments on learning rates in order to concentrate on developing computer programs for the calculation of time standards, layouts, manpower requirements, fatigue allowances, and learning rates for industrial tasks. It is forecast that, within a few years, it will be possible for firms with appropriate terminals to transmit data concerning their operations to a central computer and receive back computed values for all the above requirements.

[*] Personal communication.

II

METHODS OF JOB ANALYSIS

OVERVIEW

Job analysis; which deals with what occurs in the performance of any task is prepared at three levels with differing degrees of detail, depending on the objective of the analysis.

Industrial engineering, psychological, physiological, and physical methods of job analysis are discussed. The techniques involved in the use of each are outlined, and particular reference is made to the use of job analysis for selection and training. The use of job analysis for other purposes is briefly discussed.

The preliminary considerations that enable one to decide what type of job analysis is required are outlined.

FACTORS TO BE CONSIDERED IN JOB ANALYSIS

Nature and Scope of Job Analysis

The term job analysis is used in the published literature in a variety of senses, such as:

1. Vocational analysis—the analysis of an entire trade or profession (e.g., machine operators).

2. Occupational analysis—the study of a specialized occupation within the trade or profession (e.g., power press operators).

3. Job analysis—the study of a particular operation (e.g., changing a jig on a specific power press for a special operation or job).

These three categories are arranged in a hierarchy in which vocational analysis is a prerequisite for occupational analysis, which in turn is a prerequisite for job analysis. Because the methodology in all three groups is similar, we use the term *job analysis* to refer to the methodology employed in collection and analysis of job-relevant data regardless of the category (vocation, occupation, or job) under consideration. However, the *emphasis is on the use of job analysis for selection and training purposes only. The term as used here does not deal with applications to wage structure and method study.*

The range of problems for which job analysis has been used is outlined in Table 2.1. This chapter deals specifically with section 4 of the table; that is, with the types of job analysis that are developed for selection and training. However, we also refer here to other relevant sections (e.g., section 2).

Table 2.1   Areas in Which Job Analysis Has Been Utilized to Identify or Solve Problems

I.   For personnel specification in:

    A.   Characteristics of working environment
    B.   Clarification of job duties and responsibilities
    C.   Transfer and promotion
    D.   Study of grievances
    E.   Definition of limits of authority
    F.   Definition of limits of responsibility
    G.   Identification of consequences of wrong decisions
    H.   Identification of cases of personnel failure
    I.   Identification of cases of personnel success
    J.   Establishment of a common understanding within an organization between all levels of personnel

II.   For methods study in:

    A.   Time and motion study
    B.   Maintaining, operating, and adjusting machinery
    C.   Indicating faulty procedures and duplication of effort
    D.   Investigating accidents and near-accidents

III.   Establishment of wage structures for:

    A.   Job grading and classifications
    B.   Wage setting and standardization
    C.   Defining and outlining promotional steps

IV.   Derivation of personnel selection and training content for:

    A.   Evaluation of job content for test construction for personnel selection, placement, and guidance
    B.   Establishment of criteria for personnel testing
    C.   Evaluation of job content for establishing educational and training programs

V.   In health for:

    A.   Studies of health and fatigue
    B.   Determining jobs suitable for occupational therapy
    C.   Determining health hazards in occupations

Job analysis is frequently preceded by job description (i.e., an account of the responsibilities, duties, and activities required in a job), which is used for job evaluation and other purposes. Job analysis, if it is to serve for selection and training, needs to be much more detailed and categorized than a job description, and it requires more sophisticated techniques.

As emphasized later in the book, job analysis must be differentiated from skills analysis. The former aims at determining *what* happens objectively in the performance of a task; the latter aims at determining *how* (Chapter 3) the operator achieves it. It is also necessary to distinguish job analysis from task analysis (Miller, 1953). The latter may be considered a specialized area within job analysis, and it constitutes a specific technique for developing training programs from the analysis of the job (p. 76, task analysis).

In the last three decades, numerous books have been written about job analysis, including those by Johnson, Boise, and Pratt (1946); Stanway (1947); Jones (1948); Harrington (1949); Lanham (1955); Patton, Littlefield, and Stanley (1964); and de Jong (1969). None, however, has added significantly to those written earlier by Gilbreth (1911, 1919), Amar (1919), Viteles (1932), and others. In a sense, very little progress has been made in the last 30 years to remove analysis from the umbrella of subjectivity and bring it under objective coverage. Because of its subjectivity, and because job analysis is a prerequisite for job evaluation, the latter has been under constant attack from the trade unions; for example, the International Association of Machinists (1954) issued a 100-page manual entitled "What's Wrong With Job Evaluation?"

Despite this subjectivity, job analysis makes use of a multidisciplinary approach that requires consideration of psychological, social, physiological, physical, and industrial engineering approaches (Table 2.2), which is the pattern of the remainder of this chapter.

Job Identification

A job analysis applied to one situation is not necessarily appropriate for another situation, even a similar one. Therefore, first the job has to be identified, so that it is known *what* is to be analyzed. Job analysis is a combination of art and science; some of its components are objective analysis, and others are subjective.

In a job analysis for refrigerator assembly operators, at least the following information would be required:

1. Is the analysis to cover all manufacturers or is it only for one company?

Table 2.2   Items To Be Considered in Job Analysis

I. Factors to be considered in job analysis

   A.   Nature and scope of the analysis
   B.   Identification of the job to be studied
   C.   Number of personnel engaged on the job
   D.   Responsibilities, authorities, and effects of poor decisions
   E.   Review mechanisms for personnel on the job
   F.   Machines and tools used in the job
   G.   Physical and social conditions of the job
   H.   Aesthetics and sociopsychological surroundings of the job

II. Methods of job analysis

   A.   Industrial engineering approach
      1.   Discrete events approach
      2.   Diary methods
      3.   Recording techniques
      4.   Charting techniques

   B.   Psychological methods
      1.   Interview and questionnaire
      2.   Technical conferences
      3.   Checklist
      4.   Diary method
      5.   Work participation
      6.   Accidents and near accidents

   C.   Physiological methods
      1.   Energy expenditure
      2.   Electrical activities in muscles
      3.   Force platform
      4.   Other methods

   D.   Physical factors
      1.   Vision
      2.   Audition
      3.   Climate
      4.   Aesthetics
      5.   Anthropometry

2. If for only one company, is it for all their models or only one specific one? (Which one?)

3. Assuming that the company has more than one geographical location, is the job analysis to be prepared for a specific model applicable to all locations or for only one location?

4. If job analysis is needed for only one geographical location is the entire refrigerator assembly to be analyzed or only a specific assembly activity (e.g., fuse box assembly for model 235)?

5. Assuming the latter, are all fuse box assembly activities for model 235 the same in all stations? For example, are some work stations machine-paced with financial incentives depending on group performance and others self-paced with incentives geared to individual performance? Some work stations may use up-to-date "sophisticated" machines having relatively high mental and low physical demands on the operator, whereas other stations have older machines whose operation is characterized by relatively high physical demands and low mental requirements. Other frequently noticed differences in the environment between work stations producing the same end product could be cited.

Because of these and other reasons, *we must be very specific in the identification of the job to be analyzed.* A very frequent cause of unsatisfactory occupational situations has been lack of precision in the identification of the jobs on which job analysis has been performed. Thus the job must be very precisely and specifically identified in order to avoid mistakes that could cause human dissatisfaction and economic loss.

Number of People Employed

Once the job to be analyzed has been exactly identified, the number of people employed on the job must be learned, because some aspects (both economic and methodological) of the job analysis depend on the number of people employed on the job. There are at least three reasons for this.

1. It is often more justifiable from an economic point of view to make a thorough, detailed job analysis with cross-validations where a relatively large number of employees are engaged on a job, than in those cases where only a very few people are working. From a trade union and industrial relations point of view, however, equal attention should be given to job analysis whether one employee is concerned, or a thousand.

2. Generally speaking, the larger the population engaged on a specific job, the greater the probability of a larger variation in job description within that job, and vice versa. This of course affects the methodology employed for the job analysis in question. For example, interview may be adopted as one mode of job analysis techniques for a smaller number of people, whereas questionnaire techniques may be more appropriate for larger numbers of people. This spread in range could be affected by a host of accidental and incidental items, such as variations in tools, machinery, equipment, and physical and social surroundings.

3. If only a small number (e.g., five employees) are engaged on a specific job, the job analyst can study 100 percent of the population with

all available techniques for job analysis. When many workers are engaged (e.g., 5000 operators), it is impractical to study the activities of each with all the job analysis tools available. In the latter case, depending in part on the job in question, probably the most appropriate procedure is to adopt for all employees the questionnaire technique and merely sample (in a systematic way) a fraction of the population with other relevant job analysis techniques.

Duties and Responsibilities

When the specific job to be studied has been identified and the number of people associated with the job directly and indirectly has been determined, the workers' duties have to be ascertained with special reference to their responsibilities (i.e., what the operator has to do), their authority (i.e., what decisions can and must be made), and the effects of poor decisions (i.e., the effects of decisions made by the operator that yield negative results). In any organization, authority and responsibility typically go hand in hand, since neither is effective in isolation. Both qualities have been viewed in the light of available review mechanisms. A typical job analysis, with special reference to job duties, is illustrated in Table 2.3. This type of job analysis is incomplete and may be misleading if used as the only descriptive document for a job, since it covers only one of many items contributing to an effective job analysis and description (see Table 2.2 for a complete list).

Machines and Tools Utilized

Because skilled manual performance is so common in industry, tools and machinery form an integrated part of the majority of job activities. Therefore, a detailed description of them for job analysis is necessary and invaluable. Photographs of the tools and machinery utilized for a job, preferably made from a variety of angles in order to cover all sides of the item studied, are desirable (see, e.g., Figure 2.1). To this should be added written instructions dealing with maintenance and operation. Additional photographs illustrating the relationship of the item considered to the surrounding work area (Figure 2.2) provide additional valuable information.

It is best to record the manufacturer's name and address and the catalog serial number (indicating the year of the catalog) of the specific tool or machine. This facilitates the making of inquiries to the manufacturer if additional information is needed.

The determination of the functional requirements to operate a specific machine, tool, and piece of equipment is crucial. This could be done

Table 2.3 Part of a Popular Form of Job Analysis

Job Title: Fuse Box Assembly

Main Duties	Main Operator Decisions	Effects of Poor Decisions	Review Mechanism	
			Direct	Indirect
The operator shall assemble all four screws, washers, and nuts with two brackets to the main box. He is responsible for the maintenance of his electrical screwdriver.	Operator will decide when: 1. Tools become obsolete. 2. Finished jobs in stock have to be removed. 3. Components for his assembly activities have to be ordered. 4. A repair to his electrical screwdriver is needed, and how to accomplish it.	1. Economics loss when tools are replaced either too early or too late. 2. Economics loss due to deviations from optimum judgment of removal of completed jobs and ordering of components for assembly. 3. "Improper" repair of the electrical screwdriver resulting in electrical shock and bodily harm.	The foreman submits a yearly report to the production manager in which he evaluates his subordinates (operators) regarding their suitability or otherwise for the job.	At each stage in the production process, the operator is being evaluated by inspection and testing personnel regarding the quality of the work produced and by the foreman regarding the quantity produced.

Figure 2.1.   The workplace and immediate surrounding of an operator in the cable department. (Courtesy of Western Electric Company; photograph taken in 1971.)

under the following headings, as explained in such textbooks as those of Murrell (1969) and McCormick (1970):

1. Anthropometric considerations.

2. Gross physiological considerations, derived using energy expenditure and heart rate.

3. Local physiological considerations, derived using electromyograms (EMG), electroencephalograms (EEG), and electrooculograms (EOG). It would appear that these sophisticated techniques are not generally used in industry, in the United Kingdom and the United States, yet a number of companies do employ them, particularly EMG.

4. Psychological considerations, with special reference to mental load.

5. Social considerations, with special reference to isolation and group work.

6. Medical considerations.

7. Legal requirements.

8. Union and management policies.

Figure 2.2. Overview of the entire cable department, in which the operator in Figure 2.1 constitutes a part. (Courtesy of Western Electric Company; photograph taken in 1971.)

The anthropometric considerations should deal with such questions as: what range of anthropometric characteristics is the machine designed for? For what percentage of the working population does it provide an optimal relationship between man and machine (e.g., the fiftieth and the ninety-fifth percentile of arm-length reach)? This percentage range may be one of the factors contributing to acceptance or rejection of an applicant for the job, perhaps determining his training potentials. For example, for a job requiring a six-footer, men below this height are automatically eliminated.

Similarly, the gross and local physiological stresses associated with performance on the job must be assessed and quantified. It may be necessary to select personnel on the basis of strength. If so, endurance tests could be developed and administered as part of a selection test battery. The psychological and social factors should be considered analogously. For example, it may be necessary to make selections on the basis of suitability for individual work, suitability for group performance, or suitability for work done in isolation.

Medical and legal requirements may be crucial for the selection and training of personnel in special jobs. Tests determining these requirements cannot be a part of a test battery, in which tradeoff functions occur (i.e., high performance on one test compensates for low performance on another test if both tests have similar weighting factors). Medico-legal requirements have clear-cut lower bounds below which a person can be neither selected nor trained on the job. Specified medical requirements frequently occur for jobs in the food industry, whereas the law itself may state its minimal qualifications for practicing a profession (e.g., to practice medicine in the United States one has to have a recognized medical degree and pass the state examination). Like the legal and medical professions, trade unions typically have *minimal* requirements for those who wish to join the union and practice their profession. These requirements are the minimal functional requirements to operate·a machine, tool, or piece of equipment. The management policy is to select the operators who satisfy these functional requirements *best*. Sometimes conflicts occur between management and union requirements.

For any job, all the eight points listed previously must be considered. However, not all points are equally important for every job. For some jobs, certain points have no relevance and others are more heavily weighted (e.g., for a medical practitioner the legal requirements may be the dominant item). The importance of each point for each job has to be determined. Items 1 to 5 are dealt with in the same way as the development and validation of any test battery (Chapter 6); items 6 to 8, where they apply, are predominantly important for any job.

Conditions of Work

Another set of relevant variables in job analysis is the *conditions of work*. Favorable conditions of work presumably cause an increase in productivity, a reduction in training time, and an increase in the number of applicants per job opening. Conditions of work that may be indirectly important are enumerated under the following headings:

1. Hours of work, including the total number of hours to be worked per day and per week, the starting and completion times.

2. Shift work. Is there shift work for the specific job considered? If yes, is it voluntary or otherwise? How frequent is it? What is the bonus for those working on shift work?

3. Type and magnitude of indirect financial and nonfinancial compensa-

tions (e.g., company insurance and retirement policy, bonus plans, methods of rewarding exceptional performance).

4. Social surroundings (e.g., the nature of supervision and eating and recreational facilities).

5. Physical surroundings of the job, including:

    a. Nature of sound, vibration, light, and color. Are these harmful or annoying? (Murrell, 1969; McCormick, 1970).

    b. Nature of heat, cold, humidity, air flow, and air pressure. Are these harmful or annoying? (Brouha, 1967; McCormick, 1970).

    c. From an anthropometric standpoint, is the workplace well designed? Is it comfortable to work at? (Damon, Stoudt, and McFarland, 1966; Murrell, 1969; McCormick, 1970).

    d. What do individual employees perceive of the physical and social surroundings of the job? Do they find it aesthetically pleasing, satisfactory, annoying, or unbearable to operate in? Why?

    e. Is the operator physically isolated from other personnel during his work performance?

In the following pages, techniques are described by which answers to some of these questions can be gathered. Answers to other questions can be found in the records of the personnel, medical, or industrial engineering departments of the organization. However, an investigator should be very cautious in accepting data that have been collected by other personnel for purposes other than that of job analysis. Moreover, he must be aware of the exact methodology employed for collection and analysis of the data. Such data may be outdated and inconsistent with the present practices of the company and circumstances of the job under consideration. Therefore, before the data are utilized, it is crucial that their reliability, dependability, (see pp. 223 and 241) and validity (see pp. 223 and 237) be assessed.

METHODS OF JOB ANALYSIS

In the previous sections of this chapter, we identified the variables that should be considered for an effective and representative job analysis program; in the following sections, the various methods available to evaluate these variables are discussed, but only in reference to the methods that are essential and directly relevant to personnel selection and training.

It has been frequently emphasized that the success criterion for occupational tasks (Chapter 5) is multidimensional (e.g., Ghiselli, 1956; Seashore, Indik, and Georgopoulos, 1960). What must be stressed now, in addition, is that the methods employed for job analysis are also multidimensional, involving techniques taken from psychology (individual and social), physiology, physics, ergonomics, and industrial engineering (Table 2.2). Therefore, any job analysis that relies on only one of these disciplines is likely to be inadequate and misleading.

Industrial Engineering Methods

The purpose here is not to review all the industrial engineering techniques of job analysis, but to discuss only the techniques that are directly necessary for the establishment of a sound personnel selection and training program.

The Concept of Element Times. A technique frequently utilized by industrial engineers for job analysis is the *discrete events approach*. When an industrial engineer is faced with analyzing a job, he analyzes the operations involved in performing a job by breaking them down into functionally definable components or elements, disregarding their contextual meaning. This approach was advocated 50 years ago by the Gilbreths.

Although the elemental analysis of a task is insufficient to allow us to understand the complexity of human behavior, it has the following uses:

1. In *job description* it makes possible a detailed analysis and description of what and how the operator executes his task; that is, it serves as the basis for job and skills analysis, which in turn is used for the establishment of training programs and for the derivation of personnel selection tests.

2. In *method study* it permits the improvement of work methods (e.g., doing the same job in less time and with less effort) by indicating which elements require the greatest expenditure of effort. Methods improvement may result from elimination of some elements, from the rearrangement of other elements, or from both.

3. In *time study* it enables the establishment of work standards (Chapter 5). The job elements may be observed and timed (using a stop watch), or the analyst may apply already established Predetermined Motion–Time System (PMTS) tables of element times to each job element.

Some of the possible weaknesses of the discrete events approach to the analysis of human motions are as follows:

1. The methodology does not distinguish between the perceptual and motor aspects of a task; no proper account is taken of the time required to absorb information, process it, and plan the appropriate action.

2. The division of a task into its elements and their timing has no physiological foundation, especially when various elements make different physiological demands on the operator; the physiological work required

to execute one element does not terminate at the end of that element, but extends over the following element or elements (e.g., Welford, 1968; Payne, Slater, and Telford, 1968).

3. It does not identify the effect of physical, physiological, psychological, and social factors affecting the task.

Despite these weaknesses, the elemental approach to the analysis of human performance provides a convenient and easily measurable division of work for analyzing jobs for the purpose of improving methods of operation. The concept of elemental times is the *core of the discrete events approach, and this is what is recorded.*

Recording of Element Times. A variety of methods exist for the recording of element or using Gilbrethian terminology, therblig times. Among these are:

1. Stopwatch time study whereby each task element is timed separately. This is the method most frequently used in industry, primarily because of its simplicity and the lack of requirements for complex equipment. The method serves primarily for the establishment of work standards. It has, however, one distinguishing inadequacy; it is impossible to record with accuracy individual element times lasting less than about 5 sec. Other methods, which are more precise, but require complex instrumentation are listed in items 2 to 6.

2. SETAR (serial event timer and recorder) which records element times by current through the body (Welford, 1952).

3. The continuous recorder (Smith and Von Trebra, 1952).

4. SEMTAR (sequential electronic motion timer and recorder) (Block, 1961).

5. Electronic data collector (Hancock and Foulke, 1961).

6. UNOPAR (universal operator performance analyser and recorder) which records motion characteristics in three dimensions (Nadler and Goldman, 1958).

7. Thanks to the rapid development in computer technology in the 1960s, data taken in laboratory experimentation can be directly recorded by computer for analysis (e.g., Fliege, 1966; Kelley, 1971).

Items 2 to 6 refer to electronic time-recording equipment with capabilities of recording to 0.01 sec. These have been primarily utilized in laboratory experiments rather than in industrial situations.

Typically, the recording of elemental times by computer may be achieved in one of two ways:

1. By recording analog time signals on an analog tape recorder and converting these signals, in a central computer facility, to digital output, which in turn are fed through the computer for analysis. In this manner, records of both the original analog and the converted digital data can be kept in the tape library for further statistical analysis.

2. The data can be fed directly in its analog form through the computer, if the computer has an analog-to-digital converter built into it, from which consecutive calculations are made. The raw digital data can be produced on either magnetic or paper tapes, while the statistical analysis is printed out on a teleprinter.

Computers are also frequently utilized for on-line experiments in which immediate data feedback is required. Examples of this are found in studies by Hale (1969) and Pew (1969), in which speed and accuracy had to be instantaneously traded off; for this, the trade off calculation must be done by computer. The increased demand for utilization of on-line computers for human experimentation has increased both in the United States (Fliege, 1966) and abroad (Moray, 1969).

Diary Method. With the diary technique, all daily activities are recorded chronologically against an elapsed-time base, using logbooks or a diary in order to learn exactly what an operator is doing on the job and how much time he is spending on each activity. Times are recorded either at the beginning and end of an activity (e.g., assembling a fuse box) or at fixed intervals (typically, every 15 min).

The ultimate use of the data dictates who collects the information. When the diary method is used for documenting the work activities for the purpose of methods improvement, the data are usually collected by the industrial engineer. When data are used to document production performance (e.g., the amount produced for the day and the nature and time of interferences occurring), they are normally collected by the operator and countersigned by his supervisor.

The diary method has been used in a variety of circumstances, including the assembly of gun parts (Link, 1919), the study of drivers and electrical station operators (Viteles, 1932), and the study of communication activities of industrial research personnel (Hinrichs, 1964).

The industrial engineer uses the diary method for a variety of purposes. Among them are:

1. To improve work methods by identifying the task content and job performance methods (Barnes, 1968).

2. To establish job content for the ultimate purpose of developing

time standards based on time study, P.M.T.S., or synthetic time data (Barnes, 1968).

3. Determination of job categories for wage and organizational structure purposes (Paterson, 1969).

4. For the establishment of personnel selection procedures and training programs for a specific job (Seymour, 1966; Salvendy, 1969b). This purpose is our main interest in this book.

Whatever the purpose of the diary method, it provides the industrial engineer with a powerful and economical tool, since only a very few operators (one or two usually) need be studied for one specific job. However, the method suffers from an undue amount of subjectivity, since the determination of what constitutes a describable unit of behavior is left up to the diary keeper.

Charting and Recording Technique.   Once the basic task content and time data are available, they can be presented in a compact way that is easy to digest. In job analysis this takes the form of various types of charts (e.g., process analysis, activity and operation simultaneous motion, man–man and man–machine analysis charts, Gantt chart (Clark, 1923), flow diagrams), depending on the activity under study and the type of information required from the job. For a detailed review of these charting techniques, see, for example, Niebel (1972), Mundel (1970), and Barnes (1968). Some of these analytical tools are discussed below. They form the central starting point for skill analysis training programs and personnel selection procedures.

Some of the benefits that may be derived from the utilization of industrial engineering charting techniques can be seen from Figure 2.3, which is a *process chart* for the manufacturing sequence, "station cord." From this one-page chart presentation, the manufacturing sequence can be easily and rapidly understood, whereas many pages of writing would be required to describe it in sentences.

Since the job can frequently be performed by team of operators, by dividing the job between man and machine, or by both, it is important to know who is performing the various parts of the job. In this case an *activity chart* is used (Table 2.4), in which the operations are broken down into much greater detail than they are for process charts. Typically, an individual activity chart may be required for every item entered on the process chart. Since the two charts complement each other, the most desirable information regarding *what* an operator has to do and *when*, is most appropriately illustrated by using both process and activity charts.

Manufacturing Sequence for "Station Cord"

Insulator

- M.H. moves full take—up reel to insulator
- Staged until needed
- Remove empty supply reel
- Move full reel to work location
- Change supply
- Machine run
- Remove empty take—up barrel—conveyor
- Change take—up barrels
- Move full barrel to conveyor
- Inspect for defects
- Barrel stored until needed

Tinsel Roller

- Move supply spool to machine
- Change supply spool
- Machine run
- Remove full take—up spool
- Install empty spool
- Full spool staged in tray
- Full tray to scale
- Weigh trays
- Trays to bench
- Store on bench
- Inspect by process checker
- Tray to cart
- Stage

- Move supply spool to knitter
- Remove empty supply spool
- Place full supply spool on head
- Machine run
- Move nylon cop to machine
- Place full package on supply head
- Remove empty cop
- Move take—up reel to machine
- Remove full take—up reel
- Install empty take—up reel
- Move full take—up reel under bench
- Store until needed

- Move supply barrel to jacketer
- Reverse barrels—empty out, full in
- MOve empty barrel to conveyor
- Machine run
- Get empty take—up barrel—conveyor
- Eject full barrel, replace with empty
- Check cordage in barrel
- Store full take—up until needed

- M.H. loads racks with cords
- Move dolly to trim area
- Store until needed
- Operator moves rack into position
- Trim paper — H4CJ
- Move rack away
- Staged

- M.H. moves dolly to tube area
- Stored until needed
- Operator moves dolly to machine
- Assemble tube to cord
- Move completed dolly aside
- Store until needed

- M.H. moves dolly to coil stage
- Inspect for defects
- Store until needed
- Operator moves rack to position
- Coil cords
- Cords transported by conveyor
- Heat treated
- Cords transported by conveyor

- To area by conveyor
- Pack cords in carton
- Move packed cartons to pallet

A.S.M.E. Symbol	Name
○	Operation
□	Inspection
⇨	Transportation
D	Delay
▽	Storage

Grommet

- M.H. moves dolly to area
- Stored until needed
- M.H. moves dolly to bench
- Stored until needed
- Operator moves rack into position
- Place grommet on
- Move finished dolly aside
- Store until needed

Removal—Reversal Check

- Cords transported by conveyor
- Cords removed and reversed—checked
- Place in carton
- Cartons transported by conveyor
- Stored until needed

Servo Loosener

- Move supply spool to machine
- Change supply spool
- String tinsel in machine
- Machine run
- Move nylon supply to machine
- Remove empty nylon supply
- Install full nylon supply spool
- Move empty spool to cart
- Remove full served take–up spool
- Examine served conductor
- Move empty take–up to head
- Place empty take–up on head
- Move full take–up spool to knitting bench
- Take–up stored until needed

Nylon Doubler

- Walk to nylon twister
- Remove full spool–place on cart
- Empty spool on spindle
- Pull of empty bobbin from head
- Take bobbin to storage bin
- Return to head with full bobbin
- Place on spindle
- Return to servo loosener
- Full spool remains on cart

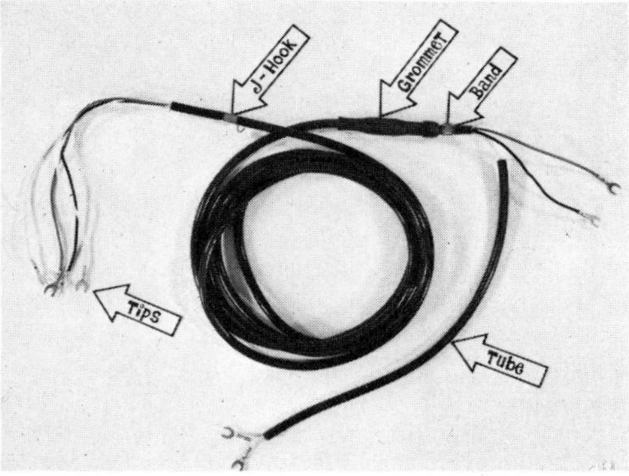

Artos

- Move take–up bárrel to artos
- Tie cable ends
- Machine run
- Graps bundles of cords and remove
- Place in bin and tie
- Inspect for defects
- Store until needed

Tip and Band

- M.H. moves dolly to tip and band
- Store until needed
- Operator moves near machine
- Store until needed
- Tip and band J–hook end
- Move finished dolly aside
- Store until needed
- M.H. moves dolly to handset tip and band
- Store until needed
- Operator moves rack into position
- Tip and band handset end
- Operator moves finished dolly aside
- Stored until needed

Figure 2.3. Process chart for manufacturing "station cord." (Courtesy of Western Electric Company.)

Operation: Tip and band H4CJ — Handset end

Man		Machine	
Operator	Time (min)	Press	Time (min)
Separate next cord from group	0.0215		
Pick up band and cord		Run	0.0318
Idle	0.0103		
Place band in next—bring cord to work area			
Loop cord			
Measure length of cord			
Place cord in band and grommet in holder	0.0719	Idle	0.0719
Tuck cord under clip and over guide			
Remove hands—activate machine			
*Get cords from rack			
Visually check quality and measurements			
Get or move racks			
Clear machine	0.0182	Idle	0.0182
Record information			
Get bands			
Housekeeping			

Work ☐
Idle ▨

* These operations do not occur each cycle.

Table 2.4. Activity Chart for Studying a Suboperation of the Manufacturing Sequence of "Station Cord" (see Figure 2.3). (Courtesy of Western Electric Company.)

Psychological Methods

The psychological approach to job analysis enables the analysis, review, and evaluation of the job from the viewpoints of *both* the operator and management. However, this approach, which utilizes interviews, questionnaires, technical conferences, checklists, work participation methods, and analysis of accidents and near-accidents, is somewhat more subjective than the industrial engineering approach to job analysis and much more subjective than the physiological and physical methods described later.

Interview and Questionnaire. Interviews can be either structured or unstructured. The structured interview has a preset standardized set of questions for all interviewees. In contrast, the unstructured interview does not have preset questions; rather, questions are developed during the course of the interview by the interviewer, based on answers to preceding queries. Since unstructured interviews are tailor-made for each interviewee, administering them requires greater competence from the interviewer than does the structured interview.

Structured and unstructured interviews are distinctly different entities; however, they are on two ends of the same scale. The unstructured interview, for all its flexibility, still revolves around prestructured topics. A questionnaire in written form, whether for the interviewee to fill out or the interviewer to ask, must be always structured, because it cannot be guided or modified during its administration.

For both structured and unstructured interviews, the end objective must be well defined and understood by the interviewer, before the start of the interview, and it must be borne in mind during the entire process of the interview. Either an individual or a group can be interviewed. The former situation primarily aims at assessing factual knowledge and psychological traits of the individual; the latter, in addition, attempts to examine social behavior and group interactions and thus is used mainly for personnel selection and appraisal rather than job analysis. Since group interviews clearly must be somewhat unstructured in order to identify social interactions, they possess a greater degree of flexibility. Because of this flexibility, their interpretation is generally more subjective than that of the individual interview.

In most organizations, interviews provide the main source of information for job evaluation and personnel selection purposes (Brierley, 1967). However, *interviews are only as effective as the interviewer*.

In this chapter, attention is focused on interviews in which *information about a specific job, rather than a specific person* is sought. The latter type forms a part of a personnel selection process and is discussed in Chapters 6 and 7. Information about likes, dislikes, and difficulties experienced in performing a specific job is typically solicited and evaluated, and a comparison is made between naïve and experienced operators.

Reliability and Validity of Interview–Questionnaire Methods. Interviews and questionnaires seek to elicit data about real-world jobs, personnel, events, and phenomena by highly indirect, subjective methods. This has initiated a major area of investigation for psychologists for more than half a century. The basic question is, how valid and dependable are these techniques? One of the earliest published studies is that of Muscio (1916), which emphasized the influence of the form of the question on the results. Scott (1916), on the other hand, indicated the low reliability and validity of interview assessment of sales potential by business executives, where validity was represented by the relation between the interview assessment and the subsequent sales records of the men selected.

Inconsistency in interviews has been further demonstrated by Hollingworth (1929) in a study in which 57 candidates for salesman posts were interviewed by 12 sales managers. For example, a candidate who was placed first out of the 57 by one sales manager was placed 57th by another. Additional evidence of low validity and reliability in these techniques was provided by Vernon and Parry (1949), in their large-scale investigations during World War II dealing with personnel selection in the British forces; by Kelly and Fiske (1951), in prediction of the performance of clinical psychologists; and by Weiss, Dawis, England, and Lofquist (1961), indicating low validity of work histories obtained by interviews (Table 2.5).

Table 2.5   Validity of Work History Information Obtained During
Home Interview of 325 Physically Handicapped Individuals
as Compared with Data Furnished by Former Employers[a]

Items Considered	Basis for Accepting Items as Valid	Index of Validity (percent)
1. Pay increase	± 10 percent	38
2. Starting pay	± 10 percent	55
3. Length of job	± 10 percent	60
4. Final pay	± 10 percent	60
5. Ending date	± one month	66
6. Training	3 categories	69
7. Promotion	4 categories	70
8. Starting date	± one month	71
9. Hours worked	± 10 percent	78
10. Reasons for separation	3 categories	83

[a] After Weiss, Dawis, England, and Lofquist, 1961.

Part of the low reliability and validity of questionnaires and interviews can be attributed to the following causes:

1. The "halo effect," a term originally introduced by Thorndike (1920). This is "a tendency to be biased in the estimation or rating of an individual with respect to a certain characteristic by some quite irrelevant impression or estimate (good or bad) of the same individual. It is a frequent source of error in employing rating scales and similar procedures" (Drever, 1965, p. 115).

2. Ambiguity of the questions asked. For example, questions that "lead" the respondent reduce his freedom to respond; ambiguity produces uncertainty about how to respond.

3. The interviewer's skills in this task can affect interview outcomes significantly. Generally, the successful interviewer (those whose records are most reliable and valid) phrases his questions to elicit the most meaningful response from the interviewee—he fits himself to the latter's characteristics.

4. Interpretation of questionnaires and interview responses tends to be subjective. This may be attributed to at least two factors:

    a. Lack of a common definition in interviews of value judgments, such as "good" performance and "bad" performance. An item response may be "good" for interviewer A and "bad" for interviewer B.

    b. Variability between interviewers in the data extracted from questionnaires and interview responses.

The need for cross-validation in job analysis with special reference to interview data and questionnaire responses has frequently been stressed (e.g., Brown and Jaques, 1965) but seldom practiced. Cross-validation of job analysis is defined as the "double checking" of the questionnaire–interview responses obtained from one group of employees, relative to a specific phenomenon, with those obtained from other groups, relative to the same phenomenon. The special value of cross-validation of job analysis lies in obtaining a more dependable and accurate description of the job than is otherwise possible. However, it is used only rarely because of the excessive time involved in the procedure.

Cross-validation of questionnaire responses is most useful when the results from one group of people are compared with results obtained from other groups of personnel, such as:

1. Those directly engaged on the particular job studied.
2. Those engaged on jobs similar to the one studied.
3. Two hierarchical levels of supervision of the particular job (e.g., foreman).
4. Those in the hierarchical structure of the company who fall below the level of the job studied (e.g., the job studied is machine fitting, and the hierarchy below it is machine operators).
5. Operators engaged in supporting services to the specific job studied (e.g., inspectors, testers, storemen, maintenance personnel).
6. The operators who are being trained for the particular job studied, and their supervisors.

Cross-validation permits a more balanced sample of subjects and additional information as well as providing a quantitative estimate (reliability index) of the confidence that is allowable in the data collected. For example, Salvendy, Cunningham, Ferguson, and Hinton (1971) utilized cross-validation of questionnaire responses to assess likes, dislikes, and difficulties on psychomotor activities in dentistry. A two-way cross-validation study was conducted, one within a university (separate responses collected from sophomores, seniors, and professors) and one between universities. With this use of cross-validation a more accurate and dependable response was obtained than otherwise would have been feasible.

Interviews and questionnaires for job analysis purposes are usually administered after the interviewer has observed the job to be studied for a short period. Interviews can then be used to gather "raw material" from which questionnaires can be constructed to collect data on a population larger than could be interviewed with economic or psychological justification.

Interviews and questionnaires can be used to identify the factors most liked, most disliked, and presenting most difficulties in a particular job. This is considered by many pioneering psychologists to be the most important information in any job analysis (Rodger, 1958), since the data thus obtained may not be discernible during job observations. It is possible to quantify these subjective impressions by categorizing them and assigning a relative weight or percentage to each of the foregoing categories for each activity performed on the job.

Interviews and questionnaires can also be used to discover "unknown features" and dimensions of a job. These usually occur because of malfunctioning machinery or tools on the one hand, or variation in quality of material and parts on the other. These "unknown features" of a job usually happen at erratic and unpredictable intervals; consequently, they may not be in evidence during a particular observation of the job. Thus the interview–questionnaire can be used to supplement the individual observation.

Technical Conference.   With changes over the last decade in modes of communication from formal to informal and with the increased emphasis in business and industry on group-centered evaluations and decisions, the role of technical conferences has increased. These events are usually either oriented toward troubleshooting or in a form of brainstorming activity (Dunnette, Campbell, and Jaastad, 1963), also called "collective intelligence" (Wechsler, 1971). Technical conferences sometimes, but not always, yield results superior to those achieved by individuals working alone. Typically, basic problems in science have been solved or best formulated by creative individuals working independently (e.g., the theory of relativity by Einstein), whereas practical problems have been solved through cooperative effort (e.g., the production of the A-bomb by the scientists working on the Manhattan Project). The group may make greater achievements because, as a unit, it has greater amounts of knowledge at its disposal than an individual within or outside the group. Moreover, as a result of the group interaction, the group members may tend to influence one another's thinking, resulting in a resonance phenomenon analogous to those used to explain intellect insight (Wechsler, 1960).

Technical conferences can be directed toward troubleshooting, or they can be concerned with job analysis.

Troubleshooting-oriented conferences deal with immediate problems in order to eliminate or reduce them. The members should include a cross-section of personnel, representing a wide range of vertical and horizontal coverage within the hierarchy of the organization.

For example, consider an electric bulb manufacturing company that experienced a sudden decline in the life expectancy of a certain bulb. This company, after being unable to solve its problem in other ways, utilized a technical conference to solve the problem. The conference had a total of 15 participants, two from each of the following groups: purchasing, inspection, testing, production supervision (first and second lines), industrial engineering, and operators. The works manager was the moderator of the conference. Two, rather than only one, individuals were drawn from each group both in order to cross-validate information derived from one person by the other and also for the most important reason—to supplement information derived from one person by another. The conference lasted three hours, and there was a two-day follow-up study by the two industrial engineers. The direct interactions of the members of the group allowed each member of the group to contribute toward the identification of the causes of the problem and effective proposals for its rectification.

Job analysis conferences are very similar in structure to, but less frequently used than, the troubleshooting-oriented technical conferences. The objectives of job analysis conferences are:

1. To analyze a job in terms of *what* and *where it is being* done.
2. To analyze a job in terms of *what* and *where it should be* done. This analysis may be explored along two avenues: by focusing on methods of improving the job, and by focusing on the distribution of job items among different categories of job occupations.

An example can be cited from a recent experience in an electromechanical concern. The topic of the conference was the interactions between assembly operators and store attendants. The conference, moderated by the production manager, was attended by seven personnel, representing the storemen, purchasing staff, foremen, superintendents, the union, industrial engineers, and the scheduling department. Although many items of discussion were brought up, the focus of the conference was to establish what the present job content of the storemen and assembly operators was, with special reference to their interactive effects. This led the conference group to recommend an increase in job content for the storemen and a reduction in the job content for the assembly operators; namely, that the storemen not only deliver assembly parts by trolley to the operator but also distribute the items to their appropriate locations for the assembly operators' direct use. Because it was felt, mainly by the union and the storemen, that this proposed additional load could not be performed with the present labor force of storemen, a follow-up study of methods improvement was assigned to the industrial engineer and was accomplished outside the regular conference meeting. However, the new work method was approved (with compromises) individually by all those who were present at the first conference. This methods improvement enabled the restructuring of parts of the job content of both assembly workers and storemen.

The specific problem could of course have been solved without the aid of the conference, but until that conference was held, it had not been solved.

Perhaps a few words of caution about technical conferences are in place. The following factors should be considered before deciding to make use of such a conference:

1. *Economic considerations* associated with the manpower utilization in the conference. Could the problem be solved equally effectively by other "less expensive" methods?

2. *Delay.* Waiting for the decisions arrived at in conference may invoke delays in circumstances where decisions need to be made immediately.

3. *Social influences* affecting disclosure and flow of information in a group setting may be either negative or positive. The social effects may prevent some personnel from expressing themselves freely when others are present; on the other hand, social interaction may result in exchange of ideas leading to a better product or solution to a problem than could feasibly be achieved by a single person.

4. *Psychological influences* (e.g., a feeling of participation and contribution in the discussions) may lead to more ready acceptance of conclusions and action requirements by all groups within the organization.

Decisions reached by consensus produce greater confidence in these decisions by participants. Precautions should be taken to include all "appropriate" representatives in the conference group to avoid hurt feelings.

5. *The rationale* for utilizing technical conferences should be considered. Such a technique might be more effective for one mode of a situation (e.g., practical problems, as a rule, can be solved more effectively by group intelligence) and less effective for another (e.g., basic problems in science are usually best formulated by creative individuals working alone). Technical conferences should be utilized only when other techniques have failed to produce satisfactory results.

Checklist. After an extensive preliminary study has been conducted to collect appropriate task statements, using some of the job analysis methods (e.g., diary method) described in this chapter, a list of these statements is prepared. The operator may check what he has to do against the list, hence the name.

A check list is used in a number of situations; among them are the sequential operation of complex machinery and systematic fault analysis of machine breakdowns. In all these cases, the main advantage in the use of a checklist lies in reminding the operator of what he has to do and what is the most effective way of doing it. Despite these advantages, the use of checklists has the obvious disadvantage that the only items checked are those appearing on the list of task statements (i.e., only items appearing on the checklist have definitely been considered in the execution of the task). Thus the use of checklists is only as effective as the list of task statements.

Checklists for job analysis purposes may be used in two different ways:

1. Check the item on the list which is present in the job studied—independently of the magnitude of its presence on the job.

2. Check the item on the list which is present in the job at its *appropriate level* (e.g., each job statement is categorized into five levels: excellent, good, reasonable, bad, intolerable).

In either case, errors are introduced because, by their nature, the items in the second method are on a continuum scale from excellent to intolerable, whereas in the first the only judgment being made is whether the items are present—which is analogous to comparing only mean values in statistical analysis, ignoring the spread of the distribution. Errors produced by the first method are self-evident (Davies, 1961).

In the second method, an obvious error is introduced by subjectivity and halo effects involved in rating procedures. The consequences of using a rating for classification purposes is well documented in the published literature. As indicated earlier, one judge has frequently ranked a phenomenon as the highest and another judge has rated the same phenomenon as the lowest (e.g., Hollingworth, 1929).

Its many weaknesses notwithstanding, and for job evaluation (McCormick, Jeanneret, and Mecham, 1972) the checklist method has been frequently used for job analysis purposes to complement other applicable techniques. Dunnette and England (1957) found checklists useful for differentiating engineering jobs, and Dunnette and Kirchner (1959) employed them for differentiating sales jobs. Whitfield (1967) has utilized this technique for the purpose of job allocation between men and machines.

Checklists have been used not only for job analysis purposes but also for job description, such as the estimated worker trait requirements for 4000 jobs listed in the *Dictionary of Occupational Titles* (U.S. Department of Labor, 1963), for industrial market research (Stacy and Wilson, 1963) see above.

Work Participation.   In the work participation method of job analysis, the analyst performs the job himself, for as long as he needs to obtain an understanding of the job performed (usually three to 10 repetitions of the task). This enables him by introspection to achieve first-hand experience of the characteristics of the job under investigation. The work participation method seldom involves any recording of data, because it is difficult to perform an activity and simultaneously record one's impressions. However, such impressions can be recorded after the job is completed. Even when no objective data are recorded, work participation can be extremely useful as a base or starting point for more objective investigations of various parts of the job that appeared in the introspective analysis as the key issues of the job. In a pioneer study of manual skills in industrial tasks, Cox (1934) used introspective analysis as a preliminary to his experiments.

Accidents and Near-Accidents

Physicians studying disease and mental breakdown have made significant contributions to the understanding of how human organisms function; similarly, industrial engineers may use the study of accidents and other malfunctioning of a system as a tool of job analysis.

Accidents or near-accidents have been defined in the following manner:

"An accident is an unexpected and undesirable event which arises directly from a work situation; that is, from faulty equipment or the inadequate performance of a person. There may or may not be personal injury and damage to equipment or property. Accidents, however, always interrupt the normal work routine and are associated with increased time delays or errors" (Chapanis, 1959, p. 77).

An illustration of a case of near-accident could be cited from an assembly shop floor where both the air and electricity cables interconnecting the assembly benches were lined on the floor in ½-in. steel tubes. Operators frequently tripped when carrying delicate asembly parts, but bodily or material harm was never caused. These events were near-accidents until one day an operator tripped and broke both his hand and the assembly items he had been carrying.

Obviously the basic patterns of near-accidents and accidents are identical, with the exception of the consequences. Because of this, we are much better off from both humanitarian and economic points of view to concentrate on the study of near-accidents rather than accidents themselves, for by so doing the latter occurrences may be prevented. Furthermore, there are many more near-accidents than accidents. Consequently, near-accident data lend themselves to more reliable analysis than do accident data.

Accidents and near-accidents have been studied extensively by Flanagan (1949), Heinrich (1950), and Cheit (1961) for the prevention of industrial accidents, and by McFarland and Moseley (1954) for long-haul trucking operations. However, the method these investigators used to determine the hazard involved and additional compensation (danger money) required, although frequently adopted by both management and workers, has not received the systematic study it deserves.

Study of accidents for job analysis purposes is valuable in pinpointing effects of poor decisions resulting in physical and material harm. Such statistical data should be collected and monitored centrally by, for example, the company's Safety Engineer or Personnel Department. Monitoring implies both the assurance that the information sheets are "properly" filled out and that periodical statistical evaluations of the data are made to determine hazards.

In order to obtain accurate accident, near-accident, or critical incident data (all accidents and near-accidents are critical incidents), the following points must be observed:

1. Have a standard reporting form to ensure that all relevant data are recorded in the same way (e.g., Chapanis, 1959, pp. 81 and 82).

2. Investigate as soon as feasible after an event to prevent loss of information through forgetfulness on the part of witnesses (Laughery, Fell, and Pinkus, 1969).

3. Get information from as many witnesses as possible and get it privately. This enables the most effective cross-validation of the information to be made.

Accidents and near-accidents may be caused by the malfunctioning of the operator (e.g., lack of motivation, inadequate skill, the inadequacy of his work procedures and/or his physical environment, or all these combined). For personnel selection and training purposes, we are interested only in those cases where the operator's behavior contributed to the accident or near-accident. With this information, operators prone to accidents can be identified and placed in jobs whose characteristics do not lend themselves to accident occurrence. Depending on the accuracy of accident investigation, the frequency of accidents can be significantly decreased. This approach was successfully employed by Viteles (1932) for taxi drivers.

Effective training methods based on skills analysis (discussed in Chapter 3) have also tended to reduce accidents and critical incidents (Simmons, 1958).

Physiological Methods

Physiological measures are utilized for job analysis to establish the stresses imposed on individuals by performing a job. This information can then be used for personnel selection by developing a test, or a battery of tests, simulating real-world working stresses. After these tests have been validated (Chapter 5), cutoff points for acceptance or rejection can be developed.

Physiological measures for job analysis can also help in personnel training by identifying muscle groupings on which stress demand is high. A training program can then be developed to improve the effectiveness of these muscle groupings.

According to Benedict and Cathcart (1913), the earliest utilization of physiology for job analysis probably emerged 200 years ago as a result of Lavoisier and Seguin's demonstration of the relation between muscular performance and the amount of carbon dioxide expired. In the middle of the nineteenth century, Scharling experimented using heavy iron bars and concluded that after heavy muscular exercise, the amount of carbon dioxide in the expired air increases. As a result of Joule's determination of the mechanical equivalent of heat and the formulation of the law of conservation of energy by Mayer and Helmholtz, it became feasible to compute the calories expended per kilogram-meter of work and thus determine the mechanical efficiency of the human body.

It was apparent that both the carbon dioxide produced and the oxygen consumed are correlated individually with the work load, but that both are needed for accurate predictive purposes (Douglas and Priestley, 1948). However, approximations to this may be made based on a formula validated by Weir (1949) for which no carbon dioxide recording is needed.

Although the utilization of respiratory indices for assessing energy expediture was advocated by Lavoisier, it was not until a century later that local muscular activities could be assessed by measuring electrical activities in human muscles. Electrical potentials produced by the muscles can be picked up by electrodes, and the nature of these electrical characteristics suggests how well the human functions physiologically. For discussion on these measurements, see the next two sections.

Energy Expenditures. Two centuries ago Lavoisier analyzed the work of musical composers by assessing the changes occurring in the amount of carbon dioxide they expired; more recently, Brouha (1954) utilized the changes occurring in the oxygen consumption between rest and the work associated with preparing papers for typing to determine energy expenditure.

These energy expenditure indices are primarily useful for analysis of jobs involving medium and heavy physical work. For this they have been utilized extensively [see the early work of Benedict and Cathcart (1913) on the bicycle ergometer, by Amar (1919) on walking, and by Hill on the efficiency of the biceps muscles (1922) and on the energy expenditure in sport (1927)]. Das (1951) and Snook, Irvine, and Bass (1969) have utilized energy expenditure for analyzing the job of manual lifting. Karpovich (1965) and Ricci (1967) have employed the concept of energy expenditure for studying the work of athletes, and Brouha (1967) has done likewise for the evaluation of industrial stresses. Åstrand and Rodahl (1970) provided a comprehensive textbook of work physiology with special reference to the regulatory mechanisms studied during physical activities.

Two excellent statistical summaries on the utilization of energy expenditure measures for job analysis purposes have been written for walking by McDonald (1961) and by Passmore and Durin (1955) for a variety of activities, which are partially listed in Table 2.6.

Recently, Salvendy (1969a) utilized the index of energy expenditure for studying the pacing effects on energy expenditure in job situations involving the bicycle ergometer, pump ergometer (also used by Corlett and Mahadeva, 1970), and a step test. Salvendy and Pilitsis (1971b) studied the effects of age on the efficiency of paced performance by way of the index of energy expenditure. This study illustrated that older operators (45 to 65

Table 2.6   Energy Expenditure for Various Activities[a]

Activities	Energy Cost (cal/min)
Sitting, listening to radio	1.0
Electrical typing 40 words/min	1.2
Watch and clock repair, trainee	1.6
Draftsman	1.8
Standing at ease	2.0
Sitting, playing cards	2.0
Dressing and undressing	2.3
Driving a car	2.8
Sheet metal worker	3.0
Walking (160-lb persons), 2.0 mph	3.2
Driving a motorcycle	3.4
Joiners	3.6
Cleaning windows	3.7
Tidying beds	3.9
Machine fitting	4.2
Walking (160-lb persons), 3.0 mph	4.4
Hewing coal	5.7
Drilling coal	5.8
Walking (160-lb persons), 4.0 mph	5.8
Forging	6.5
Tending heating furnaces	10.2
Walking on loose snow with 50-lb load at 2.5 mph	20.2

[a] After Passmore and Durin (1955).

years) have higher body efficiency and greater satisfaction working at paced performances, whereas the younger group (20 to 45 years) have higher body efficiency and satisfaction working at a "freely" chosen pace than at a paced one (for further details see pp. 301-304). (These findings are contrary to those of Belbin and Toye, 1970, dealing with the psychology of adult training.) If the results of Salvendy and Pilitsis are valid, their implications for personnel selection are that older operators should be placed on tasks associated with paced performance, and younger operators should be assigned on jobs that can be performed at their "freely" chosen pace.

In a world of rapid technological innovations and increasing automation, there are more and more jobs characterized by high perceptual and mental load rather than by heavy physical work. Newer jobs resulting from rapid technological changes make very light physical demands on the operator. Because of this, studies of gross energy expenditure utilizing respiratory indices during work and recovery (Hill, 1927; Douglas and

Priestley, 1948) or during the steady state only (Lukin, 1963), or the approximate calculation for energy expenditure proposed by Weir (1949) are now appropriate for the analysis of fewer jobs than in the past.

Heart rate as an approximate index of energy expenditure has been used in recent years for job analysis more frequently than pulmonary ventilation indices. This results from the advance in electronic technology that enables the construction of miniature and versatile heart recorders (Figure 2.4), which are markedly more convenient to use in real-world situations than those adopted by laboratory methods (Figure 2.5). Figure 2.5 shows a subject cycling on a Collins Bicycle Ergometer with which his physiological functioning is recorded, including the volume of exhaled air* and the percentage of oxygen and carbon dioxide consumed. The use of this technique has made possible the quantification of energy expenditure for a variety of diversified jobs (Table 2.6). Data are recorded on a Beckmann Biomedical Dynogram R recorder together with potentials picked up by electrodes for heart rate and EMG recording (Figure 2.5). A variety of other measures may be recorded on the Dynogram such as electrooculography (EOG) and galvanic skin response (GSR).

Electrical Activity in Muscles. Another frequently utilized physiological technique for job evaluation is electromyography (EMG) (Thompson, Lindsley, and Eason, 1966), in which the electrical potentials produced by contracting muscles are picked up by electrodes and recorded on a Biomedical recorder (Figure 2.5) for graphical analysis or fed through amplifiers into a computer for direct quantitative analysis of the data (e.g., Chaffin, 1969a; Tichauer, 1971). The theory behind the EMG is that both muscular activities and muscular fatigue are directly proportional to the electrical potential exhibited by that particular muscle. The EMG has been used for fatigue, posture, and occupational studies (e.g., Rosenfalck, 1963; Chaffin, 1969b; Tichauer, 1971).

Electroencephalography (EEC), which records the electrical potentials of the nerve cells in the brain by means of electrodes attached to the scalp, provides promise for job analysis research of vigilance, sleep deprivation, and so on (Kennedy, 1953).

---

* The laboratory gas meter shown in Figure 2.5 is not designed to measure the volume of exhaled air directly from the subject, because of the air resistance present in the apparatus which introduces some minor error in the measurements. In order to reduce this error the exhaled air should be first collected into a bag (e.g., the Douglas bag) and then the air from the bag transmitted through the gas meter in order to assess the volume of exhaled air. An equally accurate method is to measure the exhaled air from the subject directly by a gasometer. These gasometers are commercially available from such companies as W. E. Collins of Braintree, Massachusetts.

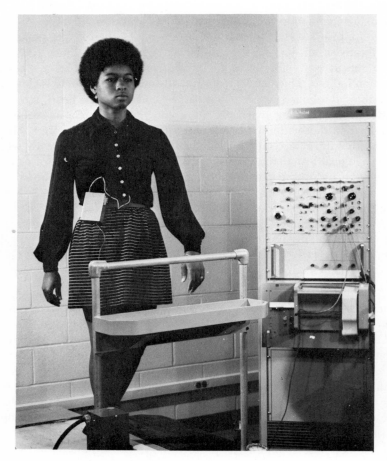

Figure 2.4. The heart beats during a walk on a treadmill are measured with a portable FM transmitter attached to the subject's waist. (Courtesy of Eastman Kodak Company, Kodak Park Human Factors Laboratory.)

EOG is also based on the measurement of the electrical potentials from the muscles (Shackel, 1961). This technique enables the determination of eye positions; consequently, eye movements can be studied for reading behavior (e.g., Woodworth and Schlosberg, 1954; Lee, 1972), for response movement (Knight, 1967), for training (Bhatia, 1957), and for manual dexterity studies using photographic techniques (Salvendy 1968, 1969b).

The utilization of EMG, EEG, and EOG for job analysis purposes

Figure 2.5.   Recording of energy expenditure, heart rate and EMG during bicycling.

provides information on *how* a job is performed, which is relevant to skills analysis and personnel training programs. It also furnishes data on the physiological stresses and fatigues associated with a job which permit the user to derive more appropriate personnel selection procedures.

Force Platform.   The force platform was initially introduced by Lauru (1957) and later developed by Greene (1957), Barany (1961), Barany and Greene (1961), and Hearn and Konz (1968) for the measurement of forces resulting from either static or dynamic actions. The device can record forces in three directions: vertical, transverse, and frontal. The principle on which the apparatus is set up is that the forces exerted by a subject through his muscular activities are measured by piezoelectric quartz crystals mounted on each of the three edges of the platform (Figure 2.6a).

It has been proved that the forces recorded approximate those obtained by the analysis of pulmonary ventilation for heavy manual work (e.g., Brouha, 1967). The technique enables not only the recording of energy expenditure without interfering with the operator's performance

Figure 2.6. (*a*) The use of the force platform, developed by Barany (1961) for studying the physiological cost associated with walking on a treadmill. (*b*) Typical force traces for two subjects walking on a treadmill. (Courtesy of Barany, Ismail, and Manning, 1965.)

(e.g., face mask for pulmonary ventilation or electrodes for heart rate) but also provides data on the distribution of forces on body members (e.g., Payne, Slater, and Telford, 1968). This feature may assist training programs by permitting more concentrated training on the parts of the body member that exert the relatively highest force, and vice versa; it may also be helpful in job redesign for redistributing job activities in accordance with force requirements.

For example, Brouha (1967) utilized the force platform for studying the forces involved in: (1) loading 50-lb bags to various heights, (2)

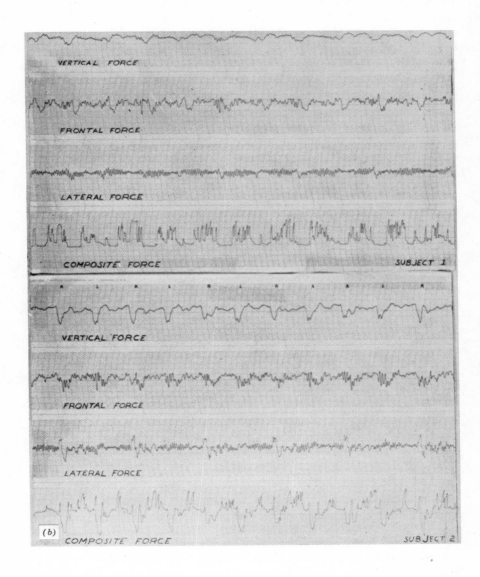

VERTICAL FORCE

FRONTAL FORCE

LATERAL FORCE

COMPOSITE FORCE   SUBJECT 1

VERTICAL FORCE

FRONTAL FORCE

LATERAL FORCE

(b)   COMPOSITE FORCE   SUBJECT 2

lowering both arms from shoulder level to full extension, (3) closing five drawers of a regular filing cabinet, (4) typing by electrical and manual typewriter. Payne, Slater, and Telford (1968) employed the force platform for analyzing sport activities, such as vertical jumps, hurdling, shot putting, and weight-lifting.

Barany and Green (1961) proposed to utilize the force platform for personnel selection and training, and Greene and Morris (1959) advocated its use for work measurement as an industrial tool.

The utilization of the force platform for job analysis purposes is most promising for light or short-duration physical work; the other techniques discussed earlier for the measurements of energy expenditure are applicable only for work of high intensity and long duration.

Other Physiological Methods.   A variety of other physiological techniques are available for job analysis purposes, but they appear to be less applicable for the study of skilled manual operations than those discussed previously. These techniques are reviewed in such textbooks as Douglas and Priestley (1948), Sidowski (1966), Karpovich (1965), Brouha (1967), Ricci (1967), Murrell (1969), Åstrand and Rodahl (1970). These additional physiological techniques for job analysis purposes consist principally of:

1. Physical and chemical measurements in muscles (Hill, 1927).
2. Chemical composition of the blood and the urine (Lauru, 1957).
3. Body temperature and rate of sweating (Lauru, 1957).
4. Blood presure and cardiac output (Dorrogury, 1950; Lauru, 1957).
5. Electroretinogram (ERG) (Thompson, Lindsley, and Eason, 1966).
6. Electrocardiogram (EKG) (Thompson, Lindsley, and Eason 1966).
7. Galvanic skin response (GSR) (Sidowski, 1966).
8. Electrodermal response (EDR) (Thompson, Lindsley, and Eason 1966).

Physical Analysis of Jobs

In the physical analysis of jobs, we evaluate the impact on work performance of such environmental variables as noise, temperature, and lighting.

Noise.   Noise is described along two dimensions; one deals with the frequency of the sound (cycles per second, or Hertz—Hz); the other is related to the measurement of the intensity of sound [decibel (dB) scale above a "zero" level of 0.0002 dynes/cm^2]. For example, speech at a 4 ft distance produces 60 dB; a typewriter at 2 ft, 70 dB, and a train whistle at 40 ft, 110 dB.

The physiology of the ear and the effects of noise on both human performance and health are well documented in the published literature (Woodworth and Schlosberg, 1954; Stevens and Warshofsky, 1965; Murrell, 1969; McCormick, 1970; and Kryter, 1970). It is by now well known that people do not like certain types of noise; noise may damage their hearing and may cause a decrease in their working efficiency. Some noises may be annoying and cause a decrease in productivity, whereas others stimulate an increase in productivity (Wyatt and Langdon, 1937; Uhrbrock, 1961; Broadbent, 1957; Gupta, Sen, and Singh, 1965).

Hearing loss is generally greater in the higher frequencies than in the lower frequencies. Burns (1960), for example, has suggested that frequencies in the range of 37.5 to 150 Hz at 100 dB sound pressure may produce deafness in humans; but the same effect is present at only 80 dB when the range of frequency band is 1200 to 4800 Hz. Similarly, McCormick (1970) cited other studies to indicate that hearing loss with advanced aging is greater at the higher frequencies. Hearing loss at 500 Hz at age 60 is only 6 dB, but at 4000 Hz it is 32 dB. Continuous exposure to a fixed intensity of noise will cause greater hearing loss, the higher the frequency and the longer the exposure time. For example, a 90-dB noise at a frequency of 4000 Hz will cause a hearing loss of about 18 dB after five years of exposure and 30 dB after 20 years of exposure.

When an individual is exposed to noise above the damage level, the first effects are likely to be temporary hearing losses, of up to 20 dB, according to Murrell (1969) in citing other studies. Most of these temporary losses occur after a time period much shorter than the working day. From this temporary damage, a complete recovery occurs overnight. However, if exposure continues, for a substantially longer time, the hearing loss may become permanent.

Present-day technology enables operators to protect their ears from any reasonable level of noise, provided they are willing to take advantage of appropriate techniques. These range from ear plugs to ear covers and head covers, depending on the severity of the noise that must be reduced. The wearing of these items requires adjustments on the part of the individual. Some workers adapt easily without any discomfort, whereas others never adjust; they either fail to wear these job aids and suffer hearing loss or they resign from the job.

Climate.   The climate variables that should be reported in job descriptions or analyses are: temperature, humidity, air flow, barometric pressure, precipitation type, light characteristics, dry or wet work environment and the degree and kind of environmental pollution. It is assumed of course that the nature of the job is such that climatic conditions impact significantly on job performance; otherwise, such detailed information is not required. The distributions for each of these characteristics are needed, both for single working days in particular seasons and for the entire working year. This is because mean values may be very misleading as far as human preference and comfort are concerned.

The effects of environmental conditions on human performance are well covered in the published literature by Bedford (1948, 1961) and Bedford and Warner (1939) on heating and ventilation. Burton and Edholm (1955) have dealt with the subject with reference to extreme cold environments, and Fox (1965) has studied hot environments in this respect. McFarland and Moseley (1954) have indicated that manual dexterity tasks can be performed at temperatures below 50°F, although Lockhart's (1966) experiment indicates that a decrease in skin temperature from 93°F to 45.8°F affected performance on manual tasks, such as knot-tying, block-stripping, and block-placing. Simms and Hinkley (1960); Crockford, Hellon, Humphreys, and Lind (1961); Fox (1965); and Brouha (1967) have discussed protective clothing in hot and cold environments. McCormick (1970) has described the effects of barometric pressure on human comfort, performance, and health; Industrial Services Company (1957) has investigated the effects of air flow on productivity; Ridker (1967) and McClellan (1970) have examined the effects of air pollution on productivity; and Fox (1965) has studied the thermal exchange (radiation, conduction, convection, and evaporation) between an individual and the work environment.

As far as protective clothing is concerned, it is clear that no job description of the furnace cleaner's work would be adequate without the reference to the need to wear this specific protective clothing during work in temperatures reaching 400°F (Figure 2.7). This information would need to be incorporated in the decision-making process regarding personnel selection so that the attributes required for operating in these temperature conditions could be assessed in advance.

THE DERIVATION OF TRAINING PROCEDURES

As a preliminary to the development of training programs, skills analysis (Chapter 3) must be performed in addition to job analysis. The methods by which this is done are explained and exemplified in Chapter 4.

However, for certain types of less complex work it is possible to derive training programs from job analysis, using the techniques of task analysis originated by Miller (1953).

Figure 2.7. Protective clothing worn by furnace workers when cleaning out furnaces under hot conditions. After working three-quarters of an hour in temperatures up to 400°F, the two men showed no fatigue or sweat loss. (Courtesy of British Steel Corporation, Cansett Works.)

In *task analysis,* which has been applied in numerous industrial situations, *jobs* are divided into *tasks* (i.e., behaviors that can be defined in terms of objectives or end products. Each task is analyzed by successively dividing it and describing each division in increasing detail, until a point is reached at which no further description is needed because new entrants can be expected to perform the individual behavior. This last subdivision, the *unit of behavior,* is designated an *operation;* such units, however, exist only in relation to the given task.

The accomplishment of a task is regarded as involving not only the *operations* to perform it but also a *plan* or strategy for combining or interrelating them. The *plan* for the task objective includes recognizing subordinate subplans; analyzing a task is viewed as the process of diagnosing the plan that is needed to achieve a stated goal (the task).

Starting from a general description of the task (i.e., statement of objective) the *task analyst* determines its main sections, restates their objectives, and continues subdividing and describing until the unitary level (as defined earlier) is reached.

For example, the task analysis of an operation involving running a chemical plant may end at the point of determining that a meter has to be read at specific intervals and that a valve must be closed if a certain point on the dial reading is reached.

Task analysis facilitates training decisions (i.e., decisions on how the task and its subdivisions are to be taught to trainees possessing an expected level of initial competence). If the task has been subdivided down to the level of *operations*, it will be necessary to provide only descriptive instructions for training beginners in the operations and to teach the structure of the task. If the task cannot be divided into operations—that is, if naïve trainees cannot identify the input or the feedback or execute the action—special training exercises will be required to enable the trainees to overcome these difficulties. An algorithm is provided to illustrate the decision making in determining training procedures.

In breaking down tasks into *operations,* task analysis rejects the time-based and movement-based forms of breakdown that have been used in time and motion study, PMTS, and skills analysis as *the basis for determining training* (though not for their other uses). It recognizes, however, that not all tasks can be subdivided to the *operation* level and that training exercises, such as those developed from skills analysis, may be required for certain tasks. (Annett and Duncan, 1971)

Task analysis is a logical and elegant means for determining systematically what has to be done in a task in terms of units or "building blocks" within the competence of trainees; it is self-determining insofar as it informs the analyst when he has broken down the task sufficiently—in this way, excessive analysis is avoided. It has generality of application insofar as it can be applied to any task, but this does not necessarily imply that it possesses universal utility. Other, speedier means for determining the appropriate level of analysis and for determining the areas of learning difficulty may be available (e.g. from PMTS data).

Superficially, task analysis in its intended function of determining areas of learning difficulty, may appear to differ from other types of analysis [e.g., skills analysis (Chapter 3)] that concentrate on how the experienced worker overcomes the difficulties. In this, as in some other respects, task analysis and skills analysis are not mutually exclusive. Normally, the skills analyst, before commencing to analyze *how* the experienced worker performs the task, uses job analysis, method study, or other available data to determine *what* happens in the performance of the task in order

to provide the initial subdivisions requisite for detailed observation and to describe what happens to time. The skills analyst from these data decides where to concentrate the emphasis of his analysis—or decides to analyze no further. Task analysis provides a more logical procedure for facilitating such decisions, but not necessarily a more economical one, since in many industrial situations existing data can be used.

The terms used in task analysis are familiar to psychologists, although the terminology is difficult for those in industry, to whom the words *operation* and *plan* already have quite different connotations and associations.

Task analysis has many applications. So far it has been applied mainly to nonrepetitive tasks (e.g., in process industries and in military occupations), and it is here that it is likely to be most useful.

III
THE ANALYSIS OF
SKILLED PERFORMANCE

OVERVIEW

Job analysis is the answer to the question *"What* does a person do?" in performing a particular task; skills analysis sets out to answer the question *"How* does the experienced person achieve the *what?"* Such analysis requires not only a consideration of the *elements* of work performed (elemental analysis) but also, in complex tasks, of the structure of the total performance (structural analysis). The relation of skills analysis to other techniques in sudying human performance is discussed.

The procedures followed in elemental analysis and the means for recording it are explained for the motor, sensory and perceptual components. For analyzing decision making, the use of algorithms is recommended.

The structural analysis of skills is discussed in terms of the pattern of information flow between man and material. Consideration of these man–material systems and the man–machine–material systems leads to a classification of work into six main categories. Each one is defined, described, and exemplified. Further subdivisions of some of the main classes are identifiable.

Further uses of skills analysis for placement and for methods improvement are outlined, and procedures for training skills analysts.

Very few people realize how they perform the innumerable tasks they accomplish—often very skillfully—every day. Few of us could report in human performance terms how we shave or how we start an automobile. The artist or sculptor, like the professional sportsman, has little idea of how he accomplishes the very skillful activities by which he earns a living. Ask a skilled workman how he does a job, and he will most likely reply, "I can't tell you—I'll show you."

The determination of how a skilled person uses limbs and senses to accomplish a task is not only an academic exercise—as such, it has a place in the curriculum of human engineering studies—it is even more important as a basis on which to build training programs. Indeed, unless the skills and knowledge employed by the experienced, skilled performer have been analyzed and understood, the training specialist has no adequate conception of where his training must lead the trainees. This dictum applies not only to industrial and commercial work, but to other areas of manual skilled performance, including surgery, dentistry, painting, sculpture, games, and the playing of musical instruments.

This chapter concentrates on the practical analysis of actual industrial operations as carried out in modern factories, but the procedures are equally applicable in the other areas of skill just cited. A knowledge of human performance at least to the degree outlined in Chapter 1 is essential and is assumed throughout.

JOB ANALYSIS AND SKILLS ANALYSIS

Before any useful analysis of performance in industrial tasks can be achieved, two simple, pertinent questions have to be answered:

1. *What* does the worker do in performing the task? What are the objective events that occur as the task is accomplished? The answer to this question is not skills analysis but job analysis (see Chapter 2); but no analysis of skills is possible until the question What? is adequately answered.

2. *How* does the skilled and experienced worker achieve what he does? To answer this question, we must (*a*) identify each pertinent item of display or cue in the task situation from which the worker receives a signal; (*b*) determine by which sensory channel it reaches the brain, to what perception it gives rise, and what decisions issue from this; and (*c*) identify what muscle groups are innervated and limb movements made to carry out each succeeding step in accomplishing the task. This may be called *elemental**
analysis.

In more complex tasks, involving a variety of constituent skills, it is necessary to determine the structure of the total performance and the temporal and other relationships between the various skill features involved; this is known as *structural* analysis.

---

* The use of this term is not intended to suggest that the psychophysiological variables of the performance correspond to specific elemental divisions of the task—among other factors, the "hierarchy of habits" found by Bryan and Harter (1897) and discussed by Welford (1958) would discount such a view. But convenient subdivisions must be found before analysis can begin.

It is important to appreciate the relation of skills analysis to other techniques in the study of human performance at work. The relation to time and methods study, to job specification, and to job analysis are clear: they deal with *what*, skills analysis with *how*. The element breakdown used in time and methods study provides a useful point of entry to skills analysis, because it is necessary to analyze how a task is done element by element or step by step, otherwise the volume of detail to be dealt with simultaneously is too great. Similarly, the therblig notations used in motion study are useful in defining particular elements of movement, providing a descriptive vocabulary for analyzing the effector output. The abbreviations or "shorthand" of predetermined motion time systems (e.g., MTM and work factor) are similarly useful in identifying and recording the movements in task performance.

The relationship of skills analysis to training within industry* TWI breakdowns is similarly clear. The latter provide an itemized list of stages or elements prescribing what occurs in performing the task, and the key points sometimes refer to features of *how* the stage is performed, but without detailed analysis. Where time and methods study job specifications do not exist, TWI breakdowns provide a useful starting point for skills analysis.

PROCEDURES FOR ELEMENTAL SKILLS ANALYSIS

Principally, skills analysis is applied to the performance of workers whose output and quality are considered to have attained the "experienced workers' standard" (EWS). This standard is expressed in different terms in different industries; it may be measured in weight of output, in numbers of articles completed, in length of fabric or, more frequently, on a time-based scale or indicator. Standard hours, or standard minutes, of work are the most generally used common basis for measuring different kinds of work, but there are at least three scales used for comparing actual performance with standard performance. On the original Bedaux (60/80) scale, EWS output coincides with the 80 point; on the 100/133 scale it

---

* This technique for job instruction originated in the United States during World War II (see *Training Within Industry Report*, War Manpower Commission, Washington, D.C., September 1945) but has subsequently been little used there. The U.K. Ministry of Labour (now Department of Employment) adopted and developed TWI, and it has been widely used in Europe, Africa, and Australia.

coincides with 100.* Even where no work measurement has been applied, seasoned supervisors are usually aware of a norm attained by experienced workers.

Normally, it is necessary to ascertain from supervisors the identities of the workers within their groups who are considered to operate at EWS, and the information can be checked by reference to performance records in the department. Before commencing to analyze the skills of workers, it is essential to obtain their agreement; this is most conveniently done by discussing the analysis, and the purpose of it, with the working group. Analysts, and others studying the performance of workers, should recognize that the skills and knowledge of the operator are the personal possession of the individual, and without his cooperation it is not only discourteous, but virtually impossible to analyze it adequately.

Skills analysis begins with gross observation and continues with increased and more detailed observations. It depends on the perceptual ability of the analyst, and this, like any other form of perceptual activity, needs to be learned. Initially, the analyst will have a few words with the operator, observe the cycle, and, if a work study is not available, determine the break points between which it will be possible to observe the individual elements of the job. An element is then selected and observed carefully each time it recurs in the cycle until the analyst can detect the hand and other limb positions (if involved) at the beginning and end of the element. Then, gradually, the intermediate movements as they recur in the element are observed and noted until the pattern of movements has been identified.

Up to this point, skills analysis is similar to motion study; that is, it is an analysis of the *effector* processes involved in performing (an element of) a task. Although receptor processes precede the effector processes in time, it is almost always more convenient to commence by analyzing the motor components before proceeding to the sensory features.

Next, and before beginning the analysis of the receptor processes, it is customary to record the observed movements in detail. Therblig or

---

* The U.K. Department of Employment *Glossary of Training Terms* defines the experienced worker standard as: "The standard of quality and output of production or services achieved by the average experienced worker over a given period of time (normally one working day at operator level). E.W.S. is normally agreed between managers' and workers' representatives and often derives from *work study* or *job analysis*. . . ." See also *Glossary of Terms* in B.S. 3138, British Standards Institution (1959) London, and McCall, R., *The Bedaux System of Labour Measurement.* The Cost Accountant, Sept. 1934.

PMTS symbols can be used for this, but for analysts unaccustomed to such shorthand, a record in ordinary words is adequate. The following simple abbreviations, however, are helpful (see also Seymour, 1966, 1967);

R	Reach	G	Grasp
M	Move	P	Position
P/U	Pick up	P/A	Place aside
RL	Release	D	Disengage
LF	Left foot	RF	Right foot
LH	Left hand	RH	Right hand
T or Th	Thumb	1, 2, etc.	First, second, third finger

An example of such a movement analysis appears in Table 3.1 (p. 90). The operation of body looping on fully fashioned sweaters and knitwear (i.e., the stitching together, loop to loop, of the sections into the complete garment) is by machine. The very intricate task of "running on" the fabric onto the points of the machine is done by the operator, however, and the job used to take 8 months to two years to learn up to EWS. The extract from the movement analysis in Table 3.1 shows the fine detail of the motions, which can be appreciated from a study of the photographs of the operation (Figure 1.2).

Where, as in this task, the movements are small and the distance moved can be related to the fabric on the machine dial, it is not necessary to record movement distance in inches. Where, as in the operations in a machine shop, the movements are appreciable, the distances should be recorded; likewise the motions of any other limbs involved (e.g., feet) will need to be similarly recorded (see Seymour, 1966, p. 34, for movement analysis of punch press operation).

With practice, the movements of an operator on most industrial tasks can be observed and recorded adequately. It is necessary to concentrate on a small part of the task at any one time and to watch for its recurrence in each cycle of the operation. Each hand must be observed separately, and likewise other limbs, for example, the feet and knees in lockstitch (power sewing machine) operation. It may be necessary to stop the operator at certain points to establish exactly where each finger is, and what it is doing, but care must be exercised to ensure that the exact positions used in doing the job are maintained. Photographs taken on a Polaroid camera can be helpful in providing almost instantaneous records that can also be used for subsequent study and reference.

Where the movements are very fast or very fine, it may be necessary to film the operation, or some parts of it, with a high-speed camera and to analyze the film by projecting at lower speeds, or by frame analysis. This procedure is especially useful for beginners in analysis, but with experience it becomes less often essential. Even when filming is used, the questioning of the operator and detailed checks on the job will also be required to ensure that all details are observed and recorded.

The exclusive observation of a very experienced worker may fail to reveal some features of the skill because performance appears to be so smooth and easy. The analyst will perceive more if he can observe, more or less simultaneously, a very good worker and an average worker or a learner. Such comparative observation enables an analyst to observe more detail and to recognize features of skill that would otherwise pass undetected. This is particularly true in the analysis of the sensory channeling as exemplified in the case of beet cutting, described in the following section.

THE SENSORY ANALYSIS

When the movements involved have been observed and recorded, it is necessary to consider the sensory channels—visual, tactile, kinesthetic, auditory, olfactory—by which the operator is receiving the information for initiating and controlling the movements. This is best achieved by considering first the *vision* channel. Usually it is possible to determine eye movements, and the point of fixation of the glance, by watching the worker's eyes. If, as in assembly tasks, the operator is looking down at the bench, it may not be easy to follow his eye movements; but frequently the essentials can be observed by watching the eyelashes, which usually reveal eye movements. If this method is not adequate, it is useful to place a small mirror at the work point, in such a position that the observer, when looking over the shoulder of the worker, can see the worker's eyes in the mirror while continuing to watch the hand movements at the same time. This use of a mirror is also very helpful when filming an operation, and the procedure may be reversed (i.e., hands photographed in the mirror reflection, and the eyes filmed directly). Such films may subsequently be subjected to frame-by-frame analysis (Barnes, 1968).

From these observations the analyst records the operator's use of vision, the locus of the cue that provides the relevant information, and the type of vision (e.g., peripheral) and its purpose (e.g., for planning, controlling, checking). It is not always possible to detect all these points by observation alone; judicious questioning of the operator may be required to establish, for example, whether a particular glance of the eyes is unnecessary or essential to check that a feature of the task has been correctly completed. It may also be possible for the analyst to attempt the task, or part of it, himself in order to determine how he needs to use his visual sense in accomplishing it.

The use of touch and kinesthesis is more difficult to identify, usually requiring indirect determination. If the operator continues to do part of the task without looking, the movements involved must be controlled by the tactile and kinesthetic senses. For example, when an operator making an electrical assembly keeps his eyes at the assembly point while reaching for the soldering iron, that movement must have been controlled kinesthetically and terminated by touch when the fingers came into contact with the handle of the soldering iron. Sometimes it is possible to distract an operator's attention to see whether he continues to perform the task satisfactorily—if so, he is able to control the activities kinesthetically at that point in the cycle. This procedure, however, should *not* be adopted unless the analyst is perfectly sure that no safety hazard can arise from distracting the operator's attention.

The distinction between kinesthetic and tactile perception is often difficult to identify; in reaching "blind" to an object and grasping it, the transition from one sense to the other is so swift that it is almost impossible to determine when one ends and the other begins. Since such nearly-combined uses of these two senses are so common and so necessary in skilled performance, there is sometimes little practical value in determining this distinction. In many situations, the essential feature is to ascertain that the particular movements are not visually controlled and that, at the moment in time, vision is free to deal with other sources of information. Such determination of the "sense channels available" and "sense channels used" is an important feature of the analysis.

The sense of touch serves principally to elicit information about the conclusion of a movement that is not visually controlled. However, touch can also be employed in a much more delicate way, to detect the shape and orientation of components, to judge the surface finish of materials, or to identify one object from among others (e.g., a crooked needle in a group of straight ones). After a few trials, the analyst becomes able subjectively to identify the use of touch if it is employed to determine shape or orientation. If touch is being used to judge surface finish or to identify faulty objects, the analyst may not be able to feel for himself the more delicate differences; but, with the cooperation of the experienced worker, he will most likely be able to sense the differences in extreme cases and thus to identify how the channel is being used.

The use of the kinesthetic channel can most easily be recognized where this sense is used to control "blind movements." A very large number of activities are controlled visually by beginners which would be controlled kinesthetically by experienced workers. Rechanneling of the information for controlling one hand, while retaining visual control for the other, enables an operator to do two things at once, and this can be observed in many occupations. For example, an analyst walking through a beet field saw two men cutting beet and noticed that one man, without apparent haste, was getting through his work some 30 percent faster than the other. The less productive worker leaned forward, visually selected a beet, speared it with his knife, raised it, transferred it to the left hand, released the knife, cut off the leaves, and finally glanced to the pile of finished roots and threw his beet on to it. The more productive worker made exactly the same movements, but he had learned to control the throw of the finished beet kinesthetically, thus saving the glance to the pile. While the left hand was throwing aside, the right hand, visually controlled, was moving to the next beet, thus saving considerable time without exerting extra effort. Innumerable similar examples can be cited from productive industry—in the loading and unloading of machines, in the two-handed operation of dual machines, and in the reaching for hand tools while controlling material or a machine with the other hand.

The close *comparative* study of operatives often reveals when kinesthesis has been substituted for vision. In the case of the beet cutters, for example, it is doubtful whether the analyst would have noticed the point if he had seen only the faster worker.

Again, in the operation of a lathe, an inexperienced analyst might correctly observe that the operator's vision was always directed to the cutting point. However, he might fail to appreciate the more important point that, because of this, all the worker's hand movements in operating the machine must be kinesthetically controlled. In other words, the operator learns proprioceptively to move his hand a certain distance in a certain direction, and he learns by association that his hand will then have reached a certain control knob or handle, from which he will receive feedback by the tactile sense when the hand touches the object. Workers at different levels of proficiency may use different channels to obtain the same information. For example, subjects on a capstan lathe experiment (Seymour, 1967) reversed the star wheel during their initial attempts, when the slide hit the backstop; subsequently, they began the reversing movement when they heard the click that preceded the hitting of the backstop. Ultimately, they learned the limb and body position associated with the point at which the reversal should take place and determined the point of reversal kinesthetically.

A second and equally important use of the kinesthetic sense occurs when the operator must judge the pressure exerted by a limb in achieving appropriate control. This is exemplified in the use of the treadle-operated clutch on a lockstitch sewing machine. Since the operator cannot see the treadle, it is quite clear to the analyst that the feet must be controlled kinesthetically and not visually; information about the rate at which the machine is sewing, however, is derived by eye and ear. Where a lever or other control mechanism is within view of the operator's eyes, it is more difficult to determine whether the operator is using vision or kinesthesis; but this can usually be decided by asking the operator to perform the action without looking at the hand. Other controls, like the knee lift on sewing machines or the knee stirrup on type-soldering machines in type-writer manufacture are likewise kinesthetically controlled. Since the extent of movement is between stops, however, the *degree* of control is predetermined, although the sensory coordination is important.

The use of the sense of hearing is not always easy to identify, since it may occur only sporadically. Many people in industry have observed a man standing with his back to a group of machines, who suddenly turns around and adjusts one of them because he has recognized by a change in the sound pattern that one of them is running abnormally. An experienced worker can detect such changes even in a very noisy shop, and even if his acuity of hearing is not abnormally good, because he is perceptually alerted to it. In a food factory, experienced operators minding pie-packing machines had less serious stoppages due to "double feed" of cartons. On analysis, it was found that even in the noise of the shop they heard the sound made when two cartons were fed into the machine; by immediately stopping the machine and removing the extra carton, they prevented further mishap that would have occurred if the additional packing material had subsequently smashed a pie. If a particular sound is very difficult to detect, its presence may be recognized by the analyst by recording the situation on a tape recorder and playing it back repeatedly till the signal can be identified.

Hearing is especially important in the musical instrument industries, where it is frequently required to ultranormal standards. Here again, the analysis of how the experienced worker derives the perceptual information is important (e.g., that the piano tuner adjusts the string tensions not by his perception of pitch differences, but beat frequency changes). In this task, the kinesthetic control of fine but powerful hand movements to turn the tuning pins is equally important.

Similarly in pipe organ tuning, fine kinesthetic control of pipe length adjustments is as important as the detection of pitch and tone differences. The auditory discrimination required in organ pipe voicing is of the very highest order, and only a small proportion of the population have the necessary ability for this work. In all these tasks, the use of electronic gear and cathode ray tube presentation has made it possible to "translate" the auditory stimuli to visual ones, but handling such equipment retards the performance of the experienced worker.

Taste and smell are critical senses in the food and drink trades. Some earn their living by tasting tea or whisky; others by smelling eggs that are to be added to cake mixture (since one musty egg will contaminate a whole batch). The particular sensory discrimination demanded in such jobs is obvious, but the level of it needs to be analyzed by experimental procedures similar to those used in psychological experiments using the method of limits. (See also Harper, 1972).

RECORDING ELEMENTAL ANALYSES

A simple and basic method of recording the *effector* processes is presented as in Table 3.1. In this case, only three columns are shown, one for the elements and one each for left-hand and right-hand movement. Where other limbs are involved, additional columns must be added. The abbreviations used are those listed previously, which are adequate for most purposes. Analysts who are accustomed to PMTS will prefer to use the abbreviations employed in the system they know, for example MTM (Maynard, Stegemerten, and Schwab, 1948), or work factor* (Quick, Duncan, and Malcolm, 1962). The motion notation recording system introduced by Laban and Lawrence (1947) and developed by Preston-Dunlop (1969) can be used for recording movements in some industrial jobs. Initially, analysts find some difficulty in sequencing activities correctly on their record sheets; it is essential to appreciate that time is recorded downward and that a left-hand movement following a right-hand movement should be recorded one space lower; clear records occupy a good deal of paper.

The example in Table 3.2 illustrates the normal form of record used in analyzing both the receptor and effector processes involved in performing industrial tasks. In certain cases it may be advantageous to provide columns for both touch and kinesthesis and, very occasionally, for hearing also. The Comments column is useful for recording important additional features or for clarifying points in other columns (e.g., small sketches to illustrate hand positions, notes on bimanual or hand-and-eye coordinations, and points affecting safety or quality). In completing the sheet, it is

* The work factor is a PMTS by which the investigator calculates the EWS from data on basic motions (see also Chapters 4 and 6).

Table 3.1   Movement Analysis Chart[a]

Job: Body Looping   Task: Run-on Front Panel

Element	Time	Left Hand	Right Hand
Run-on rest of first shoulder		Regrasp. T lying on top of points in front of fabric. 1 behind (2, 3, 4, folded away).	Release.
		Hold.	Regrasp. 1, 2, 3 under points and behind fabric, sliding along to vee neck fashioning, T on front 1, 2, 3, 4 gather fabric into palm as hand moves up to points.
		T and 1 pull fabric upward and to L, pulling stitches onto points.	Fabric between T on front and I resting under points, uncurls fabric as folds run out of palm. Fabric held loosely or pulled to R.
		Continue as above	Continue as above.
		Continue as above.	Regrasp. 1, 2, 3, 4 gather more fabric into palm.
		Continue running-on until top hole of 1st side of vee appears	
		T and 1 grip fabric over top of vee hole, holding stitches on points.	Turn wrist toward body, bringing fabric to R of vee away from points. Release and regrasp. 1, 2, 3, 4 gather fabric into palm.

[a] Courtesy of the U.K. Knitting, Lace, and Net Industry Training Board, from *Operator Training Recommendations*, 1970.

necessary again to ensure that successive movements are on successive lines and that the entries in the senses columns are aligned with the movements to which they relate.

Crossman (1956a,b) proposed a more elaborate form of skills analysis chart which he called the Sensori-Motor Process Chart; an example is given in Figure 3.1. To begin recording on this chart, the analyst lists in the outer columns the observed features of the performance. Then in the central columns he records, for each element of work, when any symbolic (see p. 12) decisions have been made and mental work performed. The perceptual activity (p. 28) is recorded using the following symbols:

Plan   ∨
Initiate   ○
Control   ⌁
End   ●
Check   ∧

Sensorimotor process charts have been recorded by Crossman and Seymour (1957) for cigar-making operations, letter sorting, biscuit packing, and hand stripping of tobacco leaves, and by the DSIR (1960) for soldering joints on electronic assemblies.

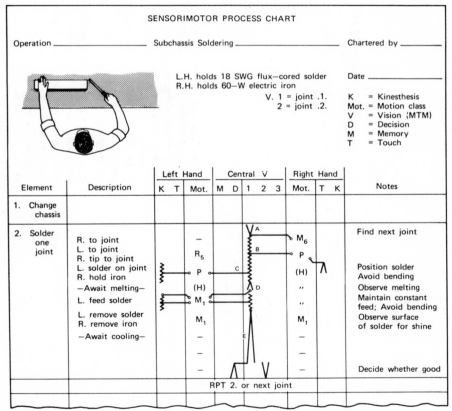

Figure 3.1   Sensorimotor process chart. (From Crossman and Seymour, 1957.)

Table 3.2 Skills Analysis Chart[a]

Job: Body Looping   Task: Run-on Front Panel

Element	Time	Left Hand	Right Hand	Vision	Other Senses	Comments
Run-on rest of first shoulder		Regrasp. T lying on top of points in front of fabric. 1 behind (2, 3, 4 folded away).	Release.	Locate correct course.		
		Hold.	Regrasp. 1, 2, 4 under points and behind fabric, sliding along to vee neck fashioning, T on front. 1, 2, 3, 4 gather fabric into palm as hand moves up to points.	Peripheral vision locates vee neck fashioning.	*Touch:* R.H.1 under points confirms gathering completed.	
		T and 1 pull fabric upward to L, pulling stitches onto points.	Fabric between T on front and 1 resting under points, uncurls fabric as folds run out of palm. Fabric held loosely or pulled to R.	Confirms correct points emerge through stitches.	*Kin:* Loose R.H. hold or tension to match stitch for point.	Smooth continuous movement.

Continue as above.		*Touch* detects grip on fabric becoming uncomfortable, indicating need for regrasp.
Continue as above.	Continue as above.	
Continue running-on until ⟶	Regrasp. 1, 2, 3, 4 gather more fabric into palm.	Locates top hole on 1st side of vee appears from under R.H.T.
T and 1 grip fabric over top of vee hole, holding stitches on points.	Turn wrist toward body, bringing fabric to R of vee away from points. Release and regrasp 1, 2, 3, 4 gather fabric into palm.	Confirms hole on front lines up with stitch on back which stands up from points.
		To ensure that front and back necks match.

[a] Reproduced by courtesy of the U.K. Knitting, Lace, and Net Industry Training Board, from *Operator Training Recommendations*, 1970.

The sensorimotor process chart is an extremely valuable method of charting the analysis of fine work where the perceptual load is high, but its use is limited to the relatively few people experienced in perceptual analysis. For the majority of industrial operations, the type of record shown in Table 3.2 is adequate.

ANALYZING DECISION MAKING

All pertinent sensory perception in skilled performance gives rise to decision making, which varies in kind and in degree. In some tasks it is quite unconscious and based on nonsymbolic information as when a sewing machinist stops the machine at the end of a seam. In others, the decision may be qualitative, although still nonsymbolic, as when the cigar maker, examining a leaf of tobacco, decides where to place it to produce another cigar. In still other situations, the decision may depend on symbolic information, as when a coil winder reads a numerical indicator to determine the end of a layer. A fourth type of decision making occurs in grading tasks, as when, at the completion of tanning, the bend of leather is graded by the selector in one of several categories; or again, in inspection tasks, as when an inspector determines the cause of noise in domestic cleaners (Seaborne and Thomas, 1964). Finally, a most important type is seen when a fitter or machine setter has to diagnose the fault in a machine and determine which of several possible causes is actually responsible for the stoppage or malfunctioning.

The first four types of decision making can be, and are, analyzed along with the sensorimotor processes already described. But the last type of decision making deserves special consideration. Often the most skillful workers are able to make better decisions because they have obtained *more* and *earlier* information and can, as a result, discriminate between possible causes or anticipate and sometimes prevent faults or stoppages. When analyzing fault finding in electromechanical systems, it is necessary to identify the locus of the cue from which the experienced worker is gaining additional information. Sometimes such information may be gained from the machine operator, as when the person responsible for setting nucleonic-controlled cigarette-making machines receives from the "catcher girl" information about what happened when the machine went wrong. He may learn even more by comparing the electrical and electronic situation (e.g., as shown on the control panel) with the mechanical situation (e.g., whether the machine has stopped at the beginning, middle, or end of a cycle) (Seymour, 1967). Such additional information makes it possible to decide more rapidly and precisely on the probable causes of any fault and, by elimination, to arrive at the true cause. Not only is time

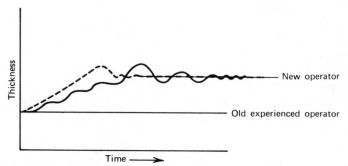

Figure 3.2.   Change of product thickness in process plant. Solid line indicates inexperienced worker's results; dashed line indicates experienced worker's results.

and production lost when the fitter is searching for a fault, but even more is lost when he "puts right what isn't wrong" (Seymour, 1968b).

In process industries, similar factors prevail—for example, the sugar boiler who detects an abnormal rise in temperature by feeling or listening to the vat and is able to take earlier preventive action than would have been possible, had he waited for information from the pyrometer. In addition, the experienced worker develops or adopts certain strategies that constitute an essential part of the overall skill, and these can be identified and analyzed. Such strategies are particularly exemplified when process workers have to achieve a change in the state of the process to achieve a change in the product.

For example, in paper or board making the operator may at some point be required to increase the thickness of his product, and this involves possible changes in water content, pulp, and chemicals. When the inexperienced worker changes thickness, his results tend to follow the solid curve in Figure 3.2. An experienced worker, on the other hand, can make the change indicated by the dashed curve—and the difference may represent hundreds or thousands of dollars worth of lost output. An analysis of the experienced operator's strategies can be made by careful observation, by identifying the cues he is attending to, and by determining the sensory information and the operator's interpretation of it, which enables him to make earlier and better decisions about the manipulation of his controls. Timing and prediction are the essence of such skill; but these factors, like others affecting human performance can be analyzed.*

* Some processes like the one just described are now electronically controlled by computer programs; but many situations still remain in which human control is paramount.

RECORDING

The recording of the sensory and perceptual cues from which an experienced worker derives special information for decision making can be done using the type of skills analysis chart shown in Table 3.2. or a sensorimotor process chart (Figure 3.1). Where the decisions in fault finding need to be made in a particular sequence in order to eliminate possible causes and to identify the true cause of a fault, the procedure is more conveniently recorded by means of an algorithm. The decision processes of the experienced worker are first analyzed in the sequence in which they must be made, and the discriminating signals are noted. The decisions are then recorded on a "yes" and "no" basis in the form of a "logical tree." "Algorithm" is defined as follows:

"A mathematical term meaning an exact prescription, defining a computational process leading from various initial data to the desired result. In logical tree analysis its meaning has been extended to cover any rule of thumb procedure, any recipe—not necessarily mathematical—for achieving a desired outcome. In this sense, a flow chart, or its list structure equivalent, provides the user with an algorithm for handling a variety of different conditions in the right way. This usage also ties in with computer programming technology. A person working through an algorithm can be likened to a computer working through a programme. In both cases the process of decision-making is reduced to a sequence of "yes/no" (either-or) responses to specific questions, stemming usually from previous decisions made and/or prior statements of action. Provided there are no ambiguities of instruction, a successful outcome is guaranteed. The technique is particularly useful for task analysis where mental skills of a diagnostic/discriminatory nature are involved, as for instance, in the process industries" (Glossary of Training Terms, Department of Employment, United Kingdom, 1971).

An example of an algorithm for determining the cause (and rectification) of a paper-feed fault on a packing machine is given in Figure 3.3. Details of how such charting is accomplished appear, with numerous and amusing illustrations, in *Algorithms and Logical Trees* (Lewis and Woolfenden, 1969).

THE STRUCTURAL ANALYSIS OF INDUSTRIAL SKILLS

The *elemental* analysis of skilled performance in industrial tasks so far discussed is basic in the understanding of such performance; but more complex and intricate tasks in industry demand, in addition, an analysis

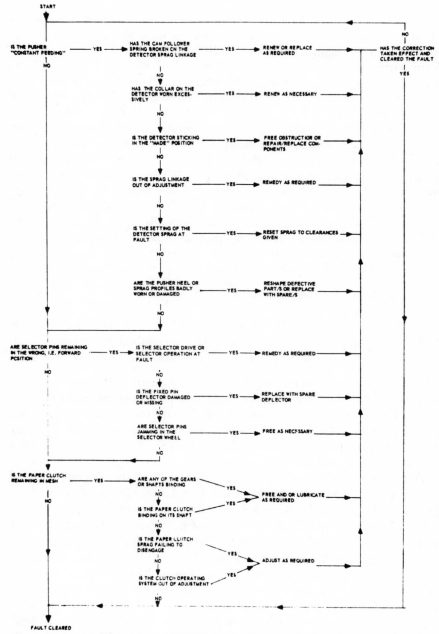

Figure 3.3. Algorithm for a D.E.F. machine paper feed fault: paper continues feeding–no product. (Courtesy of T. Wall & Sons [Ice-Cream] Ltd.

of the *structure* of the skills involved. Just as human performance consists of more than a series of discrete responses to specific stimuli, so the higher ranges of skill in industry consist of more than the ability to perform particular elements of work to prescribed standards. The skill required to drive a truck through the streets and avenues of New York involves more than an ability to operate steering wheel and pedals, and the skills of an *experienced* operator on a turret lathe involve more than pressing buttons and pulling levers. The hierarchical organization of performance as skill develops in industrial and other tasks has been emphasized (Bryan and Harter, 1897; Book, 1925; Welford, 1958, 1968), and clearly an understanding of the structures of the total skills required in the performance of complex industrial work is essential in their analysis. These skill structures differ considerably as between different types of work in industry, and they depend fundamentally upon the relationship of the worker to his material and the pattern of information flow between man and material which is involved in the task.

The structural analysis of a complex task requires the determination of:

1. The range of activities involved.
2. The principal constituent skills.
3. The hierarchical and temporal organization of the receptor, effector, and decision-making processes exercised by the skilled performer.
4. The immediate and stored information used in carrying out the task.

The first and most obvious type of work in industry is that in which the operator's hands (or other limbs) come into direct contact with the material. Widely differing examples of such activity occur—from the picking and peeling of a banana in order to eat it to the wiring of memory matrices for computers. The use of the hands to obtain food exemplifies the earliest and most primitive of human activities, but the same direct man–material relationship is to be found also in the manufacture of sophisticated modern products. Such a relationship is illustrated in Figure 3.4. Here we are concerned not with a man–*machine* interface, but with man–*material* interface—the relationship of man to the material that is undergoing change. In manual work this relationship is self-evident and readily recognized. When the potter moulds clay with his hands, the direct contact of man and material enables us to recognize the output of effort and the flow and feedback of visual, tactile, and kinesthetic information between material and man.

The second type of work is that in which the operator uses tools, held in the hand, to fashion the material for his purpose. The use of tools constituted the first stage in the development of man's mastery of his

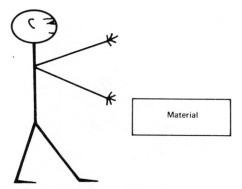

Figure 3.4.   Man-material chart.

environment, and by it man is as much differentiated from the animal kingdom as by his ability to communicate by speech and written symbols. "Man is a tool-making animal," wrote Benjamin Franklin in 1778. Man's ability to make and use tools, however, comes not from any specialized development of the hand itself, but from the development of a more refined central nervous system—the higher levels of skill and manual dexterity being of cerebral rather than anatomical origin. Tool making has been the means of man's ability to achieve survival and economic development, for it is the basis of his technology (Singer et al., 1954). Indeed, the most complex machines and equipment of today could be traced back to hand tools used by our remote ancestors. In modern industry, the man who uses hand tools seldom makes his own, and thus we are concerned now with the *use* rather than the *fabrication* of hand tools.

The ability to use tools in the hand has been for centuries the traditional criterion of a craftsman's skill, and it still forms the basis of apprentice training. It is also fundamental in the work of surgeons, dentists, sculptors, and artists. In addition to craftsmen, there are in industry today many millions of semiskilled workers who earn their living by the use of hand tools in assembly and adjusting tasks, and the like. All tasks involving the use of hand tools have in common "not only the use of the hand as a tool but also the use of tools by the hand" (Cox, 1934). Tools are fashioned to achieve what bare-fisted skill cannot accomplish; they constitute an extension of the hand not only as a motor force but, equally important, as a *channel of information*. The use of tools comprises the first stage in interposing aids between man and the material he is fashioning for his

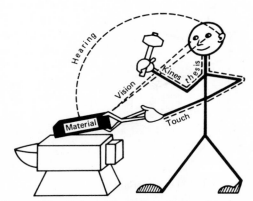

Figure 3.5.   Information flow in the hand tool work.

purpose. The now indirect relationship between man and material can be represented by Figure 3.5. The diagram illustrates not only the way in which the interposition of tools affects the way in which forces are exerted on the material, but also the way in which the tools become channels by which information flows from the material to man. In particular, the kinesthetic feedback that provides the check (see p. 91) that a perceptually recognized activity has been completed is especially important.

Thus work with the tools in the hand differs essentially from pure handwork in the differentiation of the manner in which the bodily forces are exerted (with consequent differences in the manner in which muscular contractions are made and controlled) and in the manner by which the information flow from the material reaches the brain by way of the senses. "Implements," wrote K. U. Smith, "alter the status of human learning because they introduce special modes of transformation of feedback control into motor-sensory activities" (Smith and Sussman, 1969, p. 132).

Work with the use of machines constitutes yet another category of tasks that are encountered in industry. By definition, a machine is anything that provides mechanical advantage—and in industry today there are still machines that use "muscles for motors" and derive their motive power from the operator's limbs. These are becoming increasingly rare, however, as are those powered by wind, water, or animal power; in modern industry we need consider only the devices driven by electric motors or, in remoter areas, by gasoline engines.

In machine work, the man–material relationship is different again insofar as the main motive power is provided not by muscular contraction but by external forces, as depicted in Figure 3.6. The information flow between man and material is again different and more indirect. The motor effort of the worker becomes less, but the *control* factors become more important. Control is achieved by small and easy movements which depend on sensory processes derived at a further state of remove from the material. The greater degree of intermediacy between man and material demands different channels of perception and a different phasing of the time factors—as the material is located further away and as it changes state more swiftly through the application of mechanical forces, the operator's perception and decisions need to occur earlier in order to compensate for time lags in the system.

Figure 3.6 represents one of the simplest forms of machine operation—a man operating a drill press. There are many more complex information-flow situations in which more machines or more complex machines are controlled by one man. We can however identify three main forms of man–material relationships in industrial machine systems:

1. That involved in single-purpose machine work, where the machine is used for a single purpose and where a specific group of skills is required at all times (see pp. 114-117 and pp. 162-164).

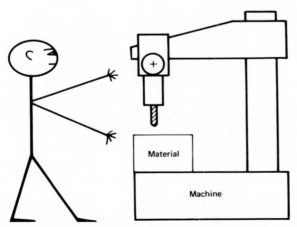

Figure 3.6.   Man-machine-material chart.

2. That involved in multipurpose machine work, where the same machine is used at different times for different types of work. In such cases, a repertory of skills is required, and these serve in different permutations and combinations when different jobs are done on the same machine (see pp. 117-118 and pp. 164-167).

3. That involved in group machine work (multimachine assignments), where the worker is called upon to produce from more than one unit of production. Here the man is more remote from his material; artificial signals such as warning lights may be introduced to draw his attention to what is occurring, and he is required to spread his attention more widely. In contradistinction to handwork, perception of the operator is almost wholly exteroceptive and rarely proprioceptive (see pp. 118-121 and pp. 167-170).

In addition to tasks already enumerated, there are others in industry that involve the preparation and maintenance of machines, plant, and equipment for work, and the operation of process plants.* These may be comprised under the heading *nonrepetitive* work and divided into two categories:

1. In manufacturing industries, nonrepetitive work is done by fitters, mechanics, and the like, who set machines and rectify faults in them. The relationship of these workers to the material undergoing change is indirect and intermittent. In the setting of machines, the ability to recognize that the material is or is not being satisfactorily changed constitutes the prime relationship between man and material. The complex information derived by the setter on an automatic lathe from his "first off" (first component produced) is all-important in telling him what further adjustments he needs to make. This is true in all machine setting situations where the setting is determined from the product and not the product from the setting.

2. In process industries, nonrepetitive work is performed by operators who are responsible for the control of process plant in the chemical, food, and petroleum refinery industries, and so on. In such situations the worker is remote from the material, which he usually cannot see; his manual activities are restricted to adjusting valves and making records, and he receives sensory information indirectly by way of gauges, meters, pyrometers, and the like. The change in the material itself is accomplished by nonhuman means but involves *control* skills on the part of the operator,

---

* Work of these kinds is becoming increasingly important as a result of changes in skill profiles due to technological change; see, for example, Crossman and Laner (1966, 1969) and Crossman (1966).

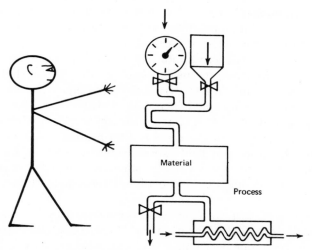

Figure 3.7.   Man-material chart for process work.

whose relationship with the material can be represented by Figure 3.7. A similar situation exists in electric power stations where the changes involved are not those of material, but of energy forms. In studying human performance in productive industrial tasks, then, the ultimate consideration is not the man–machine system, but the man–material system, which may involve a direct interface, an interface mediated by tools, or a man–machine interface in differing forms, capable of affecting the nature and degree of information flow.

Even this brief survey of man–material and man–machine–material relationships in industrial work and the accompanying differences in information flow, makes it possible to appreciate the need for another type of analysis of industrial skills—namely, structural analysis, which enables us to identify types of industrial work and facilitates our understanding of them in terms of the man–material interface. After completion of a job analysis, when the skills analysis of a task is being initiated, structural analysis should precede elemental analysis, since the former enables the analyst to recognize the likely salient features, the types of work that are similar in other industries, and the way in which the elemental analysis, can best be tackled. Furthermore, through structural analysis it is possible to categorize the many varied types of work in industry, with the following advantages:

1. By determining the particular class of work to which a given task belongs, the analyst can appreciate the hierarchical structure of the skills required and the relationship of particular features to the whole.

2. By classifying tasks *across* industry and not just *within* industries, the analyst can gain access to analysis performed in similar but different fields. As experience in skills analysis has increased, it has become ever more necessary to classify this experience so that it can be used and so that it provides students with a system of ready access to what is already available. In other biological sciences, classification is as important a discipline as laboratory and field experimentation. Thus in the study of industrial skills, a taxonomy is equally important not only for theoretical reasons but to provide an index and ready reference to existing knowledge in the subject.

3. By the use of *structural* analysis, economies can be made in the *elemental* analysis required (see pp. 107, 111 and 118). Of course elemental analysis is very time-consuming, and can be quite costly; but if the structure of the skills in a task is appreciated, ways can be found of achieving the necessary understanding of the skills without analyzing every variation in the work. This is especially important in situations such as assembly and machine shop work, where operators do many different jobs, each one consisting of a different permutation or combination of specific elements.

A classification of occupational skills based on the type of information flow involved, and hence of skill structure, has been put forward (Seymour, 1959, 1967, 1968a). In this classification, machine work has been subdivided into the three parts enumerated earlier: single-purpose machine work, multipurpose machine work, and group machine work. This distinction is useful because, although in each case the change in the material is accomplished by machine, the degree and manner of control and of information flow differ. This classification results from a consideration of human performance in the whole range of industrial work situations. It classifies man–task relationships by differentiating tasks in terms of the differing patterns of behavior attributable to the nature of the work and in terms of sensorimotor and perceptual activity. However, it does not attempt to cover theoretical considerations, and thus it differs from some other taxonomies of skill such as Fleishman's (1962) approach to the classification of tasks by means of ability variables, Fitts's (1962) task taxonomy, and the task descriptions of Miller (1962), Gagné (1965), and Annett and Duncan (1968).

Tilley (1969) emphasized the need for classification when he wrote: "Behavioural analysis requires some general system for classifying tasks, a task taxonomy, although it may be somewhat pretentious to use the term 'taxonomy' at the present time" (p. 585). He illustrated with great clarity the use of an information-processing model in understanding skilled performance, summarizing three noteworthy features of a system of job classification based on an information-processing model:

1. It emphasizes that the concept of task difficulty is multidimensional.
2. It indicates appropriate training methods.
3. It provides a language for describing any human skill.

Fitts and Posner (1967) have designated the various ways in which information is transformed in different types of activities, and especially in perceptual motor skills. They have thus indicated a common basis, in terms of information processing, for both mental and motor skills.

Main Classes of Occupational Skills

The six main classes of occupational skills and their principal subdivisions (Seymour, 1967) are as follows: handwork, handwork with tools, single-purpose machine work, multipurpose machine work, group machine work, and nonrepetitive work. Let us discuss these individually.

Class 1: Handwork. Work that is done exclusively with the operator's bare hands, without the intervention of any tools or machinery, is called handwork. (For this purpose the word "tools" includes any apparatus used as an extension of the fingers but excludes anything that might normally be found in a home, e.g., pieces of paper, dusters, or brushes.) In this group of operations, which still employs a large number of operators, are wrapping and packing operations, some assembly work, pottery decoration, and other examples of very fine work. Some types of inspection work also fall into this category.

Even in the highly mechanized and automated industry of the 1970s, handwork constitutes an important part of industrial employment, and millions of workers today earn their living by "bare-fisted skill." This is in part due to the continued high market value of fine products "made by hand," in part to the need for ancillary work that cannot economically be mechanized and in part to the desire for a final examination of products (especially food stuffs) by people. In the case of the last, it is sometimes advantageous to perform minor handwork operations at the same time.

Handwork operations in manufacturing industry can be subdivided into four main groups: traditional, ancillary, packaging and assembly, and viewing and examining tasks.

1. *Traditional Handwork Tasks.* Some traditional tasks are component parts of ancient craft skills; others, although calling for great skill and dexterity, do not require full apprenticeship. Old established industries like needle making, spring making, textiles, pottery, leather crafting, and glass making provide the majority of examples of this type of work. The task may be presented to the worker in various forms or sizes; for example, in china cup handling, a preliminary survey of the range of the operation (Seymour, 1966) is required. High product quality and consistency of standards are necessary (in, e.g., glass tableware); hence the determination of the quality specification is particularly important, if seldom easy. For these tasks, training exercises that permit the worker to practice the appropriate skill features in isolation, have been more often useful than special training devices.

Two detailed examples of training for hand work have been published (Seymour, 1967) dealing with the sponging of cast ware of moulded clay and the enameling (i.e., hand painting) of Wedgwood china. The pottery and fine china industries, with their wide variety of skillful and highly dexterous operations, present a fascinating field for the study of manual skills. In particular, the levels of sensory perception involved are unusually high both for vision and kinesthesis. The handling of cast ware in sponging requires very delicate kinesthetic sensitivity, since the articles, being still unfired, are extremely fragile. In enameling, fine control of the pressure on the brush is necessary to achieve the correct depth of color in paling and shading. This task also involves very considerable job knowledge, since the range of designs for flowers, leaves, and stems is very large, and the appropriate point of entry, type of enameling, and strength of color must be known for each pattern and consistently maintained throughout every piece in a set (Seymour, 1967).

2. *Ancillary Operations.* Many industrial products, produced in the main by highly mechanized processes, also involve some ancillary work done by hand and, if productivity in such handwork sections is inadequate, overall production and profitability falls. Often the training time for handwork operations is longer than that required for operators on the mechanized sections, and hence more attention needs to be given to organizing effective tuition.

In some parts of the food industries, it is common for the main production work to be done by men and the ancillary operations by women. In meat preparation, for example, female operators "look up" the skirts of beef that have been boned by butchers, removing gristle, bone, and excess fat before slicing the joints into specified pieces. Since there are some nine different main joints to be "looked up," and since the total time for the whole operation is about 40 min, the analysis of the entire procedure is very time-consuming. As in many similar cases, however, it was found that the experienced workers used a limited repertory of angles and movements in the handling of the knife. Once the total pattern of work had been structurally analyzed, the elemental analysis of each knife movement could be accomplished much more quickly (Seymour, 1967).

Prior to the manufacture by machine of cigars and high-grade pipe tobacco, it is necessary to remove the stem of the leaf by hand in order to prevent the damage to the leaf that might result from the machine-stemming procedure used in making cigarettes. Hand stemming is a highly repetitive task which anyone can learn very quickly to do *somehow*. However, to do it to the production standards of the experienced worker, to avoid three common faults, and to ensure that no part of the leaf is removed with the stem (and hence wasted) is quite difficult; it takes new recruits some eight weeks to master the task to EWS. Skills analysis showed (Seymour, 1967) the importance of the kinesthetic control of left-hand movements in spreading the leaf, in removing creases, and in holding the leaf while the right hand removed the stem. Systematic training based on this analysis made it possible to reduce the training time to two and a half weeks.

3. *Assembly and Packaging Tasks.* Many industrial products are assembled by hand—without the use of tools or machines—from components that have been made by machine. Similar tasks occur where completed products are packed by hand at the end of a machine line: the product is, in effect, assembled into the packaging or container. These two types of work can thus be conveniently considered together.

One of the most delicate hand industrial assembly operations is the wiring of computer matrices, which is described in some detail in Chapter 4. Most handwork assembly jobs are much easier, and those encountered in mechanical and electrical engineering (e.g., consumer durable subassemblies and switch assemblies) seldom require long training periods. Miniaturization and microelectronics, however, have presented other skill training problems as difficult as those of computer matrix wiring.

Most packaging tasks done by hand are relatively simple, but considerable dexterity is required if the speed and consistency of quality of the experienced worker are to be attained. The tasks may be subdivided into those which are *unpaced* and those which are *paced* (i.e., have to be performed to keep pace with a conveyor belt).

In *unpaced packaging*, the operator works at his own speed on batches of work obtained by him or supplied to him. The range and complexity within the task may be considerable, as with the hand wrapping of screws, where the operator may be called upon to pack and wrap any of some 2000 different types of woodscrews (Seymour, 1959). The knowledge content of the job is considerable; the worker needs to know the different types of screws and screwheads, and which screws go into which boxes with which type of label and wrapper. The element that demands most careful analysis is the weight counting of the screws, in which the worker measures the quantity by balancing against a counted quantity. Experienced workers are able to judge the correct number of screws to put in the weigh pan by kinesthetic discrimination and can get the number right to ±1 screw almost every time. Unsurprisingly, the EWS cannot be attained if the worker has to add or subtract several screws to the lot.

Unpaced hand packing is replaced by machine or paced packing wherever the quantities make it more economical. But numerous examples can be found elsewhere in industry, including the packing of high-grade toiletries and pharmaceutical products, and the weighing and packing of tobacco and some foodstuffs.

In most mass production industries, packaging is done either by machine or on some form of conveyor, and the operator must keep pace with the flow of work. Such *paced packaging* tasks appear to be easy—anyone can do what is required; but new entrants can seldom maintain the preset pace, and their inability is responsible for delays, damaged work, and wasted materials. Detailed analysis of biscuit packing, using Crossman's sensorimotor process chart (Seymour, 1967), reveals the visual, tactile, and kinesthetic planning and control by the operator.

In some examples of paced packaging, operators are obliged to carry out work from time to time at different "stations" on the line and to perform different tasks. In order to train future workers for flexibility in such instances, it is necessary first to analyze the structure of the total skill patterns required from operators. This is exemplified in toiletry packing, where different products are packed at different times on a number of belts. The range of subtasks may include some three types of bottle loading, two types of filling, and two types of capping and cap tightening, followed by any one of five types of cartoning. Each of these needs to be analyzed before training can be established that will enable trainees to learn, *before* they go on to production, to do any of the subtasks at line speed.

Many examples of paced packaging occur in the food industry, where, although often the packing could be done by machine, handwork is preferred in order to ensure inspection of the product before it is dispatched to the customer. In such operations hygiene training is of great importance in addition to the normal skill and knowledge features. An account of a typical training procedure—for ice cream packaging—has been published (Seymour, 1967).

4. *Viewing and Examining.* Since viewing and examining are primarily perceptual activities; the motor component of such tasks is usually minimal. Elementary forms of viewing occur in the engineering industry, where operators check that an operation has been completed on components. The work, which gives rise to acceptance or rejection, is usually visually controlled; but wherever possible it is transferred to sensing devices or other methods not involving human decision makers. More difficult perceptual situations arise in the examination of material for faults and for quality grading. Faults are detected either visually (as in warp knitted fabric examination), tactile (as in wood finishes), kinesthetically (as in grading bends of sole leather), or by a combination of these senses.

Although the perceptual characteristics of viewing and examining are more important than the motor activities, it may be necessary to analyze the latter carefully, since the manner in which the hands are used to present the material to the senses is frequently important. Thus in hand-sewing needle inspection (Seymour, 1966), the precise procedure for rolling the needles must be mastered before faulty needles can be tactilely detected. Similarly, in the inspection of television screens, analysis showed the need for careful training in handling the TV screens to ensure proper inspection of all surfaces (Singer and Ramsden, 1969).

In analyzing the perceptual component of an examiner's work, a useful first approximation can be made by posing the question "Can the untutored perception of the novice detect the differences in material on which the experienced workers' decisions are based?" If the answer is in the affirmative, the analysis and subsequent training can be relatively simple, based on quality specification and fault analysis (see p. 136). If the answer is in the negative, it will be necessary to analyze much more carefully the experienced workers' perceptual processes. For example, tactile and kinesthetic perceptions as exercised in the inspection of sewing needles must be analyzed in detail (Seymour 1966). Also calling for precise analysis are the various forms of visual perception used in woven cloth examination (Belbin, 1964; Kirk and Feinstein, 1967), in the examination of cotton textiles and warp knitted fabric, and in printed carton examination.

---

* It is useful to distinguish between viewing (i.e., the checking of work without special equipment) and inspection, where measures, gauges, micrometers, and other tools, are used. (Inspection is considered under Handwork with Tools.)

Additional problems arise when products are presented continuously for viewing on belts or conveyors (e.g., for warp knitted fabrics, pipe tobacco, milk bottles, and vegetables in canning factories). In such situations, the vigilance and attention factors affecting the detection rate in human performance need additional investigation. These problems have been the subject of many researches in recent years; results have been summarized by N. A. Mackworth (1950), Murrell (1969), and J. Mackworth (1970).

Class 2: Handwork with Tools. All types of manual work in which hand tools are used, but in which the use of mechanical power is not involved, are called "handwork with tools." In spite of the increasing mechanization of modern industry, very large numbers of workers are still engaged in operations with hand tools; these may be of a general nature (e.g., screwdrivers and pliers), or like the wig-maker's hook, they may be specially designed for the purpose. Examples are provided by most types of assembly work, pottery figure making, telephone wiring, coil fitting on electric motors, and so on.

The handwork with tools category comprises tasks involving the type of information flow exemplified by Figure 3.5; that is, the sensory information reaching the operator from the material is no longer entirely direct but is partly mediated by the tool, and the forces are exerted on the material not directly by the limbs but through the end point of the tool. Thus the tool in the hand of the experienced worker becomes an extension of the hand itself, not only as a means to achieve what the hand alone cannot do, but as a channel for the reception of information from the material. An appreciation of this unity of hand and tool is essential to all understanding and analysis of tool work.

Traditionally, the mystery of a craft centered around the making of tools and the use of them. Even today, the initial stages of craft training frequently include the making of hand tools, gauges, and similar equipment. But the vast proportion of handwork with tools performed in industry is done by persons—whether they be craftsmen or semiskilled workers—for whom the tools are already made. The skill of using tools is thus the principal skill to be analyzed—and to be taught—for this type of work.

Similarly, very few products in modern industry are basically made by hand tools; yet hand tools play a most important part in completing and finishing products from material that has been fashioned on power-driven machines. In the main, hand tools are now used in manufacturing on partially finished components in order to:

1. Fasten parts together to make whole products (fastening tasks).

2. Adjust components of a product to achieve its purpose (adjusting tasks).

3. Rectify faults in a product (rectifying tasks).

4. Determine the correctness of products by means of inspection "tools" such as gauges and calipers (inspection tasks).

Such tasks are to be found throughout the whole range of industry; they vary in difficulty from those involving the simplest use of a screw-driver to complex work such as wiring telephone equipment or fine work such as assembling electronic tubes. The difficulties of these tasks arise from one or more of three principal sources:

1. From the need to use perceptual discrimination at near-threshold levels (e.g., fine vision in electronic assemblies, or kinesthetic discrimination in wig-making or pottery figure making).

2. From the need to derive instructions in the form of symbolic information during the performance of the task from another source (e.g., blueprints, wiring diagrams, running lists).

3. From the range or complexity of the operations required of an operator, calling for a wide repertory of subskills, involving numerous different tools and their selection. Such difficulty is exemplified in type-writer aligning (described later) and many mechanical assemblies.

In situations involving the first difficulty, detailed *elemental* analysis must be performed, with particular reference to the two-way traffic of motor force and sensory perception through the hand and tool; in situations involving the second difficulty, the analyst must determine how the experienced operator coordinated the input of symbolic and nonsymbolic information and the degree to which temporary storage is used for the former.

In situations characterized by the third difficulty, which is common to a great many tool jobs, it is necessary first to ascertain the overall range and structure of the skills involved. This can be done by considering, throughout all the tasks required of an operator, how many tools he will have to use and in how many ways each tool is to be used (if more than one way). It is then postulated that, if each of the ways in which each tool is used has been analyzed, and if trainees have been taught such uses to the EWS, they will be able to perform work within the given range; that is, tasks can now be considered not as uniquely different, but as different permutations and combinations of particular tool usages. By such a structural analysis of the overall skills required, it is possible to econ-omize on the number of elemental analyses performed; indeed, in many instances it would not be feasible to carry out elemental analyses on all the jobs to be done.

Let us consider in order the four main uses of hand tools previously listed.

1. In *fastening tasks*, parts are attached together by the use of hand tools. Such tasks are quite widespread, but they occur principally in the light engineering, electrical engineering, and electronics industries. The mass production of consumer durables calls for numerous assemblies of components into products, and many of these cannot be economically achieved by machine. A typical example is the assembly of automobile door handles, and a summary of the training procedures for this job, which involves the use of a screwdriver, socket wrench, mallet, and other tools to produce a wide variety of door handles, has already been published (Seymour, 1967). The electrical industry provides many examples of a similar degree of difficulty [e.g., assembly of light fittings (Singer and Ramsden, 1969), switch and fuse boxes, and domestic appliances]. More complex examples occur in telephone manufacturing industry in bank, plate and transmission equipment wiring, in which the principal tools are special pliers and soldering irons. In the stator winding of fractional horse power motors, some half-dozen tools are used in the extremely varied types of special motors still assembled by hand (Seymour, 1959).

In the electronics industry, the fineness of the work demanded by many jobs made training times by traditional methods very long. In electronic tube assembly, the manipulation with tweezers of very small components, such as grids and cathodes, takes a high level of dexterity and kinesthetic perception; the detailed analysis of tweezer control is fundamental to the acquisition of the skills that have been described (Seymour, 1959) and illustrated in film and television programmes (B.B.C., 1968). Even finer assembly work is encountered in transistor manufacture and in the assembly of miniaturized electronic components. Another very fine, but more unusual, fastening task involving hand tools is the knotting operation in wig-making; the critical feature is the control of the hair by means of the special hook.

2. *Adjusting.* Numerous industrial products that are assembled from machine-made parts are not of any use for their purpose until, after completion, they have been set and adjusted with hand tools. Such adjustment is often intricate, requiring minute movements and delicate perception, a considerable and specialized knowledge of the components, and the capacity to use a variety of special tools. Examples of these tasks occur in telephone manufacture (dial adjusting and relay adjusting) and in the aligning of typewriters and centralizing of typing bars.

A detailed study of the analysis and training procedures required for telephone relay adjusting has been published (Seymour, 1967). The distinguishing features of skill of the most experienced workers revealed by analysis were:

(a) Ability to diagnose, from an initial examination of the relay, the extent and character of the corrections to be made. This did not appear to be symbolically recognized, however, for workers could not express the diagnosis in words.

(b) A repertory of plier movements that would adequately "bow" the springs to increase or decrease tensions, along with the sensory recognition by kinesthetic feedback that the correct tension had been achieved.

(c) Ability to recognize visually very small differences in the "bow" of springs.

(d) Ability to distinguish kinesthetically through the pliers minute differences in spring tension and to judge such tension within approximately the limits required, thus reducing the frequency with which the gauge has to be used.

(e) A repertory of precise grasps for holding the relay to present it to the tool, and precise and consistent methods of holding the tools.

An account of the analysis of, and subsequent training for, typewriter aligning is given in the next chapter. Other examples of this type of work occur in the electronics industry, where operators are required to adjust the values of specific components to enable the system to achieve its specific purpose. (See also the following item.)

3. *Rectifying.* In several industries some workers are fully engaged on rectifying products that have been made by others, either because the faults could not be detected at earlier stages or because they could not be so easily corrected at the stage at which they occurred.

Examples are seen in the textile industry for both knitted and woven fabric. With the former, *mending* of fabric (i.e., the reconstitution of the pattern) is achieved by the use of a hook and a needle; hose and fashion-knitted and circular-knitted fabrics also require mending. On woven fabrics, the operation of *burling* and *mending* is carried out with a needle; it has been the subject of study by E. and M. Belbin (1972) and others. Analysis of the mending task indicated that successful performance depended on not only the acquisition of the correct method and the required motion patterns with the needle; correct perception of the cues that make the desired motion pattern possible is also needed. Sufficient perceptual skill for recognizing each pattern of weave had to be acquired before the fabric could be correctly mended.

Fault rectification tasks on electronic systems provide other examples of this type of work. For example, in the manufacture of electronic modules for use in various types of control gear, it may not be possible to adjust the values of components to conform to the required levels (see item 2). Normally, the apparatus is then passed to other operators to be rectified. Rectification requires the use of tools, meters, and so on, to enable the operator to diagnose the cause of the faults; the rectification itself is usually less difficult—hand tools and a soldering iron often suffice to remove and replace the faulty component. The use of tools for this work can be analyzed and taught like other hand tool work, but it has been found that algorithms are advantageous for analyzing the strategies and communicating the procedures used in diagnosing faults.

4. *Inspection.* Both adjusting and rectifying tasks may contain elements of inspection; but other tasks consist entirely of inspection with the use of "tools" (i.e., gauges and other measuring apparatus held in the hand). In analyzing such work, the structure of the total skill may be assumed to consist of an ability to use each of the inspection tools to EWS. Analyses have revealed markedly different ways of using the same inspection tool in different industries; micrometers, for example, are used differently in the electronics industry and in mechanical engineering. The level of kinesthetic sensitivity required in the use of gauges is subject to variation in different situations and must be checked by analysis.

The attainment of *consistency* by inspectors and between inspectors by training and retraining is a constant aim of production managers. Few inspectors realize their variability, or that they differ from their colleagues in method or result—until a machine that has been passed by one inspector is stopped by another. Inspectors more readily recognize their differing results if they discover them for themselves (e.g., by measuring standard pieces with a micrometer and noting the variations in the results) (Seymour, 1967). The use of analyses as a basis for inspector training has been reported by Belbin (1962) and Simmons (1958); ways of developing the skills and knowledge of inspection staff were discussed by Harris and Chaney (1969).

Class 3: Single-Purpose Machine Work. All operations in which a mechanically or electrically driven machine is used for one specific purpose are considered to be single-purpose machine work. The increasing use of special-purpose machines tends to augment the number of workers employed in this category, although the numbers working on any one type of machine may be small. Examples are provided by hosiery seaming and linking machines, coil-winding machines, and cigar-making machines.

Many kinds of single-purpose machine work in industry can be mastered quickly and do not justify detailed skills analysis. Besides these, however, there are a considerable number of very difficult jobs that take several months and sometimes more than a year to learn. The difficulties encountered in such tasks arise from one or more of the following features:

1. The fineness of the work, which may require ultranormal levels of perceptual discrimination.
2. The variations in material (especially natural raw material), which call for rapid decision making.
3. The vigilance required in minding the machine.

Three subdivisions of single-purpose machine work may be identified:

(a) Loading of power-driven machines, in which the operator has only to start and stop the machine and keep it fully and correctly loaded with work. The simplicity of this description is deceptive, since a great deal of skill is often involved in loading, and errors in the work create heavy penalties for productivity, yield, and output.

An analysis of part of one such task—fully fashioned garment looping—has been given previously, and a similar example on fine-gauge seamless hose linking has been discussed at length by Seymour (1966). A case study on coil winding was quoted by Singer and Ramsden (1969), and two from the tobacco industry—cigar making (Seymour, 1959) and pipe tobacco spinning (Seymour, 1967)—have been described in detail.

Special difficulties arise when the raw material to be loaded into a machine is of natural origin, as with tobacco leaves, since each unit differs slightly from the others, and dimensional and other characteristics are normally distributed. This demands of the operator a repertory of slightly differing responses. Visual and kinesthetic sensitivity need to be highly developed to enable the worker to recognize restrictive features in the material and to feel its condition. The understanding of the import of these features leads the worker to make rapid decisions about the action to be taken. For example, in cigar making, the operator has only the cycle time of the machine to observe and feel a particular half-leaf and to decide whether its condition is satisfactory, whether any blemished parts need to be rejected, and how many cigars can be made from it.

Other examples of machine-loading tasks in single-purpose machine work occur throughout industry; for example:

Case making in the automobile tire industry.
Electrical upsetting machines.

Coil winding.

Pressing of records and other items in the plastics industry (where more than one press is controlled by each operator, this task must be considered under Group Machine Work, below).

Electrical porcelain pressing.

Board stitching in carton making.

Crate making.

Bristle fixing in the brush-making industry.

(b) In the control of manually operated mechanisms, the motor power of the machine is provided by the operator, who is also responsible for loading and unloading. Examples of such work can still be found in the food industry (Seymour, 1967), in spring making, and in electronics and instrument making. Because of the increasing rarity of this "use of muscles as motors" in industrialized countries, the work is less important than it was in the past. Nevertheless, in certain jobs in this category detailed analysis is significant in the attainment of high performance and productivity.

Capacitor winding, as practiced in the electronics industry, is one example of this type of work (see p. 21). This task is characterized by special difficulty in the initial element— starting the wind. This element is notable first insofar as it is very variable, even with some experienced workers; this factor, indeed, indicate the perceptual stringency involved. More precise training could be given only following detailed analysis of the exact finger positions, of the angle at which pressure was exerted, and of the kinesthetic sensitivity required to appreciate the correct pressure. This resulted not only in shorter training time and higher overall performance, but in a higher "yield," or proportion of capacitors wound that were within the tolerance limits of capacitance (Seymour, 1967).

(c) Minding of Special-Purpose Machines. The manufacture and packaging of products in large-scale production is increasingly performed by special-purpose machines that are individually looked after or "minded" by operators. The work seldom involves much physical activity, and to the casual observer the employees might appear to be doing nothing for a good deal of the time. But if such machines fail to operate at full productive capacity, the minders need to exercise considerable vigilance and perceptual skill. The effects of the required skill, or its lack, are indicated by the wide differences in performance between experienced and inexperienced workers looking after the same machine (e.g., operators on alternate shifts). The output of the machine is to some extent outside the control of the operator, but different levels of workers' skill and performance produce considerable divergences in results.

Typical examples of machine minding are found in cigarette manufacture and in the packing of bakery products. (In these situations, one worker is responsible for each unit of production. The situation in which a worker is responsible for several units of production is considered below under Group Machine Work.)

A comparison of the performance of the very best workers with that of less successful ones indicates that the former incur less machine stoppages and/or stoppages of shorter duration. An analysis of stoppages usually reveals that the most experienced workers are able, from additional cues, to detect oncoming stoppages at an earlier point and either to prevent them or to reduce their duration. A previously mentioned example is applicable here. In the packing of pies, newly hired operators experienced long stoppages when carton flats were double fed and pies, on being forced into the double carton, were broken. The resulting mess took up to a quarter hour to clean up so that the machine could be restarted. Older workers had few such stoppages. They had learned to recognize the characteristic sound of a double feed and, acting instantly, could stop the machine and remove the extra carton flat before any pies were damaged. Once this feature had been revealed by the analysis, it did not prove difficult to incorporate it in the training of new workers (Seymour, 1967).

Class 4: Multipurpose Machine Work. All types of work done on power-driven machines that can be adapted for a variety of purposes come under the rubric of multipurpose machine work. Typical examples are the operation of the capstan lathe and the industrial sewing machine.

Although for any given operation, multipurpose machine work involves an information flow between man and machine and material similar to that entailed in single-purpose machine work, the structure of the total skills required is different, because no single task manifests the worker's ability or level of performance. The ability to do a number of different jobs on the machine is as much a measure of the operator's skill as his ability to perform a given task.

Multipurpose machine work is most commonly found in the wood working, metal cutting, garment, and footwear industries. Milling, drilling, and grinding machines, lathes, and power presses can be used for a variety of purposes, as can traditional needle machines (lockstitch, overlock, post machines, etc.); and operators must be taught to operate these machines in several of the applicable ways, with different types of material. Thus it is necessary to determine first for each industrial situation the particular structure of the overall skills required; this can be ascertained from a study of the range of the operations required.

The range of variations can be considered under the following headings:

1. Machine variations—from the number of different machines the operator may be called upon to use individually, and from the number of ways in which each machine is to be used.

2. Material variations—from the number of different metals (in a machine shop job), types of fabric (in a garment factory), or sorts of leather and other material (in a shoe factory) that an operator will have to handle.

3. Product variations—from the range to be produced. This factor affects the operator less than the first two in relation to the skills required, but it has greater effect on standards of quality and finish (e.g., as between outerwear and underwear in garment manufacture).

Once the range of operation required on multipurpose machines is determined, detailed skills analyses can be made for each element of the task in each of the main categories of variation within the task. However, the construction of a training syllabus for multipurpose machines presents certain special problems that need early examination. Since no single activity encompasses all the skills of an operator on a multipurpose machine (in other words, no whole which constitutes the summation of the parts of the task), the training syllabus must be designed to enable the trainee, step by step, to build up or "structure" the skill required for the task and to apply that skill in any one of a variety of situations. Thus in training sewing machinists, it is not the elements of work in making a particular garment that are analyzed, but each item in a repertory of skills so that, after training based on these analyses, the worker can apply the skills in any combination necessary for achieving a given task. Here again, the analysis of the structure of the total skill required permits us to achieve a considerable economy in the total number of elemental analyses to be made.

Seymour (1967) has published extensive summaries of typical training courses for three tasks involving mutipurpose machine work: for capstan lathes, power presses, and lockstitch sewing machines. A detailed account of analytical training in garment making has been published by King (1964) and examples from the United States were cited by Ladhams (1964, 1968). Other case studies on garment sewing are reviewed in Chapter 4.

Class 5: Group Machine Work. The types of work in which the operator is responsible for the output from a number or battery of automatic or semiautomatic machines is called group machine work. Although sometimes referred to as "machine minding," this type of work involves short complex operations that must be done efficiently if full productivity is to be achieved. Automatic capstan lathe work, weaving, and spinning, provide examples in this category.

When the worker is responsible for more than one unit of production, the man–material–machine relationships are again different. The flow of visual information between the material and the operator is intermittent (with relation to any given machine), and a pattern of visual "patrolling" is necessary: the exteroceptive senses of hearing and (occasionally) smell come into play, and the operator's attention has to be distributed in an organized way over the whole work area. Table 3.3 illustrates a typical pattern of structural analysis for group machine work.

Table 3.3 Structural Analysis for Class 5 Group Machine Work

From performance of experienced workers determine:[a]

I. Manual activities: inside-cycle and outside-cycle elements of work in relation to:
    A. Material
    B. Machines

II. Signal recognition
    A. Sensory channels
    B. Levels of discrimination
    C. Distribution of attention

III. Decision making
    A. Serial, sequential, or immediate
    B. Planning (e.g., changeovers)
    C. Interference and/or time sharing

[a] Items I.A, I.B, and II.A may require elemental analysis and fault analysis.

No elaborate analysis is necessary to recognize the prime essential for high performance on group machine work—namely, that production occurs only when the machines are running. Thus both analysis and training must be concentrated first on the "outside cycle" elements in the task (i.e., those which occur when the machine is stopped). In this type of work, the machines used are either automatic or semiautomatic; but in all cases there are occasions when a machine needs to be stopped, or itself stops, and the quicker the operator completes the work that must precede restarting, the less his output will suffer. But there also tends to be interference between the cycle of work on one machine and that required on

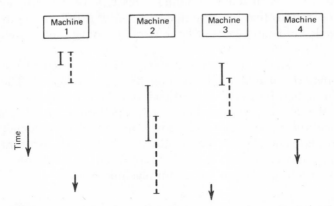

Figure 3.8. Group machine stoppages (multimachine assignments). Solid lines indicate expected duration of stoppages; dashed lines indicate time taken by operator; arrows represent stoppages that should have been remedied, but which the operator has not reached.

others—a second may stop before the operator has restarted the first; and this happens more frequently if an inordinate amount of time is used to restart after any stoppage.

Figure 3.8 shows how this situation can "build up" against the inexperienced operator. Thus if an operator falls behind on each machine in turn, he will soon lose all his productive capacity, and the frustration this creates has been one of the reasons for high failure rate and labor turnover on group machine work.

A further feature of the experienced worker's skill also must be analyzed for some of the tasks. Before the operator has restarted one machine, another may stop for a trivial reason; in this case it may pay to leave the one being worked on, restart the other, and return to finish the first job. Quite complicated decision-making situations can arise in this way if three or more machines are stopped, and experienced workers develop extremely clever strategies to deal with them with minimal loss of production. These strategies can be analyzed and—after checking to see that they are optimal —they can be used as the basis for training exercises (Seymour, 1959).

Examples of group machine work are found in the following industries:

Textiles—spinning; weaving (Lancashire and automatic looms); narrow fabric weaving.

Knitwear—circular and flat-frame knitting; circular knitting for underwear and outerwear.

Engineering—automatic lathes (single, multispindle, and chuck "autos"); automatic screw-making machines (for slotting, shaving, and threading).
Rubber industry—golf ball winding.
Plastics industry—press operation.
Fine wire drawing machines.

Examples of training courses for group machine work have been published by Seymour for woodscrew manufacture (1967) and for cotton weaving (1959); additional results on this operation were quoted by Singer and Ramsden (1969). A study of analytical training on fully fashioned knitting machines is given in Chapter 4.

Class 6: Nonrepetitive work. Tasks in nonrepetitive work involve the responsibility for maintaining production from machines, plant, and equipment and, where relevant, for setting machines and equipment into the correct condition for production. Such work occurs in many industries and is indirect in the sense that workers do not have direct contact with the material undergoing change. There are two main subdivisions of nonrepetitive tasks; those occurring in process industry and those occurring in manufacturing industry. The nonrepetitive work of a process operator for example, involves man—material relationships rather different from those of a setter in manufacturing industry. For this reason the two groups are discussed separately.

Nonrepetitive tasks in the manufacturing industries involve the preparation and setting of machines (changeovers) for production and the adjustment and rectification of machines that are not producing correctly. No changeovers are required in the case of special-purpose machines, and the tasks comprise only adjustment and rectification. Tasks that have been analyzed in this category include:

Milling and machine-shop tasks.
Automatic lathes.
Cold forging.
Four-slide multiform machines.
Auto-coil spring-making machines.
Grid-winding machines.
Electrical upsetting machines.
Flat and circular knitwear machines.
Looms of various modern types.
Cigarette-making machines.
Packing machines (various).

Most workers trained on these tasks have had previous training or association with machines, during apprentice training, perhaps, or as operators on machines they later learn to set up (e.g., loom monitors who graduate from weaving).

Analyses have shown the following features to be specific to nonrepetitive work in manufacturing industries:

1. Greater use of memory and ability to recall procedures, due to the occasional and sporadic occurrence of many elements of work. Thus the knowledge content is *proportionately* greater in relation to the skills content than in the first five classes of work. Greater technical knowledge is required.

2. The need for diagnostic ability for recognizing and tracing faults in mechanisms. Such diagnosis requires, in addition to knowledge of the mechanisms and detailed observation of them, an ability to recognize symptoms and to determine the true causes of stoppages or malfunction by eliminating the nonoperative causes.

The diagnostic function in this class of work is the most important additional feature to analyze. Experienced workers are extremely adept at locating and remedying the faults or stoppages in mechanisms they know well; but there are frequently marked differences in the speed and success rates of different mechanics faced with the same problems. Delays in rectifying faults grow increasingly costly as the rated output and capital cost of plant and equipment become greater.

In approaching the analysis of fault diagnosis on electric–pneumatic–mechanical systems in industry, we must first gain a structured understanding of the functioning of the equipment. This can be done for any system by finding the answers to the following questions (Seymour, 1967):

I. Materials
   A. How does material arrive at the machine?
   B. What processes has it passed through?
   C. What are the material specifications (i.e., quality specifications)?
   D. What happens to the material subsequently?
   E. When and how is it finally inspected?
   F. How, when, and where is the quantity of material recorded?
   G. What are the quality considerations during the operation?
II. Machine details—starting from motor and main drive with schematic drawings for each section, determine:
   A. What is the section?
   B. What does it do in relation to the operation of the machine?

    C. How does it accomplish this?

    D. How does it relate to other parts of the machine?

III. Machine adjustments—divide into:

    A. Routine adjustments and/or replacements that can be planned.

    B. Adjustments to correct faults (cf. diagnosis); for each item, determine:

        1. Purpose of the adjustment

        2. Location and accessibility of adjustment

        3. Means of adjustment—tools, direction, and degree of movement

        4. Testing adjustment (i.e., limits, trials, measurements)

        5. Side effects of adjustments

Next it is necessary to analyze *how* the most successful workers diagnose the faults that occur. There may be no direct record identifying the men who are most successful, but plant records of output usually indicate which employees suffer least stoppage per shift, if this is not already known to management. It is then necessary to make a comparative analysis of the better workers' methods of diagnosis, which they may not be able to explain. Detailed questioning of individuals may be necessary in order to obtain the information. In some cases, however, it is useful to bring a group of experienced men together with a machine, into which faults are introduced one at a time. Each man performs and describes his procedure for identifying and remedying the fault, while the rest comment and criticize. Regardless of whether individual or group means of analysis is used, it is necessary to determine the symptoms that are observed, the additional sensory data that are collected, and the optimum "eliminatory" procedure by which the true cause can be established from among numerous possible causes.

As mentioned previously, the algorithm form of presentation has been found to be most useful and comprehensible to mechanics and fitters. Where complex systems are involved, the faults and stoppages must be arranged in a systematic order. For any part of a system, the analyst can determine this systematic order by starting from the nature of the input information (e.g., operator's statements, appearance of machine product) and proceeding according to the following outline of a fault diagnosis procedure (Seymour, 1967):

    I. Start from the form in which the difficulty is seen by or reported to the supervisor; for example:

        A. Machine stopped, but was producing good work

        B. Machine running, but was producing faulty work

     C. Machine stopped, but was producing faulty work

     D. Machine running and producing good work, but behaving abnormally (e.g., noise, vibration)

II. Then proceed to record:

     A. Name of fault

     B. Appearance or indication (including gauging)

     C. Possible causes

     D. Symptoms or checks

     E. Remedy—with cross reference to sketches and machine details and adjustments

Clearly, if each adjustment has been listed in the outline for analysis previously set forth, the remedy will consist of one of these adjustments, unless the failure of the mechanical system was due to structural damage. Breakdowns in electronic systems can be more readily diagnosed by comparing panel symptoms with machine symptoms (Seymour, 1967), and they are usually remedied by replacement of a defective component. Failures in pneumatic and hydraulic controls also usually need to be rectified by replacement, and nucleonic controls are normally dealt with only by specialists.

Table 3.4 illustrates a typical pattern of structural analysis for the class of nonrepetitive tasks.

Table 3.4   Structural Analysis for Class 6 Nonrepetitive Tasks

From performance of experienced workers determine:

  I.   General outline of man–machine system or process:
        nature, purpose, and output of main sections

  II.   Machine or process details. Analyze:

      A.   Power route

      B.   Primary material route

      C.   Secondary material routes

      D.   Timing and time factors

 III.   Adjustments:

      A.   Routine

      B.   Fault correction—purpose, location, means, test limits, side effects

 IV.   Fault diagnosis: Algorithms

  V.   Changeovers

      A.   Procedures

      B.   Control skills

In process work, the analysis of the skills involved can best begin from an identification of differences in output achieved by different workers. Often it will be found that although the plant, process, and material are identical, one man or one shift may surpass the others by attaining higher output or more consistent output, with less stoppages. Such differences are the starting point for analysis—if one man can achieve more output than another, then *how* he is doing *what* he is doing is different. The identification of these differences, in terms of earlier acquisition of information or better strategic decision making, enables the analyst to recognize the features of the higher skill of experienced workers.

These skills are exercised as a result of:

1. *Sensing* by hearing, sight, or smell, the indications of change in the system.

2. *Perceiving* the meaningfulness of these signs and interpreting and comparing instrument readings.

3. *Predicting* what is likely to happen.

4. *Controlling;* that is appreciating the use and effect of controls.

5. *Deciding* what actions and strategies are likely to (a) maintain the required state within the plant or (b) bring it to that state.

Specific control skills are especially difficult if there are interactions between numerous control and display variables, if there is considerable time lag in the system, or if important variables cannot be measured but must be estimated.

Since the material is remote from the worker, he needs to develop a "model" picture of what is happening to it; he also must be aware of the indirect information channels that bring him relevant information. The analyst thus needs to determine the "geography" of the plant, the nature of the process, the background technology, and the use of the control mechanisms and display instruments (King, 1958; Crossman and Cooke, 1962; Seymour, 1967).

THE USES OF SKILLS ANALYSIS

The primary use of skills analysis is in the training and retraining of workers to prescribed levels of performance (EWS), and methods for doing this are described in Chapter 4. Skills analysis is also used as a basis for the development of selection and placement procedures (see Chapter 6) and for methods improvement.

Methods Improvement

Skill analysis can reveal hitherto unrecognized improvements in motion economy, particularly when it shows significant differences between the movements used by different experienced workers. Such improvements are taken into account when determining the teaching method to be used (Chapter 4). More substantial improvements may be suggested from a scrutiny of the analysis (i.e., by the substitution of a movement pattern not used by any present employee). Changes within the job itself by the use of better jigs, fixtures, tools, and so on, normally arise from job analysis (Chapter 2). However, if adequate consideration of ergonomic principles has not been given to the operator's work, these improvements may not be suggested until the skills analysis has been scrutinized.

A more likely area for improvement lies in the perceptual, rather than in the motion, content of task performance. An ergonomic study of how the worker is called upon to use the senses often reveals opportunities for redistributing the perceptual load or for improving the pattern of attention (especially visual attention) throughout the task.

This is particularly important in tasks involving viewing or inspection where the motor output is extremely low but the perceptual discrimination is very high. With increased mechanization, it is often possible to reduce the number of man hours per unit of manufacture, but inspection time may remain constant. In such circumstances it is advisable to make a detailed skills analysis by sensorimotor process chart to determine possible improvements in information flow, with a view to reducing the time taken for inspection.

THE TRAINING OF SKILLS ANALYSTS

The specialist function of analyzing skills is normally undertaken by training officers, senior instructors, industrial engineers, ergonomists, or full-time analysts. Irrespective of occupation, the analyst needs specific training in order to be able to analyze industrial skills, and training directors must find the most appropriate means of providing this in each individual case. It is likely that only the larger firms will employ full-time analysts, and a typical personnel specification for use in their selection has been given by Singer and Ramsden (1969). These authors listed the following topics for training full-time analysts and others who are going to carry out skills analysis training:

The principles of skills analysis training.
How to make analyses of skills.
Analyzing the quality aspects of work.
Structuring a training course, program building, and devising special exercises.
Preparing training manuals.
Tactics of investigation in analyzing work.

Training needs analysis.
Criteria for evaluating training results.

Programs for training in skills analysis have been conducted in the United States in the Department of Industrial Engineering, State University of New York at Buffalo. In the United Kingdom, a six-week practitioners' course has been held once or twice a year in the Department of Engineering Production, University of Birmingham. Specific courses are organized by several U.K. Industrial Training Boards* for their own staff and for training officers in their industries. Appreciation courses in skills analysis training have also been organized by government and professional bodies e.g., the Institute of Personnel Management in Britain, the National Development and Management Foundation in South Africa, and the Department of Labour in Australia. Several international firms of industrial consultants provide training courses on skills analysis training—particularly Urwick Orr and Partners Ltd., P.A. Management Consultants Ltd., and the P.E. Consulting Group (S.A.) Ltd. Such courses sometimes incorporate sessions on "Improving Operator Performance" by better methods and supervision.

* Under the U.K. Industrial Training Act (1964) twenty-eight *Industrial Training Boards* have been set up by the Department of Employment, covering all the main areas of productive industry. Each board is responsible for ensuring that adequate training is available for all workers (including operators, craftsmen, supervisors, and managers). A board is financed by a levy payable by all firms within the industry.

IV

DEVELOPING
WORK PERFORMANCE
BY ANALYTICAL
TRAINING TECHNIQUES

OVERVIEW

The procedures to be followed in designing a training course and the means available for determining the depth of analysis to be pursued are explained.

The "two-pronged" attack (featuring structural analysis and elemental analysis) in the current approach to training design is outlined. The procedures for analysing the knowledge content and the skills content and the use of the results of analysis to formulate training programs are detailed, and modern methods for imparting skills and knowledge are summarized.

Case studies exemplifying each of the six main classes of work are provided, showing how the principles already enunciated have been developed into practical training programs; the results achieved are summarized, as well.

The benefits for managers and workers to be derived from analytical training are described, and further examples of such benefits are quoted. In addition, the role of the training specialist is discussed, and the potential contribution of such central bodies as the Industrial Training Boards in the United Kingdom is indicated. Finally, the place of skills analysis in a rapidly developing technology of training is outlined.

How can we mobilize our knowledge about skill and its acquisition and about the analysis of skilled performance in industry to improve occupational training? This question has exercised the minds of occupational psychologists, industrial engineers, ergonomists, and human factors specialists for many years, and especially since the original concepts of analytical training were enunciated by A. H. Seymour (1904–1965; brother of the author) during World War II. In the past 30 years, knowledge about the acquisition of skills and about their analysis has expanded phenomenally; and, over the same period, the tasks that workers are called upon to perform in industrial and other occupations have changed considerably. These factors together have led to a continuing growth and expansion in analytical training techniques within the emerging field of training technology.

DESIGNING A TRAINING COURSE

The variety and complexity of human activities at work make it difficult to see how to approach the preparation of a training course and how to encompass all that a worker does in many occupational situations.

The need for preanalysis groundwork has been rightly emphasized by Donnelly and Kenney (1970), who provided an algorithm covering the questions to be answered before initiating job training analysis for semiskilled work. The analyst determines first the basic parameters of the job qualitatively and quantitatively; second, the probable incidence of technical or methods changes; and third, the type of approach—by TWI, skills analysis, or task analysis—which is most desirable.

This determination of the type of analytical procedure to use and the depth to which it should be carried is clearly of paramount importance. Analytical work is always time-consuming and costly, and it should not be undertaken unless the probable economic benefit outweighs the cost. A simple guide for determining when skills analysis is likely to pay off has been proposed (Seymour, 1968b):

1. If new workers can attain EWS within one week, explanation, demonstration, and safety and induction training (p. 134) will probably be adequate.

2. If new workers take two or three weeks to attain EWS, then TWI, with target times (p. 141) and fault analysis training added, will usually suffice.

3. If new workers take three weeks or longer to attain EWS, the most economical method is likely to be skills analysis training, although sometimes this approach is more economical even when learning times are shorter.

Even when detailed skills analysis is to be used in the development of a training program, it is seldom required for all the parts of a task. Those that can probably be performed immediately to the experienced workers' standard of output and quality will not need detailed analysis. Those elements that are considered to need analysis will usually be found to contain some limiting factor. There are three main types of limitation.

1. A physical limitation, as in heavy work (e.g., drill operation in gold mining) or work involving abnormal use of one part of the anatomy (e.g., wear on the skin of the fingers in hand winding fractional horse power motors).

2. A perceptual limitation, due either to the need to discriminate beyond normal levels with one of the senses (e.g., looping or needle inspection) or to novel situations in which recognition of differences is not immediate (e.g., printed carton inspection or fabric mending).

3. A decision-making limitation observed when new recruits are unable to make the right decisions because they cannot identify the locus of specific information or because they lack knowledge of the system, plant, or machine involved (e.g., in fault rectification in electronic apparatus or in machine maintenance).

Annett and Duncan (1971), who designed an algorithm covering these considerations and others involved in the breaking down of a task for analysis, postulated three main questions:

1. Can the trainee identify the input? If not, improve input coding or prepare perceptual training exercises.

2. Can the trainee execute the action? If not, develop training exercises.

3. Can the trainee identify feedback? If not, provide substitute feedback, improve coding, or prepare perceptual training exercises.

In discussing the general problem of designing training courses, Tilley (1969) outlined a systems approach (based on Anglo-American experience in training defense personnel) which, he said, "demands a thorough analysis of the various interacting processes involved in designing a training course; it also regards training itself as simply one subsystem within a larger system, the operation of the parent organization." Figure 4.1 sets out the various steps in the process. Each step represents an attempt to answer certain questions. Some of the more important ones discussed below are paraphrased from Tilley (1969, pp. 584, 585).

1. *Analysis of the overall system: Is training the best answer?* Training is not the only way of improving job performance. In some cases it may be more appropriate to simplify the work men are expected to do, possibly

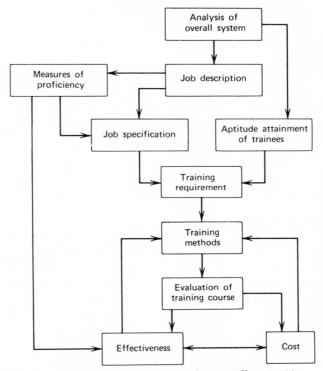

Figure 4.1.   Steps in designing a training course. (From Tilley, 1969).

by reorganizing the job, by providing job aids, or by improved equipment design.*

2. *Job analysis: What tasks will men have to perform?* What elements make up the overall job? How frequently do they occur? How important and how difficult are they? The end product of job analysis is job description, a statement of the activities of the experienced workers. (See Chapter 2.)

3. *Measures of job proficiency: What evidence is acceptable as proof of competency to do the job?* Is it sufficient for the man to be able to give a verbal description of how the equipment functions? Must he be able to diagnose and rectify faults on the equipment or even build the equipment

---

* The training specialist normally must refer these considerations to the industrial engineer or to the human factors specialist. See also Barnes (1968), McCormick (1970).

from a kit of components? These are all possible ways in which the individual could demonstrate his competency, and each has its own implications for training. (Criteria are discussed in Chapter 5.)

4. *Behavioral analysis: What knowledge and skills are associated with successful job performance?* Concern here is less with formal job content than with inferring the psychological processes involved in its performance (i.e., producing a job specification). We want to know what "cues" indicate to the experienced man that there is a need for action. How does he combine and relate these "cues" to decide upon an appropriate course of action? How complex are the actions themselves?

These remarks apply to all types of training courses. For those specifically concerned with industrial work, the approach must be elaborated. Some of the needed details are enumerated as follows:

5. *Determining the capabilities of prospective trainees: What relevant knowledge and skills do men already possess?* Training will be ineffective if it fails to concentrate on the critical elements of the tasks to be learned. It will also be ineffective if it does not take account of the knowledge and skills already possessed by men entering training. The difference between the attainments, aptitudes, and attitudes needed for success at the job and those possessed by the trainee defines the training requirements. (See Chapter 6 on personnel selection tests.)

6. *Selecting appropriate training methods: How can the necessary knowledge and skills best be acquired?* Having defined the objectives of training and the existing capabilities of trainees, we must decide how the required changes in behavior can be achieved. The major problems are those of determining how best to structure the material to be learned (sequencing and type of presentation) and how to let the trainee know what kind of progress he is making.

7. *Evaluating the training course: Is the training cost effective?* If trainees fail to pass the criterion test, it may be necessary to review the training course. Even methods that have proved effective in the past may be inefficient in terms of the utilization of resources. We also want to know about the possibility of tradeoffs between effectiveness and cost.

Further Predesign Considerations

It is generally accepted that performance at work depends upon three main factors—*skill, knowledge,* and *attitudes*—and that the results of training can be ascertained only in terms of behavioral response; that is, that the worker on completion of training behaves (or performs) in the desired way and manifests the appropriate skills, knowledge, and attitude required in the performance of the work to adequate standards. The skill and the knowledge requisite for performing a task can be determined from analyzing the performance of an experienced worker. This cannot be done, however, in the case of attitudes, since some workers (in all walks of life) do their jobs adequately but may not have the attitude toward the job that is desirable in their own or in the organization's interests. The analytical approach to the development of work performance stems from the simple recognition that experienced workers *can do* and *do know* the job, whereas novices *can't do* and *don't know*. Thus the basic requirement is to determine *what* it is that the experienced worker does (job analysis), *how* he does it (skills analysis), and what *knowledge* he uses in performing the various tasks. Having determined these points, a training program is prepared covering the skills and knowledge required. The program is designed, in accordance with what is known about the acquisition of skills and knowledge, to enable the trainee to attain the EWS, step by step, in the minimum time.

This analytical approach has developed under various names since its origination by A. H. Seymour, who called it the *process analysis* method of training. In the United States, largely as the result of the work of Geoffrey Ladhams (1952, 1964, 1965, 1968), it is generally known as analytical method (AM) training. In Australia the same basic approach is sometimes referred to as the deep analysis method, and in Europe and the United Kingdom the terms "specialized operator training," "skill development method," and, usually, "skills analysis training" have been used.

The "Two-Pronged" Approach. In recent years, added experience from the application of these analytical methods to the training of workers in many industries has indicated that, although the basic principles provide a common approach to the preparation of training courses for any type of productive work, the way in which the principles are applied varies according to the type of task being considered.. Thus there has developed the "two-pronged attack" technique in the preparation of training. The first prong is the determination of the class of work to which the given task belongs. (As explained in Chapter 3, these classes are differentiated by the type of information flow involved). Having ascertained the class of work he will be dealing with, the analyst can determine the *structure* of the skills involved, their major features, and the identities of any typical operations within the class that have already been tackled by skills analysis training (Seymour, 1967).

PROCEDURES IN PREPARING ANALYTICAL
TRAINING COURSES

The second "prong" of the attack consists of the determination of the skills and knowledge used by the experienced worker and the preparation of means whereby these can be taught. A preanalysis survey may be needed to find out the depth and detail of analysis that will be required for different parts of the task (Donnelly and Kenney, 1970). A preliminary survey of the range of operations involved may be necessary, as well (Seymour, 1966, 1967). In the documentation of the analyses and the development of the training program for any given task we must consider both the knowledge content, outlined below, and the skills content, which is discussed next.

The Knowledge Content

When we observe an experienced worker performing a task, it is not immediately possible to recognize the knowledge he is bringing to bear on the performance of the task. It is, however, quite clear that he must have knowledge of various different sorts, acquired perhaps at different times. The experienced worker himself seldom realizes just how much knowledge he is using and when he is using it; moreover, it is unlikely that he can express that knowledge in a systematic form.

If an observer is to determine the knowledge used, he must formulate a number of clear and careful questions by means of which he may elicit from the worker and from others a composite statement of the knowledge that is being used. In almost all situations in industry, this knowledge can be categorized under three main headings:

1. The knowledge required by the worker to get himself to the workplace and be prepared to work (sometimes referred to as induction training).

2. The job knowledge itself, which may be partly technical and partly knowledge of tools, machines, materials, and so on, used to accomplish the task.

3. Quality knowledge, which comprises knowledge of the standards required and of the meaningfulness of deviations from such standards.

Workplace or Factory Knowledge. If we were to ask an experienced worker how he manages to get to his workplace and to be prepared to work, he would probably consider the question ridiculous. But such knowledge can readily be determined if we learn the layout of the factory road system, the route from entrance gate to clocking-in station, cloakroom location, washing facilities, the position of the canteen, and so on. Similarly, the worker needs to know the working hours, shop procedures, meal and break times, surgery hours and location, and like details. Again he needs to know to whom he is responsible and the immediate chain of command, the method of work recording, the pay system, and, most important of all, where and when he collects his salary. Some aspects of safety training (e.g., safe behavior on factory premises) must come under this heading, although other aspects of safety training are dealt with under Job Knowledge.

Typical programs for induction training covering the items given in the preceding paragraph have been published by Pearson, Simmonds, and Keene, (1950); Bass and Vaughan, (1966); and Mills, (1967).

Job Knowledge.   Logically enough, job knowledge is the knowledge specific to the job; it normally includes the following areas:

1. The names of parts of the machine or tools to be used and the names of the materials handled.

2. Safety knowledge, in terms of any specific hazards of the job (in addition to general safety training).

3. Particulars of how to obtain and dispose of work.

4. The derivation of information from work tickets, dockets, instruction sheets, drawings, plans, tallies, and the like, and how such documents are to be read and understood.

5. Work records, comprising the information the worker is required to keep about his work.

6. Technical knowledge of the plant, process, machine, or material, which may be very elementary and may not be in the form taught in technical institutions. The technical knowledge needed and used by an experienced worker is sometimes more difficult to determine. Many extremely competent workers have very little technical knowledge. There are obvious advantages for a man who knows more about his job, if thereby his interest is extended. Yet in some industries (e.g., electronics and computer manufacture), the technology is so complex that only a handful of experts understand it, and in such instances neither the experienced worker nor his immediate supervisor has, or needs to have, any appreciable knowledge of the manufacturing processes or of the technology behind them. What is much more important is a knowledge of the particular ways in which the job is done in that particular factory; and this knowledge may well have been handed on by word of mouth from supervisor to worker, or from worker to new hand. Such specific information may not be officially or completely recorded and may reside in the

notebooks of supervisors or experienced workers. Although this information is sometimes jealously guarded and difficult to discover, failure to locate it and communicate it to trainees may undermine successful training. Therefore, in analyzing the specific job knowledge required for the performance of any task, it is necessary to be cautious about taking at face value any written documents that may exist. These constitute a starting point, but they must be checked and rechecked with supervisors, inspectors, production control staff, and so on. As in other walks of life, it is also valuable to "ask the fellows who cut the hay."

Quality Knowledge. Few will question the statement that in industry today it is just as important to train for quality as to train for productivity. Emphasis on quality and reliability has highlighted the benefits that accrue from doing a job right the first time. The right standards of quality need to be inculcated from the very beginning of the training procedure, but this cannot be made effective until management's determination of quality standards has been adequately detailed and clarified for training purposes. This can be done in two steps by means of a *quality specification* and a *fault analysis.*

1. *Quality Specification.* Management cannot expect workers to produce to the right standards of quality unless those standards have been made clear and explicit. It is therefore necessary to determine precisely the quality standards that apply to the particular *task* which the individual worker is doing, and to express the standards in terms that are communicable to trainee workers (Harris and Chaney, 1969). Such standards usually exist for the final product, but less often for the individual stages of manufacture.

This process is seldom very difficult when the product of the task is rigid and the characteristics can be determined in mensurable terms (i.e., in dimensions, tolerances, hardnesses, or brightnesses). The determination of quality standards is more difficult for products that are not rigid, such as textile products; but here standards can be determined and expressed in comparative terms and described adequately for the instruction of trainees. Numerous examples of quality specification for both rigid and nonrigid products have been published and one for the wiring operation on computer matrices is given on page 155.

2. *Fault Analysis.* However well a factory is run, faults from time to time occur, and it is essential to provide instruction about the recognition of faults during training. To do this, it is necessary to collect examples of such faults and to analyze them under the following subheadings:

Fault   Responsibility
Appearance   Action
Cause   Prevention
Effect

A brief note should accompany each of these headings for guidance of trainees. The entries under every heading may not be meaningful in all circumstances, but, unless each is considered, the main problems concerned with the recognition and rectification of faults will not have been covered. Numerous examples of fault analysis have been published (Seymour, 1966, 1967) and extracts from them for fully fashioned garment knitting are given in the Appendix (Table A.1).

Programming the Knowledge Content. When the material under the headings of factory knowledge, job knowledge, and quality knowledge has been analyzed and compared, it constitutes the *syllabus* that has to be taught covering the job knowledge required for repetitive manual tasks. It is then necessary to subdivide the material into suitable "chunks" and to program these to be taught in a systematic order. Subdividing the material, programming it, and fitting it into a timetable is an art, and without especially careful consideration of this phase, training time will not be utilized to the best possible advantage.

Knowledge content cannot be considered entirely by itself; rather, periods of knowledge instruction should precede the appropriate periods of skill practice. Some knowledge and explanation should be given before the trainee can start to work, but it is best to keep this to the minimum, so that trainees can become active as soon as possible—otherwise they soon become bored. For this reason it is advisable to postpone, if possible, some of the material to be covered in factory knowledge or induction training until the trainees have made progress in practicing the skills of the task. Talks and explanations given at a later stage can be more meaningful to trainees and will serve the additional purpose of providing periods of physical relaxation between periods of manual work. It will also be necessary in programming both the knowledge content and the skills content parts of the course to schedule adequate periods of revision in order to ensure that both skills and knowledge have been thoroughly mastered.

A good program also contains adequate time for "feedback," to satisfy the instructor that the trainees have learned the material to which they have been exposed. The training of cotton weavers, for example, includes test periods during which the trainees examine samples of faulty cloth and record the faults they have identified under each of the seven headings listed earlier. By this means the instructor assures himself that trainees are capable of recognizing faults and of understanding their effects.

Nonrepetitive Tasks. The considerations just enumerated apply to all types of work in industry, but especially to repetitive tasks involving considerable manual skills, whether the work itself is performed by hand or on machines. These considerations apply also to a greater or lesser extent to nonrepetitive work, although here additional features also must be taken into account.

Under the heading of nonrepetitive work we include the activities of persons engaged in preparing machines, plant, and so on, for manufacture, and maintaining plant and equipment in full productive order. In manufacturing industries such tasks are undertaken by fitters, mechanics, millwrights, and electricians; in process industries, workers of the same type and also process operators, whose work is likewise nonrepetitive, bear the same responsibilities.

The training of workers in nonrepetitive tasks involves certain additional considerations due to the nature of the work and because, except for process operators, all persons engaged in nonrepetitive work will have had previous training and experience before proceeding to this new stage, and often they will have acquired some of the necessary "tool skills." As a result, the new knowledge content covered in training for nonrepetitive work tends to be proportionally higher than the new skills content. Again, workers in this category are required to undertake more responsibility for expensive plant and equipment than are repetitive operators, and specific training for this needs to be incorporated in the course.

The nonrepetitive workers' additional responsibility is exemplified by their need to carry out *fault diagnosis* as well as understanding fault analysis. Fault diagnosis—the determination of the causes of faults in the functioning of machinery, plant, and equipment, and the speedy and appropriate remedy of such failures—is a complex mental skill for which a higher degree of knowledge of the structure and functioning of machines and equipment is essential.

We have previously outlined how this knowledge content can be analyzed (p. 122). The use of algorithms for analyzing fault diagnosis procedure was described on page 96, and algorithms as exemplified in Figure 3.3 have been most useful for teaching fault diagnosis (e.g., Tilley, 1969; Langham-Brown, 1971).

The Skills Content

Ascertaining the skills content of a task begins, as we know, by finding the answer to the question *What* does the experienced worker do? The procedure for this is job analysis. Next we must determine, by way of skills analysis, *how* the experienced worker achieves what he does. When the analyses have been completed in sufficient depth, two stages for the preparation of a training course are required: scrutiny of the analysis and formulation of syllabus and instruction schedules.

Scrutiny of the Analysis. It is first necessary to study the analysis and consider the following questions:

1. What method, in detail, is to be taught? The analyses of different experienced workers may show that each differs from the others in the details of performing the job. Before training can commence, these differences must be considered, and a *method for teaching* determined in the light of good motion study practice, ergonomics, safety, quality standards, and perceptual patterning. Seldom does any one operator use the best method in every respect, and the method chosen is apt to contain elements from several analyses. It should be noted that this determination of a method for teaching the task in no way presupposes that there is "one best way"—the 50-year-old controversy between the efficiency engineer and the psychologist (Myers, 1922) does not need to be reopened. Rather, we want to provide a basis from which the accumulated skills of the most experienced workers—who have derived their expertise in the course of thousands or even millions of repetitions of a task—can be communicated to trainees.

2. Does the task, as revealed by the analyses, involve any unusual movements or abnormal use of the senses? If so, it may be advantageous to provide preliminary training exercises or devices to develop the requisite movement or level of sensory perception (Seymour, 1966). Such exercises or devices share the purpose of supplying an opportunity for practicing skill features of the task in isolation and obtaining knowledge of results. However, they differ in that the exercises can be performed without special apparatus (e.g., in lockstitch training; Seymour, 1967), whereas training "devices" are specially produced for the purpose (Seymour, 1959, 1966).

3. How can the task be subdivided so that the parts or segments can be practiced and mastered separately? Laboratory experiments and industrial experience have shown that the EWS can be attained more rapidly on complex jobs if sections are mastered separately before the entire task

is performed. Part versus whole methods of training have been the subject of many experiments (McGeogh and Irion, 1952), with differing results. But in the development of work performance on complex industrial tasks, the advantages of part methods are clear, not only from experimental results but from the nature of the problem. When an instructor starts to teach not only *what* has to be done but also *how* an experienced worker does it, there is so much to communicate that the trainee can assimilate only in small amounts. Second, the subdivision of the task enables knowledge of results to be provided more frequently and, third, where there are differing levels of perceptual stringency in different parts of a task, the parts requiring most practice can be given more time than those in which the requisite standard is attained more quickly. Parts are combined when EWS has been achieved on two adjacent ones; this procedure has been shown to involve little drop in performance (Seymour, 1967).

Where there is any likelihood that difficulties will arise at the meeting points of successive parts, they may be combined by the progressive part method (i.e., by progressively adding the parts together, first in pairs, then in threes, and so on). This procedure is schematized in Figure 4.2.

Holding (1965) concluded from experimental evidence (e.g., on maze learning) that progressive part methods have little advantage over part methods, as proposed by Pechstein (1917), who first experimented with their use. In industrial tasks, however, the essential breakdown of tasks into parts or elements is never as simple as the diagram suggests, and combinations of part and progressive part synthesis of the task may be more advantageous. (For a more realistic representation of the synthesis of a typically complex industrial task from its parts, see Figure A.1.)

Syllabus and Instruction Schedules.   When the steps for training workers for a job have been determined, it is necessary to prepare an instruc-

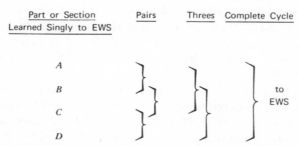

Figure 4.2.   Synthesis by the progressive part method.

tion schedule for each step. This document is a detailed specification of what is to be taught in each exercise or element of the task, how each is performed by an experienced worker, and what the target time is (i.e., how long an experienced worker takes to do it). Instruction schedules for parts of the job are, in effect, a "playback" of part of the analysis in terms that can be used by an instructor. If only the hands are involved, three columns (detailing the right-hand and left-hand movements and the attention points) will suffice; if other limbs are used, additional columns are needed. In the attention points column are noted the cues from which the trainee should derive information for controlling the movements listed in the left- and right-hand columns, as well as the sensory channel by which the information can be acquired. (An example of an instruction schedule, is given in the Appendix as Figure A.6.)

The instruction schedules, taken together, comprise the syllabus for the skills content of the task, to match the syllabus for the knowledge content. The timetable, as previously mentioned, weaves together, step by step, the knowledge and skills contents (Seymour, 1966). The timetable is planned on a "waves and tide" basis; that is, trainees progress through several stages of the task, then revise and repractice the same exercises, and continue forward to the next new stage before going back to cover the old ground again (Figure A.1*b*). When any element or stage has been mastered to EWS it is combined with the next until, progressively, the whole task has been combined (Seymour, 1966).

Summary

The procedures to be followed in preparing an analytical training course for any task can be summarized thus:

1. The knowledge content and the skills (or activity) content are separately identified and analyzed.
2. The knowledge content can be epitomized under the headings:
   (a) Factory (or workplace) knowledge.
   (b) Job knowledge.
   (c) Quality knowledge, which requires both a quality specification and a faults analysis.
3. The skills content is determined by considering *what* the worker does, and *how* the experienced worker does it, in terms of movements, sensory perception, and decision making. From a scrutiny of the analysis in these terms are derived instruction schedules, which detail what an instructor can suitably teach in each step of the training procedure.
4. The syllabus of knowledge content comprised in item 2 and the syllabus of skills content (the instruction schedules) are "interwoven" into

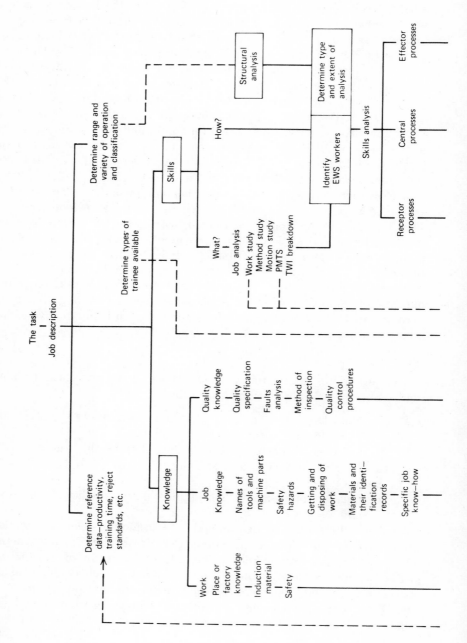

142

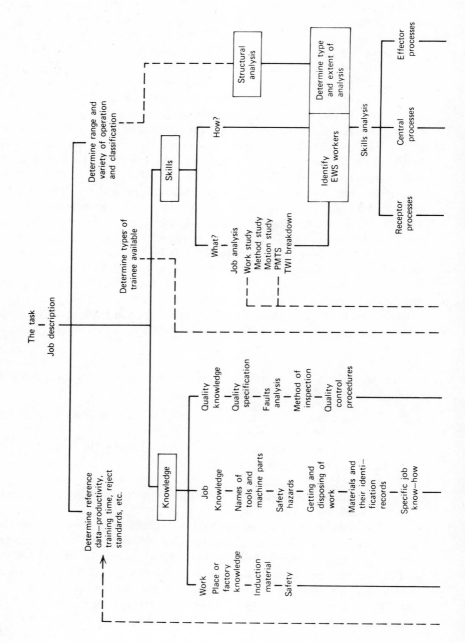

The task

Job description

Determine range and variety of operation and classification

Structural analysis

Determine type and extent of analysis

Determine types of trainee available

Skills

How?

Identify EWS workers

What?

Job analysis
  Work study
  Method study
  Motion study
  PMTS
  TWI breakdown

Skills analysis

Receptor processes

Central processes

Effector processes

Knowledge

Quality knowledge
  Quality specification
  Faults analysis
  Method of inspection
  Quality control procedures

Job Knowledge
  Names of tools and machine parts
  Safety hazards
  Getting and disposing of work
  Materials and their identification records
  Specific job know—how

Work Place or factory knowledge
  Induction material
  Safety

Determine reference data—productivity, training time, reject standards, etc.

142

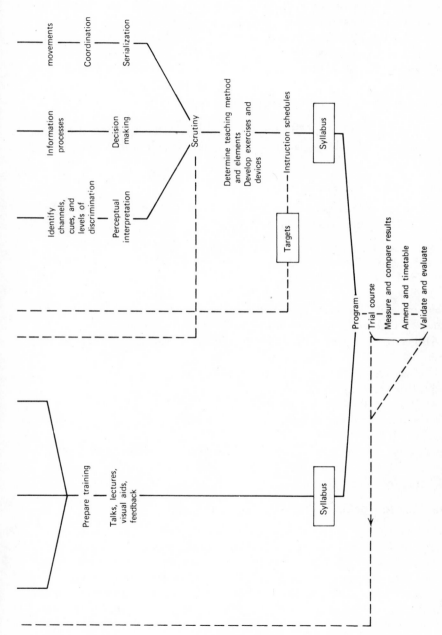

Figure 4.3. The preparation of a skills analysis training program.

a program that will enable trainees to progress as quickly as possible, covering each item of the knowledge content slightly in advance of its being required, and subsequently learning and practicing each element of the job until the EWS is attained. It is thus possible to amplify, and to detail for industrial tasks, the type of chart proposed by Tilley (1969), reproduced earlier as Figure 4.1, in the manner illustrated by Figure 4.3.

IMPLEMENTING A TRAINING COURSE

Advance preparation for the implementation of the training program while it is being developed involves five main considerations. These are discussed in turn.

Selecting an Instructor

The man or woman chosen for the post of instructor is viewed in the light of the following criteria:

1. Ability to perform the task. If trainees are to attain EWS, it is important that the instructor be able to demonstrate this level of performance at least for a cycle or short period.
2. Ability to communicate. Verbal facility is essential. Equally necessary is a capacity to understand the trainees, who may speak a dialect or may not be receiving the instruction in their mother tongue.
3. Ability to observe detail. (This quality, however, can be developed by training.)
4. Knowledge of the job at least sufficient to appreciate what is included in the training course.
5. Ability to take a leadership role.
6. Behavioral habits (in appearance, punctuality, etc.) that will constitute a model to trainees.
7. Attitudes toward fellow workers, supervisors, and managers. Typical personnel specifications for instructors are given in Singer and Ramsden (1969) and Seymour (1966).

Training an Instructor

Numerous courses of training for instructors are available in colleges and through TWI courses. The cooperation of an instructor designate in preparing an analytical training course constitutes an invaluable contribution to his training to use it. Perkins and his colleagues (1969) of the U.K. Department of Employment have summarized the requirements and exemplified some of the means available for instructor training; Singer and Ramsden (1969) described methods of training and coaching instructors;

Gentles (1969), in addition, stressed the value of work study and PMTS appreciation in training instructors, and Holding (1965) discussed the importance of verbal guidance in instruction. The means whereby instructors may impart the skills content and the knowledge content of a course are discussed in Seymour (1968b). A programmed text covering the work of an instructor on analytical training courses has been issued by P. A. Management Consultants (1969). A typical syllabus for a training course for instructors is given in the last section of this Chapter.

Training Area and Equipment

Before a training course is implemented, it must be decided whether the training is to be given on the job, off the job, or by combining both approaches. The advantages of training *at* the factory but *off* the job, in providing less distracting conditions in which the instructor can teach and the trainee learn, are generally recognized, and the provision of a training section or "vestibule" is common today in many firms. These advantages have been summarized thus (Seymour, 1966; Singer, 1969):

1. Trainees are not distracted by the inevitable interruptions that occur in the factory.
2. Trainees do not feel so nervous as in the large, strange factory building and do not have the same sense of inferiority they may experience when surrounded by competent operators.
3. It is possible to train recruits to use the most suitable method of operation, which may be a combination of various methods, or one specially adapted to the individual trainee, whereas in the factory each operator knows only his own method (which is not always in all respects the best). Moreover, in a special training section, the recruit is prevented from acquiring bad habits by imitating less skilled operators.
4. Individual instruction can be given in reasonably quiet conditions by trained instructors.
5. Training can be done systematically to a program.
6. The right attitude to work and to the firm can be inculcated from the beginning, and an interest in the firm can be fostered by talks and other means.
7. Team spirit can be more easily developed, as well as a sense of individual confidence.

In some factories, owing to the size, cost, and noise of the machines and plant, it may not be feasible to train for machine operation off the job. In such circumstances, the knowledge content may be taught off the job and the skills content on the job (an example of this is discussed later in the chapter). Details of training areas and equipment required for many factory jobs are given in Seymour (1966). Provision also needs to be made for the supply of material to trainees, for the supply and servicing of their machines, and for the making of devices and supply of equipment for them.

Records

The records required for controlling training need to be prepared and reproduced, and instructors must be told how to use them, before training begins. These records constitute the control *information* from which a training officer can determine whether the training is being properly conducted and whether each individual trainee is making normal progress or needs special attention. Typical records and the manner of completing them are given in Seymour (1966). In the United Kingdom, the form of such records is sometimes stipulated in the recommendations of the Industrial Training Boards (Garbutt, 1970), and those of one industry are presented in the Appendix (Figures A.2 to A.5). In addition, the U.K. Textile Council Productivity Centre has issued a programmed text (undated) for training instructors in the completion of the daily work sheet.

Recruitment and Selection of Trainees

The factors to be considered in selecting trainees are discussed in Chapter 6. The recruitment situation and procedures required differ for every industry and geographical region and are not discussed here.

PLANNING THE INTRODUCTION OF ANALYTICAL TRAINING

Numerous activities comprise the preparation and implementation of an analytical training course. The success of the training depends not only on the thoroughness of the preparation but also on the time scheduling of the activities involved. A fairly simple plan will suffice for training for replacement of workers or for expansion in existing production premises. If a new production unit or satellite factory is to be established, of course, more comprehensive, detailed planning will be required, and it may prove feasible to use network analysis (see, e.g., Moder and Phillips, 1964). In such situations, the financial value of speedy and effective training (and of effective selection) is predominantly important—the costs of new premises, new plant, new staff, and new equipment are incurred early; but the recovery of these costs is seldom achieved until the workers are producing at EWS or another level of planned performance.

In most situations the type of planning sheet suggested in Figure 4.4 will suffice. The left-hand column lists the main activities in preparing

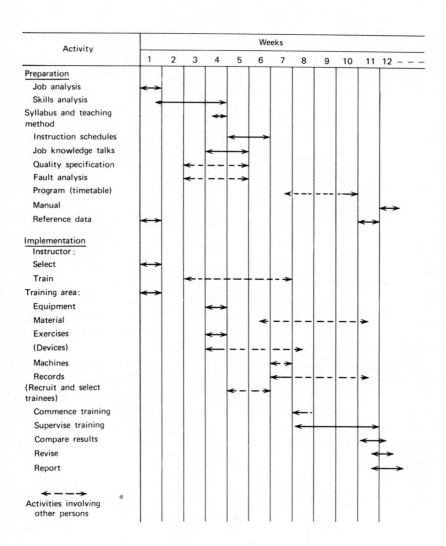

Figure 4.4. Skills analysis project planning sheet.

and implementing a skills analysis training project, and subsequent columns are headed with as many numbered weeks as are necessary. First "D" day—the date on which training is due to commence—is determined; the decision may depend on the date trainees will become available (e.g., youths leaving school) or on the date new plant is to be commissioned. Then we work back from this date to ensure that all facilities will be available when required—fortunately this is less complicated than planning the first landing on the moon. Unless a job analysis is already available, this item must receive priority; but other essentials may need to be initiated almost simultaneously (e.g., the selection and training of instructors, if they will be sent to participate in external courses). Early decisions are also needed on training area and equipment, which must be fitted into programs of works' engineers and others and may involve bought-out parts.

The time periods and deadlines ascribed to other activities will depend on the man-hours available and the interdependence of the activities accompanying the preparation of the training facilities. For example, the fault analysis can be undertaken by an instructor, if he is available while the training officer is undertaking skills analysis. Obviously the equipment and material cannot be installed until the training area itself is ready, but an earlier beginning will help to ensure readiness once the space is available. Forms for records may have to be designed well ahead of time if they have to be printed outside the firm. The detailed presentation of reference figures can be left till the end, but it is important to ensure right from the start that all records and data are carefully preserved—it has been known for such information to be destroyed shortly before it was needed.

IMPARTING THE SKILLS AND KNOWLEDGE CONTENT

When a training course is being prepared, the means by which the skills and knowledge content are to be imparted to the trainees must be specified. The content has to be divided into suitable steps or lessons and programmed so that the communication of the knowledge parallels the development of the trainee's skill.

Methods and techniques for imparting the skill and knowledge content have been described (Seymour 1968b, Chapters 5 and 6). Face-to-face communication by the spoken word, whether individually or to groups, is usually essential, and always advantageous; but instruction directed at more than one sense channel is preferable. Thus in the planning of the training, consideration should be given to the selection of appropriate visual aids, which may range from the simplest chalkboard diagram or chart to sophisticated projections. Forms of visual aid and their use were comprehensively described by Taylor (1966). The use of visual aids and the design of projection material was covered by Powell (1969), who devoted a chapter to audio communication aids.

Programmed Learning

The work of B. F. Skinner on linear programs and of Crowder on branching programs has led to the adoption of programmed learning, both by teaching machines and by scrambled books, in industrial as well as in educational institutions. At the Industrial Programmed Instruction Centre for Industry at Sheffield University, a register is maintained of programs available for industrial use, and particulars of the design and use of programs appear in numerous text books (Markle, 1964; Kay, Annett, and Syme, 1963; Mackenzie, Davey, and McDonnell, 1964; Powell, 1969; Davies, 1971).

Unlike training devices, which are concerned only with certain features of a task, simulators are used particularly in the process industries (e.g., for demonstrating the operation of chemical plants). Computer-assisted training aids, in which knowledge of results is fed back to the trainee by computer processing, are at present not in general use in industry, but simpler devices are being developed and are gaining currency in the United States.

Case Studies

The way in which work performance can be developed by training based on ergonomic principles and on the analysis of skilled performance is best illustrated by case studies. Numerous examples have already been published covering a wide variety of tasks and industries. These include garment manufacture (King, 1964); small-batch, medium-batch, and mass-production operations in engineering (Singer and Ramsden, 1969); tobacco manufacturing operations (Seymour, 1959, 1967); textile and hosiery (Ladhams, 1965); food manufacturing tasks (Seymour, 1967); and operator tasks in the electrical industry (Gentles, 1969), in the pottery industry (Seymour, 1967), and in the textile and knitwear industries (Seymour, 1959, 1967). The U.K. Engineering Industry Training Board (1968, 1969, 1970) have reported more than 100 case studies of the application of systematic analytical training leading to economies for firms in the industry.

To illustrate the outline of analytical training in the present volume, six case studies have been selected, one to illustrate each of the six classes of skills in work (presented in Chapter 3).

Class 1, Handwork: Computer Matrix Wiring. Although other means of storage are available, the majority of present generation computers use wired matrices. Typically these consist of a core mat some 2 in. square on which are placed 64 rows of 64 columns of ferrite cores on end. Each core is at 45° to the edge of the mat, but at 90° to each adjacent core. Four wires each of some 0.004 in. (0.08 to 0.1 mm) diameter are threaded through the cores (which have internal diameters of 0.014 to 0.020 in. (0.35 mm.) according to type) as follows:

First wire—Y drive—vertically through each column.
(for this the plane is turned through 90° and threaded left to right).

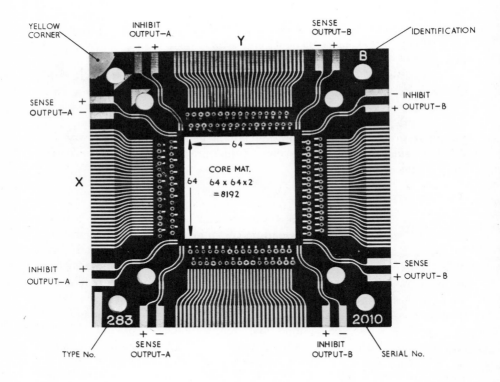

Figure 4.5.   Matrix plane, "A" side. (Courtesy of Mullard Blackburn Ltd.)

Second wire—X drive—horizontal through each row.
Third wire—first and second sense—through alternate diagonal rows.
Fourth wire—inhibit—horizontally, as X drive, but leaving the second
    sense wire uppermost.

A typical matrix plane and a portion of a wired core mat are presented
in Figures 4.5 and 4.6, respectively. A "needle," consisting of a short length
of stiffer steel wire of the same diameter, is soldered to the end of the
plastic-coated copper wire to provide a lead into the cores, and is subsequently removed. The operation, which is carried out "with bare-fisted

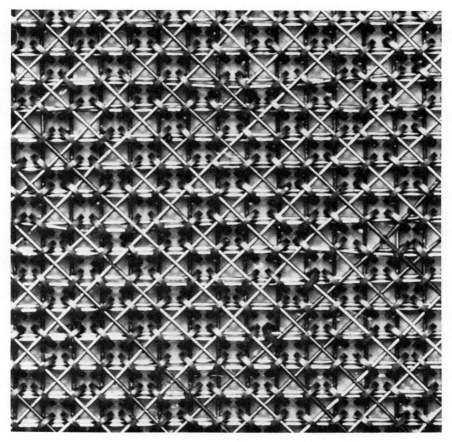

Figure 4.6.   Wired core matrix 20 thou. magnified 1150 times. (Courtesy of Mullard
Blackburn Ltd.)

skill and the naked eye" (although binocular magnification is used to in-spect for faults), exemplifies the assembly type of handwork.

Theoretically an operator must be able to see clearly a wire 0.08 mm in diameter, and also detect variations in depth of the same order. Ergo-nomics of the layout determine the visual working distance, but this should not be less than 150 to 200 mm if accommodation strain is to be avoided in prolonged work cycles. At these distances the wire subtends angles of 1.4 to 2.4' of arc—since visual acuities better than 1' cannot be expected, lighting and contrast are of paramount importance. The mat on which the cores are mounted is firmly held in a jig fixed to the bench, to give a working distance of the order just defined. The plane of the mat can be adjusted, and a hand support is provided by the edge of the jig. A light unit using "white light" fluorescent tubes is mounted above the jig and can also be adjusted for inclination. A maximum illumination of 300 lumen in the work plane is available, but lower values are available at the operator's discretion. Incident light is normally near perpendicular to the work plane to avoid shadow; and wire, core, and mat colors are chosen to give a degree of contrast. Reflectivity of the wire is higher than that of the mat or cores.

Selected operators must possess good acuity and also good accommoda-tion, since the latter has to be sustained for long periods.* These proper-ties must exist equally in both eyes, and the two eyes must be able to converge precisely on a point at the working distance without muscular strain if good stereoscopic vision (essential for fine depth perception) is to be attained.

Conventional methods of vision measurements are used and the follow-ing standards set:

1. *Visual Acuity:* distant (Snellen chart), 6/6 both eyes; near (National Type Face at 30 cm), N5 both eyes.

2. *Accommodation* ("RAF Binocular Gauge"): read N5 at 150 mm or less.

3. *Phoria* (Maddox Wing): within range 4 deg exophoria to 3° eso-phoria; no hyperphoria or cyclophoria acceptable.

4. *Refractive Error* ("fogging test" with + 1D lens): lowest line read on Snellen chart to lie between 6/18 and 6/9 (inclusive).

Some of the original theoretical concepts have been modified by ex-perience and observation on the production unit, as follows:

* Dr. D. J. F. Munro, the Medical Officer of Mullard Blackburn Ltd., which pro-vided the illustrations, has kindly furnished the notes on visual factors in the task.

1. It was thought that virtually all feedback information to the operator would be conveyed by the visual channel, with consequent problems of fatigue on an essentially long-cycle operation. This is probably true in the initial training stages, but it is now evident that the touch and proprioceptive sensory pathways play a very important role in feedback despite the very low signal intensity level that must be received.

2. Determination of the correct threading level for second and subsequent wires through a core was expected to depend principally on a very high quality of depth perception, even though depth discrimination of the order envisaged might take a long time to develop. In practice, each wire has a "highlighted" center bright band down its length, bordered by two relatively darker bands. The interruption of this bright band by ferrite core or other wire crossing above it gives a very useful indication of position and level, even though the bright band is only about 0.03 mm wide.

3. Considerable time was spent experimenting with a variety of optical magnifying aids in the belief that these would improve operators' performance, but none was either acceptable or beneficial.

4. An appreciable relaxation factor is built into the work, and it is essential that operators use this. Trainees are instructed not only that they should look up from the work at fairly frequent intervals, but also that they should deliberately focus the eyes on a "distant" object—this achieves the necessary relaxation and the resting of the accommodation muscles within the eye.

Some trainees, after a rigorous selection procedure, are recruited directly for the job; others are transferred from jobs that are also exacting (e.g., television tube assembly). All operators are female, and the age range is from 15 to 35 years. The operation is performed to work factor standards and under rigorous quality control.

Training for such fine work had presented numerous problems; learning periods were in excess of 30 weeks, and standard performance had not been attained by any of the operators at the time detailed analytical studies were initiated. However, it was possible to analyze the skills of experienced workers on similar types of work in another factory, which was visited by instructresses and more advanced trainees, who were thereby able to convince themselves that the job could be performed to standard.

The existing job breakdowns were checked and were found adequate for all but the most difficult feature of the task—the insertion of the wire needle through a row of cores without displacing them or other wires. Detailed analysis of this critical feature, which was more difficult for sense and inhibit wires than for drive wires, showed that although very fine vision was required to initiate each insertion, an equally important factor was the detection, by kinesthesis, of obstacles obstructing the tip of the "needle." The operator was then obliged to choose a movement for circumventing the obstacles and to recognize, by kinesthetic feedback, that the movement had been successful (this seldom needed visual reassurance in the case of experienced workers). The most usual strategy was to roll the "needle" until the tip could enter a core or circumvent an obstacle; sometimes the needle-holder (a fine sewing needle fixed in a holder) was used to adjust the position of a core or of the "needle."

A scrutiny of the analyses indicated that preparatory exercises were necessary to develop visual and kinesthetic sensitivity to the very fine levels required. A visual exercise [as described in the Appendix of Seymour (1966)] and pin board dexterity exercises were already available. The exercises were practiced on a jig containing slots equal in size to the inner diameter of cores. First the trainees threaded the "needle" through the slot in the same manner as through a core. The second exercise was to practice making the loops, which have to be formed at the end of each row of cores, so that the loops were long enough to provide continuous wire sufficient to complete a section. The manipulation of the wire in these loops, which may be 4 ft long and only 0.004 in. thick (0.08–0.1 mm.) demands a highly developed kinesthetic control that is best acquired by isolated practice.

Other exercises were developed for training the use and focusing of the binocular microscope. This instrument cannot be used when threading wires, because the image around the immediate magnified area is distorted and the magnified area is too small; however, the microscope is used for checking faults and making final inspection and repairs.

After preliminary training on the exercises and after the necessary job knowledge has been covered in a series of talks, new workers begin their training as either drive or sense–inhibit wirers. Certain ancillary elements, such as fixing the mat in the jig and finishing off the job, are taught separately. The pattern of wiring to be followed is also taught, and trainees have diagrams and a finished matrix in front of them as guides.

Even after detailed analysis, the essential element of threading—with the associated element of looping the loose wire—constituted the main difficulty for trainees. Initially, the element could be attempted only for short periods, and the frustration arising from repeated failures to overcome obstacles was considerable. Even when the task was broken down to its minimal steps, and even when these were preceded by preliminary exercises, the trainees' success and continued motivation depended greatly on the skill of the instructress. The instructresses concerned were already experienced in teaching other jobs, and they had to absorb the analysis very thoroughly, identifying in their own performance the features written into the analysis. In addition, they needed to develop a diagnostic ability to understand the difficulties encountered by trainees, so that they could indicate to each puzzled trainee how the particular type of obstacle was recognized and how best to circumvent or remove it.

When trainees can thread individual rows successfully, they proceed to longer runs of 8, 16, 32, and 48 rows, and then to a complete side; the target for a side may be from 30 to 50 standard minutes according to type. Trainees are taught the standards of quality from the following specification:

1. The wiring shall be in accordance with the wiring diagram.
2. The wiring shall be in correct position with respect to the frame.
3. The sense wire shall not be under a Y-wire.
4. The wires shall not contain far thinner portions.
5. The mat shall not sag excessively; the cores must be at least 1 mm from the table top.
6. The wires shall not show kinks, serious torsion, or sharp bends on which the insulation is damaged.
7. Interruptions in the wiring must not be present.
8. The wires shall be in the correct grooves.
9. Wires wrapped around the lower tags must lie in the middle of the space between the upper tags.
10. When necessary, the wires must be pressed against the side members immediately above and between the two rows of solder tags.
11. The insulation of the wire must not be damaged in such a way that the copper wire is uncovered.
12. The loops formed by the sense and inhibit windings shall be of almost equal size and regular.

The following faults are included in the fault analysis:

Cores	Overlapping wires
Drives	Rethread cores
Insulation	Splice
Kinks	Twist
Loops	Reversed core
Missed cores	Cut wires

The introduction of training based on the detailed analysis resulted in a one-third reduction in training time. The average productivity of the group increased by 30 percent, largely as a result of a reduction in time spent on correcting errors.

Class 2, Handwork with Tools: Type Aligning. Numerous jobs involving handwork with tools are concerned with adjusting mechanisms that have already been assembled. In Chapter 3 (p. 110) some of the main features of such tasks are described, and more detailed studies have been published (Seymour, 1967).

One of the most interesting examples of adjusting tasks is aligning typewriters. A machine that has been completely assembled from machine-made components (usually on line production methods), is of no use to the typist. First the characters must be aligned to print evenly all over, with correct spacing, in an upright position, and in a straight line. The goal is to present a line of typing that is pleasing to the eye and technically correct. For this, an aligner uses a kit of tools, and he must know which to use, and when and how.

In this case study of type aligning, the typewriters were portables, manufactured by an American company, operating in the United Kingdom, for United States and some other overseas markets; the machines were assembled by women in 2-min stages. At the end of the assembly line, the machines were aligned by men who, at EWS, took an average of 20 min to align one typewriter. Since training of the female assemblers could be accomplished fairly quickly, replacing an assembler presented a manageable problem. However, training an aligner to full proficiency took more than six months, and the early stages were characterized by chaos on the line because so many machines were held up by the slow work rate of the trainees. Quicker and more effective training became essential to make the lines operate efficiently and to allow the men to earn enough money soon enough to make it worthwhile for them to stay on the job.

The company therefore decided to introduce systematic analytical training and to carry out the greater part of this "off the job." The company selected an experienced aligner and trained him as instructor. His work (and that of other experienced men) was analyzed in order to determine initially the structural pattern and then, in greater detail, determine the movements, decisions, sensory channels, and cues. As in other handwork-with-tools jobs, the structural pattern of the skill could be considered in terms of how each tool was used; each subsequent skills analysis was based on a particular use of a particular tool. Since no two successive typewriters needed the same adjustments, no two successive cycles of work were the same; clearly, then, serial analysis was not possible. However, analysis of how each tool was used was not only feasible but formed the basis and pattern for systematic training.

The preliminary activity consists of loading a sheet of paper, typing a test line on it, deciding whether the machine is in proper condition for aligning, and (if so) what has to be done. The actual operation of aligning is divided into five main stages:

1. Centralizing (A.C.) (i.e., ensuring that the bar goes centrally into the bar guide).
2. Flattening (A.F.) (i.e., making type print of even thickness).
3. Spacing (A.S.) lowercase [small] letters.
4. Spacing capitals. (A.S. caps)
5. General alignment. (G.A.)

Each activity in aligning is initiated by the recognition of a fault, its identification, and the determination of its cause and the following courses of action: how the fault can be remedied, which tool should be used, and which of the various uses of a tool must be selected from the repertory. The input of the initial information is visual—namely, the appearance of a fault in a typed character or line of type; but the perceptual appreciation of what a fault implies in terms of means of correction is of predominant importance.

On their first day new recruits (men, usually between 20 and 25 years old) are given a brief induction. The analytical training course itself starts with a demonstration of the job, a talk on safe handling, and exercises on safety and on loading paper and typing a test line. This is a most important subskill, since if the line is not correctly typed it is not possible to judge correctly what adjustments are needed. A talk and exercise on the names of parts and tools follows, and an introductory job knowledge talk on the five stages of aligning is accompanied by demonstrations.

Since each stage of aligning is associated with particular tools, it is possible to train the use of each tool in relation to the stage for which it is used. Centralizing comes first and involves the use of a guide gauge, large pliers, and three-prong pliers. The first exercise involves recognition only. The trainees go through the bars, recording which need centralizing, and the instructor checks. Next, from a detailed instruction schedule based on the analysis, the trainee learns to make the required corrections with three-prong pliers. The instruction schedule and an illustration of plier positions are presented in Figures 4.7 and 4.8.

The trainee performs typing and centralizing exercises for two days, but the program is interspersed with further talks on machine parts and tools and on company products, facilities, and rules. As the trainee progresses on centralizing, he times himself against targets for one bar, two bars, and so on. On the third day, in addition to continuing to increase

Exercise:	Alignment centralizing	Training course for: Aligning	
Requirements: Machine, paper, pair of 3-prong pliers		Ref. no.:	A.C.
Purpose:	To centralize bar to bar guide.	Target:	6 sec/bar

Left Hand	Attention Points	Right Hand
If machine on upper case, depress large shift lock keytop with 1.	Make sure guide has been checked with gauge.	
	See that shift lock on lower case. Look for letter H keytop.	While holding 3-prong pliers in palm and T.2.3.4. with 1 depress H keytop.
Catch H type bar as it rises, with T, and push base of bar forward with pad into bar guide. Release pressure and "feel" twice. If contacting, release T and hold type bar with 1. Release when correctly adjusted.	Feel for bar contacting either side of bar guide. Feel for bar clearing bar guide both sides. See that bar falls back into basket. Repeat for each of 42 bars.	Adjust position of typebar with 3-prong pliers (see Figure 4.8) until correct.

Figure 4.7. Instruction schedule for typewriter aligning—centralizing. (Courtesy of SCM Corporation.)

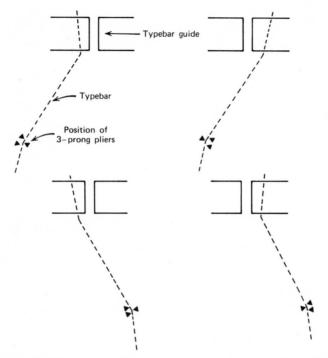

Figure 4.8.   Alignment centralizing: diagrams for recognition and adjustment exercises. (Courtesy of SCM Corporation.)

centralizing from 8 to 42 bars (one machine), the trainee does a flattening recognition exercise and practices flattening with a twister and small lever for one, two, four, and eight blocks.

The same pattern of programming is presented each day; namely, revision and extended use of what has been learned, plus initiation on the next stage by knowledge talks, recognition exercises, and tool training exercises. Except for talks, which are limited to 40 min, the day's work is divided into 1-hour periods, and detailed instruction schedules or notes are provided for each. Trainees proceed from one character to two, and so on up to 42 characters as target times are achieved.

After learning centralizing, trainees learn to set the H correctly (for the other letters are aligned to the H). They then proceed to spacing and practice that until targets are achieved for each stage. Next the stages are combined until the trainees can perform all the activities required correctly and at EWS. Fault analysis for the six operator faults and the 22 machine faults is taught from charts featuring the seven headings we have previously enumerated: fault, appearance, cause, effect, responsibility, action, and prevention.

Two further steps remain in the training. The more important involves learning to deal with combinations of faults and positions; this, of course, cannot be tackled until each individual fault has been mastered. There are 21 position faults and 139 combinations of faults to be learned. The first six are presented in Figure 4.9.

In the final step, aligners are trained to work to shop procedure and method of working, which involves, additionally, loading and unloading to the belt conveyor, checking that machine is ready for aligning, keeping records, and other activities.

Trainees remain in a training section until they have mastered all the skills of the job. For the stamina training (from one machine at EWS up to a day's run), it is more convenient for trainees to work on the line, since this accustoms them gradually to shop conditions and saves the transportation of the machines.

As in all other training, the effectiveness of aligner training depends on having a good instructor as well as thorough analysis and an adequate program. The later stages of the training demand thorough and patient teaching, since there is much to remember in how to tackle the 139 combinations of faults. In such situations it is obviously important to secure an instructor who can demonstrate the job and who has cooperated on the analysis and in building the program.

Results.   The progress of previous learners on the line appear on the lower curve on the graph of Figure 4.10; the progress of the first batch of trainees given analytical training is charted on the upper curve. At this stage the instructor divided his whole time between two trainees; later, when he became more experienced in instruction, he was able to attain even better results when devoting only about one quarter of his time to each trainee.

The benefits of the program can be summarized thus:

Reduction in training time: from 24 to 10 weeks.
Increase in earnings: 20 percent.
Increase in productivity: 44 percent.

Fault	Position	Description of Fault	Tools	Action
H Q H h q h	1	Capital and small high	Tip squeezers, levers T.14035, 3-prong pliers, peeners	A.C. bar. Pull down with levers as in G.A. Part 1 or peeners as in G.A. Part 3. If block blurrs squeeze tip. A.C. bar, space cap, A.C. bar. Only use levers on first and last 8 bars.
	2	Capital leans left	Levers	A.C. bar, space cap as in A.S. caps, A.C. bar.
	3	Capital leans right	Levers	A.C. bar, space cap as in A.S. caps, A.C. bar.
H Q H h q h	4	Small too far to the left	Side-aligning pliers, levers, 3-prong pliers	A.C. bar. Side align block to the RIGHT just over half way between small h's (block will appear FAINT on the RIGHT-HAND SIDE). Twist block FLAT as in A.F. also space cap as in A.S. caps.
H Q H h q h	5	Small too far to the right	Side-aligning pliers, levers, 3-prong pliers	A.C. bar. Side align block to the LEFT just over half way between small h's (the block will print FAINT on the LEFT-HAND SIDE). Twist block FLAT as in A.F. also space as in A.S. caps. A.C. bar.
H Q H h q h	6	Small and capital low	Levers, file, block cutters, peener, pliers	If first and last 8 bars are low proceed as follows: Pull up bar with levers as in G.A. Part 1. A.C. bar, after this adjustment the block will print FAINT all over or NOT at all. FILE TIP as in G.A. Part 2 Block cut if necessary. A.C. bar.
			3-prong pliers	If other 26 bars are low proceed as follows: A.C. bar. Peen the bar UP when level. Space cap. If too HIGH squeeze tip but make sure block is NOT hard on RING and block cut if block is FAINT TOP. A.C. bar.

Figure 4.9. Fault chart for typewriter alignment. (Courtesy of SCM Corporation.)

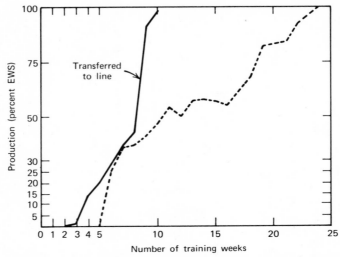

Figure 4.10. Results of typewriter alignment training course. Dashed curve, results of 5 previous learners; solid curve, results of the first pair of trainees given analytical training. (Courtesy of SCM Corporation.)

> Economy per trainee in direct labor: equivalent to 6 weeks' wages.[*]
> Economy in increased overhead recovery: equivalent to 7 weeks' wages.
> Total economy per trainee, (after deducting cost of instruction) equivalent to 11 weeks' wages.

Class 3, Single-Purpose Machine Work: Capacitor Winding. Electronic systems usually consist of large numbers of very small components assembled by hand or by assembly machines. The components themselves (e.g., television tubes) are often subassemblies of still smaller components. The basic components are usually manufactured in quantity by automatic or semiautomatic machines, but some are made from materials, purchased elsewhere, on single-purpose machines by individual workers. Certain special types of capacitors found in the last group are made from aluminum or other metal foil wound inside polystyrene, terylene, or other insulating materials.

In the case described, the operator sits at a winding machine loaded with reels of insulation material and she is provided with strips of foil

[*] Owing to devaluation and differences in British and American levels of wages, it is not meaningful to quote financial economies in sterling or dollars. Therefore, these economies are given in equivalent weeks' wages of a worker on the job.

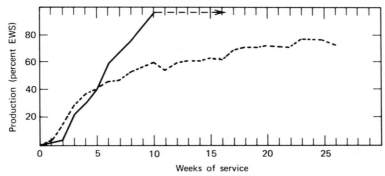

Figure 4.11. Comparative learning curves in capacitor winding. Dashed curve, results of 21 previous learners; solid curves, results of 18 trainees given analytical training. (Courtesy of General Electric Company, Telecommunciations Division.)

to which lead wires have already been welded. As in most single-purpose machine work, the critical element is the loading of the machine. The materials being very thin and lacking rigidity, this is particularly difficult, and errors of alignment prevent the capacitor from operating correctly; moreover the capacitance is affected if the wind is not commenced at the right point. Exercises were developed to enable trainees to learn setting the machine to zero and starting the wind. The determination of the completion of winding was also critical and depended on a meter reading. This, like other elements involving judgment, presented difficulty, and errors could lead to faulty production or reduction of performance through the need to rewind. Separate practice of this element was arranged until trainees could attain the correct setting without readjustment. From single elements, the trainees proceeded to groups and to the winding of single capacitors. Subsequent steps involved short runs, runs of half an hour, runs of one hour, and so on, until the daily target output could be maintained.

Prior to the introduction of analytical training, workers had taken more than 6 months to attain standard performance; the average weekly performances of 21 starters for periods up to six months are represented by the dashed curve of Figure 4.11. The corresponding performances of 18 starters given analytical training are indicated by the solid curve. From the curves it can be seen that the operators who had received analytical training attained after 10 weeks a productivity standard 25 percent higher than previous learners had attained after 25 weeks. The comparison of production and costs can be summarized thus:

Reduction in learning time: from 25 + to 10 weeks.

Increase in production over six months: 32 percent.

Increase in earnings over six months: 16 percent.

Decrease in unit cost (direct labor) over six months: 16 percent.

Economy in direct labor: equivalent to 5 weeks' wages per trainee.

Economy in increased overhead recovery: equivalent to 5.7 weeks' wages per trainee (assuming overheads at nominal 100 percent on direct labor).

Total economy per trainee: equivalent to 10.7 weeks' wages.

Subsequently, workers with three to six months' service were retrained for periods of approximately two weeks; this resulted in increases in performance of 25 to 30 percent. Eventully, the combined efforts of training and retraining yielded an increase in the average shop production from 57 to 96 percent of EWS.

Later it was found that there was an appreciable difference in the "yield" of different workers (i.e., the proportion of capacitors that came within the tolerance limits of capacitance). A statistically controlled experiment indicated that these differences were not significantly related to any factor but the operators. Two operators whose performance showed a high and a low yield (although the number of capacitors they wound was similar) cooperated in a very detailed analysis that revealed a minute but important difference in one element. The instructor was able to train the operators to reverse their methods of performing this critical element, and the yield figures were correspondingly reversed. When all operators were retrained to use the special skill of the better operator on the critical element, the overall yield from the whole department was improved appreciably.

Class 4, Multipurpose Machine Work: Garment Sewing. Garment making by means of needle machines is practiced almost all over the world, and the machinery used varies considerably. Many machines are designed and/or used for a single purpose (e.g., seaming machines for seaming tights). Other needle machines for garment making, and in particular the lockstitch or power sewing machines, are generally used as multipurpose machines (i.e., the operator uses the machine for different purposes at different times). It is thus necessary for the trainee to acquire a repertory of skills and to be able to perform any combination of these at EWS. The total possible range within the repertory on a lockstitch machine is so great that it would not be economic to train workers on each skill; indeed, unless garments involving particular elements of a given skill are available, that skill cannot even be practiced.

Several case studies of power sewing machine training have been published (Seymour, 1966, 1967; Blain, 1956, 1958, 1959; Singleton, 1957, 1959; King, 1959, 1964; Belbin and Sergean, 1963). The U.K. Shoe and Allied Trades Research Association has issued a comprehensive manual for machinists on closing room operations in the shoe industry, and a briefer manual has been produced by the Clothing & Footwear Industry Training Board (N.I.) for sewing machinists (undated). In the United States, Blain (1961) and others outlined methods of training sewing machinists, Solinger (1961) devoted a section to training machinists, the American Apparel Manufacturers Association (1968) published a report on operator training in the trade, and Wheatcroft (1971) summarized and up-dated views on analytical training for machinists.

The skills of a lockstitch machinist can be lodged under three headings (Seymour, 1959):

1. Skill in controlling the machine.
2. Skill in handling the fabric.
3. Skill in forming a garment by putting together fabric pieces with apparently unrelated shapes.

In the work of a machinist, the second item, handling the fabric, occupies most of the time, and the machine is actually operating for only a fraction (up to 25 percent) of the total time. The analysis and training of fabric handling is thus preeminently important. Variations in material constitute a particular difficulty even if the same seams are being produced, since the kinesthetic control is different for different fabrics; for example, when sewing pockets in men's suits, the changes from tweed to worsted or from worsted to vicuna have more effect on performance than changes in the shape.

The analysis and preparation of training for machine control is more standardized, and such "basic" training is available in technical institutes (Belbin and Sergean, 1963; Martin, 1959; Wellens, 1962, 1963), needle trade schools, and the like, in numerous places.

Basic training consists initially of exercises designed to aid the trainee in controlling the machine:

1. Speed control. A revolution counter is fixed near to the needle and the trainee practices maintaining the revolutions per minute (rpm) at different levels for periods of up to 15 sec until the necessary kinesthetic control has been acquired.

2. Stopping and starting must be done without using the handwheel. Trainees practice without thread on lined paper, starting with a needle

hole on one line and stopping at the next, then shifting sideways and repeating to the next line, forming a series of steps.

3. Needle positioning. A similar exercise is used to develop the ability to finish with needle up or down, as required.

4. Threading up.

Second, the trainees are given exercises relating to fabric handling, which usually include:

1. Clipboard exercises. A series of clips is fixed to a board and trainees fold pieces of fabric of appropriate length and place them under each clip, as they would under the foot of the machine. There is an exercise for each type of basic seam, as indicated by the analysis, and strips of different fabrics are used.

2. Machine and fabric exercises. Similar exercises are performed by feeding the fabric to the machine and running it through without thread, or with a chain stitch that can be pulled out. Paper shapes sometimes serve for such exercises, but these should not be used beyond the initial stage, since the kinesthetic control is not the same as when using fabric.

3. Basic seams. On strips of waste material, trainees produce the basic seams that, according to the analysis, constitute parts of the garments.

Thirdly, exercises in the following areas are used to develop the requisite form relations:

1. Geometric shapes. Circles and triangles of fabric are divided unevenly into three parts, which trainees assemble, noting the right and wrong faces of fabric.

2. Garment assembly. Exercises are assigned on pinning together the parts of the garments, which are usually cut to one-third size.

Garment training begins when trainees can make all basic seams to EWS. At this stage, they are taught to perform the seams in production sequence to make one unit of work. A unit of work may be one garment or, more frequently, one complete cycle of the individual worker's part of the garment. Thus, in making brassieres, a unit of work may be 24 cups, followed by 24 straps, followed by sewing together 12 brassieres. Targets are provided for each stage of a unit as performed under factory conditions.

Stamina training is the final stage. Here the machinist increases the working period at EWS from one unit to two, and then to one hour, two hours, four hours, and a full working day.

Results. Results of the application of systematic analytical training on sewing machine (lockstitch) operations have been published by several writers. Seymour (1966) gave the comparative curves of progress of 12 previous learners, who attained target standards after 40 weeks, with those of 10 trainees who, with analytical training, reached the same goal in 13 weeks. The results can be summarized thus:

Reduction in training time: from 40 weeks to 13.
Increase in output: 110 percent.
Increase in earnings: 50 percent.
Economy per trainee: equivalent to more than 30 weeks' wages.

The reduction in learning time was followed by a reduction in labor losses. Previously 49 percent of the new employees had left within one year, the figure was subsequently reduced to 12 percent.

King (1964) made graphs of improvements of trainees on exercises and individual elements of work in shirt making and comparative curves of previous learners (who had taken 50 weeks) and those given systematic training (who took 14 weeks).

Belbin and Sergean (1963) have quoted results from training sewing machinists in a firm whose systematic training method was responsible for reducing the losses, or cost per machinist, from more than $100 to between $35 and $42. The most detailed cost-benefit study of operative training is that of Thomas, Moxham, and Jones (1969). In an overall factory, the introduction of systematic training resulted in a reduction in training time from 17 to seven weeks and an increase in output of 30 percent over the first 60 weeks of employment. These improvements were small compared with that resulting from reduced labor turnover, which was nearly halved. The last benefit, although substantial, cannot always be predicted because other factors in the labor market may offset the effect of improved training (see p. 178).

Class 5, Group Machine Work: Full-Fashioning Knitting Machines. Full fashioning knitting machines are very expensive, and if the workers are not fully productive, the finished garments are excessively costly. The time taken by trainees to reach performance standard is thus critical, and learning by traditional methods is expensive.

The work of a knitter on full-fashioning machines exemplifies group machine work (i.e., the operator must produce from more than one unit of production). Although normally an operator has no more than two machines, each one is apt to have 12 or 16 sections, so that he may be responsible for as many as 32 production units.

The course described here was designed for men aged 21 to 35 years with some previous experience of bar loading (an ancillary operation in the trade). They were trained to work two 16-section, 21-gauge, full-fashioning automatic knitting machines. The trainees completed basic machine exercises on a sample machine before progressing to the automatic machine, where changeover sequences were learned. With the cooperation of the knitting manager and the quality control staff, it was possible to incorporate these exercises into the regular work cycle.

After all the elements of the task had been mastered, trainees ran one machine for periods of half an hour and one hour before proceeding to two machines. Practice on one machine was not continued beyond this period, since the pattern of distribution of attention required was different from that associated with two machines. Trainees, after practicing patrolling and the correct distribution of attention, ran two machines for 1, 2, and 4 hours until the EWS could be maintained for a whole shift. Men were trained on ladies' and children's outerwear (cardigans and jumpers) in groups of three (one for each shift); one recorded for another while he was carrying out a run. At the conclusion of the course, trainees were given a proficiency test.

Main Activities. The elements of work to be carried out were as follows:

1. Check work order and ribs;* issue instructions to barfiller and barloader.
2. Change yarn accordingly.
3. Set up console and knitting machines to required conditions as specified on style card.
4. Knit garment fronts, backs, and sleeves.
5. Patrol two machines, checking and adjusting for machine and knitting faults.
6. Break ends on every fabric piece.
7. Position ribs on take-up hooks.
8. Clear fly from machine and keep carrier rod oiled.
9. Bundle work in dozens (fronts and backs) and sleeves in two dozens and store in racks.
10. Enter information on Production report and on Breakdown and Stoppage report.
11. Enter name on work ticket.

To the foregoing must be added the following patrolling activities:

1. Check that ribs are positioned on machine take-up hooks.
2. Verify correct garment styling by checking the machine rhythm during the knitting cycle.
3. Prevent faults by observing warning signs (see fault prevention).

---

* The ribbed portions of the garments were preknitted on separate machines.

4. Check fabric for faults (see fault analysis). In order to detect faults, it is necessary to subject the fabric to stretch. With a short-cycle sequence (e.g., children's and short sleeves), a program of checking should be arranged so that at least four heads are checked every cycle.

5. Check at least one fabric length against the sample every cycle, to verify that the console is working satisfactorily.

Syllabus. The syllabus included 34 knowledge talks, covering the following topics:

1. The purpose and products of the machine, the names of parts, safety.
2. Needles and needle faults.
3. Loop formation, fashioning, and widening.
4. Setting up of carrier and console (see below), auto drum, and hand panel.
5. Quality specification and fault analysis.
6. Derivation of information from style card and preplanning activities for changeovers.
7. Patrolling and records.

Also, there were exercises covering the skills content; these included:

1. Threading machine and carrier, changing yarn, stopping and starting.
2. Removing, inserting, and pliering needles (see below).
3. Removing, aligning, and replacing points.
4. Aligning sinkers and knockovers.
5. Setting fashioning box, carrier, and console.
6. Changeovers: sleeves to plain, bodies to plain, and vice versa.

The instruction plan for the knowledge talk on setting up a carrier appears in the Appendix (Figure A.7); the instruction schedule for pliering needles and part of the fault analysis are also presented in the Appendix (Table A.1 and Figure A.6, respectively). The remainder of the knowledge talks and instruction schedules were similarly detailed.

Proficiency Test. At the conclusion of their training, the men underwent a proficiency test covering all aspects of the job, since productivity alone is not an adequate measure of proficiency. The test was in four parts:

1. Skills. Trainees carried out 15 exercises, from threading the machine to completing a changeover, under the supervision of the head mechanic. Each exercise had to be completed within a target time and to specified standards.

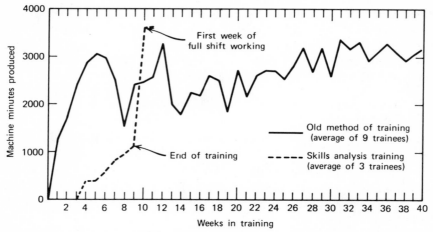

Figure 4.12.   Comparison of learning periods for fully fashioned knitter training. (Courtesy of Bairnswear Ltd., a member of the Courtauld group.)

2. Knowledge. Trainees were expected to answer verbally any of some 60 questions covering all aspects of the knowledge content. Those being tested drew lots to choose between an even- and an odd-numbered set of questions. The knitting manager supervised.

3. Fault Analysis. Trainees were expected to give the analysis under seven headings for any six faults from a list of 17 fault samples. Again, they selected their own questions by drawing numbers from a hat. Again, the knitting manager supervised.

4. Stamina. Trainees did a 4-hr run on full work load with the following requirements:

(a) Machines must attain 87 to 92 percent efficiency (EWS).

(b) Quality must be within tolerance.

(c) Machine breakdown must be nil.

This part of the test was supervised by the instructor, with the assistance of the quality control staff.

Results. The results of applying the foregoing training scheme (see Figure 4.12) can be summarized as follows:

Training time: reduced from 40 weeks to 10.

Increase in productivity: 10 percent.

Increase in knitter earnings: 10 percent.

Economy in cost per trainee: equivalent to 5 weeks' wages.

Class 6, Nonrepetitive Work: Setting Multiple Presses. Nonrepetitive tasks in industry are very varied, and none completely epitomizes the whole class. Several examples have already been published (Seymour, 1967) both from manufacturing industry and from process industry. However, the advancing technology of modern industry constantly changes the profiles of work and the training requirements within the same industry, as shown by Crossman and Laner (1966, 1969) in their study of the impact of technological change on manpower and skill demand.

One of the most common situations requiring training on nonrepetitive manufacturing tasks arises when a step forward in mechanization or automation falls short of full automation. A typical example of this occurs in medium-batch manufacture of components for semidurable products such as household equipment and cameras. Such components, traditionally made on punch presses, are now more frequently manufactured on automatic presses of varying degrees of complexity. Naturally the introduction of such machines involves the training of men to set them up, maintain them in correct running order, and perform changeover operations. In many instances, the training is actually retraining or additional training for men who have already had experience as punch press setters or in a similar job. Not being novices, these men already have acquired the tool skills and knowledge of the materials and product and quality standards; but they are incapable of using the new plant effectively without appreciable further training.

The course cited in the present example was designed to train punch press setters to set C.V.A. Air Clutch type High Speed presses of 50-ton capacity. These machines are fed with steel strip from a reel through a roller and into a cross-head unit, in which free-positioned die-sets operate to cut and shape the metal into components that fall into a tray. An outfeed roll unit then transmits the unwanted strip to a scrap-cutting unit and into a waste tray. Setters are required to be able to set the machine to make any one of numerous components from the specification on a setting card, to adjust it till components are to specification, and to make running adjustments to correct any subsequent deviations.

The job knowledge content demanded on the job was analyzed and arranged for teaching in two main sections:

1. Machine, general—the principal parts of the machine, their names and their operation, following first the power route and second the strip route.

2. Machine, details—description of each main mechanism with drawings, following the same routes.

The setting procedure was broken down into 42 steps, in which there were eight main related adjustments. Each adjustment was detailed in the following manner:

Ejector units
    4a)   *Knockout bar*

Adjustment
    Positioning of knockout bar.

Location
    Screwed into the bed of the machine are two support bars, located diagonally opposite. Over these fits a rigid member, and through its center is screwed the knockout screw, which has its end fitting through the crosshead. Locknuts are fitted, on either side of the rigid member, on the support bars and also on the knockout screw above the member.

How made
    Note:
    The machine *must* be at the *top* of its stroke, and the crosshead should have been set in position to suit the tools.
    Screw the lower locknuts right down the support bars, then place the rigid member in position, making sure that the bottom of the knockout screw contacts on the ejector pin of the tools through the crosshead.

    Note:
    The position can also be checked by operating the press on *Repeat* and placing the hand on top of the knockout screw. A slight jarring should be felt each time the press reaches the top of its stroke.

Effect
    Enables the components to be ejected from the portion of the tools.

Correct Adjustment
    The rigid member should be positioned on the support bars so that the bottom of the knockout screw contacts on the ejector pad just before the press reaches the TOP of its stroke.

Side effects
    1. If the knockout screw is set too low, as the press returns to the top of its stroke, the ejector pad will contact the screw too early, and the unit will be broken as the press continues to move up.
    2. If the screw is not set low enough, the components will build up one on top of the other. When this occurs, if the micro is set correctly, it will stop the press; if not, damage to the tools could be caused by the big buildup of components.

Arrangements were made for the verbal part of the training to be given in a separate room and for the practical instruction to be done on a "tool try-out" machine situated in the tool room, which was relatively quiet. In order to minimize disruption of normal work, the training began in the afternoon and extended into overtime. All the arrangements were discussed in advance with the foremen concerned and with the shop steward (who was the first trainee).

The training began with an outline of the project and of the training method. Then the general operation of the machine was explained, following the power route and the material route. Next came the name of essential parts: unless the names are known, communication between instructor and trainee is difficult. Then each detail of the machine was studied in order, until its function was understood, and instruction was given on safety, guarding, maintenance, and materials. Next each machine adjustment was taught, following the same sequence as in the machine details.

There followed the procedure for changeovers, and practice in removing, replacing, and resetting a set of tools for a selected series of jobs, exemplifying the range of multiple and compound tools used on the section.

Interspersed with the practical training were periods of verbal instruction and practice on gauges and inspection standards, the reading of setting cards, and the planning of a changeover. The quality requirements of the task were taught from a quality specification and from the fault analysis (i.e., a list of faults, with examples, detailing their appearance, cause, and effect, and action to be taken).

Last, and most important, it was necessary to teach the diagnostic procedure—the eliminatory thinking process—by which an experienced setter diagnoses a fault before attempting to correct it. This procedure, which had been carefully analyzed in conjunction with the foreman and instructor, was taught systematically from a fault diagnosis diagram (see Table 4.1).

This part-time course extended over three weeks, with some minor interruptions.

Results. When training is for tasks with measured work, it is possible to determine whether the training has been successfully accomplished to the EWS from the trainee's performance index. Nonrepetitive tasks such as setting are seldom based on measured work, and in such cases it is less easy to determine the results of the training.

At the conclusion of training, a proficiency test was administered which occupied rather more than half a day. In the morning the trainee was

Table 4.1   Part of a Fault Diagnosis Diagram for a Misfeed

Machine stopped	Check	Indication	Action
First check			
Is the micro connection faulty?	Reverse machine to TOP of stroke and observe strip.	1. If strip is all right, micro is faulty. 2. If strip is damaged, a misfeed has occurred.	Reset or replace micro. (See adjustment No. —) Continue below.
Second check			
Is the material size correct?	Remove strip from the machine and check size with a MIC.	1. Oversize on width or thickness. 2. Correct.	Reject, and replace coil. Continue below.

given a verbal test by the manager and the foreman. Thirteen questions covering the knowledge content of the task had been prepared, and three numbers were drawn out of a hat to determine which three would be asked. When the manager and the foreman were completely satisfied with the answers, a practical test on three fault diagnosis problems was introduced. The next task was to strip a machine and to put on a set of tools that had not been seen before, although it belonged to one of the types covered in the instruction. The foreman watched this test throughout, without giving aid or comment, and timed it. The test finished at the moment when the inspector passed off the components as correct; the net setting time was 1 hr 50 min, which compared favorably with the foreman's estimate of 2 hr for an experienced setter to do the job.

Next, while the trainee's back was turned, the foreman "put wrong" the first of three preselected faults on the machine which had just been set. Then, before the trainee picked up his wrenches to correct the fault, the following questions were asked:

What is wrong?
Why is it wrong?
How will you correct it?

The procedure was repeated for each of the other two faults, and on each occasion the time taken was recorded. Each fault was correctly diagnosed and rectified.

It was agreed by management and the shop steward that it would have taken at least four months to attain the standard reached with three weeks of analytical training. It may be noted, however, that the analysis and teaching of fault diagnosis can usually be more readily achieved by the use of algorithms.

THE BENEFITS OF ANALYTICAL TRAINING

As the case studies indicate, numerous benefits to management and workers and, ultimately, to the economy of a country, arise from improved occupational training. Let us discuss eight of the most notable advantages.

Reduced Learning Time

In many industries in many countries it has been found that the time required for workers to achieve EWS can be reduced, generally, to a half or a third of that previously required (King, 1964; Singer and Ramsden, 1969; Géntles, 1969; Seymour, 1959, 1966, 1967, Simmons, 1958; Thomas, Moxham, and Jones, 1969; Ladhams, 1965; O'Hara, 1962). This reduction in training time is the basis of the other benefits that accrue from improved occupational training.

Higher Earnings Sooner

Where payment by results systems are in operation, the reduction in learning time enables workers to achieve higher earnings sooner. This applies with straight piecework systems, bonus and premium payment plans, and also where merit rating awards depend on proficiency in performance. The possibility of earning higher wages sooner is an asset in recruiting new labor and may help to reduce labor turnover (see section, "Lower Labor Turnover," below). Similarly, higher earnings after retraining are equally beneficial to workers.

Increased Productivity

When training periods are reduced, production in unit time and productivity are increased. In the manufacture of tire moulds, training and retraining of workers in a British factory resulted in outputs higher than those achieved in the U.S. parent company.* Again, by also retraining workers presently employed, standards can be raised. Increases in average departmental performance are quoted by Ladhams (1964), Seymour

---

* An unsigned article in *Engineering*, London (January 1967), "A Case History of Operator Training in the Skill Development Method," quoted results showing a reduction in training time to 4 months as compared with 2 years in the parent company, and an increase in productivity to a level 10 percent higher than that in the U.S. company.

(1959), and King (1964). Thus, in addition to benefiting the worker, reduced learning time benefits management.

Increased productivity leads in turn to the following advantages for management.

Lower Unit Costs of Production

As shown in the case study examples, the increase in productivity results in a reduction in unit costs of production, even after the increase in earnings has been paid. This benefit to management—in reduced *direct* labor cost—is usually small and sometimes marginal where the primary benefit from increased output goes to the workers.

Increased Overhead Recovery

The major benefit to management from improved training is increased overhead recovery, and its importance increases as the capital cost and on-costs per worker are augmented by technological and social change. If an increased throughput of work can be produced by the same labor force, and the recruitment of additional labor is obviated, considerable savings ensue. If, in addition, the cost of existing plant, machinery, floor space, and services can be offset by higher production from the same labor force, even greater savings can be realized.

Because most companies are hesitant to publish their overhead figures (whether expressed as a percentage of direct labor cost or otherwise), it is customary to calculate savings in increased overhead recovery from improved training on the basis of a nominal 100 percent fixed overhead on direct labor cost. In most companies, the actual figure is very much in excess of this; nevertheless, the calculation on a nominal basis is useful. Without seeking confidential information, any manager can calculate, with a simple mental sum, the similar savings that would be possible in his own case. In the foregoing examples, the nominal figure of 100 percent was used, although this was by no means the actual figure in every firm concerned.

Variations in wage rates within and between countries, differences between rates in different industries, and inflationary changes and changes in exchange rates make it difficult to communicate in dollars, pounds, or any other currency the real saving resulting from improved training. It is convenient, therefore, to express such economies in terms of equivalent weeks' wages saved—any manager reading the figure can readily ascertain what that would currently mean to him in his own currency.

It must be emphasized that the financial benefits from reduced learning times and increased overhead recovery can be attained only where the increased production is sold at prices within the normal range.

Shorter Delivery Time

Shorter delivery times are important to firms engaged in contract work. In such cases the time that can be quoted for delivery will be shorter if the training time of new workers recruited to execute the orders is reduced. Contract orders are often more readily obtained in competitive markets when precise delivery times can be quoted (e.g., in the sale and manufacture of batches of products in light engineering components, fractional horse power motors, or electronics). These considerations apply particularly to contracts for supply to governments and large institutions.

Improved "Yield" and Reduced Scrap

Improvements in quality and reliability through improved training are particularly advantageous because they are achieved not by greater effort but by reduction in waste. Ladhams (1965) quoted examples of reduced waste in garment and other manufactures. Simmons (1958) reported the reduction in scrap rate in a bolt mill following the introduction of analytical training, and the figures over eight months are plotted in Figure 4.13. In the case study on group machine work, at the stage of the proficiency test and subsequently, the fault frequency of trainees was appreciably lower than the factory average, and similar results have been attained in the food, electronics, tobacco, and other industries. Although such reductions in scrap and faulty products are always advantageous, the benefits cannot always be translated into financial terms. For example, in a garment manufacturing firm the production of seconds was considerably reduced, but this gave the company no financial benefit because it had already been selling seconds in the factory shop at the same price as that paid by wholesalers for perfect goods.

Improvements in "yield" can be as advantageous as reductions in scrap. This particular form of waste reduction occurs, for example, in the manufacture of electronics components that must be produced within limits and cannot be measured until completed, as in the case of the capacitors referred to earlier. Another example occurs in the manufacture of cigars. The cost of leaf is very high, and the economics of manufacture depend primarily on the number of cigars, of the right standard, produced from each ounce of leaf. In countries where taxation is high, the price of cigar leaf after tax can be greater than the cost per ounce of silver. In the training of cigar makers, detailed analyses of how the best workers achieved a high yield enabled trainees to attain high standards even within the greatly reduced training period, and the financial benefit from increased yield considerably exceeded that resulting from the reduction in training time (Seymour, 1959).

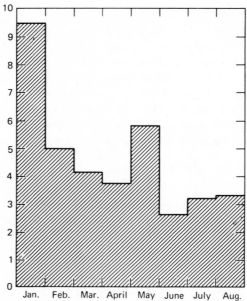

Figure 4.13.   Reduction in bolt scrap returns after training. (From Simmons, 1958.)

Lower Labor Turnover

When new entrants can master a job more quickly, earn more money sooner, and attain competence and confidence more readily, it is to be expected that labor turnover during the first few months—which is usually the period of highest incidence—will diminish. Such changes in average retention time of trainees have been recorded. In training sewing machinists, for example, it was found that only 63 percent of the new employees had remained after six months and only 51 percent after one year prior to the introduction of specialized analytical training. Subsequent to the special training, however, these figures were 93 and 88 percent, respectively (Seymour, 1966). Simmons (1958) published figures showing labor turnover in a screw mill over a 10-year period; systematic analytical training had been in use during the second half, and labor turnover had dropped to approximately half (60 to 30 percent) during this five-year span.

The most detailed cost-benefit analyses of improvements in operator training have been published by Thomas, Moxham, and Jones (1969) in a study of machinists in a factory making heavy-duty clothing—jeans, boiler suits, and overalls. The authors considered the benefits derived from change in the length of training period to EWS (which was reduced to a half), the change in average performance levels (which exceeded 30 percent), and the change in average retention time (which was almost doubled). They found that the ratio of total cost to total benefit from the improved training was about 8:1; of the benefit, 75 percent was attributable to a decrease in labor turnover, giving a longer average retention period.

It must be pointed out that the benefits derived from training improvements in terms of reduced labor turnover are occasional and not inevitable. In some cases similar degrees of improvement in reducing training time and increasing productivity have *not* led to similar reductions in labor turnover, owing to changes in the local labor market. Thus, although benefits from reduced learning time and increased productivity are calculable and assured (given a continued market for the product), benefits from reduced labor turnover may be adversely affected by nontraining factors.

Reduced Accidents

It is extremely difficult to obtain the necessary data on which to establish the effect of improved training on accident frequency, and many factors other than training could affect the statistic. Unpublished data have indicated a reduction in accidents rate in the sewing department of a sports shoe firm following the introduction of analytical training. Simmons (1958) published a chart (Figure 4.14) showing the accident frequency among female operatives in a screw mill before and after systematic training, which included "good housekeeping" and safety programs. He noted:

"Any training scheme can only be judged, ultimately, by what it achieves, and this may be difficult to determine accurately, since factors other than training may be involved. For this reason . . . the facts quoted refer either to the training itself, or to circumstances in which operator training is the only item which had been changed" (Simmons, 1958).

THE ROLE OF THE TRAINING SPECIALIST

The role of the training specialist in the prediction and development of work performance is largely that of catalyst; but this catalyst has certain specific additional functions to perform. The predictive function—selection and placement—is dealt with in Chapter 6. The development of performance encourages the training specialist to cooperate closely with production and personnel management to achieve the following aims (See also Singer and Ramsden, 1969; Singer, 1969).

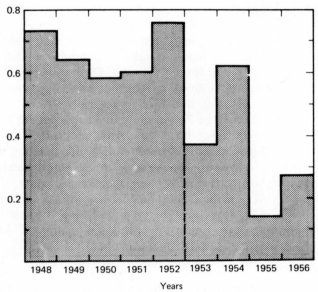

Figure 4.14. Reduction in accident frequency (1500 female workers) following introduction of training. (From Simmons, 1958.)

1. The determination of training needs. This requires the collation and digestion of all data available from marketing, sales, and production sources to determine which tasks are going to require more workers trained (for expansion or for replacement), which jobs will retain members of the present work force, and where technological or other changes will necessitate transfer training of current employees. The data collected must then be quantified numerically, qualified in types of manpower required, costed in relation to length of training time, and presented in terms of an annual or quarterly budget.

2. The identification of tasks. The training specialist is next obliged to identify more precisely who has to be trained for what, and this necessitates job analysis and personnel specifications. If every requirement could be met by hiring a fully trained man completely competent for each job, no training problem would exist. Since this is never the case, however, the training specialist's next job is to determine what types of manpower are likely to be available and to what specific capacities of skill and knowledge the personnel need to be trained. The latter question has to be answered in detail by analyzing the skills and knowledge used by *experienced workers* presently employed.

3. The depth of analysis and type of training to be used. Training managers are often uncertain about the depth or detail with which such analysis should be undertaken. Do we always need to use full skills analysis? is a frequent question. Or, How far do we need to go with our analysis? The ability to determine which analytical technique is most appropriate is a highly significant part of a training specialist's expertise, and it is as important for him to know when *not* to use skills analysis, for example, as to know *how* to use it. The basis for such decisions must be economic: Would the use of more sophisticated techniques of analysis and of training result in more effective use of resources and reduction in cost? If this question is unlikely to receive a positive answer, skills analysis or other advanced techniques should not be entertained. Because the time and cost involved in preparing analytical training are considerable, the investments probably will not be recouped unless the previous training time is appreciable and can be reduced by a significant amount. As a useful rule of thumb to decide whether skills analysis training is likely to pay off, the guidelines given on page 129 may be used.

4. Training of instructors. A training specialist will have responsibility for training instructors. External courses are available for this in some countries, but it may be advantageous to provide in-plant courses for instructors, possessing the abilities previously listed, engaged in analytical training. Such courses would normally cover the following syllabus:

(a) The role and responsibilities of an instructor.

(b) The job specification of the individual instructor.

(c) Techniques of instruction (as required for item b).

(d) The principles and practice of skills analysis training.

(e) Imparting the knowledge content:
    Induction
    Job knowledge
    Quality knowledge, quality specification, fault analysis

(f) Imparting the skills content:
    Enabling the trainee to learn
    Teaching *"what"* and teaching *"how"*
    Element training

(g) Teaching the steps from elements to total job:
    Teaching the steps
    Stamina training
    Retraining

Details of instructor training are given in Chapter XI of *Industrial Training for Manual Operations* (Seymour, 1966) and in Chapters 5, 6 and 7 of *Skills Analysis Training* (Seymour, 1968b).

In Britain, the Department of Employment's Training Development Service has added to their TWI training the use of fault analysis and target times (Perkins, 1969). In conjunction with training recommendations for operators, several of the Industrial Training boards have issued model courses and analyses exemplifying the use of skills analysis training. Thus training specialists who are acquainted with the principles and practice of skills analysis training can compare the model analysis with the task as done in their own firm and proceed to modify it and the training course to meet their firm's specific needs and to suit the levels of skill and knowledge of the trainees available. Hence the advantages of analytical training can be achieved with much less expenditure of time and effort than would be required if the analysts had been forced to prepare a course from scratch. By this means, economies of scale can be realized with benefit to all firms in an industry; indeed, the (U.K.) Engineering Industry Training Board (EITB, 1969, 1970) has already identified some $2 million savings from widespread application of operator training schemes.

The Engineering Industry Training Board commenced its projects for applying skills analysis training by commissioning consultants to train members of its own staff (EITB, 1967). The EITB staff, in turn, carried out projects and conducted courses for training staff from industry. The EITB found that, in addition to a six-week practitioner course for training officers, a management appreciation course was required, as well as a course on the identification of training needs. They found that successful practitioners needed to have:

1. The full support of management.
2. The ability to understand engineering processes.
3. The ability to work alone for sustained periods.
4. The ability to communicate well in the written and spoken words.
5. The ability to get along with people at all levels.

In the first year, more than 100 projects were carried out. In the second year (EITB, 1969), 163 projects were launched, and subsequently (EITB, 1970) the previously cited economies exceeding $2 million were identified. The 1969 report illustrates 20 of the jobs by photographs and summarizes results for five cases as follows:

1. Specialized coil winding: training time halved.
2. Ball-bearing assembly: training time reduced to one-third.
3. Electrical component assembly: training time and scrap almost halved.

4. Hand grinding: labor turnover halved; training time reduced to less than a quarter.

5. Machine setting: training time reduced to a quarter.

More recently, Woodcock (1972) has given further details of E.I.T.B. projects carried out at the Creed factory of I.T.T., where savings of 50 thousand dollars have been achieved by improved training and re-training of workers.

Similar recommendations and procedures have been adopted by the Ceramics, Glass, and Mineral Products ITB, the Furniture and Timber ITB, and the Knitting, Lace, and Net ITB, whose recommendations (see Appendix) and results have been issued.

SKILLS ANALYSIS AND THE TECHNOLOGY OF TRAINING

Following the earlier work of Wolfle (1951) and Glaser (1962), Wallis propounded a "technology of training" and put forward a model of an instructional system, whose human and physical components are designed "to achieve a measurable output of acquired human behaviour whose characteristics have been explicitly prescribed beforehand" (Wallis, 1966, p. 83). The purpose of a technology of training is to construct such instructional systems, and there exist numerous "tools and techniques" which can be applied by the practitioner while he is implementing them. Some of these techniques are already well known and well tried—the lecture, the printed book, visual aids, and the like. Others are relatively new, such as programmed instruction and skills analysis training. The former is particularly appropriate where symbolic responses are to be acquired; the latter where nonsymbolic information is to be processed (Seymour, 1968a).

Davies (1971), developing the ideas of Lumsdaine (1964), and others, identified three forms of a technology of education and training. The first is concerned with instructional aids and the application of physical science to training—audiovisual equipment, teaching machines, and similar forms of hardware. The second involves the application of learning principles in the development and changing of behavior; it is based on the application of the behavioral sciences, emphasizing the determination of precise objectives, the selection of appropriate learning strategies, and the repeated evaluation of the process. The third, which takes into account also modern organization theory and the systems approach (see p. 130 and, e.g., Tilley, 1969), regards educational technology as an interactive process of task variables, organization variables, and learner and instructor variables, in addition to the first and second forms of training technology. The changes in appreciation of the roles involved in instruction are neatly illustrated by the development from instructor-dominated (doing things to the learner) to permissive (doing things for) and to inquiry-centered (do things with) forms of instruction, in parallel with the development from teaching aids to audiovisual techniques and, ultimately, an instructional technology.

The work of K. U. Smith and his associates (summarized, e.g., in Smith and Sussman, 1969) has clarified certain principles of learning and behavioral change bearing direct relevance to the development of the technology of training. The cybernetic, experimental systems approach to the study of learning has provided principles and methods for the application of feedback research to the design of learning, training, and educational devices. Feedback research has also extended into *social teaching* and thus underlies, in part, the third form of training technology; namely, learner and instructor variables and relationships. The social skills involved in these and similar dyadic relationships have been analyzed by Argyle and others (Argyle, 1967; Argyle and Kendon, 1967). As a result, the importance of nonverbal factors in interpersonal relations is now more generally recognized.

The occupational training specialist of the future, whether engaged in industrial, institutional, or military fields, must be master of the technology of training; he must be aware of the tools and techniques available for designing and implementing an instructional system, and he must know how to employ each of them to the best advantage.

V

CRITERIA AND
THEIR MEASUREMENT

OVERVIEW

Criteria—the standards by which things are to be judged—need to be determined and measured before training and selection procedures can be evaluated. The identification of relevant criteria and the development of dependable measures of criteria, which have occupied psychologists in the field for more than half a century, are discussed.

Problems of the dimensionality and nonlinearity of criteria measures are illustrated, and the implications of these qualities are set forth.

The variability and dependability of production output are considered individually and as they relate to the establishment of work standards.

A criterion is an evaluative standard which may be used to "measure" a person's attitude, aptitude, and performance. Thus any method of evaluation has the potential for becoming a criterion measure, providing the method is sensitive enough to discriminate among individuals (Blum and Naylor, 1968), and always assuming that the measure is relevant to the task studied.

This chapter is concerned only with the use of criteria for personnel selection and training purposes. *Selection* criteria are described by the degree of correlation between selection test scores and performance measures (in real-world situations), which represent the degree of an employee's success in performing his job. *Training* criteria refer to measures utilized in evaluating the effectiveness of a training program (i.e., the measures that express the degree to which the attainment of the behavioral objectives of the training program have been met).

USE OF CRITERIA IN PERSONNEL
SELECTION AND TRAINING

Personnel selection serves to predict a person's suitability for a job, whereas the purpose of personnel training is to derive a predetermined work standard, or other criterion, in the shortest possible training time. Both purposes can be achieved by analyzing and quantifying the content and skills associated with the job. For personnel selection a test battery based on this information can be constructed and other procedures can be designed to simulate the job. For personnel training, on the other hand, a training program can be constructed based on the same information. The validation of each process can be evaluated as follows:

1. The validity of a personnel selection system can be evaluated by the degree of the relationship, or correlation, between test scores against the criteria measures (e.g., see Chapters 6 and 7).

2. The validity of a training method can be evaluated by comparing a variety of different training methods with a set of the same criteria for all cases (see Chapter 4).

The training method that yields the highest desirable criterion performance in training time with lowest cost is the most valid one. If the difference between the various training methods is not clear-cut, a tradeoff function between cost and time of training on the one hand and level of criteria achieved on the other is exercised. The specific function of this tradeoff depends on the particular job training under consideration.

The validity of selection and training programs alike is affected by the following factors, which are merely listed here because they have received individual treatment elsewhere in this text:

1. The degree to which personnel selection tests or personnel training procedures simulate real-world criteria.

2. The dependability of personnel selection tests and training under study.

3. Dependability of the criteria considered, true and not merely correlational.

4. Relevance of the criteria considered for (a) the job studied, and (b) the test batteries adopted for selection or training purposes.

5. The stage (initial, ultimate, or rate of learning) at which criteria are measured may affect validities significantly. Typically, criteria measures at the early stages of the acquisition of a skill exhibit higher validity coefficients than those we find when the measures are correlated with terminal performance (Ghiselli, 1966).

6. Because job performance is multidimensional, taking only one criterion as an index of job performance may result in artifactually high or low validity coefficients. Therefore, a multidimensional approach is essential in the measurement of job performance and criteria utilization in personnel selection and training.

7. Evidence indicates that criterion and test measures are typically nonlinear. Since, moreover, assuming their linearity increases the error variance of the validity coefficient, the validity of the assumption must be tested before linearity is assumed.

8. Fluctuations in the individual's physiological and psychological health condition, need of achievement motivation, and so on, affect the validity coefficient of personnel selection programs as well as training programs.

In summary, it is hardly possible to overstress the importance of a sound criterion measure against which personnel selection and training programs can be evaluated effectively. In order to achieve this objective, emphasis must be placed *at the outset* on the development of such measures. Without sound criteria, the true validity of personnel selection and training cannot be assessed properly.

TYPES OF CRITERIA

Criteria for the purposes of personnel selection and training lie on a continuum scale, which has two interactive dimensions: objectivity–subjectivity and employee–employer satisfaction. Some criteria are entirely subjective; others are entirely objective. Most, however, involve a mixture of the two. Interacting with the objective–subjective dimension, we find criteria of two types: those describing the satisfaction of the employee's needs and those identifying satisfaction of employers in their employees. The ideal is to have a highly objective criterion that reflects the satisfaction of employee needs (this criterion is used most frequently for personnel guidance purposes), as well as employers' satisfaction in their employees (this criterion is used most frequently in personnel selection and training). Such an ideal composite criterion is rarely found in industry, although the gap between criteria of employees' satisfaction and employers' satisfaction in employees is narrowing (Rodger, 1965).

However, the most important criterion remains the performance of a task that has been described clearly and comprehensively. Yet such performance criteria may not adequately reflect the employees' satisfaction or dissatisfaction with the job, and there may indeed be a conflict— a person can do well in a job he does not like, and vice versa.

Table 5.1   Types of criteria utilized for personnel selection and training[a]

I. Criteria reflecting employees' competence

    A. Quality of performance

        1. Quality of output
        2. Spoiled work: (a) amount, (b) cost
        3. Accidents: (a) number, (b) cost (financial and human)
        4. Breakages (tools, etc.): (a) number, (b) cost
        5. Mistakes in operation: (a) number, (b) cost
        6. Variability in performance
      *7. Rate of advancement
      *8. Standard trade examinations
      *9. Training: (a) cost; (i) to employer, (ii) to employees; (b) duration

    B. Quantity of performance

        1. Quantity of output
        2. Earnings on a commission basis
        3. Earned bonus
        4. Peak performance
        5. Lowest performance
      *6. Rate of advancement
      *7. Standard trade examinations
      *8. Training: (a) cost; (i) to employer, (ii) to employees; (b) duration

II. Criteria reflecting employees' circumstances

    1. Length of service
    2. Labor turnover (broken down to categories according to their cause)
    3. Lateness (categorized according to how late): (a) numbers, (b) cost
    4. Absenteeism: (a) certified; (i) number, (ii) cost; (b) uncertified; (i) number, (ii) cost

III. Criteria reflecting employee's satisfaction from job

    1. Rating of employee's liking for his present job
    2. Rating of employee's satisfaction with job content and desire for job enlargement or job simplification

---

[a] Starred items may reflect quality and/or quantity of performance. Since their relationship to performance is indirect, they are less valuable and important than the others.

Although it is essential to aim at utilizing the *most appropriate criterion* (for a specific job), *rather than the most convenient criterion*, it is not always feasible to assess the former or to obtain data on it. Thus the analyst is frequently faced with the practical issue of utilizing the most appropriate criterion on which data are available or can readily be collected.

Occupational jobs differ, and the *reason* for utilizing a criterion also varies; consequently, a variety of criterion measures have been developed and used over the last century, each with its charactertistic weaknesses and strengths. However, any criterion may be the most appropriate one for a specific occupation (or for a task within an occupation), depending on circumstances and purpose. The majority of the criteria relevant to today's occupational circumstances and competence are listed in Table 5.1. The most relevant criteria and those most frequently utilized for studies on psychomotor performance, such as quantity and quality of production output, are reviewed more extensively.

For some of the criteria in Table 5.1, objective data can be gathered (e.g., length of employee's service); others require subjective assessment (e.g., rating or ranking by supervisor, subordinates, members of equal status, and the employee himself). For some criteria (e.g., quality of output) both subjective and objective techniques can be utilized. Many of these can be related to training progress at the following stages: (*a*) immediate, at the beginning of training; (*b*) intermediate, at the end of training; (*c*) ultimate, in real-world operations, after completion of training.

CRITERIA MEASURES

There are basically three types of methods by means of which criteria data can be collected:

1. Rating or ranking.
2. Counting (e.g., the number of items produced, the number of latenesses, the duration of service).
3. Establishing work standards (e.g., Barnes, 1968).

In the following pages, the three methods of gathering data on criteria measures are examined with special reference to their dependability.

Rating and Ranking

Both rating and ranking have the objective of assigning a position or mark to an individual. Ranking arranges individuals in a hierarchical order, where no two persons can occupy the same placing; rating groups individuals into categories (each constituting a number of personnel), whereby categories and not individuals are arranged in hierarchical order. Consequently, ranking is the finer classification of individuals within a group. Rating enables us to compare individuals from different groups. However, it would be feasible to make such comparisons for ranking only if the groups are the same, or comparable, considering the phenomenon being ranked or rated.

Historically, rating was developed 20 years prior to ranking. It was Galton (1883) who first reported the development of a rating scale, which he used to quantify the vividness of images; Cattell (1902, 1903) presented the first ranking method.

Rating and ranking are employed as criteria measures in assessments of the relative effectiveness of workers, the relative capabilities of supervisors, the utility of different methods of work, and so on. Comparative preferences of persons for different types of occupations can also be made using ranking and rating. Other illustrative uses include the assessment of working conditions and preferences for color of surrounding and levels of lighting. Usually such preferences are recorded on scales of 5 to 10 points varying, for example, from very heavy to very light, extremely slow to exceedingly rapid, or poor to excellent (Guilford, 1954). To each assessment, a numerical value is given, and the factors to be ranked are arranged in hierarchical orders.

For rating, the factors are arranged in groups of scores. This may either be done using fixed intervals (e.g., 0 to 9 percent, 10 to 19 percent, etc.) or at intervals approximating to normal distribution (e.g., 0 to 10 percent, 11 to 30 percent, 31 to 70 percent, 71 to 90 percent, and 91 to 100 percent).

Rating and ranking are used where more objective criteria measures (e.g., direct measures of production output) either cannot be used or are not economically feasible.

The subjectivity of rating was realized early. For example, to counteract subjectivity, Link (1919) attempted to increase the objectivity of rating by utilizing rating of job performance from *two* supervisors.

Thorndike (1920), discussing subjectivity in rating, referred to the so-called "halo effect" defined (Drever, 1965) as a tendency to be biased in the estimation or rating of an individual with respect to a certain characteristic by some quite irrelevant impression or estimate (good or bad) of some individual. This frequent source of error in employing rating scales is the principal reason for the low dependability of ratings.

The subjectivity and resultant low dependability of rating and ranking is stressed by almost everyone who writes on this subject (e.g., Hollingworth, 1929; Viteles, 1932; Woodworth and Schlosberg, 1954; Tiffin and McCormick, 1966). For example, a recent study (Salvendy, 1968) of 181 female operators in three British firms performing (or being trained to perform) fine manual repetitive operations in industry negates the value of rating for psychomotor operations (Table 5.2).

Table 5.2 illustrates that the operators, in all the three firms, rated themselves (on average) 50 percent higher than did their supervisors

Table 5.2 The Value of Rating for Psychomotor Operations

	Electronic Firm, Television Tube Assembly ($N = 80$)			Electromechanical Firm, Manufacturer of Car Components ($N = 52$)			Confectionery Firm, Chocolate Packing and Wrapping ($N = 49$)		
	$\bar{x}$	S.D.	r[a]	$\bar{x}$	S.D.	r	$\bar{x}$	S.D.	r
Overall self-rating[b]	3.30	0.72	.46[c]	3.60	0.89	−.36[d]	3.89	1.02	.51[c]
Overall supervisor's rating	2.32	0.91	.19	2.38	1.39	.12	2.40	1.51	.17
Aptitude—supervisor's rating	2.04	1.01	−.13	—[e]	—	—	—	—	—
Ability—supervisor's rating	2.17	0.99	−.02	—	—	—	—	—	—
Actual production performance (where 100 is standard)[f]	127.81[g]	24.80	1.00	157.13[h]	29.91	1.00	153.25[i]	82.08	1.00

[a] Product-moment correlation coefficient with actual production performance indices.

[b] All the ratings in this table are on a five-point scale, where 1 is the "worst" and 5 the "best."

[c] $p < .001$.

[d] $p < .05$.

[e] Indicates data not available.

[f] When operator starts to produce above standard, he starts to earn money above his guaranteed minimum. This bonus earning is directly proportional to the production output above standard.

[g] Standards based on work factors (Quick, Shea, and Koehler, 1945) with lower and upper ceiling on earnings set by the company—the PPP system (Westwood, 1965).

[h] Standards based on MTM (Maynard, Stegemerten, and Schwab, 1948) or time study (Barnes, 1968).

[i] Standards based on time study (Barnes, 1968).

($p < .001$). Furthermore, none of the supervisors rated their operators validly; that is, the correlation between the "actual" production performance index and the supervisor's rating of what the operator had actually done never exceeded $+ .2$ (Table 5.2).

This highlights the relative uselessness of a supervisor's rating as a criterion of performance for psychomotor operations, since it grossly misleads and misrepresents the factual data; the supervisors' ratings in this study accounted for less than 5 percent of the "actual" performance of operators in real-world situations in these companies (a chance effect, not statistically significant).

A recent study conducted on the validity of performance criteria for classifying semiskilled operators (Amaria, 1968) indicated that the reliability of supervisor's ratings on a 5-point scale of 110 operators on 10 job criteria, such as quality and quantity of production performance and overall rating, is between .59 to .94 ($p < .001$) with a mean value of .78 using the paired comparison technique (Thurstone, 1927; Guilford, 1928) and .38 to .96 ($.001 > p < .01$) with a mean value of .72 using the retest method.

The mere apparent reliability of the ratings as demonstrated by correlational statistics does not eliminate the fact that they are affected by constant errors. These errors are constant for each person, but vary between persons. Although they do not affect the reliability coefficient, they do reduce validity.

Despite this, rating and ranking have been used in the great majority of the published studies dealing with the validation of personnel selection tests. The reason is the comparative ease with which rating and ranking scales can be developed and used.

Counting

The counting and classifying into groups of factual data constitutes a well-known method of collecting criteria. Typical types of counted data include *type* (classification) and *frequency* of accidents, lateness, absenteeism, scrap, and number of work units produced. The data derived by this method are, expectedly, highly reliable, subject to the following constraints:

1. Classification of a data category into its subparts (e.g., the categorization of lateness as short, medium, and long) is often highly subjective. On the other hand, errors are introduced when the criterion data are not divided into its subgroups, since unequal variables may be counted under one heading. For example, even though latenesses may vary from 5 minutes' duration to as much as 5 hours, each incidence might be counted

in the frequency analysis as one lateness. Failure to fractionate such data is questionable; one may ask: (*a*) Are the two types of latenesses causing the same economic damage to the employer? (*b*) Did the two latenesses occur for the same or similar reasons?

2. Human errors may be introduced in the recording and collection of data. The magnitude of these errors will depend on the individual collecting the data. Typical errors in this category are: (*a*) data recorded under an inappropriate category, (*b*) data recorded for the wrong person, and (*c*) part of the data unknowingly lost.

3. The same data to be used for different criterial purposes may require different degrees of accuracy. Thus if historical data collected in the past are to be utilized, the nature and purposes for which the data were originally collected must be known before it is possible to assess their reliability. For example, the use of historical data on climatic conditions during a calendar year may be acceptable for the prediction of a trend in manpower utilization in the construction industry, but not for the determination of a missile-launching date.

4. Historical data may be reliable but at the same time not representative of or relevant to a present situation because important influencing variables have changed.

PRODUCTION OUTPUT AND STANDARD PERFORMANCE

Standard performance is defined by the British Standard 3138 (1959) as the rate of output that will be achieved naturally, without overexertion, by *qualified workers,* * as an average, over the working day or shift, provided they know and adhere to the specified method and provided they are motivated to apply themselves to the work. This is denoted by 100 on the British Standard scale. No similar American standard has been established or recommended, and each American firm either uses its own index or adopts an index described by authors such as Barnes (1968), Mundel (1970), or Niebel (1972). The main purpose of such an index is to enable the comparison on a standard scale of different types of production outputs at different levels.

Performance standards can be established using a variety of techniques. These techniques can be grouped in five categories, although as part of each category a variety of methods are available:†

---

* Qualified workers are defined as those who have the necessary physical attributes, who possess the required intelligence and education, and have acquired the necessary *skill* and knowledge to carry out the work in hand to satisfactory standards of safety, quantity, and quality.

† Further details on these techniques are provided on pp. 205-218.

1. *Time study* is a work measurement technique for recording the elements and rates of working for a specified job carried out under specified conditions; it also serves for analyzing the data in order to obtain the time necessary for doing the job at a defined level of performance.

2. *Synthetic times* is a work measurement technique for building up the time required to perform a job at a defined level of performance by summating element times obtained previously from time studies on other jobs containing the same job elements. The technique may make use of tables and formulas derived from the analysis of accumulated work measurement data and arranged in a form suitable for building up standard times, machine processing time and so on, by synthesis.

3. In the *PMTS technique,* times established for basic human motions (classified according to the nature of the motion and the conditions under which it is made) are used to build up the time for a job at a defined level of performance.

4. *Rated activity sampling* is an extension of activity sampling, in which a list is made of the job elements comprising the worker's job; this describes the job to be performed. In addition to the time required to do each job element, an effectiveness rating of these elements is made which permits the establishment of a work standard for that job.

5. *Physiological techniques* serve for assessing work standards by establishing the physiological cost associated with performing a given job.

The choice among the foregoing techniques is usually determined by one or more of the following:

1. Competence of individuals establishing the performance standards. It becomes apparent that some individuals are familiar with (and consequently make use of) certain techniques, while other individuals are familiar with others.

2. Policy of the company requires the adoption of a specific technique, and no others may be used.

3. The nature of the job (e.g., duration of elemental and cycle times, the total quantity of each product to be produced, and economic and dependability considerations of the technique utilized).

No clear-cut evidence is available to indicate exactly when each of the five techniques for establishing performance standards could most effectively be utilized. However, the following appear to be appropriate:

1. For highly repetitive short operations, in which each cycle lasts not more than 5 min, any of the standardized predetermined motion time systems, such as MTM (Maynard, Stegemerten, and Schwab, 1948) or

work factors (Quick, Duncan, and Malcolm, 1962) could be appropriate. Such tasks are found in light assembly work (e.g., television and radio manufacturing).

2. For repetitive operations lasting longer than 5 min per cycle, typically the work standards could be most economically assessed by time study. Such tasks are found in smaller companies manufacturing products similar to those in item 1; however, because of their lower level of production, the tasks are not broken down into the shorter elements of item one.

3. For operations in which activities occur randomly, where no systematic repetition of a task is present, and in which the same workers may be engaged in several different tasks, rated activity sampling may be the most suitable to assess the work standards. Such tasks are to be found among auxiliary nonproduction operations such as storing and fork lifting, and in repair shops and automobile garages.

4. When sufficient data have been accumulated for a variety of tasks by time study, PMTS, or rated work sampling, mathematical models, including multiple-regression equations may be developed for the prediction of work standards, for which no time-values were available. The use of these synthetic times may be most appropriate for nonrepetitive tasks, provided these times are within the range covered by the mathematical model. Examples may be found in small-batch production (e.g., machine tools) and repair shops (e.g., automobile).

The determination of performance standards, utilizing any of the five techniques previously listed, has two main objectives:

1. To determine how much the output should be for a fair day's performance of a specific task.

2. To compare, using a common index, the relative performances of different operators on a variety of different tasks.

Before the validity and reliability of the various techniques can be compared, we must understand the nature, characteristics, and reliability of production performance.

Correlational Reliability of Production Performance

One of the earliest studies aimed at assessing the reliability of production performances was reported by Hayes (1932). When the first 4 weeks' output was correlated with that of the second 4 weeks, a mean reliability of .82 was obtained.

In a later study reported by Tiffin and McCormick (1966, p. 39) on 79 unit wire operators, the effects of training were more readily controlled;

here a mean intercorrelation of .87 between the odd and even weeks of production performance during a 10-week period was obtained. Relying on these data, the authors concluded that production performance data are reliable, consistent, and stable.

However, this concept of the stability of production data was not supported in a series of studies by Rothe (1946a, 1946b, 1947, 1951, 1970) and Rothe and Nye (1958, 1959, 1961) on the output patterns of operators performing repetitive tasks such as butter wrapping, chocolate dipping, coil winding, and machine operation. These studies indicated strikingly the lack of consistency in production output of operators from one period to another, especially when no financial incentive system operates. This inconsistency is illustrated by low intercorrelations of successive weeks' performance, ranging from negative intercorrelations for some groups of operators to highly positive ones (e.g., + .9) for other groups. This wide range of "consistency coefficients" of production output data could mislead an investigator if he happened to select a period of unusually high or low consistency.

The mean reliability of the production performances for all these studies was + .7, which is considerably lower than that found by Tiffin and McCormick (1966) and Bellows (1940), who reported values of .89 to .96 for card-punch machine operators and .87 for coding clerks. Other reliability figures, correlating two successive weeks, were reported by Ayers (1942) for textile inspectors. The criteria (with reliability figure in parentheses), were as follows: failure to discover defective units (.73); units that should not have been put aside for foreman's decision (.83); average hourly production (.85); total units set aside for foreman's decision (.91). Similar reliabilities were obtained for other occupational fields, such as bookkeeping, where reliabilities of .72, .78, and .83 were reported by Hay (1943), and for life insurance agents, where reliabilities of .74, .81, and .84 were reported (Strong, 1934–1935, 1943).

Salvendy (1970) studied the reliability of production performance of female operators working on financial incentive schemes in chocolate wrapping (N = 43) and car subassemblies (N = 30). Since each worker had at least one year's experience on the job, the effects of learning were reduced. The data for the first 10 days were correlated with those of the next 10 days; this resulted in intercorrelations of .92 and .88. When the odd and even days of the 20-day study were intercorrelated, lower values were obtained (.77 and .74), which suggests that day-to-day fluctuations in production output tend to be larger than week-to-week fluctuations for the same operators. This is understandable, since day-to-day variations represent a mean production value of 8 hr, whereas week-to-week variations represent 80 hr (2 weeks). The size of the sample naturally affects the reliability because, the greater the number of performances, the more likely it is that the operator's variability will be reduced as a result of the correlation of data below the mean performance with data above it.

In spite of the relatively high correlations obtained by some investigators, the reliability of production performance indices needs to be treated with caution, not only because of the possible effects of learning but also because within the same industry certain variables may in one period counteract each other and augment each other in another period.

Variability of Production Output

Variability in production output for a given operator during a working day varies markedly (Dudley, 1968), being low at the beginning and end of the working day and relatively stable from midmorning to midafternoon (Figure 5.1). This phenomenon can be explained as an early morning warmup and late afternoon slow-down of the operator.

Operator variability has been further examined in terms of a number of factors. For example, Murrell (1962), Van Beek (1964), and Sury (1967) emphasized the industrial consequences of operator variability. Klemmer and Lockhead (1962), as a result of studying more than 1000 key punch operators, concluded that individual variability was about 6 to 10 percent of the group mean and that this variability of the individual is independent of the production level.

Variability in production output during a working day may be due more to ancillary work and operational and personnel delays than to the variability of the human operator (Figure 5.2). Delays that are mainly operational occur at the start of the working day, just before and after lunch, and toward the end of the working day. These delays result in decreases in production output and increased variability in production output during the day. Operator variability usually arises as a result of complex interactions among the following factors:

1. Changes in levels of motivation (Vernon and Wyatt, 1924; Viteles, 1953; Herzberg, Mausner, and Snyderman, 1957; Vroom, 1964; Atkinson and Feather, 1966).

2. Psychological and physiological fatigue (Bartlett, 1953; Karpovich, 1965).

3. Organizational factors, such as variations in quality of material, inspection, and quantity of stock in progress (Bittner and Rundquist, 1950; Thomas, 1965; and Van Beek, 1964).

4. Chance effects and variability in the "internal clock" of the human operator (Bills, 1931; Broadbent, 1958; Bertelson and Joffe, 1963).

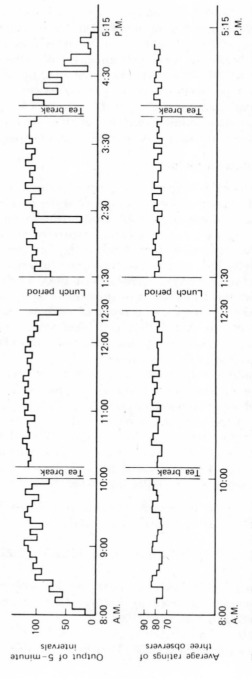

Figure 5.1. Comparison of output curve and ratings made on one operator during a repetitive manual operation (Thread-roll bulbholder) during a working day, utilizing continuous time studies. Similar results were obtained for other manual repetitive tasks and for other operators. (After Dudley, 1968, p. 55.)

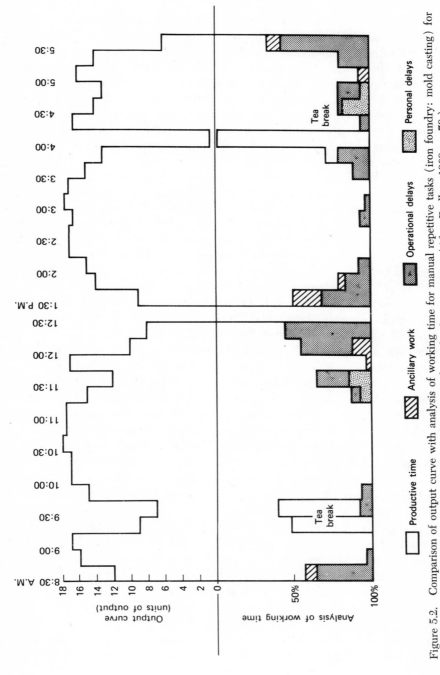

Figure 5.2. Comparison of output curve with analysis of working time for manual repetitive tasks (iron foundry: mold casting) for one operator. Similar results were obtained for other tasks and other operators. (After Dudley, 1968, p. 78.)

199

As a result of a series of industrial output studies, Rothe and Nye proposed that the incentives to work may be ineffective when the range of intraindividual differences is greater than the range of inter-individual differences (Rothe, 1946a, 1946b, 1947, 1951, 1970; Rothe and Nye, 1958, 1959, 1961). If such a hypothesis could be validated (the present studies have provided only very tentative clues), it could furnish a unique tool for evaluating the effectiveness of incentive schemes in industry. The effectiveness of work incentives could also be increased by the retraining of less productive workers, which would lead to a decrease in individual differences (Simmons, 1958).

Although these studies indicate that the magnitude of the extreme differences between individuals varies markedly, depending on the nature of the job and the operators studied, together with the place at which they are compared, it would appear safe to conclude that a ratio of 1:2.5 in production output between the lowest and the highest per-formers exists in the majority of circumstances. These conclusions are supported by a series of studies such as those of Tiffin and McCormick (1966, p. 37) on mechanical assemblers, unit wire operators, and cablers, and on such manual dexterity tests as the Purdue Pegboard (Tiffin and Asher, 1948; Salvendy, 1968) and the One-Hole Test (Salvendy, 1968), and on other manual repetitive tasks (Wiltshire, 1967).

However, as Figure 5.3 illustrates, this ratio of 1:2.5 between lowest and highest performers does not hold in real-world situations when the sam-ple is based on a larger group engaged in different and diversified tasks. All the operators whose output is portrayed in Figure 5.3 worked on direct financial incentives; they were all guaranteed by management a minimum salary that corresponded to an efficiency index of 100, independent of the actual index achieved by the operator. The distribution represents one week's performance of the operators and corresponds to their take-home salaries (with the exception of 27 operators who were absent up to 30 min each during the week, who had a proportionate amount deducted from their salaries).

During this week the 1413 operators performed 213 different operations; the standards were derived by time study on 181 operations and by MTM on the remaining 32. There were no significant differences in the distribu-tion of the efficiency index between performances on the jobs studied by MTM and those investigated by time study methods. The ratio in this case was 1:6, although the ratio of 1:2.5 was evident for 95 percent of the operators. This study also revealed that nearly 1 percent ($N = 13$) of this total labor force earned more than twice the minimum daily guaranteed income, whereas 0.2 percent ($N = 3$) earned more than three times their

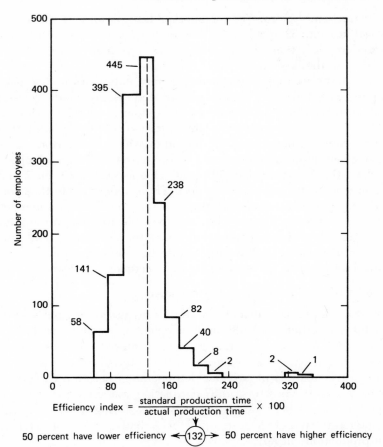

Figure 5.3. Distribution of efficiency index of 1413 female industrial operators aged 16 to 61 (x = 37) with 1 to 38 years' (x = 7) experience at an electro-mechanical concern.

daily minimum guarantee. If such an efficiency index were maintained for their entire working year, the salary of the latter group would be more than $20,000 per annum (£8000). At the other extreme, nearly 15 percent (N = 199) of the labor force earned no bonus and received only the minimum guaranteed payment; slightly more than half of the labor force (N = 712) earned incentives up to an additional one-third of their guaranteed minimum daily salary.

On one task (N = 32) there was a ratio of 1:1.5 between an operator with the lowest performance and an operator with the highest performance in the same group. Yet for another task performed the following week for the same 32 operators, a ratio of 1 : 4.5 was found. Furthermore, the standard deviation in the second case was more than three times larger than in the first case.

In accounting for these differences, we must note that the first task had been performed for only 2 years and consisted of very short cycles of 53 seconds (standard time) in which there were four identical activities, each consisting of eight basic elements (thus the complete cycle had a total of 32 basic elements). In contrast, the second task had been performed (with only some very minor modifications) for more than 25 years (7 operators worked on this for more than 20 years; 11 operators between 2 and 20 years; 14 worked for less than 2 years). The standard cycle time for the second task (87 basic elements) was 194 sec (nearly four times longer than the previous operation). Thus it is possible that the variability between efficiency indices for industrial operators performing light manual operations in industry is less attributable to inherent variability in the operator and more to organizational work methods and learning factors.

Constant Errors in Production Performance

It must be emphasized that all the studies discussed previously in terms of reliability of criteria (in the sense of repeatability and variability) do not deal with one most important aspect of criterial reliability: constant errors and the degree of homogeneity in the criteria. This point was illustrated in a recent study of two machine operators (electric cable coating process). For both operators, a .87 correlation was obtained for production performance when odd and even weeks during a one-year period were intercorrelated. However, operator A had a mean of 23 percent higher production output.

At first sight this discrepancy might not seem important because such differences could easily be due to individual variability. However, a closer examination of the situation revealed that the machine of operator B was markedly less versatile and more difficult (more fatiguing and requiring longer time) to operate than that of operator A. Furthermore, the machine of operator B was less accurate (consequently he had more spoiled material) and had a higher breakdown rate than that of operator A; in addition, operator A was always favored in the quality of raw materials he received. These and other variables (not associated with the operator's traits) helped operator A to produce about a quarter more than he would have been able to produce otherwise.

Although the repeatability correlation indicated satisfactory reliability coefficients for the production performances of operators A and B, the production indices carried a constant error of such a magnitude that the production index of operator A became significantly lower than that of operator B.

The degree of homogeneity of a criterion may also affect its reliability; for example, when the criterion is the frequency of operational mistakes. Of course mistakes can vary in magnitude with different consequences, which can be arranged in hierarchical order. Now if the variations in magnitude and consequences are eliminated, like is not being compared with like, and the nonhomogeneity of the criteria makes the results of parametric statistics less powerful than they would be otherwise. In this situation, one driver who made 10 driving mistakes (each causing only very minor scratches to the car and no bodily harm) might be considered equivalent in criterion performance to another driver who made 10 driving mistakes, each one resulting in heavy bodily and material harm. The two naturally are not alike.

The previous discussion indicates that production performance is affected by many variable factors whose possible influences should be considered as a precaution against error. The principal variables are as follows:

I. Organizational: Differences in
    A.   Quality and supply of material
    B.   Layout, mechanization, and speed of machinery
    C.   Effectiveness of supervision
    D.   Working conditions
    E.   Errors in recording quantity or quality
II. Individual: Differences in
    A.   Level of worker competence
    B.   Worker morale
    C.   Domestic circumstances

For example, if the reliability of a criterion is .90, this means that on the average there is 19 percent error variability in the production performance ($100 - (.90)^2 \times 100 =$ percent error variance). However, if the .90 coefficient has a variance of 15 percent attributable to the nonhomogeneity of the criteria and 31 percent attributable to the total biased constant errors (not including effects of individual differences), the true reliability is not .90, but only .67: $(.90)^2 \times 100 - (15 + 31)(.90)^2$. In this case, the production data carry a total of 56 percent error variance $[100 - (.67^2 \times 100]$, instead of the 19 percent reported earlier, and only 44 percent of the production index can be attributed to operator's performance.

Broadly speaking, this means that a typical operator who has a mean efficiency index of 132 (Figure 5.3) might have an actual efficiency index anywhere from 104 to 153, considering the 19 percent error variance, and from 48 to 200, considering the 56 percent error variance.

This emphasizes the need to establish not only the reliability of production performance data but also the extent of any constant error and the homogeneity of the data. Otherwise, the reliability figures may be artifactually inflated.

DEPENDABILITY OF TIME STUDY

Times for work standards are customarily calculated by a single industrial engineer who observes the work of a typical operator, selected to represent the characteristics of the average operator. The engineer breaks the operations down into smaller units called elements and times each element separately, usually by stopwatch. Simultaneously he rates* these elements on an efficiency index scale and assesses performance interference allowances.† From these data, the industrial engineer establishes the standard time in the following way:

$$\text{standard time} = \frac{\text{observed time (OT)} \times \text{observed rating (OR)}}{\text{standard rating (SR)}}$$

$$\times \frac{100 + \text{percent performance interference allowance}}{100}$$

and

$$\text{base time} = \frac{(OT) \times (OR)}{(SR)}$$

For example, observed time   = 25 sec
           standard rating   = 100
           observed rating   = 80
           performance interference allowance = 13 percent

Then he can write

$$\text{base time} = \left(\frac{25 \times 80}{100}\right) = 20.0 \text{ sec}$$

---

* Rating applies to the process during which time study analysts compare the performance characteristics of the operator under observation with the analyst's own concept of normal performance.

† Because it is not expected that a person will work without interruptions for his entire employed working period (e.g., working day), performance interference allowances are allowed. These consist of the following subcategories: (a) fatigue allowances (usually 5 to 15 percent of the base time); (b) personal allowances (usually 3 to 5 percent of the base time); and (c) unavoidable delay allowance, which may occur from zero to any percent of the base time.

and

$$\text{standard time} = \left(\frac{25 \times 80}{100}\right) \frac{\times (100 + 13)}{100} = 22.6 \text{ sec}$$

Although a number of rating scales are in use (see Barnes, 1968), the rating scale in which 100 percent equals normal performance is the one most widely employed. On this scale it is expected that 50 percent of the entire working group will be around 130 percent (Figure 5.3). This means that operators who produce 30 percent more than normal will earn 30 percent extra pay for this extra performance. An operator who is producing 10 percent below standard will still be paid the amount equal to normal performance. No operator is paid less (independent of his performance) than the guaranteed rate, which is equal to 100 percent normal performance.

The reliability of standard times derived by time study is affected by the following factors:

1. Reliability of production data.
2. Reliability of ratings.
3. Individual differences among time study engineers.
4. Representativeness of the operator whose performance is studied.
5. Size and nature of the sample studies (i.e., whether the study was performed on one or more operators, and the number of repeated studies on the same operator and the same task).
6. Time of the study (i.e. day or night shift, beginning or end of week; beginning, middle, or end of the working day).
7. Compensation relaxation allowances, usually based on company's policy rather than on scientific determination. Even in the latter case, however, the reliability of each allowance is extremely low, especially for perceptual and mental tasks.

The low dependability of work standards derived by time study has been long recognized [e.g., Anson, 1952; Rodgers and Hammersley, 1954; and the society of the Advancement of Management (SAM), summarized by Gomberg, 1954).

These studies indicated that the average time study is somewhat inaccurate. For example, the study of SAM summarized by Gomberg (1954) involved 24 manipulative operations that were rated by more than 1000 experienced time study engineers from some 200 companies. The results indicated that about two-thirds of the time study engineers in this study had both systematic and absolute errors of 20 percent.

The effect of this, for example, is that if time standards have been established (using a stopwatch) for 500 different jobs where the standard time for each is equivalent to an index of 100, then for two-thirds of all the jobs (333) the true index actually varies from 79 to 121, whereas for 95 percent of all jobs (475) the index would actually be from 58 to 142.

Obviously, the reliability of the time standards would be increased if they were cross-validated. One way to achieve this is to assign a number of time study engineers to study the same job with a number of operators on several occasions. Cross-validation study is more expensive, of course, but the benefits derived make the added expense worthwhile.

DEPENDABILITY OF PMTS

A predetermined motion time system (PMTS) is a work measurement technique whereby times established for basic human motions (classified according to the nature of the motion and the conditions under which it is made) are used to build up the time for a job at a defined level of performance (British Standards 3138, 1959; no U.S. standard definition of PMTS has yet been developed).

The first PMTS was developed nearly 50 years ago, and since then well over 10 independent methods have been developed. However, the two most frequently utilized methods are the work-factor system (WFS) developed by Quick, Duncan, and Malcolm (1962) 35 years ago, and methods–time measurement (MTM), developed by Maynard, Stegemerten, and Schwab (1948). The latter is the one most popular. Like other PMTS methods, it analyzes any manual operation into the basic motion elements required to perform the operation, assigning to each of these a time standard that is determined by the nature of the motion and the conditions under which it is made (Table 5.3).

The dependability of PMTS is affected by the following factors:

1. Low reliability of the production data.

2. Compensation relaxation allowances, which may be as unreliable in certain circumstances as those utilized in stopwatch time study.

3. The grouping effect; that is, a number of different work activities are grouped under one category for which one unified time is allocated. This process introduces error in the case of activities near the limits of a category. Such errors may be cumulative but are more likely to be self-balancing.

4. The question of the additivity of elemental times, which has been mentioned before (and has never been satisfactorily resolved). The amount of error introduced by additivity is measurable but small (Sanfleber, 1967).

As a result of the availability of anthropometric data (e.g., Samon, Stoudt and McFarland, 1966), PMTS values (e.g. see table 5.3) and rapid advancements in computer technology, it is now feasible to utilize computer assisted workplace layout and work standards for psychomotor activities (Chaffin, Kilpatrick and Hancock, 1970).

Table 5.3 Sample of MTM data for the prediction of work standards: 1 TMU = 0.0001 hr = 0.006 min = 0.036 sec (Association for Standards and Research*)

Table I—Reach—R

Distance Moved (in.)	Time TMU				Hand-in Motion	
	A	B	C or D	E	A	B
¾ or less	2.0	2.0	2.0	2.0	1.6	1.6
1	2.5	2.5	3.6	2.4	2.3	2.3
2	4.0	4.0	5.9	3.8	3.5	2.7
3	5.3	5.3	7.3	5.3	4.5	3.6
4	6.1	6.4	8.4	6.8	4.9	4.3
5	6.5	7.8	9.4	7.4	5.3	5.0
6	7.0	8.6	10.1	8.0	5.7	5.7
7	7.4	9.3	10.8	8.7	6.1	6.5
8	7.9	10.1	11.5	9.3	6.5	7.2
9	8.3	10.8	12.2	9.9	6.9	7.9
10	8.7	11.5	12.9	10.5	7.3	8.6
12	9.6	12.9	14.2	11.8	8.1	10.1
14	10.5	14.4	15.6	13.0	8.9	11.5
16	11.4	15.8	17.0	14.2	9.7	12.9
18	12.3	17.2	18.4	15.5	10.5	14.4
20	13.1	18.6	19.8	16.7	11.3	15.8
22	14.0	20.1	21.2	18.0	12.1	17.3
24	14.9	21.5	22.5	19.2	12.9	18.8
26	15.8	22.9	23.9	20.4	13.7	20.2
28	16.7	24.4	25.3	21.7	14.5	21.7
30	17.5	25.8	26.7	22.9	15.3	23.2

Case and Description

A. Reach to object in fixed location, or to object in other hand or on which other hand rests

B. Reach to single object in location which may vary slightly from cycle to cycle

C. Reach to object jumbled with other objects in a group so that search and select occur

D. Reach to a very small object or where accurate grasp is required

E. Reach to indefinite location to get hand in position for body balance or next motion or out of way

Table 5.3 (Continued)

Table II—Move—M

Distance Moved (in.)	Time TMU				Weight Allowance		
	A	B	C	Hand in Motion B	Weight (lb.) Up to	Factor	Constant TMU
¾ or less	2.0	2.0	2.0	1.7	2.5	1.00	0
1	2.5	2.9	3.4	2.3			
2	3.6	4.6	5.2	2.9	7.5	1.06	2.2
3	4.9	5.7	6.7	3.6			
4	6.1	6.9	8.0	4.3	12.5	1.11	3.9
5	7.3	8.0	9.2	5.0			
6	8.1	8.9	10.3	5.7			
7	8.9	9.7	11.1	6.5	17.5	1.17	5.6
8	9.7	10.8	11.8	7.2			
9	10.5	11.5	12.7	7.9	22.5	1.22	7.4
10	11.3	12.2	13.5	8.6			
12	12.9	13.4	15.2	10.0	27.5	1.23	9.1
14	14.4	14.6	16.9	11.4			
16	16.0	15.8	18.7	12.8	32.5	1.33	10.8
18	17.6	17.0	20.4	14.2			
20	19.2	18.2	22.1	15.6	37.5	1.39	12.5
22	20.8	19.4	23.8	17.0			
24	22.4	20.6	25.5	18.4	42.5	1.44	14.3
26	24.0	21.8	27.3	19.8			
28	25.5	23.1	29.0	21.2	47.5	1.50	16.0
30	27.1	24.3	30.7	22.7			

Case and Description

A. Move object to other hand or against stop
B. Move object to approximate or indefinite location
C. Move object to exact location

Table 5.3 (Continued)

Table III—Turn and Apply Pressure—T and AP

Weight (lb.)	Time TMU for Degrees Turned										
	30°	45°	60°	75°	90°	105°	120°	135°	150°	165°	180°
Small: 0 to 2	2.8	3.5	4.1	4.8	5.4	6.1	6.8	7.4	8.1	8.7	9.4
Medium: 2.1 to 10	4.4	5.5	6.5	7.5	8.5	9.6	10.6	11.6	12.7	13.7	14.8
Large: 10.1 to 35	8.4	10.5	12.3	14.4	16.2	16.3	20.4	22.2	24.3	26.1	28.2

Apply pressure case 1–16.2 TMU.   Apply pressure case 2—10.6 TMU.

Table IV—Grasp—G

Case	Time TMU	Description
1A	2.0	Pick up group—Small, medium, or large object by itself, easily grasped
1B	3.5	Very small object or object lying close against a flat surface
1C1	7.3	Interference with grasp on bottom and one side of nearly cylindrical object; diameter larger than $\frac{1}{2}''$
1C2	8.7	Interference with grasp on bottom and one side of nearly cylindrical object; diameter $\frac{1}{4}''$ to $\frac{1}{2}''$
1C3	10.8	Interference with grasp on bottom and one side of nearly cylindrical object; diameter less than $\frac{1}{4}''$
2	5.6	Regrasp
3	5.6	Transfer grasp
4A	7.3	Object jumbled with other objects so search and select occur; larger than $1'' \times 1'' \times 1''$
4B	9.1	Object jumbled with other objects so search and select occur; $\frac{1}{4}'' \times \frac{1}{4}'' \times \frac{1}{8}''$ to $1'' \times 1'' \times 1''$
4C	12.9	Object jumbled with other objects so search and select occur; smaller than $\frac{1}{4}'' \times \frac{1}{4}'' \times \frac{1}{2}''$
5	0	Contact, sliding, or hook grasp

Table 5.3 (Continued)

Table V—Position†—P

Class of fit		Symmetry	Easy to Handle	Difficult to Handle
1—Loose	No pressure required	S	5.6	11.2
		SS	9.1	14.7
		NS	10.4	16.0
2—Close	Light pressure required	S	16.2	21.8
		SS	19.7	25.3
		NS	21.0	26.6
3—Exact	Heavy pressure required	S	43.0	48.6
		SS	46.5	52.1
		NS	47.8	53.4

†Distance moved to engage—1″ or less.

Table VI—Release—RL

Case	Time TMU	Description
1	2.0	Normal release performed by opening fingers as independent motion
2	0	Contact release

Table VII—Disengage—D

Class of fit	Easy to Handle	Difficult to Handle
1. Loose—very slight effort, blends with subsequent move	4.0	5.7
2. Close—normal effort, slight recoil	7.5	11.8
3. Tight—considerable effort, hand recoils markedly	22.9	34.7

Table VIII—Eye Travel Time and Eye Focus—ET and EF

Eye travel time = 15.2 x T/D TMU, with a maximum value of 20 TMU.

where T = the distance between points from and to which the eye travels
D = the perpendicular distance from the eye to the line of travel T

Eye focus time = 7.3. TMU

Supplementary MTM Data

Tables 1 and 2 are supplementary data. For proper explanation and usage, refer to MTM Application Training Supplements No. 8 and No. 9.

Table 5.3 (**Continued**)

Table 1—Position—P (Supplementary Data)

Class of Fit and Clearance	Case of‡ Symmetry	Align Only	Depth of Insertion (per ¼″)			
			0	2	4	6
21 .150″–.350″	S	3.0	3.4	6.6	7.7	8.8
	SS	3.0	10.3	13.5	14.6	15.7
	NS	4.8	15.5	18.7	19.8	20.9
22 .025″–.149″	S	7.2	7.2	11.9	13.0	14.2
	SS	8.0	14.9	19.6	20.7	21.9
	NS	9.5	20.2	24.9	26.0	27.2
23† .005″–.024″	S	9.5	9.5	16.3	18.7	21.0
	SS	10.4	17.3	24.1	26.5	28.8
	NS	12.2	22.9	29.7	32.1	34.4

*Copyrighted by the MTM Association for Standards and Research. No reprint permission without written consent from the MTM Association, 9-10 Saddle River Road, New Jersey 07410.

†Binding—add observed number of AP.

Difficult handling—add observed number of G2.

‡Determine symmetry by geometric properties, except use S case when object is oriented prior to preceding M.

Table 2—Apply Pressure—AP (Supplementary Data)

Apply force (AF) = 1.0 + (0.3 x lb). TMU for up to 10 lb
= 4.0 TMU maximum for 10 lb and over

Dwell, minimum (DM) = 4.2 TMU	Release Force (RLF) = 3.0 TMU
AP = AF + Dwell + RLF	APB = AP + G2

Table 5.3 (Continued)

Table IX—Body, Leg and Foot Motions

Description	Symbol	Distance	Time TMU
Foot motion—hinged at ankle	FM	Up to 4″	8.5
with heavy pressure	FMP		19.1
Leg or foreleg motion	LM—	Up to 6″	7.1
		Each additional inch	1.2
Sidestep:			
Case 1—complete when leading leg contacts floor	SS-C1	Less than 12″	Use Reach or Move time
		12″	17.0
		Each additional inch	.6
Case 2—lagging leg must contact floor before next motion can be made	SS-C2	12″	34.1
		Each additional inch	1.1
Bend, stoop, or kneel on one knee	B,S,KOK		29.0
Arise	AB,AS,AKOK		31.9
Kneel on floor—both knees	KBK		89.4
Arise	AKBK		76.7
Sit	SIT		34.7
Stand from sitting position	STD		43.4
Turn body 45 to 90 degrees:			
Case 1—complete when leading leg contacts floor	TBC1		18.6
Case 2—lagging leg must contact floor before next motion can be made	TBC2		37.2
Walk	W-FT	Per foot	5.3
Walk	W-P	Per pace	15.0
Walk obstructed	W-PO	Per pace	17.0

Table 5.3 (Continued)

Table X—Simultaneous Motions

Motion		Reach			Move			Grasp			Position			Disengage	
	Case	A,E	B	C,D	A,Base	B	C	G1A G2 G4	G1B G1C	G4	P1S	P13S P2S	P1NS P25S P2NS	D1E D1D	D2
		W	W O	W O	W O	W O	* O	W	* W	* O	** E	** E D	** E D		** E D
Reach	A,E														
	B														
	C,D														
Move	A,Base														
	B														
	C														
Grasp	G1A,G2,G4														
	G1B,G1C														
	G4														
Position	P1S														
	P13S,P2S														
	P1NS,P25S,P2NS														
Disengage	D1E,D1D														
	D2														

*W Within the area of normal vision
  O Outside the area of normal vision
**E Easy to handle
  D Difficult to handle

☐ Easy to perform simultaneously

☒ Can be performed simultaneously with practice

▓ Difficult to perform simultaneously even after long practice. Allow both times.

Motions not included in above table

Turn—normally *Easy* with all motions except when *Turn* is controlled or with *disengage.*
Apply Pressure—May be *Easy, Practice,* or *Difficult* Each case must be analyzed.
Position—Class 3—always *Difficult*
Disengage—Class 3—normally *Difficult*
Release—always *Easy.*
Disengage—any class may be *Difficult* if care must be exercised to avoid injury or damage to object.

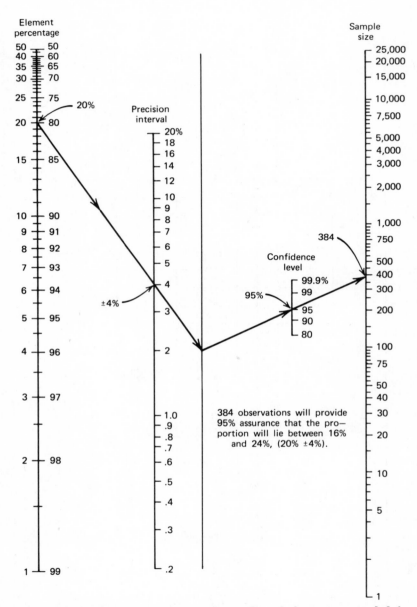

Figure 5.4. Nomograph for determining the number of observations needed for a given precision interval (absolute error) and confidence limits (relative error). (After Moskowitz, 1965.) To use the nomograph: (1) Estimate the average percentage

DEPENDABILITY OF OTHER METHODS
FOR ESTABLISHING WORK STANDARDS

Besides the establishment of work standards derived by stopwatch studies and PMTS, three other less frequently employed methods are available for the establishment of work standards. They are rated activity sampling, synthetic times, and physiological techniques.

Rated Activity Sampling

Work sampling was originated by Tippitt (1935), and from it rated work sampling was derived (Graham, 1966; Connolly, 1967; Minter, 1968; Gibson, 1970). Activity sampling is a technique by which a large number of instantaneous observations of machines, processes, or workers are made over a period of time. In rated work sampling an effectiveness rating is applied to each observed work element so that work standards can be derived.

Normally, an observer records (or takes a time lapse photograph for later analysis) the activity that is to be studied at intervals (varying usually from 15 to 30 min) and notes whether the machine, process, or worker is operating. The observer then applies a rating to the performance observed and proceeds by statistical calculation to determine the frequency and work standards for each element. In order to determine the number of observations required for a work sampling study, both the relative error and the absolute error have to be assessed from data such as that given in the nomograph (Figure 5.4).

From a nomograph, we can determine the absolute error (i.e., the accepted confidence interval) and the relative error (i.e., the tolerance error associated with the confidence interval). For example, if it is desired to have a work sample that represents 95 percent of all the working possibilities (i.e., absolute error) and if we want to be assured to the extent of ±4 percent (i.e., relative error) that the sample size will provide the required 95 percent confidence interval (i.e. absolute error), the number of required observations can be read from the nomograph as shown by the arrowed lines.

Both these errors can also be calculated from a mathematical equation

---

(mean value) of the element to be measured (e.g., 20 percent). (2) Select the required precision interval (e.g., ±4 percent). (3) Draw a straight line from the element size, through the precision interval, to the center reference line. (4) Select the required confidence level (e.g., 95 percent assurance). (5) Draw a straight line from the reference line, through the selected confidence level, to the sample size line, and read the required sample size (e.g., 384).

(from which the nomograph is derived) for the establishment of the required sample size. The required sample size is given by the following equation:

$$N = I^2 \frac{(1 - P)}{S^2 P}$$

where N = total number of random observations required (sample size)
    I = desired level of confidence interval (expressed in terms of standard deviation)
    P = percent (expressed as a decimal) occurrence, within the study, of an event
    S = desired level of relative accuracy (expressed as a decimal) for the confidence interval

Once the required number of observations have been collected to meet the desired accuracies, the data can be summarized for the derivation of work standards in the following way:

$$W = \left(\frac{T \times P \times I}{N} \right) \times (100 + A)$$

where W = work standard (per unit)
    T = total time of the entire work sampling study
    P = total working time (percent)
    I = mean rating index (percent)
    N = total number of items produced
    A = interference allowance (percent)

Synthetic Times

We derive synthetic times by building up the time for a job at a defined level of performance, either by totaling elemental times obtained previously from time studies and other jobs containing the elements considered (e.g., by the utilization of regression analysis*) or by other relevant statistical methods.

The following case study illustrates the use of synthetic time standards in industry.

The XYZ Company, which manufactures electric cables, has purchased

---

* Regression analysis refers to the relation between paired variables (e.g., the height and weight of individuals) where the relation is expressed in the form of an equation—the regression equation—which expresses the value of x to be expected for a given value of y, or the value of y for a given value of x. For the mathematics of regression analysis, see such standard textbooks as Kendall and Stuart (1967) and Davies (1961).

a new multicore winding machine. The machine is used for twisting together any of 50 different wires ranging in diameter from 0.001 to 0.01 in. It draws the wires from two or more drums up to a total of 128 drums (i.e., 127 different variations of the number of drums are possible). Since all manufacturing operators in the plant are working on financial incentives based on their production output above work standards, a work standard is required for the new machine. Hower, the company has only one of the machines (working two shifts, with one operator a shift), and therefore it is not economically feasible to time-study each job combination separately. But it does appear feasible to develop work standards based on time study for a limited proportion of the task variables. From these standards, mathematical equations could be developed for use in the establishment of synthetic times covering the other task variables and job configurations. Specifically, this was achieved in the following way.

Work standards, based on time study, were established for twisting 100-yard wires of 0.01 in. diameter made up of 2, 8, 16, 32, 48, 64, 86, and 128 wires, each wire being taken from a separate drum. When the logarithm of these work standards was plotted against the logarithm of the number of wires (i.e., drums) used, a linear relationship was established from which estimates of work standards for any number of 0.01-in. diameter wires could be derived. (The statistics and the mechanics of utilizing linear equations for estimation are dealt with in Davies, 1961.)

Because it was thought that the diameter of the wires might affect the work standard, wires with diameters of 0.001, 0.002, 0.004, 0.006, 0.008, and 0.01 in. were studies with 2, 8, 16, 32, 48, 64, 86, and 128 drums of wires. This study indicated that neither the time lost per wire drum because of wire breakage nor the time required to position the wire drum in the machine was affected by the number of drums involved. The time lost because of wire breakage increased linearly as the dimension of the wire decreased, whereas the proportion of time for drum changing increased linearly as the wire diameter increased. By the addition of these two equations, a new linear function was obtained expressing the increase in time per 100 yards of wire as the wire diameter decreased. For this, as in the previous case, a linear equation was fitted from which times for any wire dimensions could be assessed. The times taken from this equation, multiplied by the number of drums used, plus the time already determined for the 0.01-in. diameter wire, provided work standards in standard minutes per drum (for any number of drums and wire types).

Both synthetic times and rated work sampling methods are less dependable than either work standards derived by stopwatch or PMTS, since they are only approximations of the latter and an estimate can never be more dependable than the actual measure.

Physiological Techniques

The purpose of physiological techniques is to determine relaxation allowances and to establish work standards in terms of energy expenditure. Extensive experimental studies by Müller (1953) from the Max Planck Institute on a cross section of German industrial communities concluded that, in order to prevent fatigue, the overall rate of energy expenditure should not exceed 5 kcal/min. This is equivalent to walking on level surface at about 3.8 mph and covering 30 miles daily. (According to Müller, a person should be able to keep up this pace for six days a week, week after week and year after year.) This, in effect, is the expected average incentive work performance. Thus if the average efficiency index of operators working on incentive is 132 (as has been indicated earlier—Figure 5.3), then 3.8 kcal/min or walking at 2.9 mph is equal to the standard time. The establishment of work standards utilizing physiological techniques becomes more complex in the majority of real-world work situations because we must consider both muscular and psychological fatigue.

The establishment of work standards utilizing physiological techniques is highly time-consuming and expensive and can be executed only by highly skilled personnel. At the same time, it is a relatively dependable technique for establishing energy expenditure based work standards (Salvendy and Pilitsis, 1971a).

In conclusion, whenever a production performance or efficiency index is utilized as a criterion for evaluating training progress or for validating personnel selection processes, it is necessary to establish its overall *true* dependability and to indicate the methodology employed for the derivation of the criterion.

The phenomena identified in the following pages are those which affect the true dependability of a criterion; namely, nonlinearity and dimensionality of criteria.

CRITERION LINEARITY—FACTS OR ARTIFACTS?

When a criterion is used to validate a selection procedure (e.g., correlation of test scores with a criterion) or a training procedure, the linearity of the criterion is usually assumed, both in the design of the experimentation and in the statistical treatment of the data. Are such assumptions valid? This question can be examined along three avenues, namely:

1. Do criteria measures increase linearly? That is, if criterion data are collected on a large population, will there be a linear trend? Evidence

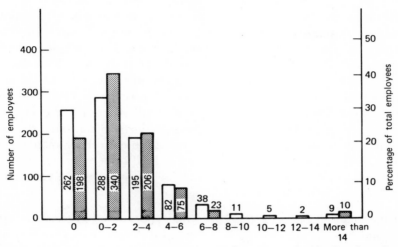

Figure 5.5. Distribution of absenteeism and latenesses of 852 female industrial operators, aged 17 to 62 ($\bar{x} = 38$) at an electromechanical concern. Solid bars: number of latenesses exceeding 3 min; open bars: number of unpaid single-day absences. The data were collected during one year through which all operators were working on financial incentives.

accumulated in industrial situations indicates that the criterion of rate of learning in a training school is exponential and not linear (e.g., Glover, 1966a, 1966b; Salvendy, 1969b). Exponential rather than linear trends were also found for criterion data such as lateness and absenteeism (see Figure 5.5). The general concept of the nonlinearity of the criterion has been stressed by a number of investigators (Kahneman and Ghiselli, 1962; Dunnette, 1963).

2. Does an equal percentage increase or decrease in a criterion measure at the lower end of the distribution have the same impact on an organization as the change at the higher end of the distribution? That is, does an increase in the productivity index from 80 to 100 have the same impact on the company as an increase from 100 to 120? Is an operator who has a productivity index of 160 worth twice as much to the company as an operator who has only 80? In the majority of industrial concerns, overhead costs exceed by far 100 percent of direct costs. However, an operator with a 160 productivity index does not consume twice the overhead as the operator with an 80 index (in the majority of cases, only 50 percent more); consequently, an operator with a 160 index is worth much more to his company than two operators each with an 80 index.

3. Does an equal increase or decrease in a criterion at the lower end of the distribution have the same physiological and psychological impact on the operator as a similar increase or decrease in the higher end of the distribution? The evidence indicates the contrary. For example, a person weighing 160 lbs walking at 2 mph expends 3.2 kcal/min, whereas walking at 3 mph (a 50 percent increase in productivity indices) requires only 4.4 kcal/min; a 4-mph walk consumes 5.8 kcal/min (Passmore and Durin, 1955). Thus, within the frequently utilized range of energy expenditures in industrial setups, the increase in the efficiency index does not relate linearly to the physiological changes resulting in the human system. Other experimental evidence (e.g., Salvendy, 1973) indicates, as well, that changes in production output do not relate linearly to psychological variables such as intellectual abilities.

In the majority of cases, then, it would appear that criteria are nonlinear and that the data should be analyzed that way; for example, when the subject population involves age as a primary criterion, the data would have to be grouped by age categories before analysis.

DIMENSIONALITY OF CRITERIA AND THEIR QUANTIFICATION

The question arises whether a single criterion associated with the job of an operator is descriptive enough to pinpoint on the one hand his satisfactoriness to his employer and on the other hand his satisfaction from the job.

The study by Yerkes (1921) on graphotype operators was probably the first to pinpoint the low correlation (.11) between output and accuracy; and Pond (1926) showed the low intercorrelations of four criteria and the highest output with foreman's ratings. These correlations of Pond ranged from the − .30s to the .50s and illustrate the multidimensionality of the criteria.

It was the work of Horst (1936a, 1936b) and Hotelling (1935, 1936) that made possible the effective mathematical combination of the criteria that should be derived which Bird (1931) named the "efficiency index." The mathematical development of these investigators, which is called canonical correlation, comprises the linear maximum correlation between the functions of two sets of variables having several possible linear combinations. Each pair of functions maximizes the correlation between the new pair of canonical variates, subject to the restriction that they be independent of previously derived linear combinations.*

Experimental evidence on the multidimensionality of criteria is available for nearly all occupational fields, such as sales (Rush, 1953); chocolate wrapper, assembly, and machine operators (Salvendy, 1968); and for the tradeoff function between quantity and quality of performance (Pew, 1969). Severin (1952) indicated, as a result of summarizing 150 studies in which correlations were reported between different measures of job performance, that the median of all correlations was .28—which indicates that it is impossible to substitute one measure of job performance for another without first knowing the degree of equivalence. This indicates the multi-dimensionality of criteria.

Similarly, in a study of 975 drivers and lorry-men employed by 27 organizations, Seashore, Indik and Georgopoulos (1960) found low inter-correlations betwen five job performance variables (productivity, effectiveness, rank-order, individual and station, and accidents and absences). They interpreted this as contradicting the validity of "overall job performance" as an unidimensional construction and as a basis for combining job performance variables into a single measure having general validity.

It can be said that merely the inclusion of a single criterion in a group of composite criteria is inadequate if the single criterion is either undependable or irrelevant for the purposes for which the composite criteria is to be used.

Besides the canonical correlation techniques, two other statistical methods frequently serve to cope with the dimensionality problem of criteria. These are factor analysis and discriminant analysis techniques.

Factor analysis is a term pertaining to a variety of procedures with the purpose of analyzing the intercorrelations within a set of variables, whereas the principal component technique of factor analysis determines the minimum number of independent dimensions accounting for most of the variance in the original set of variables (Harmon, 1960; Cooley and Lohnes, 1971). Although in certain cases factor analysis can make a significant contribution in the analysis of data (e.g., Vernon, 1950), the psychological and physiological meaning of the factors and their theoretical foundations is considered to be one of the weakest parts of this

---

* For the mathematics of canonical analysis and their utilization with computer analysis, see Hotelling (1935, 1936), Dubois (1957), Harris (1963), and Cooley and Lohnes (1971). The dimensional problems of criteria resulting from the mathematics of the canonical correlation are discussed by Ghiselli (1956).

technique (Thompson, 1939; Thurstone, 1947, 1948; Hull, 1951; Zangwill, 1965; Glaser, 1967).

McQuitty, Wrigley, and Gaier (1954) used this approach to isolate dimensions of job success in which, out of a descriptive inventory of 264 items, they extracted 23 factors that accounted for slightly more than 50 percent of the variance, while McCormick, Jeanneret and Mecham (1972) used the technique for job evaluation.

Discriminant analysis is a procedure for estimating the position of an individual on a line that best separates classes or groups (Cooley and Lohnes, 1971). This position is obtained as a linear function of the individual's N scores. It is further explored with examples in Chapter 6 dealing with validation of selection mechanisms.

VI

DEVELOPMENT
AND EVALUATION
OF PERSONNEL
SELECTION TESTS

OVERVIEW

The methods and concepts utilized to develop a test battery for personnel selection are discussed, with emphasis on commercially available tests, test manuals, and statistical–cost-benefit principles.

The manner of evaluating personnel selection tests is considered, and we pay particular attention to the use of norms and the importance of assessing the dependability and validity of test scores. Social implications of administering the same test to culturally advantaged and disadvantaged groups are related to test use, administration, and interpretation.

DEVELOPMENT OF THE TEST BATTERY

Test batteries in personnel selection are utilized to simulate, quantitatively and qualitatively, how a person would perform in a real-world situation. They may include psychological, physical, physiological, medical, social, and other tests. Obviously, before a real-world situation can be simulated, the task must first be analyzed (as described in Chapter 2). Once we know *what* has to be done, skills analysis (Chapter 3) is performed in order to determine *how* the task will be done. Information derived from both these analyses is the main source for the development of the test battery.

Naturally, the validity of the test battery (its success in predicting real-world performance) depends on how well the task and skills analyses

have been carried out, and on how effectively the resultant information has been used in the development of test battery. For maximum validity, a test battery must accurately simulate real-world situations. This statement assumes that *each* test in the battery is 100 percent dependable.*
In the majority of cases, however this is not a valid assumption; hence a completely valid test battery is rare indeed. The degree of validity depends on the magnitude of the reliability of each test within the battery. We can determine V, the maximum validity of a test battery by means of the following expression:

$$V = \frac{R_1 + R_2 + R_3 + \cdots + R_{n-1} + R_n}{N}$$

$$\times \frac{r_1 + r_2 + r_3 + \cdots + r_{n-1} + r_n}{n}$$

where $R_1, \cdots, R_n$ = reliability of the tests in the battery

r_1 = reliability of the criterion (e.g., coefficient of the correlation between odd and even days of production)

n = number of items in the criterion

N = number of tests in the battery

Thus V can be 1 only if all the tests in the battery and each of the items constituting the criteria have a reliability of 1. For example, suppose there are four tests in a battery with reliabilities of $R_1 = .60$; $R_2 = .70$; $R_3 = .78$; $R_4 = .92$; and three criteria are utilized with the following reliabilities: $r_1 = .45$; $r_2 = .60$; $r_3 = .75$. Then we can write

$$V = \frac{.60 + .70 + .78 + .92}{4} \times \frac{.45 + .60 + .75}{3} = .40$$

and the maximum validity of the test battery cannot exceed .40.

In making use of test battery, we can choose between either of the following two approaches, either individually or in combination:

1. Use of commercially available tests.
2. Construction of new tests.

Whichever method is utilized, we must begin by placing equal emphasis on the establishment of *relevant, dependable,* and *reliable* criteria for the task for which the test battery is to be employed as a predictive tool.

* Dependability encompasses reliability, homogeneity, constant and random errors, and chance effects associated with the measure being investigated rather than the individual performance studied.

Use of Commercially Available Tests

A vast amount of information can be had concerning commercial tests. The most comprehensive list, although not completely updated,* is to be found in the *Sixth Mental Measurements Yearbook*, edited by Buros (1965). This encyclopedic collection of more than 5000 pages covers a total of 2171 different tests (Table 6.1). Each entry includes a synopsis of the information in the test manual on the administration and use of the test, the name and address of the publisher, and the cost of the test. A comprehensive list of references on the construction, reliability, validity, and use of each test is provided with a brief (about 400 words) critical review by an authority (who is not the test developer) on the specific test considered. Valuable indices are provided for publishers, test titles, and authors of tests; there is also a classified index of tests.

Another excellent source to consult on the value, administration, reliability, and validity of the more frequently used tests is Super and Crites (1962). Although the book was published more than a decade ago, the majority of the material it covers has not altered significantly since then. This work provides a very comprehensive discussion on the use and value of some of the widely used tests, with a list of organizations from which specific tests may be obtained.

Table 6.1   Major Classifications of Tests Available Commercially as of mid-1964[a]

Classification of Tests	Total Number in Print
Personality	312
Vocations	307
Intelligence	243
Miscellaneous	229
Mathematics	201
English	184
Reading	164
Foreign languages	120
Science	109
Social studies	106
Sensory–Motor	57
Business education	50
Achievement batteries	41
Fine arts	28
Multiaptitude	20
Total	2171

* Just as this book went to press The Seventh Mental Measurements Yearbook, edited by Buros (1972) was published.

[a] From The Sixth Mental Measurements Yearbook, O. K. Buros, Ed., New Jersey: Gryphon, 1965, p. xxxiii.

Not all commercially available tests are scientifically sound, and no test should be adopted without the assurance that it is accompanied by a manual providing sufficient information to enable a qualified user to judge the usefulness and interpretation of the test. The standards described by the American Psychological Association (APA, 1966)* should be followed.

The part of this chapter dealing with test manuals should be consulted both by those who intend to use only commercially available tests and by those who intend to develop their own. Before a test is sold commercially, it should have been systematically developed and validated. The test manual should furnish information relative to its validation. For the individual who develops his own test, the knowledge of what should be in a test manual indicates the variables that should be considered during the test development.

It is usually safer and cheaper to use tests already available than to construct new ones, since the development of the test—and, particularly, the validation—are clearly major undertakings, requiring a number of lengthy and complex activities, as follows:

1. In order to accept a test as valid it is necessary to:

   (a) Secure a representative sample of subjects to take the test.

   (b) Test a variety of groups in order to cross-validate the predictive efficiency of the test.

   (c) Establish the reliability and dependability of the test.

   (d) Determine the relevance of performance criteria to the task being predicted (e.g., school grades, work output).

   (e) Establish the dependability and reliability of the criteria, as these affect the error variance of the validity coefficient.

2. Personnel who construct and validate new tests must be much more highly skilled than those who merely administer existing tests. Therefore, an effort must be made to secure the services of such individuals.

3. Construction and validation of a test usually takes several years; thus a new instrument cannot be utilized immediately for the selection of needed personnel, and long-range planning must be begun.

4. Since it costs significantly more to develop and validate new tests than to adopt commercially available ones, appropriate budgetary measures must be taken.

* A revision of these standards is under way. The third draft of "Standards for Development and Use of Educational and Psychological Tests" was published in the February 1973 issue of *APA Monitor* (4, 2, I–XV). Further information regarding the formal publication of the revised booklet can be obtained from the American Psychological Association, Inc., 1200 Seventeenth Street, N. W., Washington, D.C. 20036.

Consequently, there are only two cases when construction and validation of new rather than adoption of already available tests should be considered. These are:

1. When no "off-the-shelf" tests are available to assess and forecast the human traits required to perform a task.

2. When new information, concepts, or theories have been accumulated which, if incorporated into a test format, would provide test scores significantly more reliable and valid than those presently available. The One-Hole test (Salvendy, Seymour, and Corlett, 1970) is an example of such a methodological improvement.

The main factors to consider in the construction of a scientifically sound test are outlined below.

The Manual of a Personnel Selection Test

The same rules apply whether the construction of new tests or the modification of existing tests is being considered. In either case, a test published for commercial use should be accompanied by a manual that gives the qualified user sufficient information to judge the usefulness of the test and to interpret its data. The manual should make every reasonable effort to follow the recommendations outlined in Table 6.2, which are based on the Standards for Educational and Psychological Tests and Manuals developed by the American Psychological Association (APA, 1966). Table 6.2 could be used as a checklist both for test developers (in order to remind them of the operations they must perform in developing their tests) and for test users (as the basis for selecting scientifically sound tests).

Statistics of the Test Battery

The test items constituting a test or a test battery in personnel selection are selected on the basis of job analysis (see Chapter 2), skills analysis (see Chapter 3), and also frequently, by the "hunch" of the experimenter. Then the test is administered to a group of subjects for whom the test items were designed. Although ideally, all the applicants who apply for a job should be tested (so that the test can be evaluated against their subsequent performance), this is rarely practical. However, test scores and criterion measures should be analyzed for at least 100 personnel in order to assess both dependability and validity measures. Assuming that a satisfactory number of representative subjects has been tested, we arrive at the point of statistically analyzing the test results to determine if our test is valid and dependable.

Table 6.2   Items to be Included in Test Manual

I. Dissemination and interpretation

    A. Purpose and applications for which the test is recommended should be clearly stated.

    B. Qualifications required to administer and interpret the test correctly should be outlined.

    C. Periodic revision of the test and its manual should be made.

    D. For an abbreviated version of a test, new validation data should be reported.

    E. The test, the manual, record forms, and other accompanying material should assist users to make correct interpretation of the test results.

    F. Systematic errors arising from testing conditions should be discussed in relation to their probable magnitude and direction.

    G. Relationships should be stated quantitively, and it should be made clear whether the term "significant" is implied for practical situations, for statistical situations, or for both.

II. Dependability

    A. Dependability of the test should be reported and should apply for every score, subscore, or combination of subscores.

    B. The dependability sample should be described.

    C. Dependabilities should be expressed in terms of variances for error components, standard errors, of measurement, or product moment reliability coefficients.

    D. The extent to which test scores are stable should be indicated (i.e., the effect of repeating the test after lapse of time).

    E. Cross-dependability studies should be made and reported in the manual.

III. Validity

    A. Validities for each type of inference for which a test is recommended should be reported. For example, if a personality test is recommended as measuring both extroversion and neuroticism, evidence for separate validities for each inference is essential.

    B. The population for which the validity was established should be indicated, together with the adequacy of the sample studied.

Before the statistical procedures employed for this purpose are discussed, the user must be aware of the limitations of statistical methods. Some of these limitations are as follows:

1. The use of statistical techniques is or should be restricted to the mathematical assumptions underlying the characteristics of the data utilized. Violation of these assumptions may lead to misleading statistical results.

2. The phenomenon of "significance" in statistics (Kendall and Stuart, 1967), which is the usual basis for acceptance or rejection of test results, may be misleading.

Table 6.2   Items to be Included in Test Manual—Continued

C. The criteria should be described in terms of:
   1. Relevance
   2. Representativeness
   3. Dependability
   4. Dimensionality; that is, usually more than one measure is required to describe fully all the components of a criterion; thus using only a single criterion is frequently inadequate and may result in a misleading validity coefficient.
D. Central tendencies and variabilities of the sample should be described.
E. Where time limit tests are used to measure psychological attributes not specifically related to speed, evidence should be presented indicating the effect of speed on test scores and on their correlations with other variables.
F. Cross-validity studies should be conducted and the results reported in the manual.
G. Figures should be provided for content, construct, and criteria-related validities, and the type of validity discussed should be emphasized.

IV. Administration and Scoring
   A. Procedures for test administration and scoring should be written in sufficient detail and clarity to avoid administration and scoring errors.
   B. The test description should be clear enough so that the conditions under which norms, reliabilities, and validities were obtained could be duplicated.
   C. The test should be understood in the way the author intended.

V. Scales and Norms
   A. The scales on which scores are entered should permit the test results to be accurately interpreted and understood.
   B. Norms should refer to clearly described populations, to whom users of the test will wish to compare the persons tested.
   C. The number of cases on which the norms are based should be reported.
   D. Whether scores vary for groups differing on age, sex, ethnic origin, amount of training, and other equally important variables should be indicated.

(a) There may be a statistically significant relationship between two measures that has no theretical or practical meaning. For example, in a recent study (Salvendy, 1970) statistically significant differences ($p > .01$) occurred in the slope of the learning curves on the One-Hole test between left- and right-handed subjects. A further examination of the data revealed that the right-handed subjects had a 200 percent faster learning slope than the left-handed subjects. However, these differences were *practically* insignificant since the slopes of the left-handed and right-handed subjects were $-.006$ and $-.002$, respectively. Any conclusions drawn from this study regarding slope would be misleading, and it would appear to be more appropriate to say that, within the practice periods studied and in terms of practical implications, no learning occurred for either the left- or the right-handed subjects.

(b) The meaning of a statistical significance is affected by the "power of the test," which is a measure of the probability that a hypothesis may be wrongly accepted when it is false* (Kendall and Stuart, 1967, p. 164). The greater the power of the statistical tests utilized, the more confidence can be had in the statistical meaning of the significance. Typically, parametric tests (e.g., Davies, 1961; Kendall and Stuart, 1967) are more powerful than nonparametric instruments (Siegel, 1956; Walsh, 1968); and the fewer assumptions a test makes about the population and data studied, the less powerful the statistical test is.

(c) Statistical significances obtained on small sample sizes have to be interpreted with caution, specifically when the variances of the distributions are large.

(d) Statistically significant results are meaningful only if they can be explained in terms of real-world implications; otherwise, the results may be artifacts.

A number of statistical methods are available for the evaluation of a test battery. Our purpose here is not to review all the techniques available, nor to discuss the mathematical derivations and assumptions, but to indicate some of the more powerful statistical methods that can serve for this purpose. Naturally these statistical techniques can be utilized effectively only if their underlying assumptions are met.

A variety of statistical analyses of a test battery are feasible; one is illustrated in Figure 6.1. As a model of the procedure to be followed, the diagram is a step-by-step sequential evaluation, in which each step is a prerequisite for the next.

Initially, both the test battery and the criteria measures are selected intuitively on the basis of information derived from the job and skills analyses. At this stage of the experimentation, the numbers of test battery and criteria measures are larger than will ultimately be used when the test has been refined. This is because overlapping, redundant, and invalid

---

* A critical region of a statistical test must be judged by its properties both when the hypothesis tested is true and when it is false. Thus it can be said that the errors made in testing a statistical hypothesis are of two types: (a) it may be wrongly rejected when it is true, and (b) it may be wrongly accepted when it is false. These are known as type I and type II errors, respectively. The probabiltiy of a type I error is equal to the size of the critical region used, α. The probability of a type II error, which is a function of the alternative hypothesis considered, is denoted by β. This complementary probability, $1 - \beta$, is called the power of the statistical test of hypothesis.

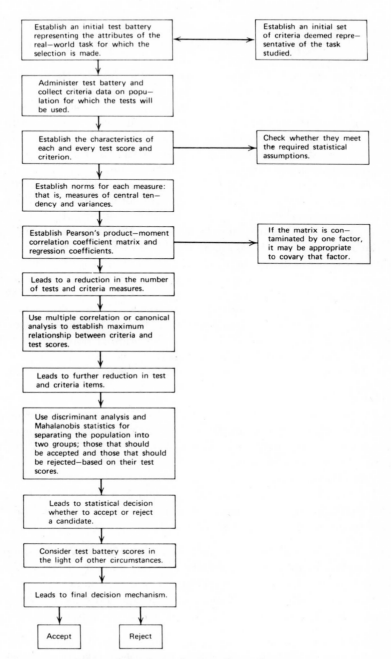

Figure 6.1.   Use of statistics for the evaluation of a test battery.

items have been included in the original test battery, and these must be eliminated—thus shortening the test and the test battery—before item analysis and other techniques are applied.

It is important that at the experimental stage data be collected on the population on which inferences will be made at the selection stage. Suppose, for example, that the tests are to be used eventually for selecting inexperienced personnel for training on a specific task. The experimental population then, must consist of untrained subjects, because test validities with experienced groups of subjects will be significantly different from and lower than those with trainee subjects (Ghiselli, 1966).

Because of the many asumptions of data characteristics underlying the use of parametric tests, such as Pearson's product-moment correlation and analysis of variance (Davies, 1961; Kendall and Stuart, 1967), it is mandatory that these assumptions be tested on the data considered before any statistical analysis is applied. If the underlying assumptions are met, then the next step in the statistical evaluation of a test battery may be undertaken. Otherwise, the data have to be converted,* or less powerful statistical tests, such as nonparametric statistics (Siegel, 1956; Walsh, 1968), have to be substituted. However, it is questionable whether a statistical procedure applied to converted data (e.g., logarithm of performance time) is directly applicable to the original nonconverted data.

The next step in the statistical analysis is the derivation of norms (i.e., test score distribution for a group, or type, of people). This has the following purposes:

1. To determine whether the tests and criteria are sensitive enough to discriminate among individuals. If they are not sensitive enough (e.g., if all the results are bunched at one end of the scale), they are of little value in the selection process and should be eliminated from the test battery or criteria measures.

2. To assess the relative standing of people in a group with regard to specific performance and behavior characteristics so that the statistical method of discriminant analysis (Rao, 1952) may be employed.

Measures of central tendency and variability are reported in norms, which may be expressed in a variety of ways (Figure 6.2), each way being most suited for a specific measure and circumstance.

Next in line is the establishment of interrelationships between and within the test battery items and criteria measures. Such a relationship

---

* For example, by taking the logarithm or reciprocals of skewed and nonhomogenous performance time distributions, frequently normal and homogeneous distributions of performance times can be derived (Salvendy, 1968).

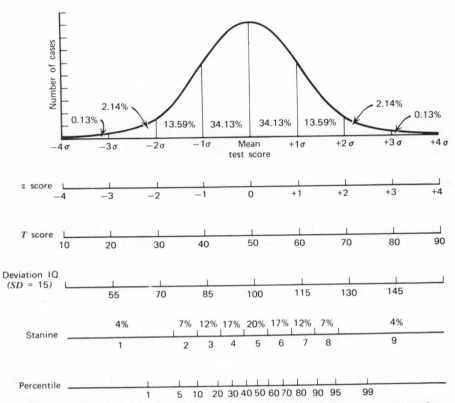

Figure 6.2. Relationships among different types of test scores used in describing norms in a normal distribution.

may be expressed in correlation* forms utilizing Pearson's product-moment correlation (Spearman, 1904), point biserial correlation (Thorndike, 1949), or other statistical measures depending on the data adopted.

From the resultant intercorrelation matrix, it is possible to derive the principal components (Cooley and Lohnes, 1971) that account for the most important test battery and criteria variables, thus resulting in a reduction in the original size of the test battery and criteria measures. This is accomplished by keeping the test measures that have the highest

* Correlation coefficients have to be interpreted in the light of the slope of the regression coefficient (Davies, 1961). A correlation coefficient accompanied by a regression slope of zero degrees is meaningless for a selection mechanism; the same correlation coefficient with a 45° slope could be a powerful instrument for personnel selection.

indirect correlation with the criteria measures and eliminating those having the lowest correlation. The highest indirect correlation is determined by the product of the direct correlation between two variables and the correlation of each of the variables with the already accounted one. For example, if a measure has a Pearson product moment correlation of .30 with the scores of a personality extrovert–introvert scale and .40 with those of a neurotic–stable scale, and the correlation between the two personality measures is .71, then the neurotic–stable scale has both a .40 direct and a .40 indirect correlation with the criteria (first starting with the highest direct correlation). The extrovert–introvert scale had a .30 direct correlation with the criteria and a .15 indirect correlation.*

When the correlation matrix is seriously affected by one dominating factor, such as age of the subjects on which data were collected, and the object of the study is to assess human performance and behavior, it is appropriate to extract the influence of the age factor from the correlation matrix, by analysis of covariance (Cochran, 1957). In this way the "true" performance of the subjects can be exhibited. These statistical manipulations of the data lead naturally to further reductions in criteria dimensionality and the size of the test battery (i.e., elmination of the age dimension).

The next stage in the analysis of test battery results is to assess the validity of the battery against the criteria for which the battery was developed. If only a single criterion is utilized, then multiple correlation, jointly with multiple regression analysis (Dubois, 1957) can be utilized; however, if a *set* of criteria measures was used in developing the test battery, then canonical correlation (Hotelling, 1935; 1936; Bartlett, 1941; Horst, 1961) must be employed, where the canonical correlation is the maximum correlation between linear functions of two sets of variables.

In either case, the relative weights (or the percentage of the total sum of squares) of each test item in the test battery must be established, and their statistical significance indicated, utilizing F-values. This process may enable further reductions in the test battery size by eliminating those test items which have only marginal contributions to the total sum of squares or to the criterion-oriented validity of the test battery.

A validity coefficient (relating test scores to criterion measures) that has not been established in the context of a conceptual structure provides no information about *why* the correlation is high or low or how the test

* Since the two personality measures have an intercorrelation of .71, 50 percent $[(.71)^2]$ of the extrovert/introvert scores has already been accounted for in the neurotic/stable score, and thus the .30 direct correlation is equivalent to only .15 indirect correlation.

measures might be improved. Therefore, *construct validity* is frequently used to evaluate the qualities of test measures. Construct validity, which is defined as evaluation by investigation of the qualities a test measures, aims at determining the degree to which certain explanatory concepts or constructs account for the results obtained.

Construct validity is studied both logically and empirically to check the theory underlying the test. The procedure involves three steps:

"First, the investigator inquires: From this theory, what hypotheses may be made regarding the behavior of persons with high and low scores? Second, he gathers data to test these hypotheses. Third, in light of evidence, he makes an inference as to whether the theory is adquate to explain the data collected" (APA, 1966).

If the theory fails to account for the data, it must be rejected or reformulated, or the test interpretation must be revised. For both fresh evidence is required if construct validity is to be demonstrated.

It should be emphasized that construct validity verifies theory, but it does not tell anything about the adequacy of the test as a selection instrument, apart from the adequacy of the theory on which the test may be based.

The determination of construct validity presents a set of methodological problems. Typically, the factors can be identified statistically by comparing the tests with other well-established instruments and by utilizing factor analysis techniques (Harmon, 1960), when the underlying statistical assumptions are met (Guilford, 1952); however, the psychological meaning of these factors may be obscure and controversial (Thompson, 1939; Thurstone, 1948; Glaser, 1967).

The last step in the statistical analysis of a test battery is to devise a mathematical decision mechanism process capable of recommending acceptance or rejection of an applicant based on his scores on the reduced test battery items. This can be accomplished by the adoption of discriminant analysis, utilizing Mahalanobis' statistic (for the statistical significance evaluation: Rao, 1952).

The procedure for employing Mahalanobics' statistic is as follows. Depending on the availability of and demand for personnel, a realistic cutoff point (e.g., a performance of 100) is established for criteria standards which all accepted applicants are expected to reach. Then the test battery scores of the experimental group are divided into two groups —one consisting of subjects who have test scores lower than the criterion demands, the other containing subjects with criteria scores higher than the minimum accepted. From the statistical analysis of the test battery

(Figure 6.1), scores of the two groups, a mathematical equation is developed with coefficients for discriminant function variables for each test score. A discriminant function constant or equation is then obtained for the complete test battery. Thus, from a statistical point of view, an individual is recommended for rejection when his total test battery scores yield, in the mathematical equation, a value lower than the discriminant function constant. Remember that the discriminant function can only be applied to the same sample population on which the discriminant function was tested (or to a similar one); the function cannot be applied to any other population about which the discriminant function has no prior information.

The decisions dictated by the discriminant function must always be interpreted in the light of other circumstances, including the economic, which sometimes modify the function or override the implications of this function.

Economic Considerations

An effective selection mechanism must be not only psychologically sound, socially acceptable, and medically harmless, it has to be economically oriented, as well. The economic component of a selection test may be viewed in a variety of ways; but the end product must be based on two highly interrelated factors: (1) optimal use of financial resources, and (2) maximum financial return on investment (the financial interpretation of validity coefficients).

Optimal Use of Financial Resources. Some of the basic economic considerations in selection test development are as follows:

1. The merit of a test in a test battery should be considered not only on its dependability, reliability, and validity, or on its contribution to the total sum of squares of the test battery but also on the total financial cost associated with the testing (e.g., time required to administer and interpret the test; the financial cost of using the test).

2. When a single test in a preliminary test battery has more than one score dimension, and each dimension has different validity coefficients, some of these contributing only marginally (e.g., 5 percent) to the total sum of squares, the possible inclusion of these items in the final refined test battery has to be decided on the basis of the following questions:

    (a) Does the addition of such an item decrease or increase the power (statistical significance) of the discriminant analysis function?

    (b) What is the additional work for the testee, if any, for collecting and analyzing the marginal test battery items?

From a strictly statistical viewpoint, marginal test battery items should not be included in the final test battery. However, when the cost of administering and scoring is minimal, their continued inclusion might well be justified, even if the items add only a little to the "power" of the test. Furthermore, when two test scores have similar dependability and validity values (their contribution to the sum of squares for identical performance or behavior measures), the test item with the least economic cost should be selected for the final reduced test battery.

Interpretation of the Validity Coefficient. It has been frequently pointed out (e.g., Hull, 1928) that the magnitude of a correlation coefficient (with special reference to validity) is not an adequate representation of the magnitude of the relationship between the two sets of variables under consideration. Thus a number of mathematical models (e.g., Hull's measure of efficiency, 1928) have been proposed as providing a more realistic representation of the magnitude of the relationship between two variables. With these mathematical models, the size of the correlation coefficient increases the extent to which one variable can be predicted from the other. Such a correlation coefficient, representing the validity of selection tests, is a linear function of the difference between two criterion means; that is, the mean for the group above the predictor cutoff and the mean for the population. This correlation coefficient, moreover, is equal to the proportional improvement over chance that is possible with each selection ratio (Brogden, 1946). Because of the linear function of the correlation coefficient, Brogden (1946) indicated that, for predictive efficiency, neither r^2 nor $E = 1 - \sqrt{1 - r^2}$ is the best index for practical significance; the value r is the most appropriate.

This approach does not take into account the relative size of the available labor force or the selection ratio (Taylor and Russell, 1939), which is the ratio between those applied and those selected. This ratio naturally varies according to the state of the labor market, which affects the efficiency of a testing program. The greater the selectivity, or lower the ratio percent selected, the higher will be the quality of the labor force (Figure 6.3). If it is assumed that the present employed labor force is 50 percent successful, a test battery validity correlation coefficient of .70 with a 90 percent selection ratio (out of 100 personnel, 90 are accepted) increases the percentage of personnel who would be successful by only 5 percent; but a selection ratio of 10 (out of 100 personnel, only 10 are accepted) increases (above chance effect) the percentage of those who would be successful by 45 percent, indicating that 95 percent of

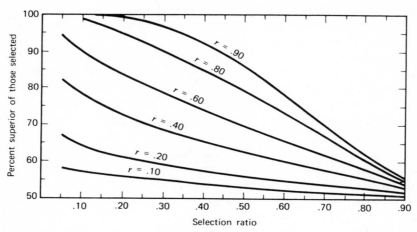

Figure 6.3. Proportion of "successes" expected through the use of personnel tests of given validity, when proportion of "successes" prior to use of test was .50. (From Taylor and Russell, 1939.)

those selected will be successful (Figure 6.3). In this case, when the percentage of satisfactory personnel is the measure of practical significance, r is more appropriate for selection test evaluation than either r^2 or E (Curtis and Alf, 1969).

Because of the limitations in the use of the Taylor and Russell (1939) selection efficiency concepts—namely, the inability of the model to handle more than two criteria dimensionalities—Curtis and Alf (1969) extended these concepts and developed a model capable of handling 18 criterion categories. Values for proportion expected in 18 criterion categories, 11 given values of r (from zero to one) and 14 different selection ratios are provided in tabular form (Curtis and Alf, 1969). From these tables it is evident that as r increases, the proportions in higher criterion categories generally increase, while the proportions in lower criterion categories generally decrease.

In a later study, Curtis (1971) put forward two different strategies for assessing predictive validity. One is a random strategy when the split is 50–50 (i.e., half the applicants are accepted, the other half rejected); the other is a blanket prediction (i.e., prediction of "high" or "low" criterion measures from test scores, when the criterion is split to "high" and "low" measures). In effect, the random strategy, which has more error of prediction than the blanket prediction, would tend to minimize the probability of erroneously accepting the hypothesis that the predictor has predictive value. The blanket prediction, on the other hand, would tend to minimize the probability of erroneously rejecting the same hypothesis.

As a result of experimental evidence, Raubenheimer and Tiffin (1971) indicated that the prediction of job success (i.e., predictive validity) can be improved beyond levels usually attainable through the more thorough study of the individuals for whom predictions are made. This was illustrated in their study by subgrouping a cross-validation sample ($N = 224$) into underpredictables* ($N = 25$), accurately predictables ($N = 51$), and overpredictables ($N = 25$). These subgroupings provided higher validity coefficients (.26, .48, and .40, respectively) than the .25 before subgrouping.

TEST EVALUATION

The cost effectiveness of a test, or a battery of tests, can be defined and evaluated from the combined information derived from the following sources:

1. Norms of each test (both general and local).
2. Norms of each criterion datum.
3. Reliability and dependability of each test and subtest.
4. Reliability and dependability of each criterion datum.
5. Validity coefficients of each subtest, test and of the complete test battery.
6. Administration and interpretation of each test and of the complete test battery.
7. Financial, psychological, and physiological costs associated with a testing program.
8. Social implications of personnel testing.

Each item listed may contribute to the cost effectiveness (or its reverse) of a testing program; thus in the following pages each of the eight categories is discussed separately, with regard to the strengths and weaknesses of the techniques utilized in the individual classification.

Scales and Norms

Both test scores and criteria measures are described by a variety of scales, including both raw and relative scores (Figure 6.2). Norms provide measures of central tendency and variability of each distribution

---

* *Underpredictable* implies that the applicant or subject had a lower test score and higher criteria measure than the average of his group. *Overpredictable* implies that the applicant or subject had a higher test score and lower criteria measure than the average of his group.

usually expressed in terms of percentile ranks or standard scores. Published norms for both criteria and test scores should be consulted in order to gain an insight into the distribution of scores. It is the local norms (e.g., those established by a company for its specific use) and not the published norms that matter, however, because the former contribute to the local validity of a testing program.

There are two principal ways in which test and criteria norms can contribute to the effectiveness of a testing program:

1. *Both test and criteria norms must be sensitive enough to discriminate between individuals* in the specific group for which the testing program applies. Assuming that individuals differ in many respects, discrimination between individuals should be achieved on each test score and criterion measure, except for the following cases:

(a) The test is too easy for the specific group studied, and everybody in the group scores high. For example, when a nonverbal intelligence test, the Raven's Progressive Matrices (Raven, 1960) was administered to 27 advanced graduate students, 24 scored the maximum of 60 and the other 3 scored 54 (.95 percentile score). The same test administered to 48 senior undergraduate college students, at another university, yielded a mean score of 39, with a standard deviation of 3. Thus the test was sensitive enough to discriminate among individuals of the undergraduate group but not in the advanced graduate group. In the same manner, a test may be too difficult for a specific group to perform. If this happens, no group members score on the test; or, if they score, the variability of the results is too small to be an effective tool to discriminate between individuals.

(b) The scores recorded on a test or job criterion are not representative of the performance of the task. When both job criteria and test scores are multidimensional, more than one measure is required to describe them. If, however, only one measure has been chosen and it represents only a fraction of the actual performance, the norms from this test are artifactual; that is, they do not represent the "true" traits and characteristics of the individual and thus cannot discriminate among individuals within a group.

(b) The score on the criterion measure is dictated not by the capability of the individual but by supply of work. For example, if a number of operators are working on items supplied by a conveyor belt, the speed of the belt is naturally constant for the entire group. Thus no individual differences in criteria productivity can be assessed reliably.

2. Where there are separate subgroups within the group, it may be necessary to treat their normative data individually. For example, norma-

tive data may be collected for individual subgroups: females or males, trainees or experienced workers, members of different ethnic groups, individuals with various levels of education and different occupations. If the collection process is thus broken down, both the individual variables contributing to high or low scores on the test or criterion and the degree of homogeneity of the sample studied can be determined. If there are no statistical and practical differences between the subgroup norms, they can be combined into a single norm having a homogeneous variance, and the data can be validated in this way.

On the other hand, if there are significant differences between the subgroup norms, each subnorm must be validated separately and the individual validity coefficients must be determined. Under such conditions, to combine the separate norms and validate the entire set of data as one distribution could provide false validity coefficients because of the nonhomogeneity of the variance.

Dependability of Test Scores and Criteria Measures

In order to achieve dependable test scores and criteria measures, which are essential in order to derive true validity, information is required on the reliability coefficient, homogeneity, transferability, and constant error. Let us now discuss these individually.

The *reliability coefficient* is a measure of consistency determined by the extent to which a second administration of the same test (to the same people as in the first administration) provides the same results; that is, the correlation coefficient between two administrations or repetitions of the same test. To save time, the correlation between two halves of one test (the split-half method) is often substituted.

Test–retest reliabilities define error variance only when there is an appropriate interval of time between tests. Immediate retest results, although often utilized, are not recommended when speed of performance is a predominant feature in the test. Test reliability is affected by the length of the test when the split-half reliability method is utilized; therefore a correction taking into account the full length of the test, is presumably accounted for by the Spearman–Brown prophecy formula (Guilford, 1954):

$$R_{nn} = \frac{nR_{11}}{1 + (n-1)R_{11}}$$

where R_{nn} = reliability predicted n times as long as the one for which
data are available
R_{11} = known reliability coefficient
n = amount by which the variable measure is increased

It must be emphasized that this formula has no physiological or psychological basis; it does not take into account fatigue and boredom, and it has no provision for including the number of items constituting the original test. Because of the last factor, this formula can at best be used only for time limit tests and not work limit tests.*

Again with regard to the Spearman–Brown correction formula, no consideration is given to whether the test is performed with or without intervals. Tiffin and Asher (1948) increased the Purdue Pegboard's reliability by trebling the original test length and introducing two intervals, and Bass and Stucki (1951) increased the reliability of the same instrument by doubling the test length without the introduction of an interval. A shortcut method for finding split-half reliability was developed by Rulon (1939), in which the estimate of the proportion of the total variance due to random error was subtracted from the total variance to be explained.

Hoyt (1941) was opposed to estimating the reliability of a test by the split-half method on the grounds that it ". . . is only one of many possible ways of splitting a test, [it] may be an unlucky division and may result in either an overestimate or an underestimate of the coefficient of reliability" (p. 155).

The Kuder–Richardson (1937) formula establishes reliability from a single administration of a test. It involves analysis of item variance, which provides the mean of all the possible split-half reliability coefficients. The Kuder–Richardson formulas are sensitive to, and their validity is affected by, the level of homogeneity of the data (Cureton, 1957). They provide reliability coefficients lower than those obtained with other measures (Guttman, 1945).

Reliabilities of personnel tests can also be derived by utilizing analysis of variance (advocated by Hoyt, 1941) or time serial analysis (advocated by Holtzman, 1963). In time serial analysis, the main emphasis is placed on the order of appearance of the events in a test.

An evaluation of the meaning and interpretation of test reliability has been outlined by Cronbach (1947); and some reliability techniques (e.g., analysis of variance) attempt to assess also the homogeneity of the test.

Homogeneity is the extent to which: (*a*) different parts of a test measure the same thing, and (*b*) different parts of a test are composed of similar constituents throughout. The utilization of factor analysis to

---

* In work limit tests, the variable studied is the time required to complete the test; in time limit tests, the variable studied is the nature of test performance or response within the time limit allowed for the test completion. The former method of testing may be used when speed of testing is of prime concern, and the latter method may be used when accuracy rather than speed is of importance.

assess the homogeneity of the test was advocated by Vernon (1950); Corlett, Salvendy, and Seymour (1971) advocated high-speed filming as a tool in the study of the internal reliability (i.e., random effects associated with the test performance which are more inherent in the test than in the individual tested) of psychomotor tests.

In assessing *transferability*, we attempt to learn the extent to which a test continues to measure the same thing when applied to different groups divided according to age, occupation, education, ethnic origin, sex, and other equally important categories.

A *constant error* is an error that appears consistently in repeated measurements. Suppose, for example, that the tire used for a car is larger than the size recommended by the manufacturer. Since the larger tire has a larger circumference (e.g., + 10 percent), each revolution of the wheel covers a distance 10 percent longer than that of the recommended tire. Thus the car speedometer, in this case, will have a constant error which shows 10 percent higher speed than the actual speed of the car. This 10 percent error will be present in repeated measures as long as the same tire is used.

Dependability of test scores and criteria measures is reflected by the following qualities:

1. Dependability of the testing instrument.
2. Intraindividual variability.

These two are not necessarily independent of each other, since intraindividual differences are the product of both test and individual characteristics, and vice versa. These individual characteristics (listed in Table 6.3) may contribute in a variety of ways to the differences in performance on a specific test.

The dependability of the testing instrument may be evaluated by several methods (Guion, 1965; Anastasi, 1968); namely, methods based on repeatability, homogeneity, transferability, and constant error. The choice among them depends on the nature and structure of the test and on the dependability dimension to be established. Since the majority of the tests have a multidimensional structure, more than one dependability measure is required for the assessment of the complete structure of the test.

Test Validity

Test validity is the degree to which the test is capable of achieving certain aims. Usually, these aims can be categorized under three headings: content validity, criterion-related validity, and construct validity.

Table 6.3   Possible Sources of Variance in Performance on a Given Test[a]

I. Lasting and general characteristics of individual

    A. Level of ability on one or more general traits, which operate in a number of tests.

    B. General skills and techniques of taking tests.

    C. General ability to comprehend instructions.

II. Lasting but specific characteristics of the individual

    A. Specified to the test as a whole (and to parallel forms of it).

        1. Individual level of ability on traits required in this test but not in others.

        2. Knowledge and skills specific to particular forms of test items.

    B. Specific to particular test items. The "chance" element determining whether the individual knows a particular fact. (Sampling variance in a finite number of items.)

III. Temporary but general characteristics of the individual (Factors affecting performance on many or all tests at a particular time.)

    A. Health.

    B. Fatigue.

    C. Motivation.

    D. Emotional strain.

    E. General test-wiseness (partly lasting).

    F. Understanding mechanics of testing.

    G. External conditions of heat, light, ventilation, etc.

IV. Temporary and specific characteristics of the individual

    A. Specific to a test as a whole.

        1. Comprehension of the specific test task (insofar as this is distinct from I.B).

        2. Specific traits or techniques of delaing with the particular test materials (insofar as this is distinct from II.A.2).

        3. Level of practice on the specific skills involved (especially in psychomotor tests).

        4. Momentary "set" for a particular test.

    B. Specific to particular test items.

        1. Fluctuation and idiosyncrasies of human memory.

        2. Unpredictable fluctuations in attention or accuracy, superimposed on the general level of performance characteristic of the individual.

V. Variance not otherwise accounted for (chance).

    A. "Luck" in selection of answers by "guessing."

[a] After Thorndike (1949).

244

Content Validity. According to the American Psychological Association, content validity is

". . . demonstrated by showing how well the content of the test samples the class situations or subject matter about which conclusions are to be drawn. Content validity is especially important for achievement and proficiency measures and for measures of adjustment or social behavior based on observation in selected situations" (APA, 1966, p. 12).

For example, content validity could be the degree to which performance on the Purdue Pegbord (Tiffin and Asher, 1948) measures the claimed (Purdue Pegboard, 1948) finger and arm dexterity required for light manual operation. Performance on the Purdue Pegboard basically consists of reaching with the hand to pins, collars, or washers on a tray, moving the items, and positioning them with the hands into holes or onto pins with close tolerances. These activities, of course, are only a sample of what might be encountered in the real-world situation. The question that must be asked is, How representative is this sample of real-world situations? To define, "representative," let us consider a group of people having a high performance on the sample of real-world tasks (in this case, the Purdue Pegboard). If the same group also exhibits high performance on other tasks in the sampled real-world situation, such as manipulating pins with tweezers in a watch factory (which is analogous to the activity performed in the O'Connor Tweezer Dexterity test: O'Connor, 1928), the sample is considered to be representative.

When the content of the test (i.e., its content validity) is not directly related to the criterion measure, a test can have simultaneously high content validity and low predictive validity. Therefore, information on the content validity of a test is of extremely limited value as a concept for personnel selection tests. However, the importance of content validity emerges in criterion measures. Since tasks are multidimensional, no single task criterion is representative of all the characteristics involved. Consequently, the utilization of a number of criteria does not necessarily make for a representative sample of the performance on the task, although the correlation between these criteria and test scores determines the predictive value of the test. If the content validity of the test criteria is low, the standard error of the predictive validity coefficient will be high; if content validity is high, the standard error of the predictive validity coefficient will be low.

A number of statistical tools such as multiple regression and factor analysis can be used in attempting to assess content validity objectively. This is important because content validity represents a subjective evaluation of the criteria; the items entering into the factor analysis study are chosen largely by intuition and subjectivity, and the possible impact on content validity of the items that have not entered into the factorial study naturally cannot be assessed.

This can be illustrated by the results of a series of factor analytic studies by Fleishman and his associates, in which the investigators wanted to determine, from a study of psychomotor skills, whether these skills are specific (to a task), general (to all tasks), or classifiable into categories of skills. All the studies supported the last hypothesis, but each had different implications (i.e., different factors were identified from different studies). For example, in one study (Fleishman and Hempel, 1954b), 12 factors of psychomotor skills were identified from the inter-relationships of 38 tests. When the number of tests studied was decreased to 23 (Fleishman and Hempel, 1956) or to 19 (Fleishman, 1953b), only 9 factors were identified; and when the number of tests, in another study (Fleishman and Hempel, 1954b), was reduced to 15 tests only 5 factors were identified.

However, the number of factors identified in a study is not directly related to the number of the tests studied, but rather to the characteristics of these tests. For example, in a study utilizing 21 tests (Fleishman and Ellison, 1962) only 5 factors were identified, whereas in another study (Fleishman, 1953b), where only 19 tests were utilized, 9 factors were identified.

This reemphasizes the need for careful selection of test items and their content validation, through factor analysis of the test correlations. If, against all reason, an attempt is made to assess test scores or items that have not entered into the factorial study, misrepresentation of the content validity of the test studied could result. It must also be recognized that the interpretation of factor meanings is highly subjective, and the data on which those factors are based frequently do not satisfy the assumptions underlying the use of factor analysis (Guilford, 1952).

Criterion-Related Validity. We demonstrate "criterion-related validity" by comparing the test scores with one or more of the external variables considered to provide a direct measure of the characteristic or behavior in question. This comparison may take the form of an expectancy table or, more commonly, a correlation relating the test scores to a criterion measure" (APA, 1966, p. 13).

Criterion-related validity is essentially of two types: predictive and concurrent.

1. *Predictive validity,* which is defined by the degree of the relation between test scores and some *future* performance or behavior on selected

criteria, is a forecast from scores of tests administered to determine how a person would perform in a given situation in the future. This forecast can be made from one test and one score, one test and many scores, or many tests and many scores. Predictive validity is important in selection for academic achievement, vocational success, and favorable reactions to therapy.

Predictive validity is determined by the "follow-up" method, in which a test is given to all applicants over a period of time but is not used for selection–rejection purposes. Performance data are collected and compared statistically with the applicants' test scores. Of course, once the predictive validity of a test has been established, test scores are no longer of interest only to research workers. For example, they become of prime concern to the applicant when they are used to make acceptance–rejection decisions.

Although the foregoing method of determining the predictive validity of a test is the one most frequently used, it has the following shortcomings:

(a) In a validation study of this nature, it is almost always true that all the applicants know that their test scores do not affect the decision of whether they are hired. Therefore, the achievement motivation of these individuals is not as high as may be expected as when test scores do affect their hiring (as would be the case after the test has been validated and put into operational use). Consequently, motivational factors within these two situations might be significantly different.

(b) No evidence is available on how applicants who withdrew, or were rejected prior to test, would have scored on the predictive task criteria.

(c) A significant limitation of the method is that it is seldom feasible in a real-world situation to hire all applicants in order to validate test–criteria comparisons for a total population of applicants.

2. *Concurrent validity* is assessed by the degree of relationship between test scores and immediate performance or behavior (e.g., training criteria) on selected criteria. The essential difference between concurrent and predictive validity is that the former makes use of immediate criteria (i.e., training scores) whereas the latter uses ultimate criteria (i.e., performance on the job after training). Concurrent validity is utilized to assess initial rather than ultimate performance and behavior, such as personality and psychiatric analysis of behavior or initial performance of an employee in a training school of an industrial corporation.

The most comprehensive statistical analysis of criteria-related validation of personnel selection tests utilized from 1919 to 1964 was reported

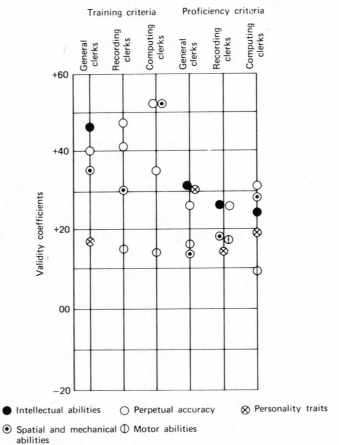

Figure 6.4. Differences in the validity coefficients of tests between training and proficiency criteria for the clerical occupations. (After Ghiselli, 1966, p. 38.)

by Ghiselli (1966). This analysis indicates that for all jobs and tests as a whole, training criteria yielded a coefficient of validity of .30, whereas for the proficiency criteria it was only .20 (see Figure 6.4). The large spread of validity coefficients of given tests for particular jobs is plotted in Figure 6.5, and Table 6.4 outlines the plausible causes for these large spreads.

Construct Validity. We evaluate construct validity by investigating what qualities a test measures, that is, by determining the degree to which certain exploratory concepts or constructs account for performance on

Table 6.4   Items Bearing on the Magnitude of the Coefficient of Criteria-Related Validity

1. Low dependability, reliability, and consistency of the criteria.
2. Low validity of the content and construct of the criteria.
3. Low dependability, reliability, and consistency of the test.
4. Deviations from optimal testing time (Horst, 1954; Horst and MacEwan, 1956).
5. Work-limit test have higher reliability than time limit tests (Fleishman, 1953a).
6. Inadequate test administration (Ghiselli, 1966).
9. Small sample size.
8. Narrow spread in the traits of the testees.
9. Proficiency criteria yielding lower validity coefficients than trainee criteria (Ghiselli, 1964, 1966).
10. Later scores on a test being more valid than earlier results (Salvendy and Seymour, 1972)

the test (APA, 1966, p. 13). The assessment of construct validity is used most frequently with projective techniques; it is of less consequence with psychomotor tests because the concepts involved in psychomotor abilities are more clear-cut.

The evaluation of construct validity can be achieved by three methods:

Method I

A. Generation of hypothesis regarding the behavior of persons with high and low scores on a test.
B. Collection of data to test the hypothesis in A.
C. As a result of B, inferences are made regarding the adequacy of the theory to explain the data collected.

Method II

Assessment of what a test measures by means of correlating the test scores with the scores from other tests validated on the same population.

Method III

Checking the hypothesized qualities in a given test against empirical performance in a situation that should require those qualities. If it is hypothesized, for example, that high performance on a certain psychomotor test indicates probable high performance on fine manual tasks, such as computer memory wiring, this inference can be checked by placing individuals in an experimental situation involving computer memory wiring and observing whether their performance corresponds to the hypothesis.

Thus construct validity is studied in order to better understand the psychological and physiological qualities measured by a test and to yield

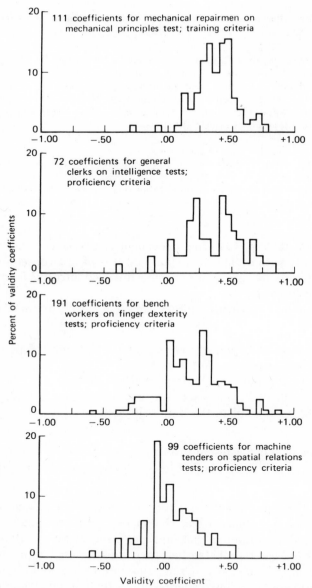

Figure 6.5. Examples of variation in validity coefficients of given tests for particular jobs. (After Ghiselli, 1966, p. 29.)

information about *why* a correlation between test scores and criteria is high or low. Presumably, if the reason for a low correlation can be determined, it would be possible to improve test score measurements by selecting or developing test items more representative of criterion qualities.

However, despite these methods, understanding of the psychological qualities being measured by a test is more a function of subjective analysis and intuition than of objective determination. A typical example is the so-called intelligence test. First, how do we define intelligence? Probably the safest answer is that intelligence is what is being measured by an intelligence test. What then, are the psychological qualities of the intelligence test? The answer is that these are the qualities inherent in the test—a completely tautological answer.

All three aspects of validity (content, criteria-related, and construct) are independent but are usually interactive; all three are relevant to all types of tests and are required for full validation of any test. For example, criteria-related validity frequently serves to predict academic success from intelligence and aptitude tests; yet the type of aptitude measured is often assessed from the content (content validity) of the items, and the place of the aptitude within the system of human abilities is derived from the correlation with other tests—concurrent validity.

SOCIAL IMPLICATIONS OF PERSONNEL TESTING

The use of personnel tests has in many instances been limited because of the public's recently expressed misgivings about personnel testing (Fiske, 1967). Indeed, there seems to have been an overall antitest revolt associated, on the one hand, with the invasion of privacy resulting from communication of test results and, on the other hand, with the negative impact of personnel testing on many of the culturally disadvantaged.

The Culturally Disadvantaged

It is by now well documented in the United States that the "culturally disadvantaged" (e.g., inner city blacks and Chicanos, and American Indians) usually score lower on tests than do the "advantaged" (Lucas, 1953; Campbell, 1964; Dugan, 1966; Tenopyr, 1967; Kirkpatrick, Ewen, Barrett, and Katzell, 1968) and that this difference is due to environmental factors rather than to innate differences (Campbell, 1965, Lockwood, 1966). However, as a result of extensive experimentation and review, Jensen (1969) concluded that environmental factors are less important in determining intelligence (IQ) than genetic factors, and he indicated that prenatal influences may well contribute the largest environmental influence on IQ. Thus, according to Jensen, *social class and racial variations in intelligence cannot be accounted for by differences in environment but must be attributed partially to genetic differences,* and he wrote that "extreme environmental deprivation can keep the child from performing up to his genetic potential, but an enriched educational program cannot push the child above that potential" (p. 2).

Kirkpatrick (1968) and his co-workers, following a recent series of extensive comparative studies on whites, blacks, and Puerto Ricans, found that in many testing situations the latter two ethnic groups are unfairly discriminated against because the majority of the presently available personnel tests have been developed on white, middle-class population. This is to say that the average criterion performance of the disadvantaged ethnic group would be underestimated from their test scores, in comparison to the advantaged ethnic group. This bias presumably resulted from having different regression lines with different intercepts for the advantaged and the disadvantaged groups. The implications are that separate test validity coefficients and regression lines have to be established for each ethnic group (i.e., validity data obtained on one ethnic group cannot be assumed to be equivalent, or similar, for another ethnic group), or, better still, culture-free tests should be developed.

TEST ADMINISTRATION

The manner in which tests are administered may affect the test scores and the resultant dependability and validity of the test. Table 6.5 presents the general guidelines in test administration.

Table 6.5   Ten Commandments for Effective Test Administration

1. Put testee at ease, and avoid a formal testee-to-tester relationship.
2. Ensure that testee is in good health (if the purpose of the test is not to measure ill health).
3. Provide an effective workplace layout with respect to such environmental factors as: (*a*) light, (*b*) audition, (*c*) climate, and (*d*) anthropometry.
4. Keep test results confidential.
5. When a test battery is utilized, establish a sequence of test administration with the least amount of transfer (behavior and skills) from one test to another.
6. The social impacts of group versus individual test administration should be considered.
7. The financial cost of testing individuals must be justified on the basis of the return on investment, which can be viewed in terms of increase in the quality of the labor force, leading to increased productivity and effectiveness.
8. Ensure that the test administrator has the required qualities, knowledge, and qualifications to administer the tests.
9. Ensure that all testees are given the test at the same academic and professional stage of their career and at the same maturity level, providing they all have a joint specific objective.
10. Ambiguity and testee bias resulting from test administration should be eliminated.

Use of the Test Battery

Because individual traits are often multidimensional (e.g., Anastasi, 1968) more than one measure may be required to describe, measure, and predict them. Since no single test can assess dependably the multidimensionality of an individual, more than one test (a test battery) is required.

However, a *test battery only supplements other employment procedures: it is not a substitute for them.* Test results always must be viewed in the light of other circumstances that could override the implications of the tests. Furthermore, it is fundamentally incorrect and misleading to assume, as some test administrators do, that an acceptable high validity coefficient will be obtained if a number of single tests are combined into a battery. Before any single test can be combined with other tests to constitute a battery of tests, each test must have demonstrated its dependability and validity. The combination of nondependable and invalid single tests into a battery does not, and will not, make the test battery dependable and valid. In order to secure the highest test battery validity with the lowest financial cost, the interrelationships (or correlations) between an individual's test scores within the test battery should be minimal; ideally, these relationships should approach zero. Under these conditions, each test could contribute *directly* to the validity of the test battery, since each test measures different traits and behavior. On the other hand, if the correlation coefficient between two sets of test scores is high, it implies that both tests measure, to a great extent, the same phenomenon.

Typically a test battery is used for three purposes, which may be outlined as follows.

1. *Guidance.* The recommendation to individuals of which occupations would suit them the best, so that they can orient their career training accordingly. This process has certain limitations, including the following:

(a) Guidance is limited in scope, since it directs individuals only to the occupations whose traits are represented in the test battery.

(b) Guidance, especially in adolescence, has low validity because of changes within the individual's trait structure as a result of aging (Bird, 1931; Kay, 1954; Welford and Birrin, 1965; Salvendy, 1972).

(c) Subjective preferences of individuals, associated with high achievement motivation, frequently override the outcome of the test battery.

This is well illustrated in the case of a colleague of one of the authors. In 1953, after graduating from high school, the individual went for career guidance to New York City where, at the conclusion of a long battery of tests, the counselor recommended that he be trained as an electronics technician. After long meditation, he turned down this suggestion and enrolled in a university to work toward his medical degree. Now he is a noted professor of plastic surgery who finds his work highly rewarding and satisfying—not to mention substantially more profitable financially than that of an electronics technician.

2. *Selection.* When the number of applicants exceeds the job openings available, some personnel are selected and accepted for the job, and others are rejected. In selection, individuals are considered only for a limited number of specific occupations; the dimensionality of the human traits and, consequently, the test battery used to predict them, is markedly smaller than that required in guidance.

3. *Placement.* There are two types of placement:

(a) Analogous and concurrent with the process of selection (i.e., an individual is selected for a specific job).

(b) A continuation of the selection process. That is, after an individual has been selected and hired by an organization, the company must decide what specific job to assign to him. A typical example of this is the person who is hired as a management trainee but will have to be placed on a specific job within the organization after the completion of training. The placement process also occurs when a job opening is to be filled with personnel already employed by the organization. This is frequently done not in terms of the level and suitability of the individual's traits and abilities for the specific task in question, but rather on a seniority basis. Placement under this condition is obviously nonscientific; it fails to make optimal use of human resources and reduces employees' achievement motivation.

Use and Interpretation of Test Results

The value to productivity of any scientific instrument, and specifically of the personnel testing process, depends on *who* uses the instrument, *how* it is used, and *what* methods are employed to *evaluate* and *interpret* the results. "Who" applies to the qualifications of the test administrator and interpreter, whereas "how" applies to the purpose and the context within which tests are used. The *evaluation* process is related to the statistical quantification of test results, whereas *interpretation* deals with the decision processes made as a result of test score evaluations.

Although the four above-mentioned phenomena associated with personnel testing are highly interactive, for simplicity of presentation each is dealt with separately below.

Some of the better-documented manuals accompanying personnel tests

give information on who should administer and interpret these instruments. However, the majority of the tests manuals do not provide this information, which is crucial in deriving the optimal use of the tests. The presentation of test administration procedures in the manual should be clear enough to allow the test user to duplicate the administration conditions under which the norms and the data on dependability and validity were obtained.

Thus it is essential that the person tested understand the test task exactly as the author of the test intended. To achieve this purpose, the test manual should indicate the required qualifications for administering and interpreting the test properly. The following categories of skills required to administer and interpret tests, identified by the American Psychological Association (APA, 1950), are to be considered as discrete rather than continuous:

1. Substantial understanding of testing and supervised experience in the use of the tests being administered.

2. Some technical knowledge of test construction and use.

3. Orientation specific to the organization and tests used. In this category might be included psychomotor tests that can be administered, scored, and interpreted with the aid of the manual and an orientation course.

The interpretation of test scores has two dimensions: one is to the testee, knowledge of results, or the lack of it; the other is to the tester, as a decision mechanism. The latter must be viewed in terms of an overall decision mechanism approach, discussed earlier. The impact of the interpretation of test results has been the subject of numerous publications. From these it appears that when the test scores are favorable, their interpretation to the testees is advantageous; otherwise, the same event is disadvantageous. However, Rothney (1952) has indicated that the interpretation of test scores during counseling interviews does not seem to cause significant negative or disturbing reactions. His results were based on a study of 869 high school sophomores, who were randomly distributed into experimental and control groups. Rothney's investigation, like most of the others that have been published, dealt only with the overall group tendencies and did not consider separately the possible impact of interpretation on individuals in the group studied.

Computer-Based Automated Testing Systems

Many personnel tests involve highly trained personnel who spend a considerable amount of time for relatively low returns in terms of relevant and useful information. Miller (1968) argued that automation of certain aspects of personnel testing, especially in clinical psychology, could serve to increase their reliability and validity, because control would be gained over the test administration. Moreover, the tests could be administered more rapidly and the psychologist's direct involvement in testing would be reduced, which is desirable because many tests take a long time to give and to score.

Elithorn and Telford (1969) described a computer-based system for analyzing intellectual skills, and Gedye and Miller (1969) developed a computer-based automatic testing system (the ts 512 model). The Gedye–Miller system consists of programmable visual (or audiovisual) display linked to a data-logger that produces a record in computer-compatible form. With the present model, when transcription is easiest, the stimuli to be presented to the subject are visual and the response is button presses. This automated testing device permits the accurate recording of response latencies and, incidentally, the accurate timing of presentation stimuli when it is required in learning and memory tests. The ts 512 model can also function as a teaching machine. Thus it can be used to instruct the subject in the test procedure and to ensure, as a result of practice items, that the subject has in fact grasped the instructions before he is subjected to the test itself.

The economic feasibility of automated testing depends on the particular situation in which it is used; this approach, however, is most likely to be ideally suited to take over routine work such as the administration of frequently used test procedures. In a busy testing center, the return on investment would be less than two years (Gedye and Miller, 1969).

Computer-based automated testing systems presently are more familiar in research than in application. In order for them to become established as an accepted psychological mode of operation, it must be demonstrated that the testing procedure leads to: (1) increases in test reliability and validity, (2) negligible or positive effects due to reduction in the testee–tester relationship, and (3) increased effectiveness of psychological assessments.

VII

ONGOING DEVELOPMENTS
IN PERSONNEL SELECTION
TECHNIQUES

OVERVIEW

This chapter discusses three research studies in personnel selection, with their concepts and related techniques.

The first study deals with the development of the One-Hole* test, a manual dexterity test aimed at assessing the rate of learning and "final" performance on fine manual repetitive tasks. The relationships of vision, anthropometric data, nonverbal intelligence, personality characteristics, and personnel data to the One-Hole test and to production performance are discussed.

The second study evaluates the possible relationships between handedness, the One-Hole test scores, and production performance.

The third study compares the effects of paced and freely chosen performances on the physiological efficiency of the human body.

Finally, future trends in personnel selection research are considered.

Whenever possible, tests should be selected from the existing repertory to meet new occupational needs (as explained in Chapter 6). In some situations, however, it may be necessary to develop new tests. The development of a testing procedure is a long, rigorous, and dynamic process, and none of the techniques so far available can be considered wholly satisfactory for the needs of occupational selection and training.

---

* The One-Hole test is now available commercially from the Lafayette Instrument Company, Sagamore Parkway, Lafayette, Indiana 47906. All royalties from the sale of the One-Hole test are channeled to the Department of Engineering Production, University of Birmingham, England.

This chapter outlines the way in which new tests are initiated, tested by experiment, modified, and tried out in pilot studies. Since this procedure is best explained by example, three case studies are included. The three studies involve: (1) selection of operators for fine manual repetitive tasks, (2) handedness and personnel selection, and (3) physiological considerations in personnel selection.

STUDY 1: SELECTION OF OPERATORS FOR FINE MANUAL REPETITIVE TASKS*

In a world of rapid technological and labor market changes, where neither the jobs nor the operators are likely to remain constant for very long, it is more satisfactory to have an operator who can improve rapidly on a task and attain a high level of performance in the early stages than one who is slower, even if he ultimately achieves an equally high level of performance. Because of the need to forecast the rate of improvement and ultimate performance on a task, the hypothesis was proposed (derived from Seymour, 1959, 1967) that by measuring elemental times during performance on a dexterity test and the rate of improvement of these times, a test validity could be obtained that was higher than the one resulting when the traditional method (i.e., measuring only the total cycle time) was employed.

To begin to test the hypothesis mentioned previously, two frequently utilized manual dexterity tests were studied (Corlett, Salvendy, and Seymour, 1971): the O'Connor Finger Dexterity test (Hines and O'Connor, 1926) and the Purdue Pegboard (Tiffin and Asher, 1948). These are illustrated in Figures 7.1 and 7.2, respectively.

Studies of Salvendy, Seymour, and Corlett (1970) and Corlett, Salvendy, and Seymour (1971) indicate that neither the Purdue Pegboard nor the O'Connor Finger Dexterity test is sufficiently controlled to constitute an adequate test of speed-skills acquisition, because of the variability inherent in grasping the pins from the tray and the different distances traveled between grasping and positioning the pin. Thus the tasks in these tests cannot be considered as repetitive. The One-Hole test (Figure 7.3) was then developed both to test the foregoing hypothesis and

* Much of the work reported here was carried out jointly by the authors and Professor E. Nigel Corlett at the Department of Engineering Production, University of Birmingham, England, under grant from the U.K. Department of Scientific and Industrial Research and the U.K. Department of Employment. Much of this study was conducted between October 1965 and September 1968 and was reported in greater detail by Salvendy (1968).

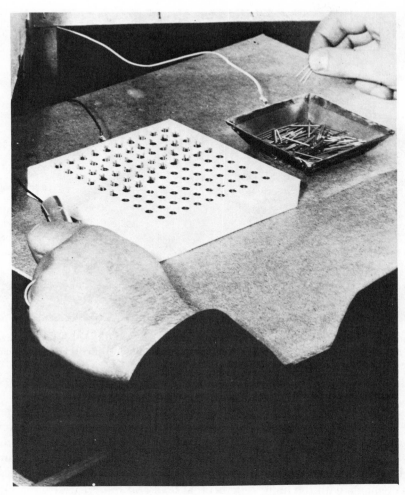

Figure 7.1. The O'Connor Finger Dexterity test. The left hand is utilized for the recording of elemental times by means of passing an electric current through the body system; this part is an addition to the original O'Connor test.

because the presently utilized manual dexterity tests have too low validity (typically around +.20 correlation coefficient between scores and criterion measures). The One-Hole test seeks to overcome the limitations of the Purdue and O'Connor tests by reduction of "noise" (i.e., by making the task more repetitive and less variable). This instrument also makes possible the recording of elemental times separately rather than merely

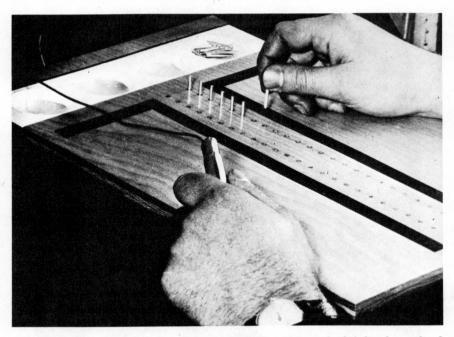

Figure 7.2.   The Purdue Pegboard. As in the O'Connor test, the left hand is utilized for the recording of elemental times; this part is an addition to the original Pegboard test.

the number of pins inserted per unit of time, because elemental times do not improve equally. During practice, some elements improve more than others (Barnes and Mundel, 1938; Barnes, Perkins, and Juran, 1940; Barnes and Amrine, 1942; Smith and Von Trebra, 1952; Wehrkamp and Smith, 1952; Seymour, 1959; Hancock and Foulke, 1963). Moreover, the elements with the highest perceptual load and the greatest variability in performance time improve the most (Salvendy, 1969b).

The One-Hole test aims to forecast those job applicants who will be able to acquire the manipulative skills most rapidly. If such a test were used successfully, those selected would be able to acquire skills rapidly, and the following advantages would be realized: (1) significant savings in training time and cost; (2) a significantly more flexible and versatile labor force could be acquired; (3) significant increases in production output could be obtained more quickly, since those who learn faster achieve a higher production output earlier; and (4) a more effective placement within an organization could be achieved by placing those with

Figure 7.3. The One-Hole test: (*a*) Test apparatus; (*b*) control console. (Salvendy, 1969b; Salvendy, Seymour, and Corlett, 1970). This test is now being manufactured and distributed by Lafayette Instrument Company, Lafayette, Ind.

high learning capabilities on jobs that require rapid and frequent shifts
from task to task, and by placing those with low learning capabilities
on jobs characterized by more stable tasks.

Since individual traits are multidimensional, a test battery is required
to measure them. The tests described below were chosen on the basis of
job and skills analysis of performance on the One-Hole test, primarily to
assess the degree to which the validity of the One-Hole test is attributable
to motor phenomena and the degree to which it is attributable to other
phenomena associated with other tests. For example, if the One-Hole test
scores have a correlation of .60 with the criterion, but at the same time
these scores correlate .90 with scores from nonverbal intelligence tests, it
is not possible to say what factor is responsible for the validity of the test.

In the present study, a total of seven tests and 110 test items were
studied. The tests were the following.

1. One-Hole test (Salvendy 1969b; Salvendy, Seymour, and Corlett,
1970; Salvendy and Seymour, 1972) (Figure 7.3). The test consists of grasping one prepositioned pin (⅛ in. diameter and 1 in. long), moving it 7 in. in
a direction 45° away from the body, positioning it into a hole with close
tolerances (of 0.025 in. between the hole and the pin diameter) and reaching to grasp the next prepositioned pin. The task is repeated for 15 trials of
one minute duration with a 5-sec interval between each trial and a 3-min
rest period between the seventh and eighth trials. The four basic elements
(Reach, Grasp, Move, and Position) were recorded electrically (to 0.01-sec
accuracy) by current through the body system* in computer-compatible
form. The data were recorded with the aid of SETAR (Welford, 1952)
for direct statistical analysis by computer.

The hypothesis that elemental times would be better predictors of learning than total cycle time could best be tested by fitting linear regression
lines for mean elemental times, their standard deviations, and then fum-
bles† over the entire 15 trials. Out of a series of alternatives, the best fitted
lines were those in which the slope of the line was the log of the total
number of cycles so far performed, and the vertical axis was the inverse
elemental times, their standard deviations, or the number of fumbles.

2. Purdue (Right-Handed) Pegboard (Tiffin and Asher, 1948; Buros,

---

* With this methodology the nonpreferred hand is holding one end of the electrical
circuit (in this case, a copper plate located on both sides of the One-Hole test)
while the preferred hand is closing and opening the electrical circuit by touching the
pin at grasp or position and thus activating the time recorder. This is achieved by
passing a minute current (7 mA in these experiments) through the body.
† A fumble was defined as the breaking of an electrical contact within the execution
of an element. Only fumbles lasting longer than 0.01 sec were identified and recorded.

1965) (Figure 7.2). The test consists of grasping a pin from a tray and positioning it in a hole. The test score is the total number of pins inserted in three consecutive 0.5-min trials.

3. Eysenck Personality Inventory (Buros, 1965; Eysenck and Eysenck, 1968) aims at assessing extravert–introvert and neurotic–stable personality dimensions; it includes a built-in scale to detect those who lie in the response. There are 57 questions about habits and attitudes, and each must be answered by yes or no. This work-limit test takes about 7 min to complete.

4. Group Test 70/23 (Slater 1941, 1942; Slater and Bennett, 1943; National Institute of Industrial Psychology, 1944; Salvendy, 1972) is a nonverbal intelligence test composed of two subsets. Each subset of GT 70/23 is designed to test general intelligence without bringing verbal or spatial abilities into play. Various geometric shapes and designs have certain meanings and characteristics which must be identified by the subject.

5. Bausch & Lomb Orthorator (the Professional Orthorator, 1943; Buros, 1965) assesses visual acuity and phoria for lateral and vertical play (for near and far vision), depth of vision, and color deficiency.

6. Anthropometric data, including height and weight and hand measurements of the preferred hand (Figure 7.4) (Salvendy, 1971).

7. A 14-item personal data questionnaire, including age, marital status, education, work experience, hobbies, and a self-evaluation rating.

These seven test measures yielded 110 test items which were correlated with 16 criteria measures representing aptitude, ability, circumstances, and productivity. Thus 126 individual items were collected and calculated for each subject.

Table 7.1   Age of Subjects According to Firm

Firm	Number of Subjects	Type of Subjects	Age (years)			
			Mean	Standard Deviation	Lowest	Highest
Electromechanical	30	Experienced	38.80	12.28	18	57
Electromechanical	8	Trainee	22.13	10.52	15	45
Confectionery	43	Experienced	37.19	13.29	15	57
Confectionery	9	Trainee	15.11	0.33	15	16
Electronic	41	Experienced	23.71	7.53	16	43
Electronic	27	Trainee	18.48	3.93	15	26

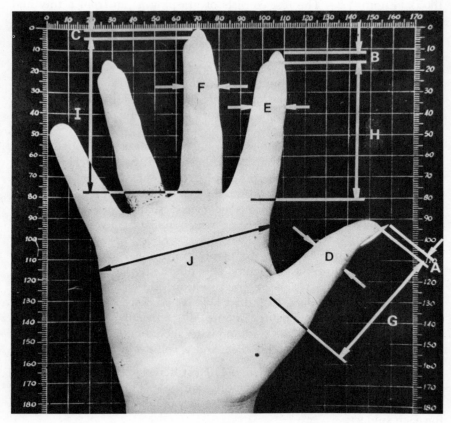

Figure 7.4.   Hand measurements taken in the study of anthropometric data (see also Table 7.11).

This study had 181* participants (Table 7.1), representing three diversified organizations (confectionery, electromechanical, and electronics). In each organization both trainee ($N = 44$) and experienced subjects ($N = 114$) were tested. The synopsis of the job content of these subjects is illustrated in Table 7.2, and the criteria of production performance against which the test scores were validated appear in Table 7.3.

The results of this experiment are discussed in terms of six separate

---

* Due to an electronic failure data on only 158 subjects is available on elemental performance on the One-Hole test.

analyses, bearing in mind that each one is highly interrelated with the others. The aspects are:

1. One-Hole test versus the Purdue Pegboard.
2. Anthropometric data (Salvendy, 1971).
3. Nonverbal intelligence test G.T. 70/23 (Salvendy, 1973).
4. Eysenck Personality Inventory.
5. Vision tester—the orthorator (The Professional Orthorator, 1943).
6. Interview questionnaire data.

One-Hole test versus the Purdue Pegboard

The reliabilities of the two tests have been studied by both correlational and internal reliability methods.

Correlational Reliabilities. The correlational reliabilities of the Purdue Pegboard (Table 7.4) obtained in this study indicate a very large discrepancy among the coefficients for the various subject groups and industries. These discrepancies could have occurred as a result of the small numbers constituting each group or because of differences in population structures. The only surprisingly low correlation, obtained from the electromechanical firm's experienced operator group, does not coincide with previous findings. The remaining correlation values, however, are within the range of those found by Tiffin and Asher (1948) (.64), and Bass and Stucki (1951) (.67).

For the gross scores, the test–retest reliabilities of the One-Hole test (Table 7.5) tend to be of similar magnitude to those obtained for the Purdue Pegboard, when different tests lengths are taken into account. Table 7.5 demonstrates that the reliability coefficients can vary significantly depending on which aspects of the test are being considered. In the present study, these varied from −.46 to +1.00. This large variation coefficients is attributable mainly to the very low relationship between initial performance, rate of learning, and ultimate performance (Salvendy, 1969b) (Figure 7.5), rather than to the statistical unreliability of the item in question. In effect, the internal reliability of the One-Hole test assessed by frame-by-frame analysis of high-speed filming of the performance on the test indicated high internal reliability of the test as portrayed below. Thus test–retest correlation reliabilities must be interpreted with caution. Without evidence regarding the internal reliability of the test and the relationship between initial and later performance, the test–retest correlational reliabilities cannot be considered to be valid indicators of the reliability of the test.

Table 7.2   Synopsis of Tasks Performed in the Three Industries Studied

Electronics Firm

Job Title	Basic Requirements of the Job	Percentage of Subjects (from one firm) Tested Who Were Engaged on this or Similar Type of Job
Cage assembly (of a tube)	1. Grasp and symmetrically or asymmetrically position very small fine objects with close tolerances. 2. Manipulate simultaneously with left and right hand and right foot. 3. Use tweezers and magnets to grasp objects.	60
Welding (of a tube)	1. Grasp and position small objects. 2. Manipulate simultaneously with left and right hand and right foot. 3. Use tweezers and magnets to grasp objects.	40

Electromechanical Firm

Job Title	Basic Requirements of the Job	Percentage
Assembly (fuse box)	1. Grasp fuse box and position in jig. 2. Grasp screws and start threading with both hands. 3. Tighten screws with screwdriver.	45
Power press operation (steel connecting plate)	1. Grasp and position object alternatively with left hand and right hand. 2. Pull up isolation with right hand and press button to start machine. 3. Press foot pedal with right foot and release.	40

Internal and Observational Reliability   It has been stressed by Jones (1966) that "Preoccupation with the relationships between psychomotor tasks has tended to obscure the equally important question of their internal structure. If a task consists of several identifiable components, how does the performance on any one or more of these components relate to performance on the whole task?" (p. 123).

Purdue Pegboard   Thus, because it was realized that a variety of different work methods were utilized during the performance on the Purdue Pegboard (and similarly on the O'Connor Finger Dexterity test), the performance of one highly skilled subject at 64 frames/sec was

Table 7.2   **(Continued)**

Job Title	Basic Requirements of the Job	Percentage of Subjects (from one firm) Tested Who Were Engaged on this or Similar Type of Job
Capstan operation (hexagon brass terminal stud)	1. Ensure "correct" speed is used and maintain "appropriate" length of metal. 2. Turn switches on and off and press and release pedal. 3. Use left hand and right hand and right foot.	15

	Confectionery Firm	
Cellophane wrapping (of a box)	1. Grasping box, wrap it in cellophane, and seal it with glue. 2. Use simultaneous movements of both hands. 3. Use brush with glue.	35
Position candies to jig	1. Grasp and position candies simultaneously with both hands. 2. Requires rapid judgment and discrimination of shapes, since different candy shapes have to be positioned into different jigs. 3. No visual senses are used for the operation.	30
Packing (chocolate blocks)	1. Grasp the "required" number of chocolate blocks and position them into the box. 2. "Arrange" cartons before and after packing.	35

filmed on 16 mm film. A total of 6000 frames was filmed, accounting for 70 complete work cycles. Groups of cycles at the first, tenth, and twentieth trial of the performance on the Purdue Pegboard were filmed and later analyzed frame by frame. The analysis of the film indicated the following points:

1. Methods of using fingers and thumb, and regardless of whether the operator looked at what she was doing, significantly ($p > .05$) affected the time required to perform the task, the standard deviation of the performance time, and the number of fumbles for the grasp element.

2. Chance effects, mainly due to the randomly distributed pins in the tray, greatly influence the time required to complete the task, and thus the scores of the test performer.

Table 7.3 Origins, Nature and Distribution of Production Performance of the Experienced Subjects

Type of Industry Considered	Methods Used to Establish Production Standards	Production Scale Equivalent to 133 (on the 100/133 Scale)a	Production Index Transformed to 100/133 Scale				Official "Ceiling" of Production Performance
			Mean	Standard Deviation	Range		
					Lowest	Highest	
Electro-mechani-cal	Time study and synthetic data based on it	225 133	159.73	28.38	87	217	Does not exist
Confec-tionery	Time study and synthetic data based on it	133	154.30	81.18	70	348	Does not exist
Elec-tronics	Work factor	75	127.85	25.19	118	160	160

a In a direct financial incentive environment; above an index of 100 the operator will be financially reimbursed and thus will earn more than his daily guaranteed income. Even if he works well below the index of 100, the operator is still guaranteed his daily fixed income.

Table 7.4 Test–Retest Reliability of the Purdue Pegboard (Right Hand)

Type of Firm	Subjects		First Trial Gross Score versus Second Trial Gross Score
	Experience	Number	
Electromechanical	Experienced	30	.21
Electromechanical	Trainee	8	.62
Confectionery	Experienced	43	.77
Confectionery	Trainee	9	.80
Electronics	Experienced	41	.59
Electronics	Trainee	27	.67

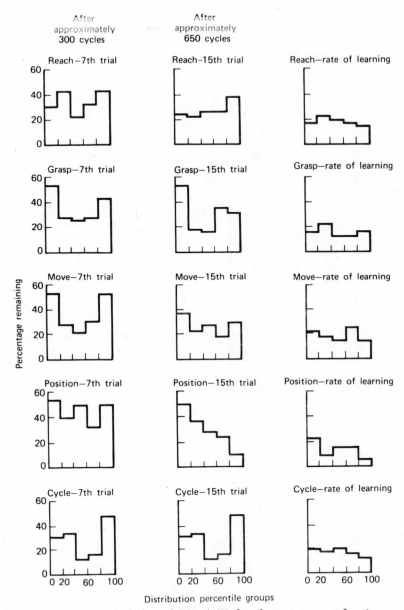

Figure 7.5. Percentage of the subjects (156 female operators performing manual repetitive tasks in industry) whose performance time remains in the same 20 percentile groups. (After Salvendy, 1969b.)

Table 7.5 Pearson Product-Moment Correlational Reliability of the One-Hole Test

Pearson Product-Moment Correlation Coefficients

Subjects	Number of Subjects	Number of Pins Inserted in First 0.5 min of First Trial vs. Second 0.5 min of Same Trial	Number of Pins Inserted in First Trial vs. Number Inserted in Second Trial	First Trial vs. Second Trial						Number of Pins Inserted in First 0.5 min of All 15 Trials vs. Number Inserted in Second 0.5 min of All 15 Trials
				Elemental Times				Number of Fumbles		
				Reach ($\bar{x}$)	Grasp ($\bar{x}$)	Move ($\bar{x}$)	Position ($\bar{x}$)	Grasp	Position	
Electromechanical										
Experienced	30	.54	.82	.06	.90	.17	.62	.63	−.46	.99
Trainee	8	.82	.82	.79	.90	.86	.96	.77	.85	.99
Confectionery										
Experienced	43	.62	.82	.56	.92	.88	1.00	.48	.73	.90
Trainee	9	.92	.52	−.09	.36	.31	.46	.03	.01	.96
Electronic										
Experienced	41	.57	.83	.73	.75	.80	.43	.52	.68	.82
Trainee	27	.74	.86	.43	.87	.67	.03	−.14	.94	.73

3. It follows that the scores on these tests are the product of at least three factors:

(a) Chance effects, which are not under the control of the subject.

(b) Work methods adopted by the performer, consciously or unconsciously.

(c) Abilities and speed-skill possessed by the performer.

4. The variable factors in these tests (e.g., differences in distance moved and grasping position) may prevent the subject from adopting any systematic method. It would appear, therefore, that the test–retest or split-half reliability, which had been considered so valuable and important in the earlier use of these tests (e.g., Super and Crites, 1962; Tiffin and Asher, 1948), may not have been attributable to a lack of learning. Indeed, in the study of Salvendy (1966), the O'Connor yielded a significant 16 percent learning. Rather, because the test-task involved so many variables, it is possible that improvements in one therblig counter balanced performance losses in others. The significance of this for the development of psychomotor selection tests is that dependable measures cannot be derived unless chance variability resulting from peculiarities in test construction (rather than from the individual's performance on the test) are reduced or eliminated as far as is feasible.

5. The Modified Purdue Pegboard, unlike the Purdue or O'Connor test, provides the same distance of travel between the elements Grasp and Position. This reduced the variability of the test slightly, but not significantly enough to constitute an adequate test of speed-skill acquisition.

One-Hole Test The internal reliability of the One-Hole test results was investigated by filming at 64 frames/sec the performance of subjects representing the extremes of their industrial groups. Two females representing the highest industrial performance group in their factory (160 on the 100/133 rating scale, where 100 represents the normal in the assembly of television tubes) and two females representing the lowest performance group in the same factory (110 on the 100/133 rating scale) were selected.

Precautions were taken to eliminate or decrease the "filming effect" on the operators and, consequently, on their performance, by obtaining the aid of the training instructors and foremen in selecting the operators who would be least affected by being filmed. As it turned out, all subjects seemed to ignore the presence of the camera while performing their task.

The subjects' performance was filmed during the first and last 10 sec, approximately, in each of the first, seventh, and fifteenth trials, a total of about 60 sec per subject. For the four subjects, this provided 165 work cycles for analysis. Since subjects differed in their performance levels and thus in the number of work cycles performed per unit of time, it was decided to analyze only the first five cycles in each 10-sec filming—30 cycles/subject. This was equal to the slowest subject's slowest rate of work.

In addition to the conditions just named, one subject belonging to the 160 group was filmed with a 16 mm high-speed camera at 470 frames/sec (28,200 frames/min) during six work cycles—three at her first trial and three at her fifteenth trial.

When the high-speed film was projected roughly 40 times slower than the speed at which it had been shot (making an actual 700 frames/min), it immediately revealed the main features of the work methods adopted by the subject during the performance on this test. This information could not be obtained from the projection of the film taken at 64 frames/sec. Furthermore, the projection of the high-speed film gave a good impression of continuity (in contrast to the low-speed film), which is often very important in the understanding of the entire task and its skill structure (Bartlett, 1958; Bilodeau, 1966).

The frame-by-frame analysis indicated that the variability inherent in the Purdue Pegboard has been eliminated in the One-Hole test. This is because there are no randomly distributed pins in the tray. In addition, the variable distance the subject has to move in each cycle is eliminated in the One-Hole test.

From this analysis it also became evident that the work methods adopted for, or during, the element *Reach*, are not necessarily characteristic of that element. They tend to be governed by the work methods adopted by the subjects in positioning and grasping the pins. The work methods adopted also appeared to affect the element Move. For example, the subjects move their fingers (and in rare cases the lower arm also) from the position that has been adopted during the element Position to the location required for the fingers and the arm for the element Grasp. These relationships indicate the interdependability of the work method elements and a slight nonsignificant interdependability of elemental times. This is a controversial factor in the published literature (Ghiselli and Brown, 1948; Smith and Von Trebra, 1952; Simon, 1955; Schmidke and Stier, 1961; Raju, 1962; Disney, Hancock, and Muskstart, 1965; Sanfleber, 1967).

The frame-by-frame analysis of the film indicated that the subjects adopted, consciously or unconsciously, at least two different methods of grasping the pins (Table 7.6). Similarly, the film reveals that the subjects adopt three different methods of moving the pin, and subjects with the highest industrial rating appear to utilize the fingers more effectively than the subjects with the lowest rating (Table 7.7). The latter, generally, have to regrasp the pins during the move element, but the former do not. This bears on statements made by earlier writers (The Industrial Self-Instructor, 1884; Seymour, 1967; Barnes, 1968) that the experienced operator utilizes his body mechanisms more effectively and uses fewer and more effective motions to execute a task, as compared with the inexperienced operator.

Table 7.6   Different Methods of Grasping the Pins During Performance on One-Hole Test

	Work Method					
	Grasps Pins with Second Finger and Thumb (frequency)			Grasps Pins with First Finger and Thumb (frequency)		
Subject	Trial 1	Trial 7	Trial 15	Trial 1	Trial 7	Trial 15
Low industrial performance						
I	0	9	10	10	1	0
II	0	0	0	10	10	10
High industrial performance						
III	10	10	10	0	0	0
IV	0	10	10	10	0	0

Table 7.7   Different Methods of Moving Pins during Performance on One-Hole Test

	Work Methods[a]								
	A			B			C		
Subject	Trial 1	Trial 7	Trial 15	Trial 1	Trial 7	Trial 15	Trial 1	Trial 7	Trial 15
I	10	3	0	0	5	10	0	2	0
II	10	10	10	0	0	0	0	0	0
III	0	0	0	10	10	10	0	0	0
IV	0	0	0	0	10	10	10	0	0

[a] The following methods were used: A, regrasps pin from first to second finger and inserts first finger on top of pin; B, grasps pin with second finger and thumb (does not move pin in hand, but inserts first finger on top or side of pin); C, grasps pin with first finger and thumb and does not alter its position during move.

It is also evident from Tables 7.8 and 7.9 that statistically significant differences occurred between and within groups of subjects relative to the number of overshots, undershots, and hits of the target hole with the pins. These differences apparently occurred because four different work methods were utilized in positioning the pins as identified by the frame-by-frame analysis of the film (Table 7.10). The table indicates that no touch feedback was necessary as the subjects progressed during the test; that is, the subject initially pushed the pin down in the hole to its very end, until the hand touched the top of the hole—which provides feedback to the subject that the pin has been positioned. However, as the subject continued with the task, her performance was carried out with less feedback, and the pins were released by the fingers (in contrast to the initial stage) after they had been inserted into the hole to about half their length. This supports the concept put forward by Crossman (1956a, 1956b) that the inexperienced worker needs more information to check his actions than does the experienced worker, who seeks and reacts to earlier information and hence saves time.

Table 7.8   Number of Hits, Overshots, and Undershots for Positioning Pins into Hole

Subject	Undershots			Hits			Overshots		
	Trial 1	Trial 7	Trial 15	Trial 1	Trial 7	Trial 15	Trial 1	Trial 7	Trial 15
I	1	3	5	1	2	1	8	5	4
II	2	4	6	6	6	3	1	1	1
III	5	8	8	3	1	2	2	1	0
IV	5	2	3	4	6	6	1	2	0

The significant effects of differences in work methods between and within operators, as shown by Tables 7.8 and 7.9 during the initial and later stages of performance include the following:

1. The work method adopted by an operator during the performance of the task is one of the most significant factors influencing manipulative personnel selection test scores. A manual dexterity selection test should therefore allow for some variation in subjects' work methods, since this will help in discriminating between high- and low-performance operators. The importance of the phenomena of work methods in psychological studies was realized more than a quarter-century ago (Seashore, 1939), but it is seldom given attention.

Table 7.9 Interaction Analysis of Number of Hits and Misses of Target Hole when Scores for Trials 1, 7, and 15 are Pooled

Type of Resultant Movement for Interactions Measured[a]	Degrees of Freedom	χ^2 Contribution	Significance Level (percent)
Undershots			
II vs. I	1	0.43	NS
III vs. IV	1	3.90	5
	1	1.92	NS
	3	7.77	5
Hits			
II vs. I	1	6.37	1
III vs. IV	1	5.26	2
	1	0.38	NS
	3	11.88	1
Overshots			
II vs. I	1	9.80	1
III vs. IV	1	0.00	NS
	1	7.54	1
Overall			
II vs. I	2	16.60	0.1
III vs. IV	2	9.16	1
	2	9.84	1

[a] Pairs of numbers represent highest industrial performance group versus lowest; all subjects.

Table 7.10 Different Methods of Positioning Pins

	Work Methods[a]											
	A			B			C			D		
Subject	Trial 1	Trial 7	Trial 15	Trial 1	Trial 7	Trial 15	Trial 1	Trial 7	Trial 15	Trial 1	Trial 7	Trial 15
I	9	0	0	0	10	10	1	0	0	0	0	0
II	10	0	0	0	10	10	0	0	0	0	0	0
III	10	7	0	0	3	10	0	0	0	0	0	0
IV	0	0	0	0	0	0	0	10	10	10	0	0

[a] The following work methods were used: A, holds pin with second finger and thumb, pushes pin with first finger until the very end; B, holds pin with second finger and thumb, pushes pin with first finger until half its length is in the hole; C, holds pin with first and second finger and thumb; D, holds pin with first finger and thumb, uses second finger to balance hand.

2. Changes occurring in work methods during the repeated performance of a test task are the main factors producing increased performance. It should be noted, however, that for a short time immediately before, during, and after the change in work method, a plateau in performance, or even a slight loss, may be observed until the change in work method starts to affect productivity.

3. From a biomechanical point of view, it appears that changes in work methods nearly always result in the more efficient use of the human body; the "better" habits, moreover, tend to be associated with less physiological cost than the previously utilized work methods.

From the preceding discussion it is possible to draw the following conclusions:

1. Detailed frame-by-frame analysis of high-speed movie films in the performance of certain psychomotor tasks can provide a greater insight into the understanding of tasks, as well as a truer picture of the dependability and reliability of a test than correlational techniques using gross scores can produce.

2. High-speed filming (e.g. 30,000 frames/min, projected at 700 frames/min) of the performance of a psychomotor task can increase understanding of how speed-skills are acquired, because it provides a continuity effect within the task that might not be found in viewing films taken at lower speeds (e.g., 4000 frames/min).

3. Test–retest reliability coefficients obtained in one situation cannot be adopted for another, even similar, situation; they have to be established for each case individually.

4. The use of the traditional reliability coefficient as an important indication in test evaluation and validation is dubious, since the coefficient measures only the statistical relationship in question rather than the internal reliability and dependability. Because of the way in which the usual reliability analysis is performed, positive and negative errors during the test performance may be canceled out. By assuming that one of the two measures is 100 percent reliable (i.e., that there is no variation within a single measure—a false assumption in most cases), a falsely high coefficient can result.

5. With regard to the specific tests used, no noticeable differences in the magnitude of reliability coefficients could be found between the Purdue Pegboard and the One-Hole test (excluding electromechanical experienced operators), when the difference in test lengths had been accounted for.

6. The chance effect and random variations that were predominantly present in the Purdue Pegboard results do not occur in the One-Hole test.

Cross-Validation of the One-Hole and Purdue Pegboard Tests

It also seemed advisable to cross-validate the results from the One-Hole and Purdue Pegboard tests. The meaningfulness and dependability of the criteria against which test results are to be compared must be evaluated in order to assess validity of the tests. The criteria for such a comparison are discussed below.

Criteria. The measure selected for validation purposes was that of production performance, since other criteria measures such as lateness and absenteeism would reflect circumstances rather than worker competence.

The production performance criteria used in this study were expressed in index form collected for each experienced subject for a cumulative period of 25 days, and for the trainees for the entire duration of their training period. The index takes into account the quantity produced at an accepted quality standard and allows up to 2 percent of unacceptable quality without affecting the level of production performance. The exact level of this allowance varies between products and firms within the limits just cited. Generally the allowances are based on the firms' past records.

The production performance standards in the electromechanical and confectionery firm were based on time study or on synthetic times deduced from the company's time study data (e.g., Barnes, 1968). For the electronics firm, the production performance standards were derived from the PMTS of work factors (Quick, Duncan, and Malcolm, 1962).

The dependability and reliability of production performance as a criterion has been investigated by earlier writers (Craig, 1925; Hull, 1928; Hayes, 1932; Viteles, 1932; Hay, 1943; Cohen and Strauss, 1946; Anson, 1952; Rodgers and Hammersley, 1954; Amaria, 1968). As a result of controlled studies, these investigators reported error variances as high as 50 percent and averaging around 20 percent. In the case of the present study, the test–retest reliability coefficients of the three firms' production data varied from .88 to .92. However, these reliabilities are highly inflated, as indicated by constant errors, internal inconsistencies, and high variability; the range of the index was from 70 to 345. Test–retest correlation coefficients for the production criterion do not measure the true dependability of the criterion, since they assume absence of a constant error, and this assumption is definitely invalid (Anson, 1952; Rodgers and Hammersley, 1954).

Predictive Efficiency of the Tests. The hypothesis proposed in this study—namely, that the measurement of elemental times during the performance on a dexterity test and the rate of improvement of these times might yield higher test validity than the gross initial scores traditionally used—was tested by means of the comparisons discussed below.

Purdue Pegboard (Right-Handed) versus One-Hole Test (First 0.5 min). The evidence from the present data (Figure 7.6) illustrates that the scores of both the tests (i.e., first 30 sec) for all groups tested cannot predict with adequate statistical significance the criterion scores with which they were associated. The highest correlation achieved is .28, and a number of the correlations are negatively associated with performance. These results are not unexpected; they are in agreement with the general trend of validity coefficients of the Purdue Pegboard and other manual dexterity tests (Figure 5.7). For example, in a previous study at the electronics firm participating in this research, based on a sample of 1200

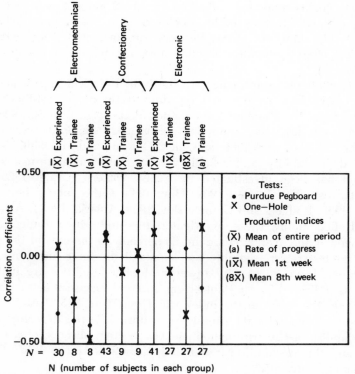

Figure 7.6. Comparison of the correlations of production performances with test scores (first 30 sec) for both Purdue and One-Hole tests. (After Salvendy, Seymour, and Corlett, 1970.)

new entrants, a statistically insignificant product-moment correlation co-efficient was found between the first trial on the Purdue Pegboard (right-handed) and any of the criteria considered, such as: quantity produced, quality produced, incentive earnings, and supervisor's ratings of aptitude and abilities. Similarly, insignificant correlations were obtained for the other parts of the pegboard test.

Thus any hypothesis that the One-Hole test has a higher validity than the Purdue Pegboard when using *equivalent* scoring methods and test length could not be upheld.

Initial versus Final Performance (One-Hole Test). Later performance on the One-Hole test is more closely associated with the criterion than is the initial level of performance. This does not necessarily hold true for each group (with each of its criteria) or for each test item separately, but it is true for the general trend of the available data(e.g., Table 7.19; Salvendy, 1968). If this view is accepted, the implications are that changes in the skill structure required to perform the One-Hole test occur with continuing performance, which would support earlier findings of Hollingworth (1913), Woodrow (1938a, 1938b), and Fleishman and Hempel (1954b).

Dynamic versus Static Scores (One-Hole Test). The central hypothesis of the One-Hole test experiment involving dynamic and static scores arose from earlier studies on the acquisition of speed-skills (Salvendy, 1966; Seymour, 1959). It was theorized that changes occurring in the distribution of performance times of certain elements, over repeated trials (especially those with "high perceptual load," where the intake of information from the task to be performed per unit of time through the sensory receptors is high) might be more appropriate for prediction than merely measuring the initial or even the final level of performance. This would also indicate that the rate of improvement is independent of the initial level of performance, which would be in agreement with Droege (1966) and Reynolds and Adams (1953).

Figure 7.5 indicates that, on the One-Hole test, the relationships between initial performance, rate of improvement, and ultimate performance were independent for about 75 percent of the subjects, and these relationships were dependent only for about 25 percent of the subject population.

In testing the hypothesis that dynamic measures of test performance might be more appropriate for prediction than measurements of the initial or final level of performance, it became clear that many of the regression lines representing rate of learning or variability in the rate of learning on the One-Hole test are significantly related to the criteria (e.g., Table 7.17, for the electronics firm). These regressions are im-

portant items in the final and reduced battery for the experienced operators at all three firms, and they are crucial in the prediction of the rate of
progress of the trainees in the electronics firm. However, they are not
useful in the item battery for predicting the first and eighth weeks' performances for the trainees in the electronics firm; nor are these regressions valuable for forecasting the rate of progress or the average performance in the training school for the trainees of the electromechanical
and confectionery firms. (Because of the small sample size of these two
groups, the results must be interpreted with caution.) Nevertheless, even
when dynamic measures were not crucial for prediction, they had higher
predictive values than traditional scoring methods.

Although the conclusions to be drawn from these experiments are not
as clear-cut as might be desired, they do demonstrate the possibility of
using dynamic measures (i.e., rate of learning) for predicting the acquisition of speed-skills in industrial tasks.

The experimental evidence adduced supports the following three concepts:

1. Both the rate of improvement during the test and the final scores
derived from the One-Hole test are more closely associated with prediction of speed-skill in certain industrial tasks than the measures derived
from the Purdue Pegboard.

2. The rate of improvement in elemental times is a more appropriate
measure of the prediction of the rate of acquisition of speed-skill on
industrial repetitive tasks than is the measure of the initial gross scores on
the One-Hole test.

3. The most powerful prediction is derived by a combined index score
of initial performance, rate of acquisition of speed-skills, and ultimate
performance on the One-Hole test (e.g., Table 7.17).

The implications for personnel selection are that the three measures—
initial scores, final scores, and rate of learning on elemental times—should
be utilized jointly for optimal prediction, bearing in mind that the index
dealing with the rate of acquisition of speed-skills carries the largest
weight in the prediction model. This implies also that the degree to
which acquisition of speed-skill can be accelerated by systematic training
depends to some extent on the initial level of skills possessed (Salvendy,
1969b).

Anthropometric Data and Production Performance

The next series of tests was performed to verify whether certain
anthropometric characteristics of an individual performing manual repeti-

tive tasks in industry have any relationship to (a) production performance and (b) performance on manual dexterity selection tests (e.g., the
Purdue Pegboard and the One-Hole test).

Twelve anthropometric indices were measured on 181 subjects (see
Table 7.11 and Salvendy, 1971). In order to achieve higher reliability and
greater flexibility, the photogrammetric method of anthropometry was
utilized (Tanner and Weiner, 1949) rather than conventional direct
recording (e.g., Martin and Saller, 1957, 1959; Garrett, 1971).

**Table 7.11   Anthropometric Norms for 181 Female British Industrial Subjects, Ages
15 to 59 ($\overline{x} = 30$)[a]**

Items Measured[b]	$\overline{x}$	S.D.	Percentile Scores				
			1st	5th	50th	95th	99th
Weight, including usual work-ing clothes (kg)	58.5	9.76	41.0	50.4	58.5	87.7	94.5
Height, including shoes (cm)	161.0	6.10	147.7	152.4	162.4	175.3	177.8
Length of thumbnail (cm)[c]	.08	.14	0	0	0	.4	.8
Length of first fingernail (cm)[c]	.07	.14	0	0	0	.4	.8
Length of second fingernail (cm)[c]	.06	.14	0	0	0	.4	.8
Width of thumb (cm)[c]	1.97	.18	1.6	1.8	2.0	2.2	2.4
Width of first finger (cm)[c]	1.68	.18	1.4	1.5	1.7	2.2	2.4
Width of second finger (cm)[c]	1.69	.19	1.4	1.5	1.7	2.1	2.5
Length of thumb (cm)[c]	5.82	.75	4.5	5.2	5.8	7.0	7.5
Length of first finger (cm)[c]	7.06	.74	5.9	6.4	7.0	8.2	9.2
Length of second finger (cm)[c]	7.90	.73	6.8	7.7	7.8	9.3	1.0
Hand width (cm)[d]	8.39	.59	7.5	7.7	8.5	9.3	9.6
Purdue pegboard (R.H.): number of pins inserted in first 3 trials	53.2	4.97	40	45	54	60	64
One-Hole test: number of pins inserted in the first 15 trials	627.0	65.01	464	571	622	700	792

[a] After Salvendy (1971).
[b] The item intercorrelations appear in Table 7.12.
[c] As portrayed in Figure 7.4.

The anthropometric norms in Table 7.11 are similar to the many studies
dealing with thousands of subjects reported by Damon, Stoudt, and
McFarland (1966) but are larger than those found by Garrett (1971).
This is presumably because Damon's and Garrett's work dealt with
young military subjects, whereas the present study is based on middle-
aged industrial operators. The norms for performance on the Purdue
Pegboard are not significantly different from that reported in the manual
(Tiffin and Asher, 1948).

Table 7.12 Pearson Product-Moment Correlation Coefficient Matrix (with p Values) for 181 Female British Industrial Subjects Whose Norms Appear in Table 7.11[a]

Tests and Criteria Items[b]		Correlation Coefficients															
		1	2	3	4	5	6	7	8	9	10	11	12	13	14	15	16
Length of thumbnail	1	1.000	.850	.658	-.181	-.158	-.201	-.181	-.073	-.038	-.138	.003	-.097	-.156	-.183	-.183	-.012
Length of first fingernail	2	.001	1.000	.730	-.152	-.113	-.134	-.152	-.066	-.066	-.120	.038	-.064	-.154	-.029	-.042	.009
Length of second fingernail	3	.001	.001	1.000	-.202	-.131	-.150	-.202	-.126	-.143	-.161	.023	-.035	-.141	.008	.037	.008
Width of thumb	4	—	—	—	1.000	.743	.665	.418	.371	.334	.503	.208	.394	.525	-.033	.094	.156
Width of first finger	5	—	—	—	.001	1.000	.920	.560	.486	.447	.614	.271	.354	.591	-.038	.084	.193
Width of second finger	6	—	—	—	.001	.001	1.000	.458	.430	.415	.598	.234	.327	.541	-.053	.077	.174
Length of thumb	7	—	—	—	.001	.001	.001	1.000	.711	.618	.490	.234	.230	.461	-.090	-.005	.242
Length of first finger	8	—	—	—	.001	.001	.001	.001	1.000	.900	.559	.284	.251	.361	-.117	-.020	.151
Length of second finger	9	—	—	—	.001	.001	.001	.001	.001	1.000	.526	.319	.225	.249	.095	-.035	.099
Hand width	10	—	—	—	.001	.001	—	.001	.001	.001	1.000	.247	.383	.403	-.104	.025	.081
Height	11	—	—	—	—	.01	.001	.001	.01	—	.001	1.000	.428	.144	.141	.013	.089
Weight	12	—	—	—	.001	.001	.001	—	.01	—	.001	.001	1.000	.427	-.121	.145	.108
Age	13	—	—	—	.001	.001	.001	.001	.001	—	.001	—	.001	1.000	-.191	.095	.479
Purdue pegboard	14	—	—	—	—	—	—	—	—	—	—	—	—	.001	1.000	.443	-.016
One-hole test	15	—	—	—	—	—	—	—	—	—	—	—	—	—	.001	1.000	.257
Production performance	16	—	—	—	—	—	—	—	—	—	—	—	—	.001	—	.01	1.000

[a] After Salvendy (1971).

Anthropometric data were utilized as far back as the nineteenth century for the selection of students at Columbia University (Cattell and Farrand, 1896). Kemble (1917) indicated that "nearly all trades and vocations have their ideas or superstitions as to the kind of hand which is adopted for their particular kind of work. . . . The piano polisher should have a padded cushion hand. The silk weaver and the watch mender should have long, slender fingers" (p. 204). However, current personnel selection concepts make little use of anthropometric characteristics.

For example, Kemble (1917) concluded, using the Matchboard test, that hand shape accounts for only about 5 percent in the variance of the average performance scores. A more controlled study was performed on 60 university students by Griffiths (1936); measurements were taken of the weight and height of subjects, the width and length of the hands, and the lengths of palm and fingers. These anthropometric measurements were tested for correlation with five psychomotor tests. Correlation coefficients ranging from —.13 to —.37, for the Matchboard were found; this low correlation supports Kemble's findings.

It is evident from Table 7.12 that individual anthropometric data have very little effect on the performance of the Purdue Pegboard, the One-Hole test, and industrial performance data. Even the pooling together of the anthropometric data as predictors of test performance yields statistically nonsignificant multiple correlation coefficients of .31 with the Purdue Pegboard and .32 with the One-Hole test. These values are in very close agreement with those of Kemble (1917), but they are lower (and of opposite sign) than those of Griffiths (1936). Presumably, the difference can be attributed to the variations between the tests utilized in the two studies and to use of college students by Griffiths and industrial operators in the present study.

However, a .56 significant ($p < .001$) multiple correlation coefficient was yielded with production performance when the effects of age and scores on the personality, intelligence, and dexterity tests were covaried[*] as influencing factors on anthropometric data with production performance. This correlation indicates that one-third of the variances predicting production performance are accounted for by selected anthropometric data; 11 out of the 12 correlations of anthropometric data with production performance are positive, indicating that big hands go with high performance. Results similar to this were obtained in an unpublished study by Salvendy on 70 female industrial operators performing repetitive soldering operations in an American company.

---

[*] For the statistics, measuring, and interpretation of analysis of covariance, see such statistical textbooks as Cooley and Lohnes (1971).

It is worth noting that it requires less than 3 min per subject to collect all the anthropometric data that served to predict production performance better than the majority of more time-consuming tests. Strangely enough, however, it is the latter and not the former which are being most frequently adopted for prediction of human performance. It is not recommended that anthropometric data be used as a sole device for selecting operators; but it is suggested that anthropometric data can be used to advantage as part of a test battery in the selection of operators performing repetitive psychomotor tasks.

Intelligence and Production Performance

The relationship between scores on a nonverbal intelligence test and production performance of the 181 female industrial operators previously mentioned was also considered.

Dependability of the Intelligence Test. The Group Test 70 (GT 70) was developed and validated by Slater (1941, 1942; Slater and Bennett, 1943) to measure general intelligence. The present study used the shorter version of this test (GT 70/23) which takes about 20 min to administer (National Institute of Industrial Psychology, 1944). The GT 70/23 is composed of two subtests, test 1 and test 2, the product-moment intercorrelation between them being .54. Each subtest is designed to measure general intelligence without bringing verbal or spatial abilities into play. Various geometric shapes and designs have certain meanings and characteristics which must be identified by the subject.

The reliability of the GT 70/23 has been assessed by three different methods, for each subtest separately, and for the total test score (Table 7.13) (Salvendy, 1973). From this it can be seen that all reliabilities for test 2 are greater than those for test 1; and these differences for the split-half reliability are significant ($F = 17.75$; $p > .01$). The test is not strictly homogeneous, since the mean number of odd items answered correctly was significantly greater than the mean number of even items answered correctly both for test 1 and for the total test scores (test 1: $t = 3.16$, $p > .01$; total: $t = 3.14$, $p > .01$).

Norms. It is evident from Table 7.14 that the norms derived from the 181 industrial subjects are significantly lower than the norms derived from the general population. Thus the median intellectual abilities of the industrial operators in this study are equivalent to the lower twentieth percentile of the general population.

Table 7.13   Reliability of the GT 70/23 Assessed by Three Methods
($N = 181$)

Method of Reliability Testing	Principal Reference for the Method	Test 1	Test 2	Total Tests 1 and 2,
Split-half	Rulon (1939)	.788	.851	.817
K–R 20	Kuder and Richardson (1937) Richardson and Kuder (1939)	.817	.842	.887
Guttman L₃	Guttman (1945)	.821	.839	.887

Table 7.14   Performance of Subjects on the GT 70/23 Compared with a Larger British Population

| | Test Scores Falling into Percentile Level ($N = 181$) | | | Unselected British Subjects, Total[a] ($N > 5000$) |
Percentile	Test 1	Test 2	Total	
.01	0	0	0	
.05	1	2	4	
.10	3	3	7	12
.20	5	5	11	
.30	6	6	13	20
.40	7	8	15	
.50	8	9	17	
.60	9	11	19	
.70	10	13	22	28
.80	11	13	24	
.90	13	15	27	36
.95	15	16	28	
.99	17	18	32	

[a] From: *Manual of the 70/23 Non-Verbal Intelligence Test, GT 70/23.* (British) National Institute of Industrial Psychology (1944).

Intelligence as a Predictor of Production Performance.   The *lack* of meaningful significant *linear* correlation between test scores and production performance criteria, when a linear model between test scores and criteria is assumed, is apparent both for test 1 and test 2 separately [$-.13$ ($t = 1.95$, $p > 0.05$)] and for total test scores [$-.15$ ($t = 2.85$, $p > .01$)]. These low validities are in general agreement with the results of previous validity studies on both verbal and nonverbal intelligence tests conducted with a variety of diversified tests, occupational tasks (requiring psycho-motor activities), and criteria measures (Super and Crites, 1962; Ghiselli, 1966). Production performance and intellectual abilities appear to lack meaningful correlation because only minimal intellectual abilities are required for repetitive psychomotor tasks; any intellectual abilities above the minimal level will not raise the level of production criteria (although if the person is too intelligent it may cause a decrease in his productivity).

In the present study, any subject who obtained a total score of seven or less on the GT 70/23 (Table 7.14)—representing the lower tenth percentile (which is equal approximately to an IQ of up to 80)—appeared to have demonstrated the minimum intellectual abilities required to perform the psychomotor operations. That is, up to this level the correlation between test scores and production criterion ($r = .46$; $p > .01$) increased significantly as the scores on the intelligence test increased. Above the lower tenth percentile, up to the ninetieth percentile, only a random relationship ($r = -.04$) was manifested between the test and production performance. The upper tenth percentile score (i.e. an I.Q. of about 120 and above) on the intelligence test yielded a significant negative correlation ($r = -.52$, $p > .05$) with the criterion. Thus it is evident that when the performance distribution of the test scores of the *entire* population is considered, an attempt to use a linear correlation method, like Pearson's R, to describe the relationship between intellectual abilities and repetitive psychomotor performance, will produce artifactual results. From this it would appear that either extremely high or extremely low intellectual abilities result in decreased productivity on psychomotor repetitive tasks; but the intellectual capabilities of the middle 80 percent of the subjects have only random effect on their productivity, although their score range on the GT 70/23 is 1 to 4 between the lowest and highest score.

Vision and Production Performance

The reliability of the Bausch & Lomb orthorator was assessed on 80 British operators from the electronics firm by checking its results against those of standard medical vision tests. The results of this comparison are in agreement with other findings on American subjects (Wirt, 1943; Imus, 1946, 1949a, 1949b; Davis, 1946; Kephart and Mason, 1950; Zeidner and Gordon, 1953; Gordon, Zeinder, Zagorski, and Uhlaner, 1954; Schwartz and Dimminck, 1958). The orthorator results revealed only small deviations from results of medical tests; the notable exception was the color test, which indicated a significantly higher percentage of color deficiency than actually existed in the sample according to the medical tests.

Although some of the vision items (e.g., near visual acruity) had statistically significant correlations with the production performance criterion, they have only restricted meaning. The two reasons for this limitation are as follows:

1. Less than 10 percent of the tested operators had deficient vision (from one to four operators in each group studied) on any one of the 12 orthorator test items. Thus with such a small number of unsatisfactory test results, it is difficult to say how much of the correlation represents a true relationship.

For example, the two experienced operators in the electronics firm who scored an unacceptable low level on a vision test item, had also the lowest rate of decrease in the standard deviation of performance time on the element Position. A highly significant correlation coefficient of .99 was present between the latter two items, indicating that in this case visual characteristics of the individual and certain performance variabilities on the One-Hole test were confounding the prediction of production performance.

2. It was noticed on many occasions during the course of the study that, although adequate vision was essential at the early stages of learning, it became virtually redundant at later stages when the kinesthetic and tactile senses largely took over and became crucial for performance. For example, an experienced operator with severely handicapped vision belonged to the highest production output group of her electronics firm; but operators at the training stage were unable to perform their jobs adequately with a comparable visual disability.

Interview–Questionnaire Technique and Productivity

As was indicated previously, the suitability of individuals for performance on specific tasks can be derived by methods other than personnel testing. One such method is the interview–questionnaire technique (see Table 7.15), which was utilized with the same 181 female industrial operators who participated in the previously reported tests.

Because there were significant differences among many of the test scores, their intercorrelation with each other, and with the criterion measures among various groups of subjects, it was not feasible to combine all six groups into one for analysis purposes.

However, there were no statistically or practically significant differences between the questionnaire analysis data for the experienced operators in the electromechanical and confectionery firms. Thus their data were pooled and reanalyzed in order to increase the sample size and, consequently, obtain a more reliable and valid response analysis.

Because the product-moment correlation assumes a normal continuous distribution with homogeneous variance, which does not hold for the majority of questionnaire items, the investigators employed the iterative multiple correlation method (Greenberger and Ward, 1956; Veldman, 1967). This method was specifically developed to analyze questionnaire responses.

The analysis of the 10-item questionnaire (Table 7.15) illustrates that between one-third and one-half of the variables (the square of the multiple correlation coefficient) accounting for mean production performance or rate of trainee improvement could be forecast by these 10 items. Not every item is important for each group in the prediction of production performance. Such items as mother's occupation have absolutely no bearing on the production performance of the daughter in any of the groups studied. Indeed, in almost all cases experience level and self-rating are the only items accounting for a significant amount of the variance. The utilization of self-rating as an effective technique of evaluating an individual's productivity is supported by a large-scale study on a variety of occupations (Pym and Auld, 1965).

Validity of the Total Test Battery

The reliability and validity of *each component* of the test battery was discussed in previous sections. In this section, we show how the discriminating items of these components can be integrated into a test battery for the selection of operators by the use of correlation, multiple-correlation, and discriminant analysis.

First, a separate statistical analysis was made for each group of subjects in order to determine whether differences in test item scores and intercorrelations of test items with themselves and the production criteria existed among the six groups. Where analysis of variance enabled the combination of the test items for different groups of subjects, further statistical analysis was carried out on the combined data; where combination was not possible, the analysis was performed for each group separately.

In order to satisfy underlying assumptions in the use of parametric statistics (Hays, 1963), such as Pearson's product-moment correlation, production figures were transformed to natural logarithms in order to satisfy the assumptions of normality and homogeneity of the data.[*]

[*] This was a more powerful transformation than taking the square, square root, or reciprocal of each production index.

To visualize how the statistical analysis of a test battery is performed, let us outline and discuss a step-by-step procedure for one group of subjects (experienced electronics operators: $N = 41$).

After the test battery items had satisfied the assumptions underlying the use of parametric statistics, the test battery items had to be reduced from the initial 110 to only the items that had a statistically significant product-moment correlation with the production criteria and to those which could contribute significantly to the multiple correlation, as indicated in the previous chapter.

Table 7.16 illustrates the eight test battery items, out of the 110 measured, that have significant product-moment correlations with the mean production performance. The purpose here is not to elaborate on the meaning and interpretation of these test items, but rather to illustrate the technique. When these test items are subjected to a multiple-correlation analysis (Dubois, 1957) (Table 7.17), a significant multiple-correlation coefficient of .63 ($p > .025$) is derived, which means that 40 percent of the variance accounting for the production performance is predictable from these eight test items.

Multiple correlation may assess the power of a test battery, but it cannot provide a mechanism for deciding quantitatively who should be accepted or rejected, based on the person's test battery scores. For this, the discriminant function with Mahalanobis' statistics is required (Table 7.18). In the study being described, when the discriminant function for an operator is −7.47 or more,* it is expected that this operator will perform in the industrial situation at an index of 115 (where 100 is the standard), whereas those scoring less than this function most probably will not be able to attain the same standard. Each discriminant function variable is multiplied with the individual test scores, and products of the multiplications are added together to form the discriminant function constant. Naturally this constant is varied according to the labor market and the level of productivity the company is wishing to accept.

When the test battery was reduced from eight to three items, by eliminating those items which did not contribute markedly to the multiple correlation (Table 7.19), a significant ($p > .01$) multiple correlation of .58 was derived with a statistically significant discriminant function constant.

---

* For the mathematical derivation and statistical use of discriminant function with Mahalanobis' statistics, see Rao (1952). When the discriminant function for an operator is −7.47, it yields a Mahalanobis' statistic of 1.81, which with 7 and 33 degrees of freedom is not statistically significant.

Table 7.15 Contribution of Each of the 10 Questionnaire–Interview Items to Multiple Correlation for Prediction of Worker's Performance
(N = 181)

	Groups of Subjects Studied					
	Trainee Operators in Electronics Firm N=27		Experienced Operators in Electronics Firm N=41	Trainee Operators in Electromechanical and Confectionery Firms N=20		Experienced Operators in Electromechanical and Confectionery Firms N=81
Variables Studied for Each Operator	Criterion 1[a]	Criterion 2[b]	Criterion 3[c]	Criterion 4[d]	Criterion 5[e]	Criterion 6[f]
	Percentage of Total Predictable Variances from Multiple Correlation Accounted for by Each Questionnaire Item[g]					
1. Age (years)	0.07	11.52	0.03	0.08	0.04	0.54
2. Marital status (married was denoted by 1 otherwise, 0)	0.85	0.03	0.68	0.00	18.26	0.16
3. Number of children	2.34	5.26	1.28	19.68	0.09	0.22
4. Spectacles (if wears, was denoted by 1; otherwise, 0)	0.02	5.01	0.68	1.75	1.30	5.16
5. Mother's occupation (arranged in hierarchy of skills, where the highest skill was denoted by 1 and the lowest by 10)	0.92	0.02	0.53	0.03	0.54	0.37

6. Knitting (when done habitually was denoted by 1; otherwise, 0)	1.19	0.15	0.62	1.87	7.02	4.63
7. Sewing (when done habitually was denoted by 1; otherwise, 0)	1.23	0.47	0.00	2.97	10.55	0.47
8. Playing musical instruments (when done habitually was denoted by 1; otherwise, 0)	5.48	2.22	2.03	8.19	22.43	0.45
9. Industrial experience (years)	30.02	7.47	1.42	1.46	0.10	5.05
10. Overall self-rating of performance on a 5-point scale (1 is denoted the lowest performance, 5 is the highest)	7.35	0.14	29.24	Not available		21.58
Total variance accounted for by the 10 questionnaire items (percent)	49.43	32.29	36.51	36.03	60.23	38.63
Multiple correlation of the 10 questionnaire items with criterion performance	0.702[h]	0.568	0.604[i]	0.601	0.776	0.622[j]

[a] Slope of linear regression line, fitted to first consecutive 13 weeks of production performance.

[b] Mean production performance during first consecutive 13 weeks of training.

[c] Mean production performance during 25 consecutive days.

[d] Mean production performance during first week.

[e] Slope of the linear regression line, fitted to the first one week of production performance.

[f] Mean production performance during consecutive 25 days.

[g] This is in effect the relative contribution of a test item to the multiple-correlation coefficient of the 10 questionnaire items with the criteria.

[h] $p < .08$.

[i] $p < .05$.

[j] $p < .002$.

Table 7.16 Statistically Significant and "Meaningful" Correlations on Performances of 41 Experienced Operators in the Electronics Firm[a]

	Significance Level							
	1	5		10				
	Correlation Coefficient with Production Means							
	.41	.31	.34	.28	.31	.28	.27	.29
	Test Measure Number							
Test Measure Number[b]	16	27	33	2	25	60	62	64
16		−.02	−.34	−.03	−.04	−.08	.17	.19
27	—		.08	.39	.34	.41	.31	.18
33	5	—		−.12	.46	.04	−.19	.12
2	—	2	—		.11	.39	.42	.16
25	—	5	1	—		.08	.31	.01
60	—	1	—	2	—		.42	.04
62	—	5	—	1	5	1		.05
64	—	—	—	—	—	—	—	

Description of Test Measure

2[c]	Number of pins inserted in second half-minute, first trial on One-Hole test.
16[c]	Slope of the fitted equation for the standard deviations of performance times on the element Reach of the One-Hole test.
25[c]	Intercept of the fitted equation for the standard deviations of performance times for element Move of the One-Hole test.
27[c]	Intercept of the fitted equation for the mean performance times for the element Move of the One-Hole test.
33[c]	Intercept of the fitted equation for the fumbles occurring during the element Grasp of the One-Hole test.
60	Number of pins inserted in the first trial on the Purdue Pegboard.
62	Number of pins inserted in the third trial on the Purdue Pegboard.
64	Scores on the extrovert scale of the Eysenck Personality Inventory.

[a] Multiple correlation coefficient of .6312 significant at 2.5 percent.
[b] The upper part of the matrix refers to values of Pearson's product moment correlation, while the lower part of the matrix refers to their significance levels (in percentages).
[c] Item refers to equation described in Table 7.19.

Table 7.17   Composites of the Multiple-Correlation Coefficients of Test Scores with Criterion Mean Production Performance for 41 Experienced Operators at the Electronics Firm

Test Battery Item Number as in Table 7.16	Regression Coefficient	Standard Error of Regression Coefficient	Contribution of a Test Item to Multiple-Correlation Coefficient F-Value[a]
2	$-.0180$	1.0015	.0003
16	$-.0706$	.0302	5.4603[b]
25	.1111	.1166	.9068
27	.0065	.0430	.0229
33	.0218	.0254	.7365
60	1.0539	1.7692	.3548
62	1.4748	1.4654	1.0128
64	1.1187	.5876	3.6238[c]

[a] With 8 and 31 degrees of Freedom.
[b] $p < .001$.
[c] $p < .01$.

Table 7.18   Composites of the Discriminant Function with Criterion Mean Production Performance for 41 Experienced Operators in Electronics Firm

Test Item Number	Coefficients for Discriminant Function Variables
2	.055
16	.010
25	$-.006$
27	$-.006$
33	$-.000$
60	$-.189$
62	$-.898$
64	$-.305$

Discriminant function content $= -7.47$

The multiple correlation and the contributions of each test item to it for all the groups of subjects are portrayed in Table 7.19. The table illustrates the need for cross-validation in personnel selection, since a test item that has a statistically significant contribution to the test battery for one group may be irrelevant for another group.

Table 7.19 Those Items from the Original Test Battery that Contributed the Most to the Prediction of Production Performance of Trainee and Experienced Operators

Group	N	Type of Production Criterion (the notations refer to those described in Table 7.15)	Test Items Utilized in Multiple Correlation (see footnote for description of notations)	Average Administration Time of Test Battery (min)	Test Battery Regression Coefficients	Standard Error of Regression Coefficient	Contribution of a Test Item to Multiple-Correlation Coefficient F-Value	Degrees of Freedom	Significance of F-Value (percent)	Multiple-Correlation Coefficient of Test Battery Value of R	Significance of r (percent)
Electromechanical											
Experienced	30	6	8	30	−.1371	.0986	1.9325	5, 23	—	.6381	2.5
			20		−.0515	.0475	1.1737		—		
			22		.0562	.0271	4.3031		1		
			48		.1068	.0615	3.0146		2.5		
			65		3.3057	1.2453	7.0468		0.1		
Trainees	8	4	108	2	−1.5156	.6276	5.8326	2, 5	5	.8923	2.5
					.6185	.6595	.8794		—		
Trainees	8	5	23	20	−.1257	.3901	.1038	2,5	—	.9068	1
			54		.6147	.2329	6.9647		5		
Confectionery											
Experienced	43	6	14	20	.9438	.5423	3.0295	2, 40	5	.4663	1
			15		.5342	.2741	3.7968		2.5		
Trainees	9	4	99	2	−.3497	.0941	3.7967	2, 6	1	.9440	0.1
			105		−.3329	.0836	5.8699		1		
Trainees	9	5	54	22	−4.4207	1.6591	7.0995	2, 6	2.5	.9032	1
			99		−24.2555	5.6073	8.7117		1		

Electronics

Group											
Experienced	41	3	16	30	−.0791	9.6027	9.6027		3, 36	0.1	.5776	0.1
			25		.0881	4.5898	4.5898		1		
			64		1.3061	5.9691	5.9691		0.1		
Trainees	27	2	21	28	.0232	3.3988	3.3988	2, 24	5	.6805	1
			25		.0313	2.2685	2.2685		—		
Trainees	27	1	25	20	.0713	.0370	3.7164	2, 24	5	.5459	2.5
			65		.7216	.8549	.7125		—		

On the first 15 trials of the One–Hole tests, each of the starred items (in the description below) relates to the linear equation $Y = a \log x + b$, when y is an element, fumble rate, or standard deviation of inverse elemental times; x is the sum of cycles in the previous trials $+ 0.5x$ (number of cycles in current trial).

Test Item	Description
8	Total number of pins inserted during the entire 15 trials on the One–Hole test
14	Slope of linear regression line fitted to number of pins inserted in each of the 15 trials on One–Hole test
15	Intercept of linear regression line fitted to number of pins inserted in each of the 15 trials on One–Hole test
*16	a for standard deviation of performance time on element Reach
*20	a for standard deviation of performance time on element Grasp
*21	b for standard deviation of performance time on element Grasp
*22	a for performance time on element Grasp
*23	b for performance time on element Grasp
*25	b for standard deviation of performance time on element Move
48	Mean performance time at 7th trial on element Move on One–Hole test
54	Mean performance time at 15th trial on element Reach on One–Hole test
64	E score on Eysenck Personality Inventory
65	N score on Eysenck Personality Inventory
99	Weight of operator (lb)
105	Length of second finger (item I in Figure 7.4)
108	Width of second finger (item F in Figure 7.4)
110	Width of thumb (item D in Figure 7.4)

STUDY 2: HANDEDNESS AND
PERSONNEL SELECTION

The main purpose of personnel selection is to discriminate among individuals. In order to achieve this objective, a battery of tests is normally administered to a set of individuals. It is possible then to discriminate among individuals on the basis of the level of their performance characteristics on specific tests. As a result of a series of recent experiments (Salvendy, 1970), it appears that discrimination among individuals, with respect to their performance characteristics, may be *partially* derived by other means than the customarily utilized personnel selection tests.

This study has been included to illustrate some of the supplementary methods that could be used to advantage in personnel selection. Even though at least one in 10 people in the United States is left-handed (U.S. Public Health Service, 1962), very little attention has been given to the handedness of an operator when he is selected for a job.

The published literature is more concerned with hand preference (Murrell, 1969; Provins, 1967; Annett, 1970), heredity, and handedness (Provins, 1956) than with handedness performance (Murrell, 1969). Hand preference is determined largely by training and environmental factors, as opposed to heredity (Hildreth, 1949). Thus social origins and development could account for the large predominance of right-handed over left-handed people (Hildreth, 1949; Horine, 1967), and would explain the origins of handedness in individuals. As a result of a series of phylogenetic studies in psychology, the existence of the phenomenon of lateral cortical dominance has been proved (e.g., Collins, 1968; Forward, Warren, and Hara, 1962; Horine, 1967). This means that the right-handed people have left-cerebral-hemisphere dominance, and vice versa. This phenomenon appears to be the product of handedness rather than its cause. The field is split ontologically; but a recent study (Horine, 1967) has shown that bilateral persons may be significantly slower on manual tasks than either left- or right-handed persons.

Five psychomotor tests were administered to 166 American university students (see Figures 7.2, 7.3, 7.4, and 7.7). Handedness was determined as a result of administering a questionnaire developed by Smith (1945). It was found that left-handed subjects have lower scores and improve less during practice than do right-handed subjects (Salvendy, 1970).

All the tests utilized in this study were designed so that they could easily be altered to handedness. For example, for a right-handed subject, the One-Hole test is situated 45° from a horizontal line parallel to his

Figure 7.7.   The blind-positioning apparatus.

body, where as the same test would be performed at 135° by a left-handed subject. It is not quite clear, however, whether the natural stereotype response on the rotary pursuit apparatus would be the same for both left- and right-handed subjects.

All the tests, for the four experiments carried out, were administered in the sequence in which they are presented in Table 7.20. The One-Hole test was administered as in the previous study, except that it was given for 10 trials only and no 3-min interval between the seventh and eighth trials. The Purdue Pegboard and the anthropometric data measures were done exactly as in the previous study.

The rotary pursuit apparatus requires the subject to follow with a stylus a 0.75-in. diameter target that rotates in a clockwise direction on a circle at 45 rpm. The duration of stylus contact with the target during a 20-sec run constitutes a trial score. Ten trials were administered with a 20-sec interval after every trial.

The hand dynamometer requires that the subject exert maximum force by the hand when the arm is outstretched horizontally and the hand is in a vertical plane. The force (kilograms) produced in one attempt constitutes a trial score. This test was performed once.

The blind-positioning apparatus (Figure 7.7) consists of a semicircular board with 21 target points (at 0, 30, 60, 90, 120, 150, and 180°), three distances (12, 20, 26 in.), and three angles of elevation (0, 30, and 60°). The subject is required to hit specific targets when blindfolded, and

Table 7.20 Synopsis of Experimental Data Used in Handedness Experiments

Experiment	Subjects[a]						Tests Utilized[b]					
	Number[c]		Age of Combined Males and Females (years)		Background	Hand Studied	One-Hole test	Rotary Pursuit Apparatus	Purdue Pegboard (R.H.)	Hand Dynamometer	Blind Positioning	Anthropometry
	Female	Male	Mean	S.D.								
I[d]	14	26	23	3	University students	Nonpreferred	X	X	X	X		
II[d]	16	16	21	2	University students	Preferred	X	X	X	X		
III[d]	—	34	22	2	University students	Preferred			X		X	
IV	70	—	41	4	Industrial	Preferred	X	X	X	X		X

[a] All subjects were caucasian Americans.

[b] Tests utilized are illustrated in the following figures: One-Hole test (Figure 7.3), Purdue Pegboard (Figure 7.2), blind positioning (Figure 7.7), anthropometry (Figure 7.4).

[c] In experiments I, II, and III, equal number of left- and right-handed subjects were in both the female and the male groups; however, in experiment IV only 14 left-handed subjects were utilized (the remaining 56 being right-handed).

[d] A more detailed report on these studies has been provided by Salvendy (1970).

deviations from the target are recorded. The mean deviations (inches) of 10 attempts at aiming on a target constitutes the trial score. The subject receives kinesthetic feedback after each trial when the experimenter redirects the subject's hand to the target point (if the subject has not hit the target).

In experiment III (see Table 7.20), utilizing the blind-positioning test, the deviations in the attempted target hits in the X and Y coordinates indicated patterns between left- and right-handed subjects similar to those of the least distance measured from the target to the attempted hit (disregarding direction of hit from target point). Therefore, only the results of the latter analysis are reported here, and unidimensional rather than multidimensional analysis could be utilized. Data for the blind-positioning experiment were grouped, since analysis of variance revealed that the relative difference between the performance of left- and right-handed subjects did not change because of this grouping.

It was learned that right-handed subjects had higher scores than the left-handed in all the three test items measured on the blind-positioning apparatus (see Figure 7.8). These differences are statistically significant ($p > .001$) except for the 12-in. distance, for which the same trend remains but at a statistically nonsignificant level.

The results of another experiment (experiment IV, Table 7.20) were somewhat deviant. Handedness of the 70 female experienced solderers was determined according to the questionnaire validated by Annett (1970). This questionnaire identified 14 strictly left-handed and 56 strictly right-handed operators out of a total population of 350 to whom the questionnaire was administered.[*]

The results indicate that the production of left-handed operators working in a right-handed environment, as determined by an analysis of 25 consecutive days (of production output), is not different from that of the right-handed operators. The right-handed operators had a mean productivity of 99.0 percent with a standard deviation of 20.7, whereas the left-handed individuals had 99.1 percent and a standard deviation of 15.2. In addition to the tests administered in experiments I and II (see Table 7.20), anthropometric data of the hand were collected from the subjects in this study, as outlined by Salvendy (1971). Right-handed operators

---

[*] This does not imply that there were 280 ambidextrous operators; instead, it indicates (according to the questionnaire response) that handedness has to be considered on a continuum scale with left-handed operators identified on one extreme and right-handed operators identified on the other. On the central line of this continuum scale were two truly ambidextrous operators. The remaining operators fell into the category that performed the majority of activities with the right hand but used the left hand for some activities, or vice versa.

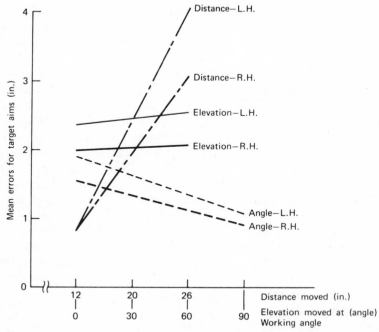

Figure 7.8. Summary of results for the blind-positioning apparatus ($N = 34$). (After Salvendy, 1970.)

scored significantly higher on the rotary pursuit apparatus than did the left-handed ones ($t = 2.35$, $p > .05$); but this result could have been due to the clockwise rotation, which is the natural direction for right-handed subjects, but not necessarily for left-handed subjects.

It is possible that the differences in results obtained between the study on university students and the study of industrial operators occurred because of the difference in the age groups investigated (mean ages of 22 and 41 for the college student and industrial subjects, respectively). These age differences may indicate that discrepancies in performance, due to handedness, diminish as skills became overlearned with aging.

It must be emphasized again that the conclusions derived from one class of subjects cannot be transferred to another class of subjects without further experimentation, since each class has its own attributes.

STUDY 3: PHYSIOLOGICAL CONSIDERATIONS IN
PERSONNEL SELECTION

It has been stated that industrial operators performing repetitive psychomotor tasks can be selected by a variety of methods, including those based on: performance characteristics on psychomotor tests, visual abilities, intellectual level, personality, anthropometric data, and handedness characteristics. In addition to these considerations, attention should be given to the physiological efficiency of the human body when performing manual activities. Since an operator with higher physiological efficiency can work longer continuously, he may have an overall daily higher productivity than his fellow worker with lower physiological efficiency.

As a result of a series of physiological investigations by Salvendy (1969a) involving the Bicycle Ergometer, the Harvard Step test, the Pump Ergometer, and psychological studies on card sorting, it has been shown that an optimum rate of work exists at a freely chosen pace. During paced performance, the natural rhythm of the operator is disturbed. Optimization occurs where energy expenditure and errors per unit of external work are minimized while human efficiency is maximized. It was revealed that working either above or below a freely chosen pace maximized the physiological cost per unit of work and minimized the body's efficiency.

A further study was conducted by Salvendy and Pilitsis (1971b) on the Arm Ergometer (Figure 7.9), in order to verify the influence of age on paced and unpaced performance. Fifteen male sedentary subjects aged 21 to 64 participated. The Arm Ergometer consists of a wooden structure containing a horizontal bar of tool steel restricted in its X–Z axis travel and interconnected at its center with a chain and sprocket mechanism supporting a calibrated 25-lb load. The external mechanical energy required in the operation of this equipment was calculated at 8.22×10^{-3} kcal/cycle (including friction). To facilitate the recording of work output for the designated work period, a work cycle counter activated by a "microswitch," located adjacent to the handle bar's track was energized by the handle upon completion of 16.94 in. of travel.

A mechanical metronome with a working range of 14 to 180 beats/min served as the pacing mechanism. The volumes of air expired and related oxygen were recorded and analyzed by a "Max Planck" respirometer and an F-3 model Beckmann oxygen analyzer, respectively.

Eight test runs were conducted for each subject, each lasting 35 min.

Figure 7.9.   The arm ergometer. (After Salvendy and Pilitsis, 1971b.)

Each subject was requested to work for a 10-min period at a rate that was representative of the performance he would maintain if he had to work at the chosen pace for 8 hr a day. These practice trials indicated the freely chosen rate for each subject ($\bar{x} = 26$ cycles/min). Three rates below and three above the initial freely chosen rate of work were administered. All test run paces were randomly selected. Subsequent to the six selected paces, the subject was once again requested to perform at a freely chosen rate of work. A .80 coefficient of correlation between the initial and final freely chosen rates of work indicated that the freely chosen pace data were reliable.

Weir's (1949) calorimetric model was used in the determination of

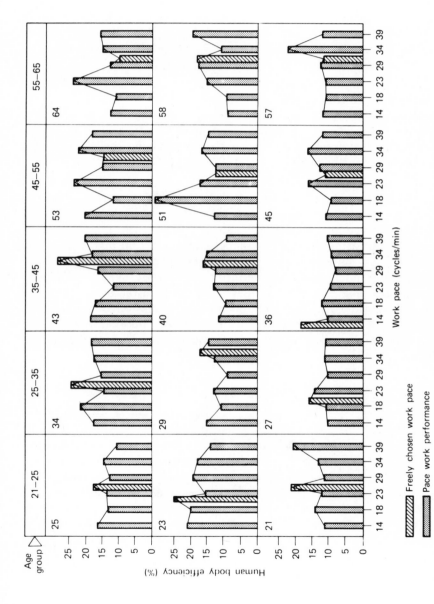

Figure 7.10. Body efficiency versus work pace for 15 male subjects. (After Salvendy and Pilitsis, 1971b.)

related expenditure of kilocalories. The results of this study indicate that the expenditure of kilocalories for young and old subjects differs in paced and unpaced situations (Figure 7.10). That is, the younger subjects (aged 21 to 45) have the highest physiological efficiency at the freely chosen pace, whereas the older subjects (aged 45 to 64) had the highest efficiency at paced performances. These results do not agree with some studies of adult training (e.g., Belbin and Toye, 1970). If our results are accepted, the implications for personnel selection will be twofold:

1. Older operators (above 45 years) appear to be more suited physiologically to work in a paced environment (such as conveyor lines) than the younger operators (below 45 years of age).

2. Because personnel vary in their freely chosen pace level, operators who have to work in a paced environment should be placed in groups according to their freely chosen pace, thus minimizing the physiological stress imposed on them by pacing.

There are other situations in which physiological indices can be used to advantage in personnel selection, including those involved in recent developments in biomechanics (e.g., Chaffin and Baker, 1970) and physical fitness tests (e.g., Fleishman, 1964). However, the greatest promise in increasing the validity of personnel selection tests by the use of physiological indices lies more in the development, validation, and adoption of an index combining performance measures and physiological or psychophysiological indices (Figure 7.11) than in the development of additional physiological tests. The hypothesis suggested in Figure 7-11 has not been yet fully validated, although tentative pilot study results to support the theory are available from some unpublished studies by the authors.

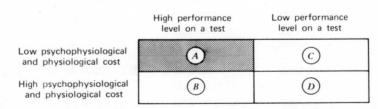

Figure 7.11. Schematization of a hypothetical interrelationship of physiology and performance. In the traditional selection mode, items falling into both boxes A and B would be accepted and C and D would be rejected. In the proposed model, only those falling into box A would be accepted; the rest would be rejected. This does not imply that more would be rejected with the new model than with the old one; since low and high performance levels are on a continuum, the cutoff point between them could be made at any stage.

RECOMMENDATIONS FOR RESEARCH AREAS IN
PERSONNEL SELECTION

The three studies just discussed illustrate three different, but inter-related, areas of development in personnel selection. Study 1 was concerned with the systematic development of performance measures in personnel selection. In study 2 we considered the use of human body structure in personnel selection. Study 3 dealt with the contribution of physiological indices to personnel selection. The direction in which present research work may effectively be extended is summarized under six main categories, which are treated individually.

Improving the Dependability of Criteria

Although the need for the development of dependable criteria measures in personnel selection has been recognizd for almost half a century (e.g., Hull, 1928), in the majority of the published selection studies this requirement receives very limited attention (e.g., Jones, 1950). Indeed, researchers frequently make only last-minute efforts to establish criteria measures and determine their dependability.

Yet it now become increasingly evident that, if theories of personnel selection and personnel training are to be truly validated, emphasis must be given at the outset to the establishment of the most appropriate performance and behavior measures or criteria against which the effectiveness of selection and training methodologies can be evaluated. Merely combining different criteria, each having low dependability, does not increase the power and overall dependability of the combined criteria index. Therefore, future research must be aimed at increasing the dependability of criterion measures, especially those of direct performance measurement and work behavior. Such studies should aim at the development of objective quantitative mathematical models based on validated theories of work performance and behavior.

Culture-Free Tests

The majority of the tests presently utilized in the United States were developed and validated on white, middle-class Americans. Favorable performance on these tests is much more readily achieved by those who have had the advantages offered by the social and cultural background that produced the makers of the tests. Groups that have not shared the testmakers' background are unfairly discriminated against because the testees cannot be expected to have made an effort to acquire cross-culturally the "knowledge" that white, middle-class subjects have automatically.

Thus these tests may discriminate unfavorably against minority groups.*
The development of new selection tests that are free both of cultural
and social status is urgently needed if human national resources are to be
distributed most equitably and effectively.

Innate versus Acquired Nature of Psychomotor Skills

At present very little is known about which components of psychomotor
skills are acquired and which are innate or inherited. Much more information is available in the general area of intelligence (Jensen, 1969,
Burt, 1972). It is believed that the experimental design to investigate the
matter could be arranged along the lines of Jensen's (1969) experiments,
and the psychomotor tests utilized should represent the factors identified
by Fleishman and Hempel (1954b), such as finger dexterity, manual
dexterity, wrist–finger speed, aiming, and positioning.

The results of such a study would have applications in personnel
selection, and they could be of great significance in personnel training,
as well. By knowing which components of the skills required for a task
can be acquired and which are innate, training programs could become
more effective by concentrating on the acquired rather than the innate
components of the task.

Use of Personnel Testing Principles for Human Experimentation

Individuals differ in many respects. Misleading results may be achieved
as a consequence of large interindividual differences (e.g., Eysenck, 1966;
Salvendy and Pilitsis, 1971a). When a significant part of this variance can
be explained meaningfully and statistically, better experimental results
can be derived. This can be accompanied in four steps: (1) the development and adoption of test batteries, analogous to those utilized in personnel selection, which attempt to represent the human traits associated
with the experimental task; (2) the establishment of the validity of the
test battery and its components by the use of multiple-correlation or
canonical analysis and selection of those components which have statistically significant predictive validity for the experimental task; (3) the
adoption of the significant components from the multiple-correlation or
canonical analysis in the analysis of covariance, in order to covary individual differences; and (4) by adopting the significant components
mentioned in item 3, achieving the reduction of the sum of squares
in the analysis of variance associated with the between subject's effects.
By the nature of the analysis of covariance, this difference in sum of

* Such discrimination has been reported outside the United States, as well. Africa,
studies have been published by Provins, Bell, Bieheuvel and Adisell (1968).

squares is distributed to the other categories of the analysis, thus resulting in a more representative interpretation of the experimental outcome.

Application of Personnel Testing to the Health Care Delivery Field

Up to the present day, personnel selection for psychomotor tasks has been primarily applied to military, industrial, and business personnel. Now, more than ever before, because of a growing demand for reducing the cost and increasing the quality of health care delivery, there is an increased need for the selection of health care personnel who can be trained in the shortest time to the highest quality of psychomotor performance.

The initial steps to accomplish this have already been initiated with regards to the psychomotor component of dental education and practice by Salvendy, Cunningham, Ferguson, and Hinton (1971) and Salvendy and Goodrich (1971) and, with regard to the psychomotor component of surgery education and practice, by Salvendy and Pilitsis (1973).

Physiological and Biomechanical Considerations in Personnel Selection

It is emphasized at the outset of the chapters on personnel selection that both human traits and task characteristics are multidimensional; therefore, a test battery, rather than merely one test, is required for an effective personnel selection mechanism. This is interpreted by some researchers and practitioners as covering no more than the psychological capabilities and limitations of the human. It is the authors' firm belief that these considerations must be coupled with the physiological (e.g., Salvendy and Pilitsis, 1971b) and biomechanical (e.g., Martin and Chaffin, 1972) evidence available; not to mention the obvious medical status of the individual and the legal requirements that must be fulfilled before the task can be performed.

The physiological and medical considerations gained greater importance in the United States with the introduction of the Occupational Safety and Health Act of 1970, which became law on April 28, 1971. The National Institute for Occupational Safety and Health (U.S.) recognizes the need not only for basic and applied research in toxicology and pathology, but also in the area of human performance and ergonomics, for which it provided seven grants for the fiscal year 1971.

APPENDIX

These forms and documents are included to illustrate individual items usually found in skills analysis training programs. A page reference to the text is appended to each Figure; specimen numbers have been included on the forms where this helped to make them more comprehensible.

This material is reproduced, by permission, from *Training Recommendations, Operatives,* of the Knitting Lace and Net Industry Training Board, Hamilton Road, Nottingham, NG5 IAU, England, whose courtesy in providing the forms is gratefully acknowledged. Other Industrial Training Boards issue recommendations for training appropriate to their industries.

BUILD-UP OF PARTS INTO WHOLE JOB

The synthesis of back panel elements that occurs in the looping of fully fashioned garments is represented in Figure A.1a. The task consists of running on (see Figures 1.2 and 3.2) the back panels, fronts, sleeves, and bodies. These are taught and practiced in the sequence shown in Figure A.1b. It is not always necessary for each of the combinations in Figure A.1b to be used. For example, it may be possible to omit the combinations in fours. Similar element breakdowns are determined for fronts, sleeves, and bodies; when these have been mastered, the main sections are combined in the same manner, until a complete garment can be looped. Appropriate target times are allocated to each part and combination of parts.

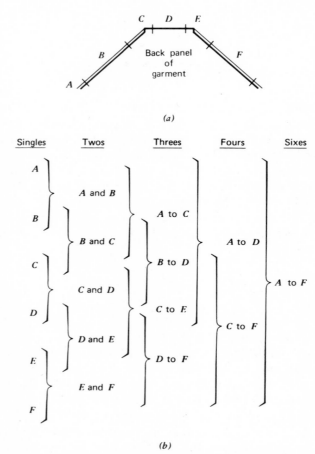

(a)

(b)

Figure A.1. (a) In running on the back panel, the main features are: A, locating the first stitch on the correct wale; B, running on an "uphill" selvedge; C, turning from a wale to a course; D, running on plain fabric; E, turning from a course to a wale; F, running on a "downhill" selvedge. (Courtesy of the U.K. Knitting, Lace, and Net Industry Training Board.) (b) Sequence in which elements A to F are taught and practiced.

* Course: Week No.:   Date: Trainee: Day No.:

Results[a]

Period	Exercise	Targets (sec)	1	2	3	4	5	6	7	8	9	10	11	12	13	14	15	16	17	Highest	Second Highest	Lowest	Attempts	Number to Target get
1	B.3	5	8/R	7/R	10/W 12/R	7/R	7/R	5/R	11/R	8/R	7/R	6/R	5/R	5/R	6/R	4/R	5/R			15	11	4	15	5
2	B.2-3	10	16/W 11/R	15/R	15/R	13/R	15/R	13/R	15/R	16/R	11/R	13/R	11/R							16	12	11	12	—
3	Talk K.14																							
4	B.1-3	15	19/R	23/R	21/R	21/R	16/R	15/R	15/R	15/R	14/R	15/W	12/W	14/R						21	14	12	12	5
5	B.5	4		6/R	4/R	5/R	5/R	3/R	3/R	4/R	5/R	3/R	4/R	5/R	5/R	4/R	3/R	3/R		16	6	3	16	9
6	M.1	—																						
7	SR. 10-12	27/90%	30/1	26/0	23/0	26/0	27/0	25/0	24/0	25/0	25/0	26/0								27	23	10	10	10
8	B.1-3	15	13/R	19/R	14/R	14/R	19/R	17/W 18/R	15/R	15/R	12/R	11/R	15/R	15/R	16/R					19	12	11	11	6

[a] R = right, W = wrong. Examples: 8/R = 8 sec and done correctly; 10/W = 10 sec and incorrect; 30/1 = 30 sec and 1 error. Quality target 100 percent in each case except period 7, where the target is 9 correct out of 10.

Figure A.2. Daily work record, stage 1 (see p. 146).
(Courtesy of U. K. Knitting, Lace and Net Industry Training Board.)

Figure A.2. Whereas the Timetable indicates the planned use of time, the Daily Work Record shows the actual use of time for each period of the day. This information is obviously needed for progress to be known and for the planning of the next day's activities. When practical exercises are performed, the time and quality score for each attempt are recorded. This can often be done by the trainee. The overall result for each period is indicated by the summary on the R.H.S, so that at a glance it can be seen how near a trainee is to reaching and maintaining target performance.

Dept:			Operation:			Trainee:	
Course: 2		Week no. 12	Day no. 59		(−6 days' absence)		Date:

Work Done	P.W. Time^a (min)	Quality	Time Start	Time Finish	Lost Time	Time Taken	Performance (B.S. scale)^b
SH 80583	23.8		7.55	8.40	10 min m/c	45	40
SL 8053	30.0		8.50	9.42	10 min break	52	44
SH 10431	31.48		9.45	10.30		45	53
SL 10431	37.9		10.31	11.15		44	65
SH 10412 $\frac{6}{12}$	15.74		11.18	11.42		24	49
SL 10412 $\frac{6}{12}$	17.16		12.30	12.52		22	59

^{a} EWS target time.
^{b} Performance on scale where 100 = EWS.

Figure A.3. Daily work record, stage 2 (see p. 146). (Courtesy of U. K. Knitting, Lace, and Net Industry Training Board.)

Figure A.3. This document serves the same purpose as the Stage 1 version, but is an alternative for use in advanced training, when production runs are being carried out. The specimen shown refers to a situation in which a piecework system is in use, and therefore it is a fairly simple matter to convert the results of each run into an Operative Performance Index. In other situations, results would be expressed in rather different terms, such as units of work produced.

Course:
Course No.:
Trainee:
Week Ending:
Week No.:

Day no.			6		7		8		9		10		Week	
Day			Monday		Tuesday		Wednesday		Thursday		Friday			
		Target	Number of Attempts	Number to Target	Number of Attempts	Number to Target	Number of Attempts	Number to Target	Number of Attempts	Number to Target	Number of Attempts	Number to Target	Number of Attempts	Number to Target
Exercise	Time (sec)	Quality (per cent)												
B.3	5	100			36	26	38	30	36	32	28	27	138	115
B.2-3	10	100			10	6	10	5	12	9	12	12	44	32
B.1-3	15	100							30	14	23	15	53	29
SR.10-27 12		90	32	27	36	34	24	24					92	85

Figure A.4.   Weekly summary sheet (timed exercises only)   (see p. 146).
(Courtesy of U. K. Knitting, Lace and Net Industry Training Board.)

Figure A.4.   This is a straightforward summary of each day's results on the practical exercises used during the week.   The figures are taken from the Daily Work Record (Stage 1) at the end of the day.   The information given on the Daily Work Record is of particular value to the trainee and to the instructor (and also perhaps to the Training Officer) but is usually rather too detailed to be of interest to the Production Supervisor or Manager.   The latter may, however, wish to consult the Weekly Summary Sheet Periodically, where the overall position is readily apparent.

Trainee's Name and Initial(s)	Sex	National Insurance No.	Date Started Training	Age at that Time	Surname and Initial(s) of Instructor	K.L.N.I.T.B. Registration No. of Instructor

Job for which being trained	Weekly Training Wage	Date Training Wage Earned	Total Training Days
Previous Employer and experience			

Record of Progress from Commencement of Training to Point at which Training Wage Is Earned.

Week No.	Week Ending	Performance Achieved or Work Produced	Equivalent Earnings	Week No.	Week Ending	Performance Achieved or Work Produced	Equivalent Earnings

Figure A.5. Sample operative training record card (see p. 146). (Courtesy of U. K. Knitting, Lace and Net Industry Training Board.)

Table A.1 Faults Analysis: Patrolling in Fully Fashioned Knitter Training[a]

Name	Appearance	Cause	Effect	Responsibility	Action	Prevention
Fly buildup	Buildup of yarn fly—occurs in 1. pot eyes 2. top of carrier tube.	Yarn rubbing, against guides.	Can eventually cause yarn breakage, tighter knitting and other machine faults.	Knitter	Blow guides clear with compressed air at first sign of fly buildup.	Frequent checking of pot eyes on guides and carrier during machine patrol.
Bent or broken points on transfer bar.	Bent or broken point on transfer bar.	Transfer bar points knocked during bar loading.	Bad transfer of rib onto machine needles (dropped stitches).	Knitter/Bar-loader	Check visible part of of transfer bar—occasionally lift out bar and check. If necessary, correct plier points.	Frequent checking of transfer bars during machine patrol and by the bar-loader.
Buildup of fly in bar transfer mechanism.	Bar not level in transfer mechanism. Does not transfer rib.	Fly buildup in transfer mechanism.	1. Machine smash—transfer bar points come down on sinkers causing severe breakage of needles, etc. 2. Bar transfers without leaving rib—causes needles to be bent.	Knitter/Bar-loader	Check alignment of transfer bars—remove any fly buildup if unlevel.	Frequent checking to see that bars are level in transfer mechanism. And check after cleaning.

[a] Courtesy of U. K. Knitting, Lace, and Net Industry Training Board (see p. 169).

315

	Dept.: Knitting Dept.		Stage: Pliering needle	

Dept.: Knitting Dept.   Stage: Pliering needle

Exercise: S7   Target: No target should be attempted until the instructor is satisfied that the trainees are pliering correctly and to the correct specification.
To plier 40 needles: 3 min, 10 sec

Materials required:
1. Pliers
2. Sample knitting machine.

Machine position: This should be carried out with the machine needles in the up position

Instruction Schedule

Left Hand	Attention Points	Right Hand
1.	First position from knitting position.	Let needle bar out to first position.
2. Move first finger-tip behind needle shank.	Eyes—check for poor alignment. Touch—feel for bowed stems and high beards.	
3. Retain first fingertip behind needle shank.	Eyes—needle required leveling backward, forward, and sideways. Placing a piece of paper behind gives a better background.	P.U. Pliers and plier at shank of needle (just below beard).
4. As above.	Eyes—check for poor alignment. Touch—feel for unevenness.	Feel along front of needles with first fingertip.
5.	Knitting position. Eyes—check that work is on top of knockovers, move up needle stem if necessary.	Replace needle bar to upright position.
6. Hold yarn tight.	Remove any kinks from yarn when replacing needle bar.	Press needle bar to original position

Figure A.6.   Instruction schedule for pliering needles (see p. 169). (Courtesy of U. K. Knitting, Lace, and Net Industry Training Board.)

Subject: Setting up carrier $\qquad$ *Talk:* K.12

Purpose: To help trainees to appreciate how the carrier is set up and how incorrect settings give rise to numerous faults.

Equipment:
1. Blackboard.
2. Fabric with selvedge faults caused through incorrect carrier settings.

Item	Explain	Show
1. Correct setting	(a) Carrier must always be in front of the sinkers. (b) Carrier should be set slightly wider than width of fabric being knitted (i.e., in middle of two sinkers to left of selvedge needle if traversing R to L, OR in middle of two sinkers to right of selvedge needle if traversing L to R.	Demonstrate the correct setting with a black-board sketch.
2. Incorrect carrier settings	(a) Too low will damage sinkers. (b) Too high will cause selvedge problems. (c) Too far back will damage brass on sinker bar. (d) Too far forward will damage needles.	
3. Adjusting carrier end setting screw	If carrier traverse is too far or not far enough on full traverse, the carrier rod requires adjustment on the carrier end setting screw (one at either end of carrier). Altering this can also affect the carrier trap, which will cause carrier bounce if not working properly. This fault, which occurs on all 16 heads, is rectified by the mechanic.	Show example of selvedge fault caused through faulty carrier setting.
4. Rectification of selvedge faults when carrier setting is correct	This is caused through the carrier being too far back or forward and is rectified by the use of the carrier cramp. This again is only carried out by the mechanic.	

Figure A.7. Instruction plan for a knowledge talk (see p. 169). (Courtesy of U. K. Knitting, Lace and Net Industry Training Board.)

REFERENCES

Amar, J. (1919). *The Physiology of Industrial Organization and Reemployment of the Disabled,* Macmillan, New York.

Amaria, P. J. (1968). Validity of Performance Criteria for Classifying Semi-Skilled Operators, MSc. Thesis, Department of Engineering Production, University of Birmingham, England.

American Apparel Manufactures' Association (1968). *A Scientific Approach to Operator Training,* Report of Technical Advisory Committee, The Association, New York.

American National Standards (1973). *Industrial Engineering Terminology: Applied Psychology: Work Measurements and Methods,* The American Society of Mechanical Engineers, New York.

American Psychological Association (1950). Ethical Standards for the Distribution of Psychological Tests and Diagnostic Aids, *American Psychologist,* 5, 620–626.

American Psychological Association (1966). *Standards for Educational and Psychological Tests and Manuals,* APA, Washington, D.C.

Anastasi, A. (1968). *Psychological Testing,* 3rd ed., Macmillan, London, pp. xiii, 665.

Annett, J. (1969). *Feedback and Human Behaviour,* Penguin, London.

Annett, J. (1971). Acquisition of Skill. In *British Medical Bulletin* 27.3.266–271. The British Council, London.

Annett, J., and K. D. Duncan (1968). Task Analysis. In *New Media and Methods in Industrial Training,* B.B.C., London.

Annett, J., and K. D. Duncan (1971). *Task Analysis.* Department of Employment, Training Information, 6, Her Majesty's Stationery Office, London.

Annett, M. (1970). A Classification of Hand Preference by Association Analysis, *British Journal of Psychology,* 61, 3, 303–321.

Anson, C. J. (1952). The Quality of Time Study Rating, Ph.D. Dissertation, University of Birmingham, England.

APA [see American Psychological Association].

Argyle, M. (1967). *The Psychology of Interpersonal Behaviour,* Penguin Books, London.

Argyle, M., and A. Kendon (1967). The Experimental Analysis of Social Performance. In L. Berkowitz, Ed., *Advances in Experimental Psychology,* Vol. 3, Academic Press, New York, pp. 55–92.

Åstrand, P. O. and K. Rodahl (1970). *Textbook of Work Physiology,* McGraw-Hill, New York.

Atkinson, J. W., and N. T. Feather (1966). *A Theory of Achievement Motivation,* John Wiley, New York.

Ayers, A. W. (1942). A Comparison of Certain Visual Factors with the Efficiency of Textile Inspectors, *Journal of Applied Psychology,* 26, 812–827.

Barany, J. W. (1961). The Nature of Individual Differences in Bodily Forces Exerted During a Motor Task as Measured by a Force-Platform, Ph.D. Dissertation, Purdue University, Lafayette, Ind.

Barany, J. W., and J. W. Greene (1961). The Force Platform: An Instrument for Selecting and Training Employees, *American Journal of Psychology*, 74, 121–124

Barany, J. W., A. H. Ismail, and K. R. Manning (1965). A Force Platform for the Study of Hemiplegic Gait, *Journal of the American Therapy Association*, 45, 693–699.

Barnes, R. M. (1968). *Motion and Time Study*, 6th ed., John Wiley, New York.

Barnes, R. M., and M. E. Mundel (1938). Studies of Hand Motions and Rhythm in Factory Work, University of Iowa Studies in Engineering, Bulletin 12, Iowa City.

Barnes, R. M., J. S. Perkins, and J. M. Juran (1940). A Study of the Effects of Practice on the Elements of a Factory Operation, University of Iowa Studies in Engineering, Bulletin 22, Iowa City.

Barnes, R. M., and H. T. Amrine (1942). The Effect of Practice on Various Elements Used in Screw-Driver Work, *Journal of Applied Psychology*, 26, 197–209.

Bartlett, F. C. (Sir Frederic) (1953). *Symposium on Fatigue*, H. K. Lewis, London.

Bartlett, Sir Fredric (1958). *Thinking: An Experimental and Social Study*, Allen & Unwin, London.

Bartlett, M. S. (1941). The Statistical Significance of Canonical Correlations, *Biometrika*, 32, 29–38.

Bass, B. M., and R. E. Stucki (1951). A Note on a Modified Purdue Pegboard, *Journal of Applied Psychology*, 35, 312–313.

Bass, B. M., and J. A. Vaughan (1966). *Training in Industry*, Wadsworth, Belmont, Calif.

B.B.C. See Annett, J., and K. F. Duncan (1968); Martin, A. (1968).

Bedford, T. (1948). *Basic Principles of Ventilation and Heating*, H. K. Lewis, London.

Bedford, T. (1961). Researches on Thermal Comfort, *Ergonomics*, 4, 289–310.

Bedford, T., and C. G. Warner (1939). Subjective Impressions of Freshness in Relation to Environmental Conditions, *Journal of Hygiene*, 39, 498–511.

Belbin, E. (1958). Methods of Training Older Workers, *Ergonomics*, 1, 3, 207.

Belbin, E. (1964). *Training the Adult Worker*, Problems of Progress in Industry Series 15. Department of Scientific and Industrial Research, London.

Belbin, E., and R. M. Belbin (1972). *Problems in Adult Retraining*, London, Heineman.

Belbin, E., and R. Sergean (1963). *Training in the Clothing Industry*, London, Twentieth Century Press.

Belbin, E., and S. Shimmin (1964). Training the Middle-Aged for Inspection Work, *Occupational Psychology*, 38, I, 49–58.

Belbin, E., and M. H. Toye (1970). Adult Training, Forcing the Pace, *Gerontology*, 25, 33–37.

Belbin, R. M. The Changing Role of Inspection, *The Manager*, July 1962.

Bellows, R. M. (1940). Studies of Clerical Workers. Chapter VII In C. L. Stead, C. L. Shartleg et al., Eds., *Occupational Counseling Techniques*, American Book Company, New York.

Benedict, F. C., and E. P. Cathcart (1913). *Muscular Work*, Carnegie Institute of Washington, Publication 187, Washington, D.C.

Bertelson, P., and R. Joffee (1963). Blockings in Prolonged Serial Responding, *Ergonomics*, 6, 109-116.

Best, C. H., and N. B. Taylor (1963). *The Human Body*, Holt, Rinehart & Winston, New York.

Bhatia, B. (1957). Eye Movement Patterns in Response to Moving Objects, *Journal of Aviation Medicine*, **28**, 309–317.

Biäsch, H. (1953). Das Anlernen und Umschulen von Hilfsarbeiten in der Industrie, *Schriften zur Arbeitspsychologie* 1, Huber, Bern.

Bills, A. G. (1931). Blocking: A New Principle of Mental Fatigue, *American Journal of Psychology*, **43**, 230–245.

Bilodeau, E. A., Ed. (1966). *Acquisition of Skill*, Academic Press, New York, p. 539.

Bilodeau, E. A., and I. M. Bilodeau, Eds. (1969). *Principles of Skill Acquisition*, Academic Press, New York.

Bird, N. (1931). Relationships Between Experience Factors, Test Scores and Efficiency, *Archives of Psychology*, No. 126, New York.

Bittner, R. H., and E. A. Rundquist (1950). The Rank-Comparison Rating Method, *Journal of Applied Psychology*, **34**, 171–177.

Blackburn, J. M. (1936). *The Acquisition of Skill—An Analysis of Learning Curves*, Industrial Health Research Board Report No. 73, Her Majesty's Stationery Office, London.

Blain, I. (1956). Speed and Quality in Sewing Machining, *The Manager*, **24**, 944.

Blain, I. (1958). Training Sewing Machinists, Clothing Institute Technological Report 1. *Clothing Institute Journal*, **7**, 2.

Blain, I. (1959). Training Garment Machinists, *The Maker-Up*, March and April.

Blain, I. (1961). A Psychological Approach to Training Sewing Machinists. In *Training Sewing Machine Operators*, F. Kogos, Ed., Kogos International Corporation, New York.

Blakenship, A. B., and H. R. Taylor (1938). Prediction of Vocational Proficiency in Three Machine Operations, *Journal of Applied Psychology*, **22**, 518–526.

Block, S. M. (1961). SEMTAR, Automatic Electronic Motion Timer. *The Journal of Industrial Engineering*, **12**, 4 (July–August), 276–288.

Blum, M. L., and J. C. Naylor (1968). *Industrial Psychology*, rev. ed., Harper & Row, New York.

Book, W. F. (1925). *The Psychology of Skill*, Gregg, New York.

Borger, R., and A. E. M. Seaborne (1966). *The Psychology of Learning*, Penguin, London.

Brierley, A. F. M. (1967). Both Sides of the Interview, *Management Today*, October, 34, 36, 40, 43.

British Standards Institution (1959). *Glossary of Terms in Work Study*.

British Standard 3138 (UDC 0001.465.015), *Glossary of Terms in Work Study*, British Standards Institution, Incorporated amendment issued June 1962 (PD 4585).

Broadbent, D. E. (1957). Effects of Noise on Behavior. In C. M. Harris, Ed., *Handbook of Noise Control*, McGraw-Hill, New York.

Broadbent, D. E. (1958): *Perception and Communication*, Pergamon Press, London.

Broadbent, D. E. (1970), *In Defense of Empirical Psychology*. C. S. Myers Lecture, British Psychological Society, London.

Brogden, H. E. (1946). On the Interpretation of the Correlation Coefficient as a Measure of Predicting Efficiency, *Journal of Educational Psychology*, **37**, 65–76.

Brouha, L. (1954). Fatigue—Measuring and Reducing It, *Advanced Management*, **1**, 9–19.

Brouha, L. (1967). *Physiology in Industry*, 2nd ed., Pergamon Press, London.

Brown, W., and E. Jaques (1965). *Glacier Project Papers:* Some essays on organization and management from the Glacier Project Research, Glacier Project Series No. 8, Vol. VII, 277 pages, Heinemann, London.

Bryan, W. L., and N. Harter (1897). Studies in the Telegraphic Language, *Psychological Review,* 4, 27 and (1899) 6, 345.

Burns, W. (1960). The Peripheral Mechanism of Hearing: The Response of the Ear to Normal and to Intense Sound, *Advancement of Science,* 17, 375–392.

Buros, O. K., Ed. (1965). *The Sixth Mental Measurements Yearbook,* Gryphon Press, New Brunswick, New Jersey.

Buros, O. K., Ed. (1972). The Seventh Mental Measurements Yearbook, *Gryphon Press,* Hyland Park, New Jersey.

Burt, Cyril (1972). Inheritance of General Intelligence, *American Psychologist,* 27, 3 (March) 175–190.

Burton, A. C., and O. G. Edholm (1955). *Man in a Cold Climate,* Edward Arnold, London.

Campbell, J. (1964). *Testing of Culturally Different Groups,* Educational Testing Service Research Bulletin 64-34, Educational Testing Service, Princeton, N. J.

Campbell, J. (1965). The Problem of Cultural Bias in Selection: I. Background and Literature. In *The Executive Study Conference: Selecting and Training Negroes for Managerial Positions,* Educational Testing Service Research Bulletin 65–57, Educational Testing Service, Princeton, N. J.

Carrard, A. (1949). *Praktische Einführung in Probleme der Arbeitsphysiologie,* Rascher, Zurich.

Cattell, J. M. (1902). The Time of Perception as a Measure of Differences in Intensity, *Philosophy Studies,* 19, 63–68.

Cattell, J. M. (1903). Statistics of American Psychologists, *American Journal of Psychology,* 14, 310–328.

Cattell, J. M., and L. Farrand (1896). Physical and Mental Measurements of Students of Columbia University, *Psychological Review,* 3, 618–648.

Chaffin, D. B. (1969a). Surface Electromyography Frequency Analysis as a Diagnostic Tool, *Journal of Occupational Medicine,* 11, 109–115.

Chaffin, D. B. (1969b). Electromyography—A Method of Measuring Local Fatigue, *The Journal of Methods–Time Measurement,* 14, 29–36.

Chaffin, D. B., and W. H. Baker (1970). A Biomechanical Model for Analysis of Symmetric Sagittal Plane Lifting, *AIIE Transactions,* 2, 16–27.

Chaffin, D. B., K. E. Kilpatrick and W. M. Hancock (1970). A Computer-Assisted Manual Work-Design Model, *AIIE Transactions,* 2, 348–354.

Chapanis, A. (1959). *Research Techniques in Human Engineering,* Johns Hopkins Press, Baltimore, p. 316.

Cheit, E. F. (1961). *Injury and Recovery in the Course of Employment,* Wiley, New York, 377 pages.

Clark, W. (1923). *The Gantt Chart,* Ronald Press Company, New York.

Clay, H. M. (1964). *Research in Relation to Operator Training,* Department of Scientific and Industrial Research, London.

Clifford, R. R., and W. M. Hancock (1964). An Industrial Study of Learning, MTM, *Journal of Methods–Time Measurement,* 9, 12.

Cochran, W. G. (1957). Analysis of Covariance: Its Nature and Use, *Biometrics,* 13, 261–281.

Cohen, L., and L. Strauss (1946). Time Study and Fundamental Nature of Manual Skill, *Journal of Consulting Psychology,* 10, 146–153.

Collins, R. (1968). On the Inheritance of Handedness, *Journal of Heredity,* **59,** 9–12.

Connolly, J. A. (1967). Rated Systematic Activity Sampling, *Work Study and Management Services,* **11,** 608–611.

Conrad, R. (1951). The Study of Skill by Motion and Time Study and by Psychological Experiment, *Research,* **4,** 8, 353.

Cooke, P. J. D. (1967). Learning Curves and Some of Their Implications for Management, *Management Today,* **148,** 72–75.

Cooley, W. W., and P. R. Lohnes (1971). *Multivariate Data Analysis,* John Wiley, New York.

Corlett, E. N. (1960). Human Factors in Machine Control, Ph.D. Dissertation, University of Birmingham, England.

Corlett, E. N., and K. Mahadeva (1970). A Relationship Between a Freely Chosen Working Pace and Energy Consumption Levels, *Ergonomics,* **13,** 4, 517–524.

Corlett, E. N., and V. J. Morcombe (1970). Straightening out Learning Curves, *Personnel Management,* **2,** 6, 14–20.

Corlett, E. N., G. Salvendy and W. D. Seymour (1971). Skill and Operative Selection for Fine Manual Tasks: The O'Connor Finger Dexterity Test and the Purdue Pegboard, *Occupational Psychology,* **45,** 57–65.

Cox, J. W. (1934). *Manual Skill,* Cambridge University Press, London.

Craig, D. R. (1925). The Performance-Interest Questionnaire in Selecting Retail Saleswoman, *Journal of Personnel Research,* **3,** 366–374.

Crockford, G. W., R. F. Hellon, P. W. Humphreys, and A. R. Lind (1961). An Air-Conditioned Suit To Wear in Very Hot Environments, *Ergonomics,* **4,** 63–72.

Cronbach, L. J. (1947). Test Reliability: Its Meaning and Interpretation, *Psychometrika,* **12,** 1–16.

Cronbach, L. J. (1957). The Two Disciplines of Scientific Psychology, American Psychologist, 12, 671–684.

Cronbach, L. J. (1960). Essentials of Psychological Testing, Harper & Brothers, New York, 2nd Edition.

Cronbach, L. J., and Gleser, G. C. (1965). Psychological Tests and Personnel Decisions, University of Illinois Press, Illinois, 2nd Edition.

Cronbach, L. J., et al. (1972). The *Dependability of Behavioral Measurements: Theory of Generalizability for Scores and Profiles,* Wiley, New York.

Crossman, E. R. F. W. (1956a). Perceptual Activity in Manual Work, *Research,* **9,** 42–49.

Crossman, E. R. F. W. (1956b). The Measurement of Perceptual Load in Manual Operations. Ph.D. Dissertation, University of Birmingham, England.

Crossman, E. R. F. W. (1959). A Theory of Acquisition of Speed-Skill, *Ergonomics,* **2,** 153–166.

Crossman, E. R. F. W. (1964). Information Processes in Human Skills, *British Medical Bulletin, Experimental Psychology,* **20,** 32–37.

Crossman, E. R. F. W. (1966). Taxonomy of Automation. In *Manpower Aspects of Automation and Technical Change.* Organization for European Co-operation and Development, Paris.

Crossman, E. R. F. W., and J. E. Cooke (1962). *Manual Control of Slow Response Systems.* International Congress on Human Factors in Electronics, Long Beach, Calif.

Crossman, E. R. F. W., and S. Laner (1966). *Evaluation of Changes in Skill-Profile and Job Content due to Technological Change.* Report to the U.S. Department of Labor, Contract 81-04-05, Department of Industrial Engineering, University of California, Berkeley.

Crossman, E. R. F. W., and S. Laner (1969). *The Impact of Technological Change on Manpower and Skill Demand*, Report to U.S. Department of Labor, Contract 81-05-66-30, Department of Industrial Engineering, University of California, Berkeley.

Crossman, E. R. F. W., and W. D. Seymour (1957). *The Nature and Acquisition of Industrial Skills*. Department of Scientific and Industrial Research, London.

Cureton, E. E. (1957). Receipe for a Cook Book, *Psychological Bulletin,* **54,** 494–497.

Curtis, E. W., and E. F. Alf (1969). Validity, Predictive Efficiency and Practical Significance of Selection Tests, *Journal of Applied Psychology,* **53,** 4, 327–337.

Curtis, E. W. (1971): Predictive Value Compared to Predictive Validity, *American Psychologist,* **26,** 908–914.

Damon, A., H. W. Stoudt, and R. A. McFarland (1966). *The Human Body in Equipment Design*, Harvard University Press, Cambridge, Mass.

Das, R. K. (1951). Energy Expenditure in Weight Lifting by Different Methods, Ph.D. Dissertation, London School of Hygiene and Tropical Medicine, University of London, England.

Davies, I. K. (1971). *The Management of Learning*, McGraw-Hill, London and New York.

Davies, O. L., Ed. (1961). *Statistical Methods in Research and Production with Special Reference to the Chemical Industry*, Oliver and Boyd, London.

Davis, C. J. (1946). Correlation Between Scores on Ortho-Rater Tests and Clinical Tests, *Journal of Applied Psyhcology,* **30,** 596–603.

de Jong, J. R. (1957). The Effect of Increasing Skill on Cycle-Time, Ergonomics, **1,** 1, 51.

de Jong, J. R. (1960). The Effects of Increasing Skill and M.T.M., International M.T.M. Congress, Scheveningen, the Netherlands.

de Jong, J. R. (1964). Increasing Skill and Reduction of Work Time, *Time and Motion Study,* **9,** 10–20.

de Jong, J. R. (1969). Opening Address, International Conference on Job Evaluation, Amsterdam, the Netherlands, September 29–October 2, 1969, pp. II-1 to II-3.

Department of Employment, U.K. (1971). *Glossary of Training Terms*, Her Majesty's Stationery Office, London.

Department of Scientific and Industrial Research (1960). *Training Made Easier*, DSIR, Problems of Progress in Industry, Her Majesty's Stationery Office, London.

Disney, R. L., W. M. Hancock, and J. A. Muckstadt (1965). The Independence of Predetermined Elemental Times. A Report of the Department of Industrial Engineering, University of Michigan.

Donnelly E. and Kenney, J. (1970). Training Analysis of Semi-Skilled Work. *Industrial and Commercial Training.* 2.6. 287–290.

Dorrogury, J., et al. (1950). Academy of Sciences, Paris, **230,** 1000, cited by A. B. Dubois (1964). Respiration, *Annual Review of Physiology,* **20,** 421–452.

Douglas, C. G., and J. G. Priestley (1948). *Human Physiology: A Practical Course,* The Clarendon Press, Oxford.

Drever, J. (1965). *A Dictionary of Psychology*, rev. ed., 1964; reprinted 1965, Penguin Reference Books, Harmondsworth, England.

Droege, R. C. (1966). Effects of Practice on Aptitude Scores, *Journal of Applied Psychology,* **50,** 306–310.

Dubois, P. H. (1957). *Multivariate Correlational Analysis,* Harper & Row, New York.

Dudley, N. A. (1968). *Work Measurement: Some Research Studies,* Macmillan, London; St. Martin's Press, New York.

Dugan, R. D. (1966). Current Problems in Test Performance of Job Applicants: II, *Personnel Psychology,* **19,** 18–24.

Dunnette, M. D., and G. W. England (1957). A Checklist for Differentiating Engineering Jobs, *Personnel Psychology,* **10,** 191–198.

Dunnette, M. D., and W. K. Kirchner (1959). A Checklist for Differentiating Different Kinds of Sales Jobs, *Personnel Psychology,* **12,** 421–430.

Dunnette, M. D. (1963). A Modified Model for Test Validation and Selection Research, *Journal of Applied Psychology,* **47,** 317–323.

Dunnette, M. D., J. Campbell, and K. Jaastad (1963). The Effect of Group Participation on Brainstorming Effectiveness for Two Industrial Samples, *Journal of Applied Psychology,* **47,** 30–37.

Elithorn, A., and A. Telford (1969). Computer Analysis of Intellectual Skills, *International Journal of Man–Machine Studies,* **1,** 189–209.

Engineering Industry Training Board (1967). *The Training of Adult Operators,* London.

Engineering Industry Training Board (1968, 1969, 1970). *Annual Reports 1967-1968, 1968-1969, 1969-1970,* London.

Eysenck, H. J. (1966). Personality and Experimental Psychology, *Bulletin of the British Psychological Society,* **19,** 1–28.

Eysenck, H. J., and B. G. Eysenck (1968). *Manual for the Eysenck Personality Inventory,* Educational and Industrial Testing Service, San Diego, Calif.

Fiske, D. W. (1967). The Subject Reacts to Tests, *American Psychologist,* **22,** 287–296.

Fitts, P. M. (1954). The Informational Capacity of the Human Motor System in Controlling the Amplitude of Movements, *Journal of Experimental Psychology,* **47,** 6.

Fitts, P. M. (1962). Factors in Complex Skill Training. In R. Glaser, Ed., *Training Research and Education,* Pittsburgh University Press, Pittsburgh.

Fitts, P. M., and M. I. Posner (1967). *Human Performance,* Wadsworth, Belmont, Calif.

Flanagan, J. C. (1949). Critical Requirements: A New Approach to Employee Evaluation, *Personnel Psychology,* **2,** 419–425.

Fleishman, E. A. (1953a). A Modified Administration Procedure for the O'Connor Finger Dexterity Test, *Journal of Applied Psychology,* **37,** 191–194.

Fleishman, E. A. (1953b). Testing for Psychomotor Abilities by Means of Apparatus Tests, *Psychological Bulletin,* **50,** 241–262.

Fleishman, E. A. (1954). Dimensional Analysis of Psychomotor Abilities, *Journal of Experimental Psychology,* **48,** 437–454.

Fleishman, E. A. (1960). Abilities at Different Stages of Practice in Rotary Pursuit Performance, *Journal of Experimental Psychology,* **60,** 3, 162–171.

Fleishman, E. A. (1962). The Description and Prediction of Perceptual-Motor Skill Learning. In R. Glaser, Ed., *Training Research and Education,* Pittsburgh University Press, Pittsburgh.

Fleishman, E. A. (1964). *The Structure and Measurement of Physical Fitness,* Prentice-Hall, Englewood Cliffs, N.J.

Fleishman, E. A. (1972). On the Relations between Abilities, Learning, and Human Performance, *American Psychologist,* **27,** 1017–1032.

Fleishman, E., and G. Ellison (1962). A Factor Analysis of Fine Manipulative Tests, *Journal of Applied Psychology,* **46,** 96–105.

Fleishman, E. A., and W. E. Hempel, Jr. (1954a). Changes in Factor Structure of a Complex Psychomotor Test as a Function of Practice, *Psychometrika,* **19,** 239–252.

Fleishman, E. A., and W. E. Hempel, Jr. (1954b). A Factor Analysis of Dexterity Tests, *Personnel Psychology,* **7,** 15–32.

Fleishman, E. A., and W. E. Hempel, Jr., (1956). Factorial Analysis of Complex Psychomotor Performance and Related Skills, *The Journal of Applied Psychology,* **40,** 96–104.

Fliege, S. (1966). Digital Computers. In J. B. Sidowski, Ed., *Experimental Methods and Instrumentation in Psychology,* McGraw-Hill, New York, pp. 699–734.

Forward, E., J. Warren, and K. Hara (1962). The Effects of Unilateral Lesions in Sensorimotor Cortex on Manipulation by Cats, *Journal of Comparative Psysiological Psychology,* **55,** 1130–1135.

Foulke, J. A. (1966). An Orientation to M.T.M. Manual Learning Curve Research, *Journal of Methods–Time Measurement,* **11,** 4, 5–6.

Fox, R. H. (1965). *Thermal Comfort in Industry,* Ergonomics for Industry, Series 8, British Ministry of Technology (Millbank Tower, Millbank, London S.W.1), pp. 20.

Gagné, R. M. (1965). *The Conditions of Learning.* Holt, Rinehart & Winston, New York.

Galton, F. (1883). *Inquiries into Human Faculty and its Development,* Macmillan, London.

Garbutt, D. (1970). The Industrial Training System, *Socioeconomic Planning Science,* **4,** 341–364.

Garrett, J. W. (1971). The Adult Human Hand: Some Anthropometric and Biomechanical Considerations, *Human Factors,* **13,** 117–131.

Gedye, J. L., and E. Miller (1969). The Automation of Psychological Assessment, *International Journal of Man–Machine Studies,* **1,** 237–262.

Gentles, E. M. (1969). *Training the Operator: A Practical Guide,* Institute of Personnel Management, London.

Ghiselli, E. E. (1956). Dimensional Problems of Criteria, *Journal of Applied Psychology,* **40,** 1–4.

Ghiselli and Brown (1948). *Personnel Industrial Psychology* McGraw-Hill, London.

Ghiselli, E. E. (1964). *Theory of Psychological Measurements,* McGraw-Hill, London.

Ghiselli, E. E. (1966). *The Validity of Occupational Aptitude Tests,* Wiley, London.

Gibson, D. (1970). Work Sampling Monitors Job–Show Productivity, *Journal of Industrial Engineering,* June, 12–19.

Gilbreth, F. B. (1911). *Motion Study,* Van Nostrand Reinhold, New York.

Gilbreth, F. B., and L. M. Gilbreth (1919). *Fatigue Study,* Routledge, London.

Glaser, R. (1962). Psychology and Industrial Technology. In R. Glaser, Ed., *Training Research and Education,* Pittsburgh University Press, Pittsburgh.

Glaser, R. (1967). Some Implications of Previous Work on Learning and Individual Differences. In R. M. Gagné, Ed., *Learning and Individual Differences,* Merrill, Chicago.

Glover, J. H. (1966a). Manufacturing Progress Functions I. An Alternative Model and Its Comparison with Existing Functions, *The International Journal of Production Research,* **4,** 279–300.

Glover, J. H. (1966b). Manufacturing Progress Functions, II. Selection of Trainees and Control of Their Progress, *The International Journal of Production Research,* **5,** 43–59.

Gomberg, W. A. (1954). *A Trade Union Analysis of Time Study,* 2nd ed., Prentice-Hall, N. J.

Gordon, D. A., J. Zeinder, H. J. Zagorski, and J. S. Uhlaner (1954). Visual Acuity Measurements by Wall Chart and Ortho-Rater Test, *Journal of Applied Psychology,* **38,** 54–58.

Graham, C. F. (1966). Work Measurement by the Use of Rated Systematic Activity Sampling, *Work Study and Management Services,* **10,** 7–14.

Greenberger, M. H., and J. H. Ward (1956). An Iterative Technique for Multiple Correlation Analysis, *IBM Technical Newsletter,* **12,** 85–97.

Greene, J. H., (1957). The Design and Initial Evaluation of A Force Platform for Measuring Human Work, Ph.D. Dissertation, State University of Iowa.

Greene, J. H., and W. H. M. Morris (1959). The Design of a Force Platform for Work Measurement, *Journal of Industrial Engineering,* **10,** 312–317.

Gregory, R. L. (1964). Human Perception. In *British Medical Bulletin on Experimental Psychology,* **20,** 21, The British Council, London.

Gregory, R. L. (1970). On How Little Information Controls So Much Behaviour, *Ergonomics,* **13,** 1, 25–37.

Griffiths, C. H. (1936). The Relationship Between Anthropometric Measures and Manual Dexterity, *Journal of Applied Psychology,* **20,** 227–235.

Guilford, J. P. (1928). The Method of Paired Comparisons as a Psychometric Method, *Psychological Review,* **35,** 494–506.

Guilford, J. P. (1952). When Not to Factor Analyze, *Psychological Bulletin,* **49,** 26–37.

Guilford, J. P. (1954). *Psychometric Methods,* McGraw-Hill, New York.

Guion, R. M. (1965). *Personnel Testing,* McGraw-Hill, New York.

Gupta, M. N., R. N. Sen, and H. Singh (1965). *Investigation of Occupational Hearing Impairment and Noise in a Nitric Acid Plant,* Report 24, Chief Adviser on Factories, Ministry of Labor and Employment, Government of India, New Delhi, India.

Guthrie, E. R. (1952). *The Psychology of Learning,* Harper & Row, New York.

Guttman, L. A. (1945). A Basis for Analyzing Test–Retest Reliability, *Psychometrika,* **10,** 255–282.

Hale, D. J. (1969). Speed–Error Tradeoff in Three-Choice Serial Reaction Task, *Journal of Experimental Psychology,* **81,** 3, 428–435.

Hancock, W. M. (1967). The Prediction of Learning Rates for Manual Operators, *Journal of Industrial Engineering,* **18,** 42–47.

Hancock, W. M., and J. A. Foulke (1961). *A Description of the Electronic Data Collector and the Methods of its Application to Work Measurement,* Research Information, Paper No. I, Methods–Time Measurement Association, University of Michigan, Department of Industrial Engineering and The Journal of Industrial Engineering, **13,** July-Aug. 1962, 227–231.

Hancock, W. M., and J. A. Foulke (1963). *Learning Curve Research on Short-Cycle Operations, Phase I. Laboratory Experiment Methods–Time Measurement Research Studies,* Report 112, The MTM Association for Standards and Research, Ann Arbor, Mich.

Hancock, W. M., and J. A. Foulke (1966). Computation of Learning Curves, *Journal of Methods–Time Measurement,* **11,** 3, 5–7.

Hancock, W M., and P. Sathe (1969). *Learning Curve Research on Manual Operations. Phase II, Industrial Studies.* Report 113A, MTM Association, Fairlawn, N. J.

Harmon, H. H. (1960). *Modern Factor Analysis,* University of Chicago Press, Chicago.

Harper, Roland (1952). Psychological and Psycho-Physical Studies in Dairying, *British Journal of Psychology,* **28,** Monograph Suppl., Cambridge.

Harper, Roland (1964). The Sensory Evaluation of Food and Drink: An Overview, *Laboratory Practice,* **13,** 7, 599–604.

Harper, Ronald (1972). *The Human Senses in Action.* Churchill Livingstone, London.

Harrington, C. C., Ed. (1949). *Job Evaluation and Wage Incentives,* Conover-Mast, New York.

Harris, C. W. (1963). Canonical Factor Models for the Description of Change. In C. W. Harris, Ed., *Problems in Measuring Change,* University of Wisconsin Press, Madison, pp. 138–155.

Harris, D. H., and F. B. Chaney (1969). *Human Factors in Quality Assurance,* Wiley, New York.

Hay, E. N. (1943). Predictive Success in Machine Bookkeeping, *Journal of Applied Psychology,* **27,** 483–493.

Hayes, E. G. (1932). Selecting Women for Shop Work, *Personnel Journal,* **11,** 69–85.

Hays, W. L. (1963). *Statistics,* Holt, Rinehart & Winston, New York.

Hearn, N. K. H., and S. Konz (1968). An Improved Design for Force Platform, *Ergonomics,* **11,** 383–389.

Heinrich, H. W. (1950). *Industrial Accident Prevention,* McGraw-Hill, New York.

Herzberg, F., S. Mausner, and B. B. Snyderman (1957). *The Motivation to Work,* Wiley, New York.

Hick, W. E. (1952). On the Rate of Gain of Information, *Quarterly Journal of Experimental Psychology,* **4,** 11–26.

Hildreth, G. (1949). The Development of Training of Hand Dominance, *Journal of Genetic Psychology,* **75,** 199–275.

Hill, A. V. (1922). The Maximum Work and Mechanical Efficiency of Human Muscles and Their Economical Speed, *The Journal of Physiology,* **56,** 19 ff.

Hill, A. V. (1927). *Muscular Movement in Man: The Factors Governing Speed and Recovery from Fatigue,* McGraw-Hill, New York.

Hines, M., and J. O'Connor (1926). A Measure of Finger Dexterity, *Journal of Personnel Research,* **4,** 379–382.

Hinrichs, J. R. (1964). Communications Activity of Industrial Research Personnel, *Personnel Psychology,* **17,** 193–204.

Hinrichs, J. R. (1970). Ability Correlates in Learning a Psychomotor Task, *Journal of Applied Psychology,* **54,** 56–64.

Holding, D. H. (1965). *Principles of Training,* Pergamon, London.

Hollingworth, H. L. (1913). Correlation of Abilities as Affected by Practice, *Journal of Educational Psychology,* **4,** 405–44.

Hollingworth, H. L. (1929). *Vocational Psychology and Character Analysis,* Appleton, New York.

Holtzman, W. H. (1963). Statistical Models for the Study of Change in the Single Case. In C. W. Harris, Ed., *Problems of Measuring Change.* University of Wisconsin Press, Madison, pp. 199–211.

Horine, L. E. (1967). An Investigation of the Relationship of Laterality to the Performance of Selected Motor Ability Tests, *Dissertation Abstracts,* Part A, pp. 1280–1281.

Horst, P. (1936a). Item Selection by Means of Maximum Function, *Psychometrika,* **1,** 229–244.

Horst, P. (1936b). Obtaining a Composite Measure from a Number of Different Measures of the Same Attribute, *Psychometrika*, 1, 53–60.

Horst, P. (1954). A Technique for the Development of a Differential Prediction Battery, *Psychological Monograph*, 68, 9 (whole no. 380).

Horst, P. (1961). Relations Among M Sets of Measures, *Psychometrika*, 26, 129–149.

Horst, P., and C. MacEwan (1956). Optimal Test Length for Maximum Differential Prediction, *Psychometrika*, 21, 51–66.

Hotelling, H. (1935). The Most Predictable Criterion, *Journal of Educational Psychology*, 26, 139–142.

Hotelling, H. (1936). Relations Between Two Sets of Variates, *Biometrika*, 28, 321–377.

Hoyt, C. (1941). Test Reliability Estimated by Analysis of Variance, *Psychometrika*, 6, 153–160.

Hull, C. L. (1928). *Attitude Testing*, George G. Harper, London.

Hull, C. L. (1952). *A Behavioural System*, Yale University Press, New Haven, Conn.

Hull, C. O. (1951). *Essentials of Behavior*, Yale University Press, New Haven, Conn.

Imus, H. A. (1946). Comparison of the Ortho-Rater with Clinical Opthalmic Examinations, *Abstract American Psychologist*, 1, 283–284.

Imus, H. A. (1949a). Comparison of the Ortho-Rater with Clinical Ophthalmic Examinations, *Journal of Aviation Medicine*, 20, 2–23.

Imus, H. A. (1949b). Comment on the Ortho-Rater. In O. K. Buros, Ed., *The Third Mental Measurement Yearbook*, Rutgers University Press, New Brunswick, N. J., Section 471.

The Industrial Self-Instructor and Technical Journal (1884). London, Ward Lock and Company.

Industrial Services Company, Israel (1957). *Establishment of Rest Allowances*, unpublished report.

International Association of Machinists (1954). *What's Wrong With Job Evaluation; A Trade Union Manual*, IAM Research Department, Washington, D.C., pp. 100.

Jensen, A. R. (1969). How Much Can We Boost IQ and Scholastic Achievement? *Harvard Educational Review*, 39, 1–123.

Johnson, F. H., R. W. Boise, Jr., and D. Pratt (1946). *Job Evaluation*, Wiley, New York, pp. vii, 288.

Jones, F. N. (1948). A Factor Analysis of Visibility Data, *American Journal of Psychology*, 61, 361–369.

Jones, M. H. (1950). The Adequacy of Employee Selection Reports, *Journal of Applied Psychology*, 34, 219–224.

Jones, M. R. (1966). Individual Differences In Acquisition of Skill. (Edited by E. A. Bilodeau), Academic Press, London, chapter 3.

Kahneman, D., and E. E. Ghiselli (1962). Validity and Non-linear Heteroscedastic Models, *Personnel Psychology*, 15, 1–11.

Karpovich, P. V. (1965). *Physiology of Muscular Activity*, Saunders, Philadelphia.

Kay, H. (1954). The Effects of Position in a Display upon Problem Solving, *Quarterly Journal of Experimental Psychology*, 5, 155–169.

Kay, H. (1955). Training in Relation to Individual Efficiency, *British Management Review*, 13, 3, 174.

Kay, H. (1957). Information Theory in the Understanding of Skills, *Occupational Psychology*, 31, 4, 10.

Kay, H. (1969). The Development of Motor Skills from Birth to Adolescence. In

Bilodeau and Bilodeau, Eds., *Principles of Skill Acquisition,* Academic Press, New York.

Kay, H., J. Annett, and Syme M. E. (1963). *Teaching Machines and Their Use in Industry,* Her Majesty's Stationery Office, London.

Keller, F. S. (1958). The Phantom Plateau, *Journal of Experimental Analysis of Behavior,* 1, 1.

Kelley, C. R. (1971). General-Purpose Equipment for Human Factors Research, *Human Factors,* 13, 487–497.

Kelly, E. L., and D. W. Fiske (1951). *The Prediction of Performance in Clinical Psychology,* University of Michigan Press, Ann Arbor.

Kemble, W. F. (1917). *Choosing Employees by Mental and Physical Tests,* Engineering Magazine Company, New York.

Kendall, M. G., and A. Stuart (1967). *The Advanced Theory of Statistics,* Vol. 2, *Inference and Relationship,* 2nd ed., Hafner, New York.

Kennedy, J. L. (1953). Some Practical Problems of the Alertness Indicator. In W. F. Floyd and A. T. Welford, Eds., *Symposium on Fatigue,* H. K. Lewis, London.

Kephart, N. C., and Mason, J. M. (1950). Acuity Differences Between the Two Eyes and Job Performance, *Journal of Applied Psychology,* 34, 423–428.

King, S. D. M. (1958). *Technological Change and the Training of Operators,* European Productivity Agency. Bulletin, Organization for European Co-operation and Development, Paris.

King, S. D. M. (1959). The Operator as a Self-Regulating System: A Factory Experiment, *Ergonomics,* 2, 2, 171–179.

King, S. D. M. (1964). Automation and the Evaluation of Training, *International Labor Review,* 90, 3 (September), 209–225.

King, S. D. M. (1964). *Training Within the Organisation.* Tavistock, London.

Kirk, N. S., and J. Feinstein (1967). An Investigation of the Relation Between Inspection and Repairing Performance of Burlers and Menders in the Worsted Woollen Industry, *Acta Psychologica,* 27, 213–222.

Kirkpatrick, J. J., R. B. Ewen, R. S. Barrett, and R. A. Katzell (1968). *Testing and Fair Employment,* New York University Press, New York.

Klemmer, E. T., and G. R. Lockhead (1962). Productivity and Errors in Two Keying Tasks: A Field Study, *Journal of Applied Psychology,* 46, 401–408.

Knight, A. A. (1967). Laboratory Studies of Response and Movement Times in Simple Repetitive Tasks, Ph.D. Thesis, University of Birmingham, England.

Konz, S. A., E. L. Dickey, C. McCutchan, and B. Koe (1967). Manufacturing Assembly Instructions: Part III, *Abstraction, Complexity and Information Theory, Journal of Industrial Engineering,* 18, 11, 658–667.

Kryter, K. (1970). *The Effect of Noise on Man,* Academic Press, New York.

Kuder, G. F., and M. W. Richardson (1937). The Theory of Estimation of Test Reliability, *Psychometrika,* 2, 151–160.

Laban, R., and F. C. Lawrence (1947). *Effort,* Macdonald & Evans, London.

Ladhams, G. H. (1952). A New Method for Training Operators, *Personnel,* 28, 6, 471–477.

Ladhams, G. H. (1964). The Analytical Method of Training, *The Bobbin Magazine,* December 1964; January and February 1965.

Ladhams, G. (1965). The Zero Defects Program in Action, *The Bobbin Magazine,* November.

Ladhams, G. H. (1968). *Developing Full Plant Potential through Systematic Train-*

ing, American Apparel Manufacturers Association, Letter 30. Washington, D. C., September.

Ladhams, G. H. (1971). The Principles and Application of the Analytical Method for Developing Operators. *The Bobbin* Magazine, Columbia, S. C. 9. 72–78.

Langham-Brown, J. B. (1971). Training for Fault Diagnosis, *British Association for Commercial and Industrial Education Journal,* **25,** 1, 9–14.

Lanham, E. (1955). *Job Evaluation,* McGraw-Hill, New York, pp. 404.

Lashley, K. S. (1951). *The Problem of Serial Order in Behavior in Skills,* D. Legge, Ed., Penguin, London (1970).

Laughery, K. R., J. C. Fell, and A. L. Pinkus (1969). *Short-Term Memory: A Collection of Three Papers,* State University of New York at Buffalo.

Lauru, L. (1957). Physiological Study of Motions, *Advanced Management,* **22,** 3, 17–24.

Lee, D. R. (1972). An Evaluation of Selected Parameters at the Microform Reading Man-Machine Interface, Ph.D. Dissertation, Purdue University, Lafayette, Ind.

Lewis, B. N., and P. J. Woolfenden (1969). *Algorithms and Logical Trees,* Algorithms Press, Cambridge, England.

Link, H. C. (1919). *Employment Psychology,* Macmillan, New York.

Lockhart, J. M. (1966). Effects of Body and Hand Cooling on Complex Manual Performance, *Journal of Applied Psychology,* **50,** 1, 57–59.

Lockwood, H. C. (1966). Critical Problems in Achieving Equal Employment Opportunity, *Personnel Psychology,* **19,** 3–10.

Lucas, C. M. (1953). *Survey of the Literature Relating to the Effects of Cultural Background on Aptitude Scores,* Educational Testing Service Research Bulletin 53-13, Educational Testing Services, Princeton, N. J.

Lukin, L. (1963). Instability of the "Steady State" During Exercise, Internationale Zeitschrift Fuer Angewandte Physiologie Einschliesslish Arbeitsphysiologie, **20,** 44–49.

Lumsdaine, A. A. (1964). Educational Technology, Programmed Learning and Instructional Science. In H. G. Richey Ed., *Theories of Learning and Instruction,* University of Chicago Press, Chicago.

Mace, C. A. (1950). The Analysis of Human Skills, *Occupational Psychology,* **24,** 3, 125.

Mackenzie, D., Davey, and P. McDonnell (1964). *Programmed Instruction,* Institute of Personnel Management, London.

Mackworth, N. H. (1950). *Researches in the Measurement of Human Performance,* Medical Research Council Special Report 268, Her Majesty's Stationery Office, London.

Mackworth, J. F. (1970). *Vigilance and Attention,* Penguin Books, London.

Markle, S. M. (1964). *Good Frames and Bad,* Wiley, New York.

Martin, A. (1968). Training the Trainer. In *New Media and Methods in Industrial Training,* B.B.C., London.

Martin, C. A. (1959). The Experiment of Training Sewing Machinists in a Technical College, in *Training of Sewing Machinists,* Tech. Report No. 5. Clothing Institute, London. (Quoted by Belbin and Sergean 1963).

Martin, J. B., and Chaffin, D. B. (1972). Biomechanical Computerized Simulation of Human Strength in Sagittal-Plane Activities. *AIIE Transactions,* 4, 19–28.

Martin, R., and K. Saller (1957 and 1959). *Lehrbuch der Anthropologie,* Vol. I and II, Fischer, Stuttgart.

Maynard, H. B., G. J. Stegemerten, and J. L. Schwab (1948). *Methods–Time Measurement*, McGraw-Hill, New York.

McCall, R. (1934). The Bedaux System of Labour Measurement, *The Cost Accountant*, September 1934.

McClellan, G. S., Ed. (1970). *Protecting*, H. W. Wilson, New York, 218 pages.

McCormick, E. J. (1970). *Human Factors Engineering*, 3rd ed., McGraw-Hill, New York.

McCormick, E. J., P. R. Jeannert, and R. C. Mecham (1972). A Study of Job Characteristics and Job Dimensions as Based on the Position Analysis Questionnaire (PAQ). *Journal of Applied Psychology Monograph*, 56, 4, 347–368.

McDonald, L. (1961). Statistical Studies of Recorded Energy Expenditure of Man, *Nutrition Abstracts and Reviews*, 3, 739–762.

McFarland, R. A., and A. L. Moseley (1954). *Human Factors in Highway Transportation Safety*, Harvard School of Public Health, Cambridge, Mass.

McGeogh, J. A. and A. L. Irion (1952). *The Psychology of Human Learning*, Longmans, Green, London.

McQuitty, L. L., C. Wrigley, and E. K. Gaier (1954). An Approach to Isolating Dimensions of Job Success, *Journal of Applied Psychology*, 38, 227–232.

Miller, E. (1968). A Case for Automating Clinical Testing, *Bulletin of the British Psychological Society*, 21, 75.

Miller, R. B. (1953). *A Method for Man–Machine Task Analysis*, Wright-Patterson Air Force Base, Ohio: Wright Air Development Center, Technical Report 53-137.

Miller, R. B. (1962). Task Description and Analysis. In R. B. Gagné, Ed., *Psychological Principles in System Development*, Holt, Rinehart & Winston, New York.

Mills, H. R. (1967). *Teaching and Training*, St. Martin's Press, New York.

Minter, A. L. (1968). Activity Sampling, *Work Study and Management Services*, 12, 342–346.

Moder, J. J., and C. R. Phillips (1964). *Project Management with CPM and PERT*, Reinhold, New York.

de Montpellier, Gerard (1935). *Les Alterations Morphologiques des Mouvements Rapides: Étude Experimentale*, Editions de l'Institut Superieur de Philosophie, Louvain.

Moray, N. Ed. (1969). On-line Computing for Psychology, N. A. T. O. Advanced Study Institute, Department of Psychology, University of Sheffield, England.

Moskowitz, A. D. (1965). A Monograph for Work Sampling, *Work Study and Management Services*, 9, 349–350.

Mowbray, G. H., and J. W. Gebhard (1958). Man's Senses as Informational Channels. In H. Wallace Sinaiko, *Selected Papers on Human Factors in the Design and Use of Control Systems*, Dover, New York (1961), paper 5, pp. 115–149.

Müller, E. A. (1953). Physiological Basis of Rest Pauses in Heavy Work, *Quarterly Journal of Experimental Physiology*, 38, 205–215.

Mundel, M. E. (1970). *Motion and Time Study*, 4th ed., Prentice-Hall, Englewood Cliffs, N.J.

Münsterberg, H. (1913). *Psychology and Industrial Efficiency*, Houghton Mifflin, Boston.

Murrell, K. F. H. (1962). Operator Variability and its Industrial Consequences, *International Journal of Production Research*, 1, 39–55.

Murrell, K. F. H. (1969). *Ergonomics*, rev. ed., Chapman and Hall, London.

Muscio, B. (1916). The Influence of the Form of a Question, *British Journal of Psychology*, 8, 3.

Myers, C. S. (1922). The Efficiency Engineer and the Industrial Psychologist, *Journal of the National Institute of Industrial Psychology*, 1, 168–172.

Nadler, G. (1967). *Work Systems Design: The Ideals Concept.* Richard D. Irwin, Homewood, Ill.

Nadler, G., and J. Goldman (1958). The UNOPAR, *Journal of Industrial Engineering*, January–February, 58–65.

National Institute of Industrial Psychology, England (1944). *Manual of the 70/23 Non-Verbal Intelligence Test, G T 70/23.*

Niebel, B. W. (1972). *Motion and Time Study*, 5th ed., Richard D. Irwin, Homewood, Ill.

O'Connor, J. (1928). *Born That Way*, Williams & Wilkins, Baltimore.

O'Hara, J. B. (1962). Analytical Training at Daylesford Woollen Mills, *Personnel Practice Bulletin (Melbourne)*, 18, 2, 12.

Paine, R. R. (1964). Experiment in Operator Learning at T.R.W., *Journal of Methods–Time Measurement*, 9, 4, 6–15.

P. A. Management Consultants, Ltd. (1966). *The Instructor.* A Programmed Text (unpublished) London.

Passmore, R., and J. V. G. A. Durin (1955). Human Energy Expenditure, *Physiological Reviews*, 35, 801–840.

Paterson, T. T. (1969). The Decision Bond Method, *Proceeding of the International Conference on Job Evaluation*, Amsterdam, Netherlands, September 29–October 2, pp. III-1 to III-12.

Patton, J. A., C. L. Littlefield, and A. S. Stanley (1964). *Job Evaluation:* 3rd ed., Richard D. Irwin, Homewood, Ill.

Payne, A. H., W. J. Slater and T. Telford (1968). The Use of Force Platform in the Study of Athletic Activities. A Preliminary Investigation, *Ergonomics*, 2, 123–143.

Pear, T. H. (1924). *Skill in Work and Play*, Methuen, London.

Pearson, F. V., A. G. Simmonds, and N. B. Keene (1950). *Induction*, Institute of Personnel Management, London.

Pechstein, L. A. (1917). Whole v. Part Methods in Motor Learning, *Psychology Review Monograph*, 23.

Perkins, F. H. (1969). *The Training and Use of Operators as Instructors,* Report of a Departmental Committee, U. K. Department of Employment, London.

Pew, R. W. (1969). The Speed–Accuracy Operating Characteristic, *Acta Psychologica*, 30, 16–26.

Pond, M. (1926). Selective Placement of Workers, *Journal of Personnel Research*, 5, 345–368.

Powell, L. S. (1969). *Communication and Learning*, Pitman, London.

Preston-Dunlop, V. (1969). A Notation System for Recording Observable Motion, *International Journal of Man–Machine Studies*, 1, 361–386.

The Professional Orthorator (1943). *The Manual*, Bausch & Lomb, Optical Company, London.

Provins, K. A. (1956). Handedness and Skill, *Quarterly Journal of Experimental Psychology*, 8, 79–95.

Provins, K. A. (1967). Motor Skills, Handedness, and Behavior, *Australian Journal of Psychology*, 19, 137–150.

Provins, K. A., C. R. Bell, S. Bieheuvel, and C. H. Adisell (1968). Cross-Cultural Measurement of Perceptual and Motor Skills in Relation to Human Adaption, *Human Biology*, 40, 4, 484–493.

Purdue Pegboard (1948). *Examiner Manual for the Purdue Pegboard*, Lafayette Instrument Co., Lafayette, Ind.

Pym, D. L. A., and H. D. Auld (1965). The Self-Rating as a Measure of Employee Satisfactoriness, *Occupational Psychology*, **39**, 103–113.

Quick, J. H., W. J. Shea, and Koehler, R. E. (1945). Motion Time Standards, *Factory Management and Maintenance*, **103**, 97–108.

Quick, J. M., J. H. Duncan, and J. A. Malcolm (1962). *Work Factor Time Standards: Measurement of Manual and Mental Work*, McGraw-Hill, New York.

Raju, C. S. (1962). An Investigation of Interaction in Elemental Times, M.S.C. Thesis, The College of Aeronautics, Cranfield.

Rao, C. R. (1952). *Advanced Statistical Methods in Biometric Research*, Wiley, New York.

Raubenheimer, I. Van W., and J. Tiffin (1971). Personnel Selection and the Prediction of Error, *Journal of Applied Psychology*, **55**, 229–233.

Raven, J. C. (1960). *Guide to the Standard Progressive Matrices, Sets A, B, C, and D, and E*, Lewis & Co., London. (Prepared 1936; reprinted with additional bibliography.)

Reynolds, B., and J. A. Adams (1953). Effect of Distribution and Shift in Distribution Of Practice Within a Single Training Session, *Journal of Experimental Psychology*, **46**, 3, 137–145.

Ricci, B. (1967). *Physiological Basis of Human Performance*, Lea & Febiger, Philadelphia.

Richardson, M. W., and G. F. Kudar (1939). The Calculation of Test Reliability Coefficients Based on the Method of Rational Equivalence, *Journal of Educational Psychology*, **30**, 681–687.

Ridker, R. G. (1967). *Economic Costs of Air Pollution; Studies in Measurement*, Praeger, New York.

Rodger, A. (1958). How Should We Think About "Interest" in Occupational Psychology? *Proceedings of the 13th International Congress of Applied Psychology*, Rome, April.

Rodger, A. (1965). The Criterion Problem in Selection and Guidance, *Occupational Psychology*, **39**, 2, 77–82.

Rodgers, W., and J. M. Hammersley (1954). The Consistency of Stop-Watch Time Study Practitioners, *Occupational Psychology*, **28**, 2, 61–76.

Rohmert, W., and K. Schlaich (1966). Learning of Complex Manual Tasks, *International Journal of Production Research*, **5**, 2, 137–144.

Rosenfalck, P. (1963). *Bibliography on Electromyography*, rev. ed., DISA Elekronik A/S, Herlev, Denmark.

Rothe, H. F. (1946a). Output Rates Among Butter Wrappers: I. Work Curves and then Stability, *Journal of Applied Psychology*, **30**, 122–211.

Rothe, H. F. (1946b). Output Rates Among Butter Wrappers: II. Frequency Distributions and an Hypotheses Regarding the "Restriction of Output," *Journal of Applied Psychology*, **30**, 320–328.

Rothe, H. F. (1947). Output Rates Among Machine Operators: I. Distributions and Their Reliability, *Journal of Applied Psychology*, **31**, 484–489.

Rothe, H. F. (1951). Output Rates Among Chocolate Dippers, *Journal of Applied Psychology*, **35**, 94–97.

Rothe, H. F. (1970). Output Rates Among Welders: Productivity and Consistency Following Removal of a Financial Incentive System, *Journal of Applied Psychology*, **54**, 549–551.

Rothe, H. F., and C. T. Nye (1958). Output Rates Among Coil Winders, *Journal of Applied Psychology*, **42**, 182–186.

Rothe, H. F., and C. T. Nye (1959). Output Rates Among Machine Operators: II. Consistency Related to Methods of Pay, *Journal of Applied Psychology*, **43**, 417–420.

Rothe, H. F., and C. T. Nye (1961). Output Rates Among Machine Operators: III. A Nonincentive Situation in Two Levels of Business Activity, *Journal of Applied Psychology*, **45**, 50–54.

Rothney, J. W. M. (1952). Interpreting Test Scores to Counselors, Personnel Guidance Journal, **30**, 320–322.

Rulon, P. J. (1939). A Simplified Procedure for Determining the Reliability of a Test by Split-Halves, *Harvard Educational Review*, **9**, 99–103.

Rush, C. H. (1953). Factorial Study of Sales Criteria, *Personnel Psychology*, **6**, 9–24.

Sadosky, T. L. (1969). *Prediction of Cycle Time for Combined Manual and Decision Tasks*, Report 116, M.T.M. Association, Fairlawn, N.J.

Salvendy, G. (1966). Skill and Operator Selection for Fine Manual Tasks, M.Sc. Thesis, Department of Engineering Production, University of Birmingham, England.

Salvendy, G. (1968). A Comparative Study of Selection Tests for Industrial Operators, Ph.D. Dissertation, University of Birmingham, England.

Salvendy, G. (1969a). Ergonomic Aspects of Paced and Unpaced Work, *Proceedings of the International Congress of Industrial Neurology*, Prague, Czechoslovakia, p. 85. Reprinted in Acta Physiologica, 1972, **42**, 267–275.

Salvendy, G. (1969b). Learning Fundamental Skills—A Promise for the Future, *AIIE Transactions on Industrial Engineering Research and Development*, **1**, 300–305.

Salvendy, G. (1970). Handedness and Psychomotor Performance, *AIIE Transactions*, **2**, 227–232.

Salvendy, G. (1971). Hand Size and Assembly Operation, *AIIE Transactions*, **3**, 32–36.

Salvendy, G. (1972). Effects of Age on Some Test Scores and Production Criteria, *Studia Psychologica*, **14**, 186–189.

Salvendy, G. (1973). The Non-Linearity Model of Operators: The G.T. 70/23 Non-verbal Intelligence Test—Norms, Reliabilities and Validities, *Studia Psychologica*, **15**, 171–187.

Salvendy, G., P. R. Cunningham, G. Ferguson, and W. H. Hinton (1971). Acquisition of Psychomotor Skills in Dentistry. Presented at the 15th Annual Conference of the Human Factors Society, New York, October 19–21.

Salvendy, G., and T. Goodrich (1971). An Electro-Mechanical Dental Simulator. Presented at the 15th Annual Conference of the Human Factors Society, New York, October 19–21.

Salvendy G., and J. Pilitsis (1971a). Physiological Learning Curves for the Establishment of Work Standards: An Exploratory Study, *Proceedings of 22nd Annual Conference and Convention*, American Institute of Industrial Engineers, Boston, May 12–15, pp. 459–465.

Salvendy, G., and J. Pilitsis (1971b). Psychophysiological Aspects of Paced and Unpaced Work as Influenced by Age, *Ergonomics*, **14**, 703–711.

Salvendy, G., and J. Pilitsis (1973). Medical Suturing—The Acquisition and Training of Related Psychomotor Skills. Unpublished study, Purdue University, Lafayette, Ind.

Salvendy, G., and W. D. Seymour (1972). Manual of the One-Hole Test. Lafayette Instrument Company, Lafayette, Indiana.

Salvendy, G., D. Seymour, and E. N. Corlett (1970). A Comparative Study of Static vs. Dynamic Scoring of Performance Tests for Industrial Operators, *Journal of Applied Psychology*, 54, 135–139.

Salvendy, G., Hershcopf, W., Boy, R. and Przybylski, P. (1971). Shielding Aspects of Signal Light Discrimination. Studia Psychologica, 13, 79–84.

Sanfleber, H. (1967). An Investigation into Some Aspects of the Accuracy of Predetermined Motion Time Systems, *International Journal of Production Research*, 6, 1, 25–45.

Schmidke, H., and F. Stier (1961). An Experimental Evaluation of the Validity of Predetermined Elemental Time Systems, *Journal of Industrial Engineering*, 12, 182–204.

Schwartz, I., and F. L. Dimmick (1958). Comparison of High Acuity Scores on Snellen and Ortho-Rater Test, *American Journal of Optomology*, 35, 309–313.

Scott, W. D. (1916). Selection of Employees by Means of Quantitative Determinations, *Annals of the American Academy of Political and Social Service*, 65.

Seaborne, A. E. M., and E. Thomas (1964). Subjective Standards in Industrial Inspection, Department of Scientific and Industrial Research, Her Majesty's Stationery Office, London.

Seashore, S. E., B. P. Indik, and B. S. Georgopoulos (1960). Relationships among criteria of job performances, *Journal of Applied Psychology*, 44, 3, 195–202.

Seashore, R. H. (1939). Work Methods: An Often Neglected Factor Underlying Individual Differences, *Psychological Review*, 46, 123–141.

Severin, D. (1952). The Predictability of Various Kinds of Criteria, *Personnel Psychology*, 5, 93–104.

Seymour, W. D. (1954a). Manual Skills and Industrial Productivity, *Journal of the Institution of Production Engineering*, 33, 248–90.

Seymour, W. D. (1954b, 1955, 1956, 1959, 1962). Experiments on the Acquisition of Industrial Skills. *Occupational Psychology*, Part 1, 28, 77–89. Part 2, 29, 82–98; Part 3, 30, 94–104; Part 4, 33, 18–35; Part 5, 36, 10–21.

Seymour, W. D. (1959). *Operator Training in Industry*, Institute of Personnel Management, London.

Seymour, W. D. (1966). *Industrial Training for Manual Operations*, Pitman, London. Obtainable in the United States from: International Publication Service, 303 Park Ave. South, New York, N.Y. 10010.

Seymour, W. D. (1967). *Industrial Skills*, Pitman, London. Obtainable in the United States from: International Publication Service, 303 Park Avenue South, New York, N.Y. 10010.

Seymour, W. D. (1968a). Note on Time Distributions for Two Elements in Capacitor Winding, *International Journal of Production Research*, 7, 2, 147–149.

Seymour, W. D. (1968b). *Skills Analysis Training*. Pitman, London. Obtainable in the United States from: International Publication Service, 303 Park Avenue South, New York, N.Y. 10010.

Shackel, B. (1961). Electro-Oculography: The Electrical Recording of Eye Position, *Proceedings of the 3rd International Conference on Medical Electronics*, London, 1960. Charles C Thomas, Springfield, Ill. 1961.

Siddall, G. J. (1954). Variations in Movement Time in an Industrial Repetitive Task. Report No. 216/54, Medical Research Council, Applied Psychology Research Unit, Cambridge.

Sidowski, J. B., Ed. (1966). *Experimental Methods and Instrumentation in Psychology*, McGraw-Hill, New York.

Siegel, S. (1956). *Nonparametric Statistics for the Behavioral Sciences*, McGraw-Hill, New York, 316 pages.

Silberer, P. (1956). La Formation fonctionelle dans l'Entreprise, *Hommes et Techniques*, 12, 143, 731.

Simmons, E. D. (1958). Operator Training: A Scheme and Its Results, *Engineering*, 185, 753.

Simms, D. L., and P. L. Hinkley (1960). *Protective Clothing Against Flames and Heat*, Department of Scientific and Industrial Research and Fire Offices' Committee Fire Research Special Report 3, Her Majesty's Stationery Office, London.

Simon, J. R. (1955). The Relation of Perception to the Component Movements in Human Motion, Ph.D. Dissertation, University of Wisconsin.

Singer, C., E. J. Holmyard, and A. R. Hall, Eds. (1954). *A History of Technology*, Vol. 1, Oxford University Press, London.

Singer, E. J. (1969). *Training in Industry and Commerce*, London Institute of Personnel Management, London.

Singer, E. J., and J. Ramsden (1969). *The Practical Approach to Skills Analysis*, McGraw-Hill, London.

Singleton, W. T. (1957). An Experimental Investigation of Sewing Machine Skill, *British Journal of Psychology*, 48, 127–132.

Singleton, W. T. (1959). The Training of Shoe Machinists, *Ergonomics*, 2, 2, 148–152.

Singleton, W. T. (1968). Acquisition of Skill in *New Media & Methods in Industrial Training*, B.B.C., London.

Slater, P. (1941). Tests for Selecting Secondary and Technical School Children, *Occupational Psychology*, 15, 10–25.

Slater, P. (1942). Notes on Testing Groups of Young Children, *Occupational Psychology*, 16, 31–38.

Slater, P., and E. Bennett (1943). The Development of Spatial Judgement and Its Relation to Some Educational Problems, *Occupational Psychology*, 17, 139–155.

Smith, K. U. (1945). The Role of the Commissurial Systems of the Cerebral Cortex in the Determination of Handedness, Eyedness and Footedness in Man, *Journal of General Psychology*, 32, 39–79.

Smith, K. U., and H. Sussman (1969). Cybernetic Theory and Analysis of Motor Learning. In Bilodeau, E. A. and Bilodeau E. A., Eds., *Principles of Skill Acquisition*, Academic Press, New York.

Smith, K. U., and H. Sussman (1970). Delayed Feedback in Steering during Learning and Transfer of Learning, *Journal of Applied Psychology*, 54, 4, 334–342.

Smith, K. U., G. Rubin, and P. von Trebra (1952). Dimensional Analysis of Motion: Complexity of Movement Pattern, *Journal of Applied Psychology*, 36, 272.

Smith, K. U., and P. von Trebra (1952). The Dimensional Analysis of Motion: IV. Transfer Effects and Directions of Movement, *Journal of Applied Psychology*, 36, 348–353.

Smith, K. U., and L. Wargo (1963). Sensory Feedback Analysis of Specialisation of Movements in Learning, *Perceptional and Motor Skills Research*, 16, 749.

Snook, S. H., C. H. Irvine, and S. F. Bass (1969). Maximum Weights and Work Loads Acceptable to Male Industrial Workers While Performing Lifting, Lowering, Pushing, Pulling, Carrying and Walking Tasks. Presented at the American Industrial Hygiene Conference in Denver, Colo., May 13.

Solinger, J. (1961). *Apparel Manufacturing Analysis*, Textile Book Publishers, New York.

Spearman, C. (1904). The Proof and Measurement of Association between Two Things, *American Journal of Psychology*, **15**, 72–101.

Stacy, N. A. H., and A. Wilson (1963). *Industrial Marketing Research*, Hutchinson, London.

Stanway, H. G. (1947). *Applied Job Evaluation; A Manual of Installation and Operating Methods*, New York, Ronald Press.

Stevens, S. S., and F. Warshofsky (1965). *Sound and Hearing*, Time, New York.

Strong, E. K., Jr. (1934–1935). Interest and Sales Ability, *Personnel Journal*, **13**, 204–216.

Strong, E. K., Jr. (1943). *Vocational Interest of Men and Women*, Stanford University Press, Stanford, Calif.

Super, D. E., and J. O. Crites (1962). Appraising Vocational Fitness by Means of Psychological Tests, Harper & Row, New York.

Sury, R. J. (1967). Operator Performance in Conveyor Based Working, *Work Study and Management Services*, **11**, 12–15.

Tanner, J. M., and J. S. Weiner (1949). The Reliability of the Photogrammetric Method of Anthropometry, with a Description of a Miniature Camera Technique, *American Journal of Physiological Anthropometry*, new series, **7**, 145–186.

Taylor, E. A. (1966). *Visual Presentation in Education and Training*, Pergamon Press, London.

Taylor, H. C., and Russell, J. T. (1939). The Relationship of Validity Coefficients to the Practical Effectiveness of Tests in Selection: Discussion and Tables, *Journal of Applied Psychology*, **23**, 565–578.

Tenopyr, M. L. (1967). Race and Socio-economic Status as Moderators in Predicting Machine Shop Training Success, *Proceedings of the Annual Convention of the American Psychological Association*, Washington, D.C.

Thomas, B., J. Moxham and J. A. G. Jones (1969). A Cost Benefit Analysis of Industrial Training. *British Journal of Industrial Relations*, **7**, 2, 231–265.

Thomas, L. F. K. (1965). *The Control of Quality*, Thames and Hudson, London.

Thompson, G. H. (1939). *The Factorial Analysis of Human Ability*, University of London Press, London.

Thompson, R. F., D. B. Lindsley, and R. G. Eason (1966). Physiological Psychology. In J. B. Sidowsky, Ed., *Experimental Methods and Instrumentation in Psychology*, McGraw-Hill, New York, pp. 117–182.

Thorndike, E. L. (1920). A Constant Error in Psychological Ratings, *Journal of Applied Psychology*, **4**, 25–29.

Thorndike, R. L. (1949). *Personnel Selection*, Wiley, London.

Thurstone, L. L. (1927). The Method of Paired Comparisons for Social Values, *Journal of Abnormal Social Psychology*, **22**, 384–400.

Thurstone, L. L. (1947). *Multiple Factor Analysis*, University of Chicago Press, Chicago.

Thurstone, L. L. (1948). Psychological Implications of Factor Analysis, *American Psychologist*, **3**, 402–408.

Tichaeur, E. R. (1971). A Pilot Study of the Biomechanics of Lifting in Simulated Industrial Work Situations, *Journal of Safety Research*, **3**, 98–115.

Tiffin, J., and E. J. Asher (1948). The Purdue Pegboard: Norms and Studies of Reliability and Validity, *Journal of Applied Psychology*, **32**, 234–247.

Tiffin, J., and E. J. McCormick (1966). *Industrial Psychology*, 3rd ed., Allen & Unwin, London.

Tilley, K. W. (1969). Developments in Selection and Training, *Ergonomics*, **12**, 4, 583–597.

Tippitt, L. H. C. (1935). Statistical Methods in Textile Research. Uses of the Binomial and Poisson Distribution. A Snap-Reading Method of Making Time Studies of Machines and Operatives in Factory Surveys, *Journal of Textile Institutes Transactions*, **26**, 51–55, 75.

Uhrbrock, R. S. (1961). Music on the Job: Its Influence on the Worker, Morale, and Production, *Personnel Psychology*, **14**, 9–38.

U.S. Department of Labor (1963). *Dictionary of Occupational Titles*, Government Printing Office, Washington, D.C.

U.S. Public Health Service (1962). *Health Examination Program of the U.S. Public Health Service*. Unpublished Cancer Association study.

Van Beek, H. G. (1964).The Influence of Assembly Line Organization on Output and Quality of Morale, *Occupational Psychology*, **38**, 161–172.

Veldman, D. J. (1967). *Fortran programming for the Behavioral Sciences*, Holt, Rinehart, & Winston, New York.

Vernon, H. M., and S. Wyatt (1924). On the Extent and Effects of Variety in Repetitive Work Industrial Fatigue Research Board Report 26, Her Majesty's Stationery Office, London.

Vernon, P. E. (1950). An Application of Factor Analysis to the Study of Test items, *British Journal of Psychology* (stat. red.) **3**, Pt. I, 1–15.

Vernon, P. E., and J. B. Parry (1949). *Personnel Selection in the British Forces*, University of London Press, London.

Viteles, M. S. (1932). *Industrial Psychology*, Norton, New York.

Viteles, M. S. (1953). *Motivation and Morale in Industry*, Norton, New York.

Vroom, H. V. (1964). *Work and Motivation*, Wiley, London.

Wallis, D. (1966). The Technology of Military Training. In *Manpower Planning*, English University Press, London.

Walsh, J. E. (1968). *Handbook of Nonparametric Statistics*, III: *Analysis of Variance*, Van Nostrand, London.

Wechsler, D. (1960). Intelligence, Quantum Resonance and Thinking Machines, *Transactions of the New York Academy of Sciences*, **22**, 259–266.

Wechsler, D. (1971). Concept of Collective Intelligence, *American Psychologist*, **26**, 904–907.

Wehrkamp, R. A., and K. U. Smith (1952). Dimensional Analysis of Motion. II: Travel Distance Effects, *Journal of Applied Psychology*, **36**, 201–206.

Weir, DeV, J. A. (1949). New Methods for Calculating Metabolic Rate with Special Reference to Protein Metabolism, *Journal of Physiology*, **109**, 1–9.

Weiss, D. J., R. V. Dowis, G. W. England, and C. H. Lofquist (1961). Validity of Work Histories Obtained by Interview, *Minnesota Studies in Vocational Reliability*, No. 12, University of Minnesota, Minneapolis.

Welford, A. T. (1958). *Ageing and Human Skill*. Oxford University Press.

Welford, A. T. (1964). Experimental Psychology in the Study of Ageing, in *Experimental Psychology, British Medical Bulletin*, **20**, 1, 65–69.

Welford, A. T. (1968). *Fundamentals of Skill*, Methuen, London.

Welford, A. T. (1970). Perceptual Selection and Integration, *Ergonomics*, **13**, 1, 5–25.

Welford, A. T., and J. E. Birren (1965). *Behavior, Aging and the Nervous System. Biological Determinants of Speed of Behavior and its Changes with Age.* Charles C Thomas, Springfield, Ill.

Welford, N. T. (1952). An Electronic Digital Recording Machine—The SETAR, *Journal of Science Instrumentation,* **29,** 1–4.

Wellens, J. (1962, 1963). Operative Training . . . The Analytical Method, *Technical Education,* December 1962 and January 1963, Evans Bros., London.

Westwood, D. F. (1965). The Premium Pay Plan, *Work Study and Management,* **9,** 8–11.

Wheatcroft, E. O. (1971). Analytical Training 1971. The Bobbin Magazine, 12.10. 48–62, Columbia S. C.

Whitfield, D. (1967). Human Skills as a Determinant of Allocation of Function. In W. T. Singleton R. S. Easterly, and D. C. Whitfield, Eds., *The Human Operator in Complex Systems,* Taylor & Francis, London, 54–60.

Wiener, N. (1949). *Cybernetics,* rev. ed., 1961. Wiley, New York.

Wiltshire, H. C. (1967). A Variation of Cycle Times with Repetition of Manual Tasks, *Ergonomics,* **10,** 3, 331–347.

Wirt, S. E. (1943). Studies in Industrial Vision: I, The Validity of the Lateral Phoria Measurements in the Ortho-Rater, *Journal of Applied Psychology,* **27,** 217–232.

Wolfle, D. (1951). Training. In S. S. Stevens, Ed., *Handbook of Experimental Psychology,* Wiley, New York.

Woodcock, J. A. D. (1972). Cost Reduction through Operator Training and Retraining, Kogan Page, London.

Woodrow, H. A. (1938a). The Effect of Practice on Groups of Different Initial Ability, *Journal of Educational Psychology,* **29,** 268–278.

Woodrow, H. (1938b). The Relationship Between Abilities and Improvements with Practice, *Journal of Educational Psychology,* **29,** 215–230.

Woodworth, R. S., and H. Schlosberg (1954). *Experimental Psychology,* Methuen, London.

Wyatt, S., and J. N. Langdon (1937). *Fatigue and Boredom in Repetitive Work,* Industrial Health Research Board, No. 77, Her Majesty's Stationery Office, London.

Yerkes, R. M., Ed. (1921). Psychological Examining in the United States Army, *Memoirs of the National Academy of Science (U.S.),* **15,** 837.

Yoblick, D., and Salvendy, G. (1970). Some Effects of Sensed Frequency and Intensity on Subjective Perception and Estimation of Times, *Journal of Experimental Psychology,* **86,** 157–164.

Zangwill, O. L. (1965). *An Introduction to Modern Psychology,* rev. ed., Methuen, London.

Zeidner, J., and D. A. Gordon (1953). A Comparison of Visual Acquity Measurements by Wall Charts and Ortho-Rater Tests (Abstract), *American Psychologist,* **8,** 459.

INDEX

Spearman, C. (1904). The Proof and Measurement of Association between Two Things, *American Journal of Psychology*, **15**, 72–101.

Stacy, N. A. H., and A. Wilson (1963). *Industrial Marketing Research*, Hutchinson, London.

Stanway, H. G. (1947). *Applied Job Evaluation; A Manual of Installation and Operating Methods*, New York, Ronald Press.

Stevens, S. S., and F. Warshofsky (1965). *Sound and Hearing*, Time, New York.

Strong, E. K., Jr. (1934–1935). Interest and Sales Ability, *Personnel Journal*, **13**, 204–216.

Strong, E. K., Jr. (1943). *Vocational Interest of Men and Women*, Stanford University Press, Stanford, Calif.

Super, D. E., and J. O. Crites (1962). *Appraising Vocational Fitness by Means of Psychological Tests*, Harper & Row, New York.

Sury, R. J. (1967). Operator Performance in Conveyor Based Working, *Work Study and Management Services*, **11**, 12–15.

Tanner, J. M., and J. S. Weiner (1949). The Reliability of the Photogrammetric Method of Anthropometry, with a Description of a Miniature Camera Technique, *American Journal of Physiological Anthropometry*, new series, **7**, 145–186.

Taylor, E. A. (1966). *Visual Presentation in Education and Training*, Pergamon Press, London.

Taylor, H. C., and Russell, J. T. (1939). The Relationship of Validity Coefficients to the Practical Effectiveness of Tests in Selection: Discussion and Tables, *Journal of Applied Psychology*, **23**, 565–578.

Tenopyr, M. L. (1967). Race and Socio-economic Status as Moderators in Predicting Machine Shop Training Success, *Proceedings of the Annual Convention of the American Psychological Association*, Washington, D.C.

Thomas, B., J. Moxham and J. A. G. Jones (1969). A Cost Benefit Analysis of Industrial Training, *British Journal of Industrial Relations*, **7**, 2, 231–265.

Thomas, L. F. K. (1965). *The Control of Quality*, Thames and Hudson, London.

Thompson, C. H. (1939). *The Factorial Analysis of Human Ability*, University of London Press, London.

Thompson, R. F., D. B. Lindsley, and R. G. Eason (1966). Physiological Psychology. In J. B. Sidowsky, Ed., *Experimental Methods and Instrumentation in Psychology*, McGraw-Hill, New York, pp. 117–182.

Thorndike, E. L. (1920). A Constant Error in Psychological Ratings, *Journal of Applied Psychology*, **4**, 25–29.

Thorndike, R. L. (1949). *Personnel Selection*, Wiley, London.

Thurstone, L. L. (1927). The Method of Paired Comparisons for Social Values, *Journal of Abnormal Social Psychology*, **22**, 384–400.

Thurstone, L. L. (1947). *Multiple Factor Analysis*, University of Chicago Press, Chicago.

Thurstone, L. L. (1948). Psychological Implications of Factor Analysis, *American Psychologist*, **3**, 402–408.

Tichaeur, E. R. (1971). A Pilot Study of the Biomechanics of Lifting in Simulated Industrial Work Situations, *Journal of Safety Research*, **3**, 98–115.

Tiffin, J., and E. J. Asher (1948). The Purdue Pegboard: Norms and Studies of Reliability and Validity, *Journal of Applied Psychology*, **32**, 234–247.

Tiffin, J., and E. J. McCormick (1966). *Industrial Psychology*, 3rd ed., Allen & Unwin, London.

Siegel, S. (1956). *Nonparametric Statistics for the Behavioral Sciences*, McGraw-Hill, New York, 316 pages.

Silberer, P. (1956). La Formation fonctionelle dans l'Entreprise *Hommes et Tech-niques*, 12, 143, 731.

Simmons, E. D. (1958). Operator Training: A Scheme and Its Results, *Engineering*, 185, 753.

Simms, D. L., and P. L. Hinkley (1960). *Protective Clothing Against Flames and Heat*, Department of Scientific and Industrial Research and Fire Offices' Committee Fire Research Special Report 3, Her Majesty's Stationery Office, London.

Simon, J. R. (1955). The Relation of Perception to the Component Movements in Human Motion, Ph.D. Dissertation, University of Wisconsin.

Singer, C. E. J. Holmyard and A. R. Hall, Eds. (1954). *A History of Technology*, Vol. 1, Oxford University Press, London.

Singer, E. J. (1969). *Training in Industry and Commerce*, London Institute of Personnel Management, London.

Singer, E. J., and J. Ramsden (1969). *The Practical Approach to Skills Analysis*, McGraw-Hill, London.

Singleton, W. T. (1957). An Experimental Investigation of Sewing Machine Skill, *British Journal of Psychology*, 48, 127–132.

Singleton, W. T. (1959). The Training of Shoe Machinists, *Ergonomics*, 2, 2, 148–152.

Singleton, W. T. (1968). *Acquisition of Skill in New Media & Methods in Industrial Training*, B.B.C, London.

Slater, P. (1941). Tests for Selecting Secondary and Technical School Children, *Occupational Psychology*, 15, 10–25.

Slater, P. (1942). Notes on Testing Groups of Young Children, *Occupational Psychology*, 16, 31–38.

Slater, P., and E. Bennett (1943). The Development of Spatial Judgement and Its Relation to Some Educational Problems, *Occupational Psychology*, 17, 139–155.

Smith, K. U. (1945). The Role of the Commissural Systems of the Cerebral Cortex in the Determination of Handedness, Eyedness and Footedness in Man, *Journal of General Psychology*, 32, 39–79.

Smith, K. U., and H. Sussman (1969). Cybernetic Theory and Analysis of Motor Learning. In Bilodeau, E. A. and Bilodeau E. A., Eds., *Principles of Skill Acquisition*, Academic Press, New York.

Smith, K. U., and H. Sussman (1970). Delayed Feedback in Steering during Learning and Transfer of Learning, *Journal of Applied Psychology*, 54, 4, 334–342.

Smith, K. U., G. Rubin, and P. von Trebra (1952). Dimensional Analysis of Motion: Complexity of Movement Pattern, *Journal of Applied Psychology*, 36, 272.

Smith, K. U., and P. von Trebra (1952). The Dimensional Analysis of Motion: IV. Transfer Effects and Directions of Movement, *Journal of Applied Psychology*, 36, 348–353.

Smith, K. U., and L. Wargo (1963). Sensory Feedback Analysis of Specialisation of Movements in Learning, *Perceptional and Motor Skills Research*, 16, 749.

Snook, S. H., C. H. Irvine, and S. F. Bass (1969). Maximum Weights and Work Loads Acceptable to Male Industrial Workers While Performing Lifting, Lowering, Pushing, Pulling, Carrying and Walking Tasks. Presented at the American Industrial Hygiene Conference in Denver, Colo., May 13.

Solinger, J. (1961). *Apparel Manufacturing Analysis*, Textile Book Publishers, New York.